The AUSTRALIAN
LIGHT HORSE

Also by Roland Perry

Monash: The Outsider Who Won a War
Last of the Cold War Spies
The Fifth Man
Hidden Power: The Programming of the President
Mel Gibson, Actor, Director, Producer
The Exile: Wilfred Burchett, Reporter of Conflict
Lethal Hero
Sailing to the Moon
Elections Sur Ordinateur
Programme for a Puppet (fiction)
Blood is a Stranger (fiction)
Faces in the Rain (fiction)
Bradman's Invincibles
The Ashes: A Celebration
Miller's Luck:
The Life and Loves of Keith Miller, Australia's Greatest All-Rounder
Bradman's Best
Bradman's Best Ashes Teams
The Don
Captain Australia:
A History of the Celebrated Captains of Australian Test Cricket
Bold Warnie
Waugh's Way
Shane Warne, Master Spinner

Documentary Films

The Programming of the President
The Raising of a Galleon's Ghost
Strike Swiftly
Ted Kennedy & the Pollsters
The Force

The AUSTRALIAN
LIGHT HORSE

The magnificent Australian force and its decisive
victories in Arabia in World War I

ROLAND PERRY

hachette
AUSTRALIA

*To Mike Guy, for his guidance through Palestine (Israel),
Jordan and Southern Arabia*

My horse a thing of wings, myself a god
From a sonnet by Wilfrid Scawen Blunt

First published in Australia and New Zealand in 2009
by Hachette Australia
(an imprint of Hachette Australia Pty Limited)
Level 17, 207 Kent Street, Sydney NSW 2000
www.hachette.com.au

This edition published in 2010

10 9 8 7 6 5 4 3

National Library of Australia
Cataloguing-in-Publication data:

Perry, Roland, 1946–
The Australian light horse / Roland Perry.

2nd ed.

978 0 7336 2748 4 (pbk.)

Previous ed.: 2009.
Includes bibliographical references and index.

Australia. Army. Australian Light Horse–History.
World War, 1914-1918–Participation, Australian.
World War, 1914-1918–Campaigns–Palestine.
World War, 1914-1918–Cavalry operations.

940.41294

Cover design by Darian Causby, Highway 51 Design Works
Cover photograph courtesy of Australian War Memorial
Map by Kinart
Text design by Post Pre-Press Group
Typeset in 12/15pt Sabon by Post Pre-Press Group
Printed in Australia by Griffin Press, Adelaide, an Accredited ISO AS/NZS 4001:2004 Environmental Management Systems printer

Contents

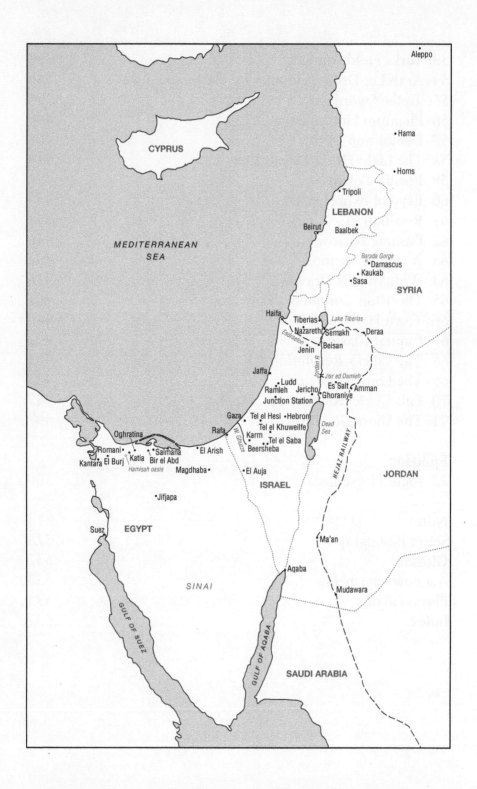

PART ONE

The Making of Harry Chauvel—Battle Commander

Charge at Beersheba

Lieutenant General Sir Harry Chauvel was glancing at his watch every few minutes now. It was approaching 3 p.m. on 31 October 1917. The sun would set in 90 minutes. At 5 p.m. it would be dark. Most of Beersheba's outskirt defences had been breached by the attacking Australian light horsemen. But the wells were the key. The horses had been without water for 36 hours.

The wells had been prepared for demolition. If they were still in enemy hands by nightfall, they would be destroyed. The British would fail to break through the Turkish defence line in Palestine from Beersheba to Gaza on the Mediterranean coast. This was the British force's third attempt since the desert campaign began 20 months earlier. If it failed this time, the war in the Middle East would be in stalemate at best. At worst, the enemy would hold the advantage. The British would never take Palestine.

The pressure mounted. The wiry, diminutive 52-year-old Chauvel consulted with second-in-command General Hodgson, Grant commanding the resting Australian 4th Brigade, and FitzGerald of the British 5th Mounted Yeomanry. A typical mounted rifles attack with the troopers dismounting and advancing on the trenches was now out of the question. Even if the assault force did brilliantly, it would be unlikely to take the town before dark. That left one option: an old-style cavalry charge over and through the trenches that carried the troopers right into the town. Such an assault is what every horseman dreamt of. They were few and far between in this war, and had all but ceased on the Western Front. Any proposed action at Beersheba would make or break the third Gaza battle. No trooper would be dwelling on glory or history at that moment. It would be the thrill of the thought of the charge, unexpected, and yet frightening, that would be on his mind.

The impulsive commander Grant was first to ask to make the charge. He pointed out that his brigade was closer to Beersheba. FitzGerald, not to be outdone, made his plea. His brigade had swords and was just behind Chauvel's HQ. Grant increased the tension, pointing out that his troopers had both rifles and bayonets, and the latter had been sharpened for an occasion just like this.

Chauvel remained ice-cool and in complete control of himself and the situation. He called for aerial photographs again. The four men hovered over them. The town was almost ringed with barbed wire entanglements and pits dug as traps for horses. There was only one approach—from the south-east—that was not defended this way. Concealed trenches were embedded in the terrain. Grant was closest to it. He and Englishman FitzGerald were asked to wait by their horses while Chauvel consulted briefly with Hodgson, also English. Chauvel, as commander of the Desert Mounted Corps, had officers of several different nationalities under him. He was conscious of not being seen to favour the Australians. If anything, he was less popular with them for not leaning their way in the campaign so far. He was aware too that his 4th and 12th Regiments had 'seen very little serious fighting'. The choice would be critical. He had to be certain that the lead regiments would do the job.

Chauvel turned to Hodgson. Placing his finger at a point on a photograph, he said:

'Put Grant straight in.'[1]

Brigadier General William Grant swung onto his horse and galloped off to gather his resting regiments. The troopers were scattered in small groups over a wide network of valleys (wadis) to avoid giving German aircraft bigger and easier targets. They had been all day in the Iswainin area, about six kilometres from Beersheba, and were frustrated that they had not had the order to saddle up. While the battle raged, the 4th (from Victoria) and 12th (New South Wales) Regiments waited and felt the effects of a scorching heat, despite winter's approach. They had not only been out of the action; they were becoming concerned. Their water was running out. As the shadows of the afternoon lengthened they were unlikely to take the wells at Beersheba. A 12-hour march to the water at Asluj or anywhere that far away seemed unthinkable. But it would be the only option if the wells were not taken.

'If they don't capture the town soon,' an older trooper said to the youngest of them, 16-year-old Harry Bell, 'we're well and truly stuffed.'

Young Harry was stunned, though he fought not to show it. He had claimed he was two years older than he was when he joined up and had done so under the assumed surname Wickham. This was to avoid being traced by his family. His father, he knew, would never have let him volunteer.

Moments later, the order came down the lines of the 4th and 12th:

'Regiments! Form squadrons, line extended . . . form squadrons, line extended.'

Harry and everyone else wondered what was happening. He was on edge. It might be action. It could mean his beautiful waler would get a drink soon. The squadrons trotted towards the area behind Chauvel's command post high on a hill with a comprehensive view of the battlefield. Harry looked around to see Beersheba in the distance before the town disappeared as they fell in behind a ridge.

A squadron sergeant major galloped along the front of the troops. A corporal called to him:

'What's going on, sir?'

The response electrified everyone within hearing:

'We're gunna charge Beersheba mate!'[2]

*

It was 4.25 p.m. before the 4th Regiment under Lieutenant Colonel M. W. J. Bourchier on the left, and the 12th under Lieutenant Colonel D. Cameron on the right, could draw up all their men behind the ridge about 1.5 kilometres north of Hill 1280. From the ridge's crest they had a clear view of Beersheba down a long, slight slope. The ground seemed clear, perfect for what was intended. The sun sinking behind them would provide light for the charge for another half hour at best.

The two regiments lined up beside each other, two squadrons wide, and three lines deep. The lines were about 400 metres apart, making about 800 horsemen in all, before the scouts at front, the artillery and ambulance men were factored in.

The last time the desert troopers had done anything like this was at Katia more than a year ago. Then the dash was across a salt pan for a forgettable end in a marsh, which made it the cavalry charge that wasn't. This time, all troopers, rifles slung around their backs and bayonets held in one hand, knew it would be different; the real thing. There was no impediment such as a stinking bog to hold them up. Everyone knew the town had to be secured in this burst forward before it was too dark.

The 4th Regiment's 33-year-old tall and broad-shouldered Yorkshire-born Major Lawson would lead the front squadron. He had a brief, cheery chat to the two scouts, Tom O'Leary and Tom Healy, stockmen and Gallipoli veterans. They would sweep wide 70 or 80 metres ahead of the rest.

All eyes were on the striking, stiff-backed and tall figure of Grant, high in the saddle. He had floated out in front of the 800. He pulled his hat down tight. He raised his right arm, his hand pointing straight at Beersheba. The biggest body of horsemen in a century to line up for a cavalry-style charge, began at a slow walk, five metres apart.

A corporal in the front squadron gave Harry Bell a wink. It was meant to reassure him. Everything was okay. This was going to be a thrill, a great moment in his short life. Yet the teenager was nervous now. His erratic energy transferred to his horse. It was unsettled. Harry stroked its neck, something that always calmed him. He glanced back to look at his packhorse carrying a machine-gun and ammunition. No-one was speaking. The air was punctuated with the sounds of explosions and weapons fire to the west, east and north. Artillery was thumping out from near Chauvel's command post. A horse snorted. It began a chain reaction. Most walers were all but symbiotically joined to their riders. They sensed nerves, energy and adrenaline. They smelt fear.

Thirty metres short of the crest and without any warning, Grant flexed his arm, extended it towards Beersheba again and bellowed:

'Forwaaard!'

The troopers expelled an enormous amount of pent-up energy in a roar that sounded like a football crowd. By the time Grant and the lead squadron topped the crest of the ridge in full view of the enemy, they were at a trot.

Grant was followed closely by his brigade major McKenzie in the lead. Bourchier and Cameron headed their regiments.

A New South Wales grazier, Major Hyman was at the head of the 12th mounted stretcher-bearers, who, as ever, were right up with the lead horses. Artillery, machine-gunners, reserves, HQs, and ambulances followed. The reserve 11th Light Horse Regiment, which had been furthest away from the forming-up place, was moving up as fast as it could. On the far left, the 7th Mounted Brigade was galloping along the Khalesa Road, in line with the vanguard of the main Light Horse force now moving at a canter.

Just after the Turkish machine-gunners adjusted the sights on their Maxims and opened up with the Light Horse three kilometres away, an Essex Battery on the left of the charging Australians spotted the source of the fire almost in line with them, on Hill 1180. The officers calibrated the range and let the big guns loose. By a fluke or good management, the first shower of shells killed all the Turkish machine-gunners. There were many others, but this direct impediment to the attack had been eliminated.

Just 2.5 kilometres from the trenches, Bourchier was now the most forward commander. He raised his right arm, pushed it out straight from the shoulder and bellowed:

'Chaaarge!'

The troopers quickly reached a near-top-pace gallop.

The next obstacle for the charging front squadron, led by the scouts, was Turkish riflemen, who were propping in front of the oncoming troopers. They hit several horses, but for many of the marksmen it was their last act as the rampaging Light Horse barrelled straight through them. If anything, the horses' tempo increased.

The troopers were 1.5 kilometres from the trenches.

Only a few had been felled by two German planes swooping low and finding targets difficult to hit with their bombs in the fading light. Enemy machine-gunners had been silenced and the snipers had been trampled on. There was a sense now among the horsemen that they were going to get there. They did not know what was in front of them, but the waves of horsemen were more or less intact.

Red and orange flashes whizzed around and above them. Young Harry Bell was hit by machine-gun fire that knocked him off his horse. He hit the broken soil hard. Instinct caused him to cover his head as the Light Horse thundered over and by him. But after a few seconds the pain of a bullet high on the femur, which had shattered the bone, and then the twisting fall to earth that left his right leg mangled, took over. He passed out.

Chauvel, on the rise close to his big guns, was inspired by the charge and excited by the view as darkness crept in. Continuous rifle fire flashes outlined the position of the enemy trenches. Their field guns beyond and above the rifles delivered the bigger, deeper light emissions. His own artillery shells burst 'like a row of red stars' over the defence lines.

'The long lines of cavalry swept forward at racing speed,' he noted, 'half obscured in clouds of reddish dust. Amid the deafening sound [right near the artillery]. . . they seemed to move silently, like some splendid, swift machine.'[3]

Grant had dropped back to keep an eye on the advancing formation, leaving Lawson and Bourchier at the front of the main body of troopers. They were all following scouts O'Leary and Healy charging straight at where the most trench rifle-fire was coming from.

Either the Turks in their panic failed to change their rifle sights at this point, or they were just poor shots, or both. But as the troopers reached the last 500 metres, none was hit. They could see the shallow front trench, with nearby earthworks indicating incompletion. There were few Turkish riflemen.

The horses, first running as hard as in a race, were now performing as hurdlers. With the scouts still leading the way, they careered over the first trench. No man or horse was shot or bayoneted from it. They thudded down and galloped on, straight at the second, deeper, wider trench 30 metres back. It was stacked with Turks. Many froze, some panicked and a few took aim with rifles or lurched up and under with bayonets, as a wall of striking hooves and muscular horseflesh flew at and over them. Several horses and riders were cut down, including two Victorian graziers, Lieutenants F. J. Burton from Minyip and B. P. G. Meredith from Colac. Most made it.

Scouts O'Leary and Healy amazed themselves by being first over the three front trenches. Healy did not hesitate or wait for the others to reach him. He dismounted and was first to run at the trenches. In a matter of seconds, Lawson and the first squadron were with him.

The maverick O'Leary, however, belted on into Beersheba. He spotted an artillery gun being rolled away by six gunners, galloped them down, fired his rifle and forced them to surrender.

He bustled the captives down a side-street and waited. He wasn't letting this 'haul' go until his mates arrived.

Back closer to the trenches, the tidal wave of horses were reined in amid an encampment of tents and huts. Then the cavalry morphed into infantry. They dismounted. One trooper in each section designated to gather the horses did his job. The rest ran back, hearts pumping hard, bayonets flaying and with a huge psychological advantage of what had just been achieved in the face of a stunned enemy. Some Turks resisted with steel and rifle, but only a few, and to little effect. About 35 were felled in the west end of the second trench. The rest there threw up their hands and begged for mercy.

'One of the troopers had galloped on to a [third] reserve trench,' historian Henry Gullett recorded, 'the Turks shot his horse as he jumped, and the animal fell into the trench. When the dazed Australian found his feet he was surrounded by five Turks with their hands up.'[4]

Major C.M. Fetherstonhaugh, a grazier from Coonamble, New South Wales, found his fine charger had been hit 30 metres from the trenches. It didn't make the first 'hurdle'. The major dismounted, took out his revolver and shot it between the eyes. It was a terrible moment for him. He loved that horse. Fired up and bent on pay-back, Fetherstonhaugh rushed to the trench firing at the Turks. He killed four before being shot in both legs.[5] Mounted stretcher-bearers arrived and attended to him with their customary calm bravery. Some explained their courage by the fact they had to save lives. It was their job *and* duty. They didn't have time to think about anything else. They just did what they had to in any accident situation. None had shirked the heaviest of fire. In the rush, some stretcher-bearers, unarmed and focused, were killed.

The Turkish trenches and redoubts (battlefield fortifications) were laid out at different angles on small hills and there was no continuity.

Major Hyman galloped on to a fort on a hill manned by 100 Turks. He dismounted and led 13 troopers in a fierce fight of bayonet, rifle and revolver. Hyman's wild attack following the reckless charge gave his small pack extra force. He was a crack shot with rifle or revolver. He favoured the freedom of the smaller weapon in close-quarter fighting. He used it with brutal, unerring accuracy felling an estimated 15 Turks of the 60 that were killed in this one action. After a 10-minute encounter, the remaining 40 Turks gave up.

Between the fort and the trenches, a Turkish crew scrambled to remove a machine-gun from a mule, with a backup crew close by. Orders were being screamed by an officer who kept turning and pointing at the trenches. The aim was clear. The machine-gunners would rake the area and slaughter the still incoming troopers. Armourer Staff Sergeant Jack Cox spotted the crews, turned his horse and headed straight for the 11 armed Turks. Cox, now a target running parallel with the trenches, charged the crews, brandishing his revolver. The officer fired at him. Cox returned fire, wounding the officer, who dropped to the ground. The aggressive approach caused the other 10 Turks to surrender.

The quick thinking and guts of Hyman, Cox and many others in hurtling at the enemy had saved many from certain death at such close range.

Acts like this were quickly turning Beersheba the way of the assaulting force.[6]

There was chaos now, and this is where the troopers thrived. Some, still mounted, raced on to Beersheba with instructions to stop the wells being blown. They heard several explosions and at first thought their mission had failed. An ammunition dump went up in flames, as did a flour mill. A locomotive was up-ended. Then, to the oncoming troopers' horror, two wells were blown. If the other 15 exploded, Beersheba would be a disaster despite the incredible charge.

*

The 27-year-old, tall, dark-haired German officer/engineer assigned to throw the switches was not sure about what he was doing. He was in a central control room in the town's centre, facing a bank of switches and wires. He had replaced the chief engineer who had set up the demolition switches, who was on leave in Jerusalem. The stand-in hesitated. He was unsure which switch did what. He had heard the result of his first few jittery slamming downs of the switches on one board and was just about to throw the rest, when two light horsemen rode up, dismounted and crashed open the door to the control room.

The troopers yelled at the German as they aimed their revolvers at him. The German turned. He could tell by the plumed slouch hats that they were Australians. He was surprised to be alive, given their reputations. In a split second, he had the choice of glory if his hand pushed down on a switch and blew up wells containing 400,000 litres of precious water. If they went up, the entire Light Horse would be forced to retreat to find water elsewhere. The Germans and Turks could hold the Gaza–Beersheba defences. The third attempt to break through would not succeed; British General Edmund Allenby would fall at his first big hurdle as commander-in-chief. The entire Middle East campaign would be lost.

The German raised his hands. He would not be remembered for his martyrdom.

The charge had broken the Turkish resistance. The advancing 7th Mounted Brigade veered off the Khelasa road from the west to hit the retreating Turks. The 1st and 3rd Brigades, which had struck fierce resistance in the east, now broke through, creating an enemy melee that surged through the town and out to the hills in the north. Some stopped and set up machine-gun and sniper posts, causing further battles as the Australians pursued them in the darkness.

The territory was as unfamiliar at night to the troopers as it was to the Turks. About 100 of the enemy became lost wandering near a remote outpost on a hill in the north. It was manned by a squadron of the 10th Light Horse led by Major Timperley. The Western Australians heard the wandering Turks coming from every direction.

'Who goes there?' Timperley challenged.

There was no response, which suggested it was the enemy.

'We will open fire unless you surrender!' he called.

Again there was no response. The Turks began to set up a makeshift fort and to dig in. Timperley ordered his machine-gunners to sweep the area almost 360 degrees. There were cries in the dark as the gunners collected targets. This was followed by the sound of the enemy fleeing the area. Later, 50 Turkish casualties were found.

It was a matter of time before those who had taken flight were killed or rounded up as prisoners. By midnight, the Beersheba streets were deserted of locals and the enemy and populated only by Anzac troopers.

An ebullient Chauvel, having a late meal in a 'fine, comfortable stone house', was presented with a wine of dubious quality by his aide-de-camp to celebrate the victory.

In one crowded hour, from the moment the two regiments had been ordered to saddle up to the minute Beersheba was penetrated, the desert campaign had had its charge in every sense. Allenby had taken over from General Murray in June 1917 as commander-in-chief of the Egyptian Expeditionary Force (EEF), and this was his first major venture.

He had not experienced at first hand Chauvel's brilliance as a commander in other major battles in the desert campaign at Romani, El Arish, Magdhaba and Rafa in the push from Egypt through the Sinai to southern Palestine. All those battles had been won *before* Allenby arrived. But now the new chief knew what power he had at his disposal with 30,000 light horsemen and cavalry under Chauvel's command. It gave the new commander-in-chief confidence that he could now dream of going on to sweep the entire Turkish/German force out of Palestine, Syria, Jordan and Arabia.

He and Chauvel would have an inkling, but not yet full awareness, that this loss would have a dramatic impact on the morale of the main enemy force of Turks. The Light Horse's audacity—the enemy saw it as 'madness'—in attacking in such a manner against huge odds created a pattern. It meant that every time the Anzacs hurled themselves and their mounts at a fort or charged a town, the Beersheba experience would be on enemy minds. Those who had not witnessed the charge would hear reports that would send chills up their spines.

Fear would be with the Turks from that day no matter what their superiority in terms of men and weaponry. This would be a crucial factor later in the campaign when pressure on the defending 4th, 7th and 8th Turkish armies was at its peak.

Though he did not think it at the time, this was the finest hour for Harry Chauvel in his battle command experience over six years and two wars. How did an Australian officer become the leader in a British army of the most potent cavalry force in history, and the most successful battle commander in the Middle East War of 1914–1918?

For answers we must go back to his roots.

2

Chauvel of Tabulam

Harry Chauvel was on a collision course with war from a saddle by his background, birth, upbringing, desire, needs and destiny. The second son of Major Charles Chauvel was born on 16 April 1865, the same year as the King

of the British Empire, George V, whom he would serve; the
Supreme German Commander of World War I, General Erich
Ludendorff, whose forces he would oppose on the Eastern
Front; and John Monash from Melbourne, the most outstand-
ing general on the Western Front.

Chauvel was 'old' at 49 in 1914, but his lean, neat frame,
small stature, and ease on a horse in any circumstance made him
appear a decade younger.

His bloodline was French Huguenot, an aristocratic line
of Calvinists, or church reformists. They were persecuted and
forced out of their homeland after 1685, when Louis XIV
stripped away their legal protections. Harry's land-owning fore-
bears from the Loire Valley, led by Simon Chauvel, fled across
the Channel to England. Simon's grandson was a Lieutenant
Colonel James Chauvel of the Middlesex Militia. In 1838, a
direct-line descendant, Charles, arrived in Australia a free set-
tler. In 1848, he bought a fabulous sheep property at Tabulam
in the Clarence River region of northern New South Wales. His
second son Charles Henry married the well-bred Fanny James,
took over the business of nearly 20,000 acres, expanded it to
8,000 sheep and added 2,000 head of shorthorn cattle. Harry
(christened Henry George) was the second born of seven children to Charles Henry and Fanny.

Most country kids in Australia of the 19th century could
boast being on a horse as long as they could remember. Harry
could go one better. He was on a horse before he could remember. Fanny sat him on a cushion on the pummel of her saddle
before he was a year old.

Horses had been part of all the colonies since their inception,
and young Harry had been raised as if they were family. They
were an essential part of living on the land, more natural than
the car is today. Horses and their capacities created the rhythms
of Australia for many generations. Even with the advent of trains
mid-century they were by far the dominant means of transport
for most pioneering families of the era. They had become char-
acteristically Australian, more even than the hot sun, the frost
of winter, the floods and droughts, the willy-willies and the dust.

They were as much the aroma of the bush as eucalypt, bushfire smoke, fresh bread and beer in a country pub. The whinnying, snorting and the steady clip-clop on hard ground or the thunder over open ground, blended with the cries of native birds by day, and noises of assorted animals such as possums, dogs and dingoes at night.

To young Harry, horses were as important as siblings, and loved almost as much. He never subscribed to the concept that his equine companions had the brains of a two-year-old child. They had done things that would baffle an intelligent man, such as guiding a rider through fire and smoke without panic, or carrying to safety a rider who had collapsed on his back. Horses exhibited features that were essential in bush life: loyalty and mateship. Without a dog, you could be lonely; without a horse in Australia's inhospitable outback, you were lost or dead. A man loved his wife, children, mates, dogs and horses with near equal facility.

Harry's first school was Belcher's boarding school near Goulburn, about 900 kilometres south-south-east from Tabulam, the family station. To reach it in 1873, Harry, aged seven, and his elder brother Arthur, eight, rode two days to the New South Wales towns of Grafton or Lawrence, protected by an Aboriginal stockman. This was his first memorable experience of a long ride. From then on, the horse was front and centre of his universe. They then caught a ship to Sydney and a train to Goulburn.

Belcher's provided the usual good training in reading, writing and arithmetic, along with history and geography. The school also added farm work and horse riding to its curriculum. More memorable still were the frightening floods of July 1876, when the Clarence River burst over its wide catchment, and threatened the farm. The entire herd was in danger and the few horses left on the property were vital in saving lives both human and bovine.

Harry and Arthur went on in 1876 to Sydney Grammar, where they were known as 'Little Shovel' and 'Big Shovel', and could not wait to return home for term and summer holidays.

City life was not as attractive as the bush, although Harry did make some lasting acquaintances, including an A.B. 'Banjo' Paterson, who, like him, came from a long line of soldiers, and who also had ambitions to continue the military tradition. They both enjoyed the cadet corps, and were inspired by the lessons on Saladin (the 12th century Kurdish general and Muslim warrior from northern Iraq), Napoleon, Wellington, and the American Civil War. Harry was well aware of his ancestry and wanted a military life above all else. It was viewed through the prism of British military history, which was romanticised as all that was good and positive in life.

He had style, and enjoyed wearing a French kepi (military cap), scarlet jacket and blue trousers in the cadets. The colour, carbine and camaraderie had brought alive his past and his future. At least that was what he believed.

Harry was much more at ease at Toowoomba Grammar in his last year of school in 1881. Now 16, he rode the entire 240 kilometres with younger brother Allan, escorted again by an Aboriginal stockman, who brought the packhorse back. The boys kept their horses at school as did most of their fellow pupils. Harry was a competitor in races and buck-jumping shows on weekends, a time when students were encouraged to ride into the mountains and live off the land, with possums and rabbits being favourite catches. At 168 centimetres (5 feet 6 inches) and 60 kilograms, he proved to be an accomplished jockey, wearing his claret and pale blue colours, and doing well enough in outback picnic races to suggest he might have taken his racing further. But Harry was ambitious for another life.

In his first decade after school, he would lead a bushman's existence in the untamed border country of New South Wales and Queensland under varying conditions of dry desert plains, rugged mountains and waterways. His main work was with the cattle and horses at Tabulam, and other family properties at Tooloom, Acacia Creek, and Canning Downs South just over the New South Wales border in Queensland.

At 21 in 1886, he already had the grounding for any future military career to do with cavalry, or mounted riflemen. His interest was generated by his father Charles, whose father, grandfather and great-grandfather had been soldiers. Charles obtained permission from the New South Wales government to raise the Upper Clarence Light Horse, and was gazetted captain on 14 March 1886. It was a family affair and a serious one. Arthur and Harry were made second lieutenants, and the two younger brothers Allan and Percy became troopers. They wore blue and scarlet uniforms with white helmets. They trained among the white gum trees on a hill on the Clarence's west bank at Tabulam, which was named 'Bugle Hill' in honour of this further inspirational military moment. The drilling led to a major event when England's Lord Carrington opened the Tenterfield Railway. The Chauvels were part of the guard of honour formed by 30 representatives of the Upper Clarence Light Horse.

This was the profession Harry wanted. The family tradition, pomp, discipline, service for empire (Australia in 1886 was still just a political promise, not a nation), and being high in the saddle providing it, was a romantic attraction. The way for someone with his background was to be trained with England's Royal Military Academy, Sandhurst, where a cadet passed out in order of merit. He had his sights set, not on the Royal Engineers or artillery, but the cavalry. He had enough money to make the trip to England for training. It was a matter of when, not if. But in 1888 the colonies ran into a recession. Much of it was to do with drought in rural New South Wales. The Chauvels couldn't sell their stud bulls. Cattle became unsaleable, except for tallow. Banks began to call in loans. Charles Chauvel had to sell Tabulam for less than half its value before the recession. This was a blow to the family. They would survive in reduced circumstances after the decades of plenty by moving north to Canning Downs South station. But it would never be the same. Tabulam had been heavenly; the new home region did not have the same appeal.

In 1891, Harry Chauvel had his first taste of real 'combat' or 'conflict' as a soldier, but in the form all honest soldiers wished to avoid with a passion: when the military is used to quell civil unrest. Maritime workers had been on strike, but their efforts had failed. This encouraged pastoralists to get tough with shearers, who had supported their dockside and ship-worker brethren. Trouble welled in Clermont, central Queensland, where shearers congregated and rejected contracts offered to them. The pastoralists threatened to bring in 'foreign' or 'free' labour from other colonies. Rumours abounded that Chinese would be invited to work in Australia. The shearers responded by promising violence against these 'scabs'. The Queensland government was forced to act. It called up the local defence force to support the police.

Chauvel with his 20 mounted riflemen was ordered to Charleville where their assignment was to escort a group of free labourers to a sheep station north of the town. He would have been apprehensive. His force was made up of farm workers with no formal military training. It was topped up with police but was never more than 25 strong. Chauvel loathed the idea of using arms against fellow Australians, and in many ways this was more a test of discipline than if he were leading men into battle. Restraint would be his watch-word. But there was always the fear that matters could get out of hand, especially when less than two kilometres from their destination they were confronted by about 220 mounted shearers.

The senior policeman, an inspector, in Chauvel's group moved first, pointing out four shearers that were on his 'wanted' list. They were arrested. One of the arrestees screamed for action. The shearers, brandishing iron bars and other weapons, swarmed around the protection party. The police were outnumbered. The inspector looked nervously to Chauvel. It was up to him.

'Soldiers . . . load!' Chauvel called with authority.

'Lieutenant,' the inspector yelled, 'take the men [free labourers] through [the angry mob]!'

Chauvel pointed his rifle outward and not at the mob. His men did the same. Chauvel, his right hand free, motioned his small force forward. He led them and the four fresh captives through the aggrieved shearers. The mounted riflemen moved with precision and intent. The unionists parted. Chauvel's party pushed on, only to be followed by the angriest shearers. The inspector, emboldened by realising that Chauvel and his force would not buckle, turned back to warn the followers he would make more arrests if they continued.

The shearers fell back, hurling abuse. The demonstrators had been faced and defeated.

In a quiet ceremony after this 'action', Chauvel handed each mounted rifleman a piece of emu hide with the long, flowing feathers attached. They were to be worn in their slouch hats as a reminder of their courage.

In the early 1890s, there was talk of economic recovery. However, a depression, not yet experienced before by the colonies, took hold and led to a run on the banks. Many hopes, ambitions and lives were ruined. Arthur Chauvel was set to be a city barrister. That aspiration expired. After a broken romance, he became a country recluse. Harry Chauvel's dream of escaping to Europe to join Sandhurst evaporated. His life, at 28, was not in tatters, but his expectations were lowered. There would be no more reverie of leading the British cavalry in some far reach of empire; just a shift from his regiment to the Queensland Mounted Infantry now that he was based in the northern state. He was still a second lieutenant.

To salve his disappointment when he had saved some money in tough times, he bought a hurdler, Beggar Boy, whose name was no reflection of Chauvel's mind or the horse's ability, especially when he proved good enough to be entered in a Queensland Turf Club hurdle race in Brisbane. It was a gamble. Chauvel couldn't afford a top jockey. He engaged one of his Canning Downs South station hands to ride him.

Beggar Boy took off like a winner, much to Chauvel's delight. The horse led the field by such a distance that the bookies looked on in horror as the long-shot from the bush seemed a certain winner. The station hand, inexperienced at big events, felt Beggar Boy had even more in him. He brought out the whip. The horse accelerated, taking a jump too fast. Animal and man crumpled to ground. The jockey was thrown clear, but six other horses ran over Beggar Boy. He was injured. The station hand, perhaps over-exuberant in the moment, jumped back on the horse and pounded after the leaders. The game animal galloped in third; remarkable given the ground he had to make up.

Beggar Boy had an injured hind leg and needed a vet. Chauvel could not afford the close attention needed to bring the horse back to racing again. Reluctantly, it was sold to Queensland's police commissioner, who promised to look after it, which he did with spectacular results. Beggar Boy went on to many race wins in Brisbane and Sydney. Chauvel had to look on with mixed feelings.

His daughter Elyne Mitchell wrote:

'Knowing the bond of affection that Dad created with any animal he owned, I realize how he must have felt . . . so there was Dad, still with a longing for the permanent [British] army, short of money, his own home [at Tabulam] sold, his beautiful horse damaged, and now owned by someone else.'[1]

Harry Chauvel's life was hardly shattered. He had work in a field he appreciated. Unlike the thousands of unemployed wandering the streets of Sydney and Melbourne, he still had hope. Yet it was a fall from the heights in his world and a test of character.

Until 1896, Chauvel more or less marked time, running Canning Downs South, and continuing with his company of volunteer mounted riflemen. Then came the first of several big changes. A few months after his father died, he applied for and was appointed adjutant for the Moreton Regiment in the Queensland Defence Force. This made him responsible for turn-out, discipline and routine, a job for which he was well-suited. He would be paid £306 a year and stationed in Victoria Barracks, Brisbane.

The life he was leading was beginning to etch itself into his fine features. Because he was lean and spare of face and body,

Chauvel, at 31, probably already had the appearance he would have for the rest of his years. He was all refinement and good breeding, from the lean aristocratic nose and flared nostrils, to the square jaw line that would never bridge a second chin. He had the thin, durable and deceptively strong body of a long-distance runner, and the fine-boned hands and fingers of a pianist rather than those of a cattle rustler. Chauvel's sharp blue eyes, however, were the key to his character. Unblinking and calm, they would never betray fear to his subordinates. They were the eyes of a self-disciplined, self-possessed man. In moments of confrontation and physical danger, they were steady; in repose, they twinkled.

With this move to further consolidate as a professional soldier, he may well have thought, indeed hoped, that life would never be quite the same as before.

3

Change of Pace

It proved to be more than just another tennis game when Chauvel met for the first time and played 16-year-old school-girl Sibyl Jopp at Newmarket Brisbane early in 1904. It promised to be even a match for life. This attractive, lean brunette was 23 years his junior. He had a penchant for younger women, and Sibyl had the 'right' pedigree for someone of his background. Her mother was Bertha Manning of the Sydney legal family, granddaughter of Arthur Wilcox Manning, who was principal under-secretary at the foundation of the colony. Her grandfather on the other side was George Keith Jopp, a surveyor who had charted much of the vast Queensland outback.

The Jopps still thought of themselves as Scottish despite having been in Australia for three generations. Sibyl's father Keith had been a friend of Chauvel's since before the Boer War.

At first he did not consider this teenager as a future partner. But he was 39 in 1904 and feeling the pressure to marry and have a family. Chauvel's experience in the Boer War in South Africa, 1899–1902, in his mid-30s had unsettled him. The excitement had caused him to be less inclined to think about settling down. After the ready availability of women of varying backgrounds on the veldt and in the town and cities, he had, like many soldiers, been affected in his attitude to partners. Young soldiers in their late teens and 20s were more inclined to return to Australia and look for a partner and start a family. Chauvel's maturity caused him to be less precipitate and more cautious. Now he had been back three years and was approaching middle age (for the time), he was feeling more comfortable about taking on responsibilities. Another factor too, that had held him back was his lack of means. His background of some wealth in the Tabulam days made him concerned about not being able to offer a partner home comforts and a good education for their children. But his new job carried a reasonable pay. He was determined, in his own undemonstrative way, to be elevated to higher positions within the army.

Chauvel's confidence was growing. He was now based in Brisbane as acting chief staff officer after being isolated for three years at remote tropical Townsville as a lieutenant colonel. He was also appointed aide-de-camp to the first Queensland governor, which added prestige, although little extra income.

He drew close over the next two years to the lovely Sibyl, who had just left school. Chauvel did not surprise her father in January 1906 when he asked for her hand in marriage. Exactly two years after that first tennis match, Chauvel, 41, proposed. They married on 16 June 1906. It was the most important change in his life. He had drifted as a single man in the years before and after the Boer War. Now both his professional and private life had direction and goals.

Another change from the past was the sale of Canning

Downs South, which severed all ties with his country life. It also delivered some moderate funds that would not go astray in the development of the marital home.

Chauvel's experience in South Africa put him in no doubt that he wanted to stay in the military. But there was a catch. He had been inspired by the actual combat, yet it seemed unlikely on any scale in the region or in support of the Empire, at least in the near future. There were scares about 'yellow hordes' (an unidentified Asian force) invading in the 19th century but that had evaporated. The Japanese were becoming increasingly adventurous, especially after their defeat of Russia in the Russo-Japanese War of 1904–05; the Germans were in the area with their eyes on certain bases close to Australia, including New Guinea. But neither of these two nations was seen as a direct threat in the first decade of the 20th century.

Chauvel was part of the struggle at home to create a professional federal armed force. Some ministers were supportive in principle, but when it came to allocating funds, they were slow. On top of that, left-wing elements in the well-organised Labor Party, which was gaining in political strength all the time, were keen to rail against an obscure 'militarism', encompassing the armed forces. It was a Marxist term linked with 'capitalism' and therefore anathema to the feverishly doctrinaire in the party. If anything, this retarded the military's development, although one of the more worldly and intelligent Labor men, Senator G. F. Pearce, was a supporter.

Chauvel was not making headway in his own career. He was a supporter of (now Sir) Edward Hutton, his commander in South Africa, who had the gigantic task of creating and leading the new Australian army. When he left for England in 1904, Chauvel was marked as a 'Hutton' man, and his successor, Major General Sir J. C. Hoad, held it against him. Chauvel was informed bluntly that he would not be moved from Brisbane, an outpost compared with Melbourne and Sydney, and therefore conveniently (for Hoad and his supporters) out of the way.

Chauvel requested secondment to the newly formed New South Wales General Staff in London. This was rejected. Once more his ambition to further his career at the seat of empire had been rebuffed.

Chauvel was not political in the sense of manipulating gains for himself within the growing army bureaucracy. This meant he had to mark time and wait for something to happen. In the lull, he did what all army personnel do between engagements: he filled in his day as best he could with boring (for him) administrative work. He hated the idea of being posted to Duntroon, the newly established military college in New South Wales; not because he did not care to be helpful to the new breed coming on. He simply preferred action, or the chance of it; more like Clancy than the office worker. Yet he was chief instructor of all Light Horse schools in Queensland and a supervisor of infantry schools. He also conducted practical examinations of units in the Brisbane area.

Chauvel did, however, lecture. He had the experience that few had in actual war. It had been instructive to him. He felt he had learned much about soldiering, especially leadership and how to handle the 'Australian soldier', that strange, ill-defined and little understood character. He had distinguished himself in battle in South Africa. His courage was not in question; his self-discipline and reliability were never in doubt.

One major problem was creating an esprit de corps, a hackneyed expression in the early 1900s, which referred to the good attitude of the soldier towards his unit. It was lacking in the Boer War, a main factor being the need for the Australians to be tacked onto British army elements where they never quite fitted in. If there had been a national army, Chauvel and all the other Australian commanders would have had a chance to create spirit in the entity. There was no chance for anything like it in the Boer War. This led to a negative image of the Australians, which was exacerbated by the Breaker Morant affair. Morant had fought with the South Australian Mounted Rifles, and he and P. J. Handcock were court-martialled and executed by firing squad for murdering several Boer prisoners and a German missionary. Whatever the merits of the case, it created an image Chauvel and the Mounted Rifles could do without.

Chauvel's lectures lauded the Australian soldier's positive features. But he concentrated on the areas of potential improvement in an attempt to overcome perceived weaknesses. He did not worry about the trivia, such as the lack of saluting which drove British officers apoplectic. Chauvel's concern centred on 'march discipline'. This was where soldiers would simply drop out of a troop formation, go off alone or in a small group for any amount of time and then drift back when they felt like it, usually when they had run out of food. They would never stray out of touch with their regiment, and would remain near enough to be safe from the enemy. Chauvel called the hundred or so Australians and Canadians who did this on the ride from Bloemfontein to Pretoria 'the Legion of the Lost Ones'.

These rogue or maverick operators often robbed and looted. They caused havoc on the local farms and in the towns.

He saw this as part of the reason for 'Australia's bad name' in South Africa. Chauvel was aware that the national army could not emulate the British layered class system, which saw the officers drawn from the middle and upper classes and the soldiers from lower classes. The set-up in Australia had to be handled differently. It had few class layers. Men would refuse to be bullied or treated without respect. There was also the opportunity for officers to emerge from among the non-commissioned if they showed leadership skills and wanted elevation, something impossible within the British structure.

Chauvel insisted officers should 'know their work', that is, know what they were doing to ensure the confidence and respect of their men. An officer should never court popularity at the expense of discipline. Rather than drawing on the Boer War, he used his 'hot' experience during the shearers' strike in 1891 as an instance of the right way to lead. He had shown his skills when the situation became nasty. After that he had the respect of the rank and file.

'The only way of instilling discipline into the Australian,' he said, 'was by appealing to his common sense and esprit de corps [once developed] when trouble comes.'

The soldier had to be imbued with the idea of 'keeping his end up'. This would run through the regiment and be the norm rather than the exception when soldiers were under pressure.

Chauvel, who had lived, worked and trained with bushmen all his life, did not agree with the promoted image of their capacities to carry on under extreme conditions without food, or to put up with the monotony of prolonged missions.

'I've never seen the oily rag,' Chauvel said, 'that he [the bushman] was meant to live off . . . the Australian man is like the Australian horse; he must have his belly half full.'[1]

This on the surface seemed harsh, but there was rarely love lost between officers and soldiers, even in the more egalitarian Australian society. Soldiers, for their part, had limited regard for officers, who were maligned for their relative inaction and 'good living'. Officers had to earn respect, either by example in the field or at least by the way they looked after their men on and off the battlefield. A trick for the better officers to learn was the thin line between being too strict for discipline's sake, and being too slack. Those who aped their British counterparts, where there was a thick line drawn between officers and men in all matters, were destined for failure.

The Chauvels' first child, Ian, was born in 1907; then Edward (Teddy) in 1909. He was becoming a family man. Without the focus of war, which had sharpened him, his career was directionless and thwarted by his being out of favour with superiors.

4

Fortune's Turning

Sir J. C. Hoad, who had retarded Chauvel's advance, died in 1911. It meant a turning of the wheel of fortune for him. In the changes that occurred, Chauvel received a boost when appointed the army's adjutant general, and would be based at headquarters in Melbourne. He also took up a position on the Military Board, which meant that he would be on top of all army developments and in line for the best appointments in the event of war. The main reason for his elevation was his support for the retention of the militia, which had been run in various forms for decades. Opposed to this were those who wished to disband it and create a compulsory or conscripted army from scratch. Chauvel felt the militia and the regular force could be merged or run in parallel, which was the thinking of Kitchener and his staff.

Chauvel, Sibyl and family moved to Melbourne at the end of 1911. He began work in an office in the bluestone Victoria Barracks on St Kilda Road. With the reshuffle at the top of the army and no obvious impediment to his aims, Chauvel, for the third time, began lobbying for an appointment to England, this time to the War Office.

While Chauvel preoccupied himself with a professional enhancement in London, the United Kingdom's First Lord of the Admiralty, Winston Churchill, 40, was making strategic moves over oil that would determine much of Chauvel's destiny. Three years earlier in 1911, Churchill had declared oil to be of paramount importance for the supremacy of the British Imperial

Navy. Marcus Samuel, the founder of Shell, was his educator in
this matter. In 1913, Churchill sent an expeditionary team to the
Persian Gulf headed by Admiral Slade to investigate the chance
of extracting oil from the region. At the same time, Churchill oversaw a secret agreement with the Sheikh of Kuwait, who
promised exclusive oil rights to the British. The latter move was
a political coup. Kuwait publicly still pledged allegiance to the
Ottoman Sultan in Istanbul. (Once war was underway in 1914,
Churchill pushed hard for Kuwait to become a British protectorate, which was achieved in November of that year.)

In July 1913 and about the time of the birth of his third child,
Elyne, Chauvel heard that he would be taking up his long-
yearned-for appointment, but not before a visit to Australia by
Sir Ian Hamilton, the inspector-general of British overseas forces.
It was important for Chauvel to be at home at this time. He had
been acquainted with Hamilton in South Africa, and would be
invaluable in advising him on Australian developments, especially in the Light Horse.

Hamilton arrived in November 1913 and began inspecting the troops as tensions in international relations worsened.
Alarm bells had been set off after the Agadir crisis of July 1911
when the Germans deployed a gunboat, *Panther*, to the Moroccan port of Agadir, which was a signal of intentions to threaten
British dominance on the high seas. The backdrop of the Balkan
Wars (1912 and 1913) added to the uncertain atmosphere. Now
the Germans were beating war drums and building up their
arms, particularly artillery, at a rate that more than suggested
war preparation.

Hamilton wished in particular to assess the Australian preparedness for conflict. He was a far more acute thinker than
Kitchener, who had looked over the Australian army in 1910.
Hamilton toured Australia in a blur of parades, lunches, din-
ners, field exercises and speeches that drove him to distraction.
But along the way impressions were made that would stay with
this erudite, urbane Scot, and these would be conveyed to the

British War Office. Of all the military personnel he met, Colonel John Monash, a part-time soldier from Melbourne, had the most impact. He was a man of 'outstanding force and character', Hamilton noted. He added that Monash had a necessary 'ruthless streak' after viewing exercises in brutal bushfire heat outside Melbourne early in 1914.

He was also taken with the Light Horse regiments above the others. In a letter to the Australian Minister for Defence, E. D. Millen, Hamilton said:

'They are the thrusters who would be held up by no obstacle of ground, timber or water, from getting at the enemy.' They were less disciplined than the British Yeomanry but had more 'go and initiative' than them. The Light Horse were 'certainly under the control of their officers. This is a great deal more than could be said for this very same type of man in the South African War.'

Chauvel's efforts in training around Australia were the main reason for this. The report would have been of some satisfaction, given his own observations and efforts for more than a decade to develop the troops' efficiency, professionalism and spirit after the Boer War.

Hamilton went on to say that in all the Australian army he thought the Light Horse were the best fitted for war, adding:

'They are the most formidable body of troops, who would shape very rapidly under service conditions.'

Coming from perhaps the most highly respected cavalryman in the empire, this was huge praise and reflected on its leaders, especially Chauvel. It would be taken into account in any future conflict. Hamilton's chief of staff, Brigadier General G. F. Ellison, writing to Kitchener's chief of staff Brigadier General George Kirkpatrick, said:

'I have great faith in Chauvel's sound commonsense, and am endeavouring to obtain his opinions on all the more important recommendations Sir Ian has in mind.'[1]

Kirkpatrick himself, on visiting Australia with Kitchener a few years earlier, made notes for Hamilton on the various army leaders he encountered. Chauvel, he said, was 'delightful, reliable, honest, slow, just. Best A.G. [adjutant-general] Commonwealth has had'.

The 'slow' remark seemed incongruous in the list. Chauvel was not someone to push himself forward. Perhaps Kirkpatrick, not himself known for sharp thinking or articulation, meant 'methodical'. Yet an overall tone of appreciation was there. Chauvel was seen as even more acceptable because he was 'sound on the Imperial Connection'. In other words, he would be compliant in doing the empire's bidding. Kirkpatrick also observed that Chauvel 'gets his own way on the [Australian] Army Board'.[2]

Most importantly for Chauvel, the top echelons of the British War Office were now more than aware of his skills and capacities.

By early 1914, Churchill was stepping up moves to secure Britain's access to oil. Tensions in Europe were building. There was now a strong possibility of some sort of conflagration. It prompted the British to take dominant holdings in any company that was exploiting oil in Iraq. The favoured organisation was the inaptly named Turkish Petroleum Company (which had no actual Ottoman participation). It had been founded in 1911 and named this way to exploit Mosul oil. The aim was to explore in three provinces (vilayets), which made up Iraq (Mesopotamia) under Ottoman rule. The names of the capitals bore the names of the provinces: Mosul in the north; Baghdad in the middle; and Basra in the south. Geologists masquerading as archaeologists began visiting the area to carry out secret surveys.

In March 1914, an extraordinary meeting took place in London at the Foreign Office. Present were British and German diplomats, along with British and German bank executives. Also present were British and Dutch oil companies. The latter wanted the Germans 'in' because they held Turkish oil concessions. The British were most assertive at the meeting, given Churchill's aggressive attitude to his nation's attempt to control oil in Iraq. It was also seen as a gateway to the British colony of India.

The upshot of the dealing was that the British walked away with nearly a 50 per cent shareholding in the Turkish Petroleum Company, which meant that they were set to exploit oil finds in Iraq ahead of anyone else.

5

War Again

The newspaper clipping was no bigger than a couple of postage stamps. It was mailed by a secret band of terrorists—the Black Hand—in Zagreb, capital of Croatia, to a run-down cafe, Zlatna Moruna, in Belgrade where their comrades congregated. In late April 1914, they sat under a flickering gas light and read the tiny announcement that Austrian Archduke Franz Ferdinand would visit Sarajevo, the capital of Bosnia on 28 June. He was to direct army manoeuvres in the neighbouring mountains. It was passed from hand to hand in silence. This was the moment they had waited years for. They would attempt to assassinate him. The crude aim was to free Bosnia from Austria so that it could be integrated with Serbia.

On the day of the visit, 22 conspirators took up positions 500 metres apart over the entire route the archduke would travel from the rail station to the town hall. The motorcade travelled too fast for the first couple of assassins to throw grenades they had tucked under coats, especially as they would most likely kill Serbians, their comrades. The line of vehicles slowed just enough for a third would-be killer to hurl his grenade. It hit the side of the car. Three officers in the car were injured but the archduke was only shaken. The vehicle did not stop. It sped on to the town hall at such a pace that no further bomb throwing was attempted by another 12 assassins in the crowd.

The brave, perhaps foolhardy archduke attended the function held in honour of him and his pregnant wife Sofia. During it, the Austrian army commander begged them to leave the city. It was seething with rebellion, he said. Sofia saw the deep concern in the commander's eyes and persuaded her husband to make a hurried exit to a waiting train.

The escorted car sped to the bridge over the River Miljacka, at which it had to make a sharp turn, which slowed its progress. A young Bosnian Serb, Gavrilo Princip, stepped from the curb. He drew an automatic pistol and fired two shots. The first hit Sofia in the stomach, killing her and her unborn child. The second struck the archduke near the heart.

'Sofia!' was his last word before he too fell dead.

These shots triggered a chain reaction of political and military moves. The blood-related royals from several countries wrote letters to each other. England's King George V (who was married to a German, formerly Princess Mary of Teck) and Germany's Kaiser Wilhelm II communicated, but the latter was keen for conflict. He had presided over a huge build-up of arms and was ready for a stoush, which could even decide supremacy over all the faltering empires. Besides, he hated George, believing him to be overly favoured by their late grandmother, Queen Victoria. If this family feud developed, it promised to be like no other in history, given the military might of the two main antagonists. There were hurried conferences. The Germans laid out a doubtful secret deal, which was as tricky as it was unworkable. In a nutshell, they said: 'If you [the British] don't enter any possible conflict, we won't come on French soil, we'll just take their dominions.' The smarter British generals and politicians felt it was simply acquisition of territory by subterfuge and stealth, methods at which they were well-versed themselves. They were certain that the Germans would take France, and once at the channel would say: 'We won't come on British soil, we'll just take your dominions.' Australia, Canada and South Africa were known already to be mineral rich and would make lovely acquisitions for the German industrial/military complex. The British rejected the German deal.

Events were swiftly moving away from any royal or political influence, which was on the wane anyway. Even if a special peace-making figure had emerged at this point, time was running out to stop the political and military fission. Russia and France were already preparing to align. Germany, Austria and Turkey were doing the same. The UK, now it had said 'no' to the Germans, felt it was being sucked into a fiery vortex, from which there was no escape.

On 4 August 1914 the UK declared war on Germany. All of England's dominions, including Australia, were expected to take part in the conflict.

Like most Australians (and Europeans), Banjo Paterson read about the brutal murder in the press in late July and thought little of it. He had given away his law practice soon after returning from the Boer War. Moving around the country lecturing and public speaking about the war was more fun than the dingy law office. When the novelty petered out and the engagements dried up, he tried newspaper editorship (the Sydney *Evening News* followed by the more leisurely *Town & Country Journal*), and international and national travelling. When his health failed, he took up farming.

He was 50 years old. He had married at 40 25-year-old Alice Walker, but not even marital bliss could prevent him being jaded. His main interest was writing. Paterson reported much himself over the years and revelled in journalism. But his true love was poetry. He found his muse sporadically in time and quality, but it was always there lurking and tugging at his pen. Even someone of his repute found it impossible to live by his inspiration. It just didn't pay enough for a coffee and biscuit, let alone a family. A poem, even a classic such as 'Waltzing Matilda', brought him a pittance in royalties.

The morning he read in the papers that a war was 'on', he dashed into the *Sydney Morning Herald* and pushed hard to be its war correspondent. So much for farming, journalism and married life. He needed the excitement of battle, travel and the 'scoop'. But times had changed in 15 years since he rushed to South Africa. That was a puny event in a colony. This new conflict promised to be a world conflagration. The still fledgling Commonwealth government would pick and choose who it wanted to report the war, and not the papers themselves, although correspondents would mostly come from the established news groups. The *Sydney Morning Herald* would use Charles Bean (who would be the official government war historian, just chosen over Keith Murdoch, who would report for the Melbourne *Herald*). Paterson, out of pocket and out of touch, had to accept what he could get. He would be a reporter via the barn door. This poet, horse-lover, reporter and farmer secured a tenuous role as an honorary veterinarian on a troop ship carrying horses and soldiers. It was a clever ploy. Once aboard, the paper would make moves for him to upgrade to correspondent status. Paterson, still a gambler and adventurer in middle age, would somehow, somewhere find something beyond being a ship's unqualified horse doctor. That would get him the trip to the other side of the world at no expense. After that, he would rely on his reputation and wits to obtain suitable work.

In the meantime, before the ship left, he visited army camps around Sydney and established contacts. He was quickly a familiar sight, scribbling on a notepad, chatting and interviewing. Paterson loved it. He felt alive again. That elusive muse was floating about him like a misty banshee. Exactly one month after the declaration of war against Germany, Paterson dropped in his first piece for the *Sydney Morning Herald*. It was called 'Making an army', but could have been entitled, 'The remaking of a war correspondent'.

6

The Call, for All

The captain of the liner SS *Ulysses* took Chauvel aside when the ship reached Durban early in August 1914.

'The situation looks bad in Europe,' he told him, 'I am under orders to skip Cape Town and head for England, lights out all the way.'

Two days later, the captain summoned him to the bridge to show him an intercepted wireless cable from the German station at Swakopmund, South West Africa. It said the British had declared war on Germany for invading Belgium. Chauvel was concerned. Sibyl, now 26, and the three children, including six-month-old Elyne, were with him. He knew that the ship was carrying some weaponry including machine-guns, which could make it a target. The captain instigated daily parades for all passengers who wore belts at boat stations.

War on the high seas began. The German liner *Kaiser Wilhelm der Grosse* captured the British liner *Galicia*. But within a day, the battleship HMS *Highflyer* stalked and sank *Kaiser Wilhelm* and rescued *Galicia*. *Ulysses* continued to sneak up the coast of Africa, lights out, for seven successive nights.

Chauvel questioned the captain about their chances of making Liverpool without being 'taken'.

'They won't bother capturing us,' he was told, 'there is no German port from here to England. They will sink us.'[1]

Chauvel was relieved to sight Lands End on the English coast. Despite the limited news on the outbreak of hostilities, all on board were awed to see British troop ships of the expeditionary force already on their way across the Channel to France.

Once docked at Liverpool, he bundled the family onto a train to London while he searched for luggage lost in the confusion of thousands of departing troops. He was able to retrieve his bags and travel to London himself, a trip that took twice as long as normal. The train was pushed into sidings three times to make way for those carrying soldiers to Liverpool.

Chauvel went straight to the War Office the next morning and requested a posting to France. But there was a cable from Australia informing him he had been appointed commander of the 1st Light Horse Brigade, making him the only Australian-born regular officer to take over a command. He would be forced to wait months for his troops, which was irritating with all the activity going on around him in England. Yet he rejoiced in his appointment and honour. It drove home how he was destined to be in the action. He was 49 years of age, and considered 'old' for combat. The Boer War had given him experience at conflict, which now would be invaluable. He had left South Africa 13 years ago and had been marking time ever since with the vivid thought that he would retire without any further major contribution in battle. In an instant, all languid ideas about a career wasted had evaporated.

Dour, bullying Colonel Bridges, who would command Australia's first division of infantry, wrote explaining that the Light Horse would be made up of a regiment each from New South Wales and Queensland; a further regiment would be raised from smaller states Tasmania and South Australia.

There was an election in Australia on 5 September 1914. The result was a new government led by Andrew Fisher. Chauvel and others in the military were pleased: George Pearce would be defence minister. He was respected by all Australia's top commanders.

While waiting impatiently for his troops, Chauvel was given a spartan room in the London War Office. His experience on the Military Board paid off for his country. His desk job entailed looking after administrative matters, including training. This led him to take train trips down to Salisbury Plain, where his troops were destined. He was appalled with conditions. The weather was cold and wet in late autumn. The fields for exercises were waterlogged. Conditions would be worse in a few months when the Australians arrived. Chauvel asked if there would be huts built to house the troops. He did not receive a straight answer from High Command, and realised that his men would most likely suffer in the dead of winter in canvas tents. He urged that the 20,000 troops, which included his Light Horse, coming from Australia should be disembarked in Egypt. Notes sent to Field Marshal Kitchener, the Secretary of State for War, who had the final say, were ignored. Chauvel lobbied the Australian High Commissioner, who in turn fronted Kitchener and had the order changed. The Australians and New Zealanders would now land in a good winter climate in the Middle East. Apart from the better conditions, they would have more time to train.

Chauvel's commonsense and care for his men had been invaluable long before a shot would be fired in battle by an Australian.

The declaration of war saw hundreds of thousands of men from every corner of the vast Australian continent form long queues at recruiting offices around the country. Birth certificates were not required. Some teenagers as young as 14 put their ages up in the hope of fooling the recruiting officers. Thousands of men over 50 years put their ages down. In all, 376,000 would enlist out of a population of about 4 million. Given half of the population were men and half again were too young, old or infirm, about 40 per cent of all eligible males in the young nation (just 13 years old when war began) would enlist. About 97 per cent were of British stock, descendants of families from England, Wales, Scotland and Ireland. The remaining 3 per cent came from a 'foreign legion' of volunteers, including Germans, Russians, Turks, Greeks, and many other nationalities. It said much about the support for the British Empire and the willingness for the fledgling 'dominion' to do its bit, display its courage and make its mark on history. The outpost wished to be noticed. Bands played 'Rule Britannia' and men were weighed, measured and issued their gear. This included the slouch hat, which carried the insignia of the Rising Sun. It had been copied from the design of the trademark for jam of the same name, a popular item for soldiers in the Boer War. Jackets were noticeable for their big pockets and non-metal buttons, which were appreciated by the men, who would not have to spend time cleaning them, which was a tedious chore in the British army.

The men joining the mounted units came out of a variety of bush activity: farmers from the rich eastern coastal belt between the dividing range and the sea; orchardists from the foothills; timber-cutters from the forests on the ranges; young men from the wheat belts on the inside slopes of west of the mountains; and those from cattle and sheep stations on the wide inland plains. Many of them lived on outback stations in remote areas of the interior and the deep north, and the far north-west. Squatters, stockmen, shearers, farmers, labourers, prospectors, itinerants, loners and the occasional vagabond rode the dusty tracks, alone or in numbers. Their destinations were towns that would take them by trains to the big cities and recruiting points.

All of them had to be resourceful. Most had initiative in living or surviving in the outback. They were mostly all horsemen; many were excellent; almost all were competent. Most had experienced breaking in bush-bred colts or wild horses. They would all say they could ride any horse put in front of them. Their skills as horsemen were as important to them as anything in life, including family, sport, religion, sex and drinking.

Many of these potential 'recruits' had little idea of the military. Yet they were in essence, ready-made for training in cavalry work. They were experts when it came to surveillance of country or judging it, whether it was topography or weather. They had such good senses of distance and direction that it seemed to be innate. These bushmen knew their territory by day or by night. A great asset from the military point of view was their ability as marksmen. Nearly all were deadly with a breech-loading rifle. Most of them were very accurate with the weapon. If they went kangaroo or rabbit shooting, they might only take six bullets and would usually come back with six 'kills'.

Mounted units were placed in camps in all states, and horses in numbers began to arrive soon afterwards. The Australian horses were mainly 'walers', originally known as New South Walers. They stood between 14 and 16 hands, and were sired by English thoroughbreds from breeding mares that were often partly draught horse. Over the generations, the walers had the benefit of genetic input from the Welsh pony, Timor pony and brumby. All contributed to their toughness and staying power, so vital in the often arid regions of Australia where stockmen had to travel long distances without water.

Veterinary scientist Dr Ian Parsonson describes the breed as 'strong-boned, with fine, clean legs and neck, short backs, long barrels and broad head'. They were a versatile animal. 'Stock-men could muster cattle or round up sheep all day, and then turn the horse loose at night to do its own thing. There was no need to corral or stable them against predators or the elements. They could live rough by night and do civilised rural jobs by day.'[2]

As long as the waler was looked after with food and water, its stamina was near limitless. What they lacked in aesthetics they made up for in spirit, courage, sharpness and dependability. Since 1830, the British army in India had provided a substantial export market for the breed. They had been used in the Boer War. In contrast to that conflict, the troopers did not have to bring their own mounts. But many did. They were paid £30 for each horse that was examined and passed by a veterinary surgeon. The animals were branded with the Australian government's broad arrow and the initials of the purchasing officer. A number was burnt into one hoof.

Men had to have a medical too. Officially they had to be at least 5 foot 6 inches (167 centimetres) and have a minimum chest measurement of 34 inches (86 centimetres). Men shorter than this were let through if they were considered strong enough, although their height would always be measured officially at 5 foot 6 inches. Yet there were fewer allowances for defective feet, bad teeth and extreme shortsightedness. Colourblindness was also tested, but charts were standard and many men with the defect cheated by memorising the positions of colours. All those accepted had to have an anti-typhoid injection.

Most men wishing to be troopers could handle a horse. Some were caught up in the romance of the cavalry and tales of derring-do on horseback through the ages.

Tall, lean Robert Ellwood, 21, from Kingaroy in Queensland

had been using the extensive private library of an ex-army captain since the age of 12.

'There was a good deal of that Army stuff on Kitchener and Gordon of Khartoum . . . and the Indian Mutiny . . . and other things of that description,' he recalled, 'and I was influenced by it . . . I joined the school cadets.'

On reflection after the war he admitted he may have been a 'little brainwashed' by his reading but he was a staunch 'lover of my country, my family, my culture . . .' He wanted to defend them in war.

Ellwood's family was from the city. His father was a businessman. But the young man already had a small country property. Ellwood mixed with country lads and could ride with the best of them.

'They were a fine type of fellow,' he said, 'brought up to develop their initiative and overcome obstacles.'

He wanted to be in the mounted riflemen and joined up with the 2nd Light Horse Regiment, passing the riding tests with ease.[3]

Ellwood had the maturity and prescience to sign over his property to his mother before he left Australia. He was adventurous, but realised there was a chance he could be killed.

Countless other city lads had dreams of the Light Horse. But some had never been on a horse. One young man entered the remount depot at Guilford, a Perth suburb, and asked for a riding test that, if successful, would see him enter the 10th Light Horse Regiment. Captain T. J. Todd looked him up and down. Slight, wet behind the ears and city.

'Sandy,' he said to his assistant, 'break out "Doctor Mac" for Mr . . . Jones, will ya?'

Sandy McPhee caught Todd's gaze for a split second, then nodded. He brought a tall chestnut into the yard. He was big, but benign looking.

'Okay, Mr Jones,' Todd said. 'Mount him.'

Jones circled the horse and decided to come at him from the off side. He almost scrambled into the saddle, but soon slid off. Todd kept a poker-face. McPhee moved close and even went to help the young man. But Todd waved him away. After six attempts, Jones slid into the saddle. Old Mac, as if in on the joke, had behaved until now. As soon as his rider was astride him, he arched his back, put his head down and bucked hard. Jones catapulted five metres forward and hit the dirt hard. He dusted himself off, shook his head and struggled to mount Old Mac again. Seconds later he was bucked off again. After Jones had been forcibly removed from the horse's back a third time, Todd beckoned him into his office.

'Have you ever been on a horse before?' Todd asked.

'No sir,' Jones replied, bruised but unfazed.

'Well, what the hell did you come here for?'

'I wanted to have a go. I wanted to join the regiment.'

Todd considered the lad for a moment. He was made of the required fibre.

'I'll tell you what, Mr Jones,' Todd said, 'you go away for a week, learn to ride, and I'll give you another chance.'

Young Jones returned to take up the offer and passed the test. He was just one of many young men around the nation who wished to join the Light Horse, which was the most romanticised of all the armed forces. Few came just for the prospect of fighting. Most were going for the adventure, the camaraderie and the paid travel. In keeping with an image of a fresh egalitarian society, the privates on six shillings a day—the so called 'six-bob-a-day tourists'—did much better than their British, Canadian and New Zealand counterparts. But the Australians of higher ranks were worse off comparatively.

In Western Australia, some came from huge distances. A 17-year-old 'Bertie' Godley rode 500 kilometres overland from Kimberley to Wyndham, where he caught a boat to Fremantle. By the time he arrived, the regiment's quota was filled.

'I've come from Broome,' Godley complained. When told he had ridden so far, Todd asked him to do a test on Old Mac. The horse remonstrated as hard as ever but could not dislodge him. Todd told him to 'hang around for a bit'.

Two days later a spot was found for him.

Another notable recruit at the 10th in Perth provided one of the more bizarre moments in the recruiting period. He could ride well enough, but a malformed big toe on his left foot ruled him out of the mounted riflemen. Todd gave him the bad news.

'I'll have to do something about it,' the young man said.

He came back a week later. He removed a boot from his left foot and pushed it at Todd. His great toe had been amputated.

'Will you take me now?' he asked with a confident grin.[4]

English-born itinerant miner Jack Cox was looking for a change in his life when war was declared. He read in the local paper that recruiting doors would open in Melbourne on 10 August 1914. He arrived in the city on the 9th and turned up at the office at 4.30 a.m. hoping he would be first to join up. Cox was surprised to find 84 in front of him. And all these early comers were determined to be accepted.[5]

He waited his turn for a riding 'test' on the patchy, muddy earth at the Broadmeadows army camp north-west of Melbourne. The long barbed wire fence that had to be hurdled on horseback was only about a metre high. Cox, an experienced horseman who had fought in the Boer War, first for the Imperial Yeomanry then the Light Horse, was not particularly concerned he would clear it, even if he obeyed the order by the commanding officer for 'arms and stirrups' to be folded. Cox's mount, a big waler, was a regulation mounted rifleman horse, about right for his 174-centimetre (5-foot-9-inch) and 74-kilogram frame. The animal was steady and not feisty. When given the signal to charge the fence he did so at a steady gallop. The horse felt his rider leaning forward in the saddle and he lifted effortlessly over the hurdle. As mount and rider galloped back to the depot entrance, Cox received the thumbs up from the commander, indicating he was officially 'in' the 4th Light Horse Regiment. He would not have to sit a written test or do any more tricks.

Nor would David Alexander Crawford, 37, a motor mechanic from High Camp near Kilmore, Victoria. He had been in the mounted riflemen at the same time as Cox in South Africa. Crawford had lost the thumb and index finger of his right hand in a sawmill accident, but he was determined to join up again. He planned to have a mate distract the recruiting officer while signing up with his left hand. His ploy worked and inspired three of his nephews, Charlie, Frank and Bill Merritt, to join up.[6]

Other recruits were also determined despite the medical restrictions. Another Victorian who passed the riding test was rejected because he had false teeth.

'I want to shoot the bloody Germans,' the man said in disgust, 'not bite them. My fangs may be false but my intentions are true.'[7]

Backing his word, he rode to the next town and did not mention his teeth. He was accepted.

7

Parting and Much Sorrow

Cox, Crawford, the Merritt brothers and the other successful applicants were asked to report at the Broadmeadows training depot 10 days after joining up. They arrived with hundreds of others, many who had also fought in South Africa, to do the barbed wire jump test. The few (including Cox and Crawford) who passed joined the 4th. The rest were transferred to infantry battalions.

The Light Horse battalions drilled at Caulfield and Flemington racecourses. Even the venerable Melbourne Cricket Ground was used.

Cox wrote to his girlfriend Agnes McKibbin, whom he had met in Lithgow, and asked her to marry him. The prospect of war had given him the courage to make this move, which otherwise may have seen him remain single. It also caused

Agnes to say 'Yes'. Cox arranged leave, travelled to Sydney and married his long-time sweetheart on his 35th birthday on 7 September 1914. They were officially man and wife at 11 a.m. After an hour of marital bliss, Cox, Lee Enfield rifle in hand and pack on his back, rushed off to board a ship that would take him to war.

Like thousands of other soldiers, he told his partner he expected to be back in a few months time. Excited, sad and tearful, Agnes waved him goodbye at the wharf, unsure she would ever see her new husband again.

Another woman left down and wondering at about this time was the stunning 25-year-old Rania MacPhillamy, the daughter of a rich grazier and racehorse breeder near the Lachlan River at Warroo, in outback New South Wales. Her man was Ronnie MacDonald, a grazier's son from Mudgee. They had met in April 1914 at a dance during the Royal Easter Show and had grown steadily in love. Rania was in Sydney's Lister Private Hospital undergoing an operation for appendicitis when MacDonald visited her on 7 September. His 1st Light Horse Regiment rode through the city streets past the Astor Hotel, where a tearful Rania, recovering from her illness, stood and waved from the entrance steps crowded with well-wishers. Against doctor's orders, Rania followed the regiment to Woolloomooloo, where it and the rest of 1st Brigade embarked on the *Star of Victoria*. It was pouring as she boarded a launch that would accompany the ship part of the way to Sydney Heads. MacDonald just managed to spot her. He gave one final wave before he was bundled below deck with all the other troops.

Rania had some comfort from knowing that MacDonald had received her going-away gifts, including a pair of binoculars, a pen, and for sentiment's sake, a small piece of blue ribbon. But the one gift she wished to go with him had to remain in Australia: herself.

Already forming in the back of her mind was a plan to join him. Rania would be similar to countless selfless country women who would involve themselves in Red Cross fundraising. But making tonnes of jam and knitting socks were never going to salve the pain of being separated, and the sense that she could do much more for the army cause. Rania enquired about the Australian Army Nursing Service. There was no official work. She would have to volunteer, arrive at a destination and hope she could help out.

Rania made the first step. She began nursing training.

The 15,000-tonne leviathans in the Australian flotilla made their way round southern Australia to Albany. Most of the boats were liners, which had been refitted to accommodate the 23,000 soldiers from Australia's 1st Division, Chauvel's Light Horse Brigade, the New Zealand Infantry led by Colonel F. E. Johnston, and New Zealand's Mounted Riflemen. Salubrious state rooms had been stripped of passenger cruise accoutrements such as elegant sofas and chairs. In their place were thousands of hammocks for the men. The holds were fitted with horse stalls.

There was a sense of excitement on board. Those hundreds who had been to the Boer War were reassuring. Of the 12,000 Australians in that conflict, only 231 had died in action, which was a low attrition rate of about 1 in 50, good odds if you were a betting man, and most of the soldiers were. After all, how many horses had won the Melbourne Cup at 50 to 1? Only two in the history of the race until then. The soldiers discounted the 257 who died from disease, as if that could have happened anywhere. But from a realist's point of view, this reduced the odds to 1 in 25; this was a much more uncomfortable gamble. The point forgotten was that disease always followed war like a persistent phantom. These Boer War comparative figures were the only ones Australians had. Very few of the soldiers would have fears and trepidation about what they were doing. On balance, this was probably a good thing.

Banjo Paterson, along with 27 qualified vets, was travelling with the medical and veterinary ship, which carried about 4,500 people. He had the 'arduous' task of commanding six young nurses and a military officer.

The convoy waited three days at Albany taking on final supplies, equipment, soldiers and horses. It sailed off again at sunrise on Sunday 1 November 1914 and steamed into the Indian Ocean with the Australian coastline a marker for some time. In the lead were the escorts; the grey, ominous cruisers: the *Ibuki*, a Japanese vessel, and three from Australia—the *Melbourne*, the *Sydney*, and the *Minotaur*. They were protecting the 38 transport ships, including 10 carrying New Zealanders with 20,000 soldiers and 7,843 horses. Smoke swirled from the convoy, with the transport ships in two long columns behind.

Paterson wrote:

'It was the most wonderful sight that an Australian ever saw.'[1]

Yet there was a different atmosphere from the earlier cruise around southern Australia. In the days the fleet came together, Turkey had declared war against Britain and France. Conflict could spread worldwide. The Australians were part of the British Empire contingent force, which would grow to 600,000 troops, and included also Canada, New Zealand, South Africa, India, Newfoundland, Ceylon (now Sri Lanka) and the West Indies. In turn, the entire British force was part of the 'Allies', which included Russia, France and Serbia. Negotiations were under way for the Japanese and Italians to join the Allies' side. They were pitted against the central powers of Germany and the Austro-Hungarian Empire. They would be joined soon by the Ottoman Empire (and in 1916 the Bulgarians).

These developments, fuelled by wild rumours, were filtering through to passengers in the convoy and changing the collective mindset. The soldiers were beginning to realise that this was going to be a very different experience from that of the Boer War. There was also the possibility that they could be in battle long before they reached the expected destination of Europe. The flotilla was now heading into dangerous waters. German boats had been sinking British ships with alarming regularity to Australia's north-west in the Indian Ocean, which was the convoy's direction.

Daily safety drills and 'lights out' at night became routine. Paterson's diary reflected the grim situation on board, but also the conviviality and frivolity which any group of young Australians on a ship would be searching for, no matter what the circumstances:

> 3 November—Sacred day: Melbourne Cup. Not much chance of hearing what won. Lifeboat parade. I am to collect the nurses and see that they get into the boats to which they are allotted.[2]

Paterson looked after his own horse, and with his vet's hat on kept a keen, concerned eye on others. All the vets worked hard to limit the loss of horses, which was expected to be about one per cent, or about 75 in all for the voyage. There were already one or two cases of pneumonia, but there was hardly any stress or colic.

Sergeant Ellwood (of the Queensland 2nd Light Horse) was a duty officer in charge of a lower deck of the *Star of England*. He remembered vividly the sickness of some of the horses: 'When one of them died, the boat slowed down. The vets slid the dead horse out through an opening in the side.'[3]

The precious animals were loaded in three decks. The upper deck was open to the air, and sometimes the sea. The middle deck was ventilated and well lit. The two holds of the lower decks were dark and not well ventilated by shafts and canvas air chutes.

Each horse was in a stall facing across the ship. Stall fittings were moveable. The routines each day included cleaning of the stalls (after each meal), and a feeding of oats, bran and chaff three times a day. There was also the essential provision of water in buckets of up to 10 gallons a day. Horses were groomed after the midday feed. Their feet were attended to, and the sheaths of geldings were cleaned. In the afternoon, matting was laid down on the decks for exercise. The horses enjoyed their brief freedoms; some were let loose to parade around. They adapted well. Paterson made sure pickets were on duty on the horse decks all the time. He added in his diary:

4 November—Horses very drowsy. My horse goes to sleep and falls down.

5 November—Put big horse in a sling. He went to sleep, lay in the sling and nearly pitched out. An American Tommy on board was in the Philippines War. He got in the stalls and was hustling a tricky pony about.

I said: 'Look out man; that horse will kill you!'

He said: 'Nossir, me and this hoss is vurry well acquainted.'

9 November—Man died last night of pneumonia: Private Kendall, aged 21, ex-policeman. Funeral very impressive.

10 November—They serve out 300 pints of beer in an hour daily at the canteen . . . One old soldier said: 'I'm going to see Lord Kitchener about this one-pint-a-day business.'

He was promptly made a prisoner, and beer will not trouble him for a time.

Each night, Paterson bustled his nurses and the military officer below deck. The door was shut in the companionway. The heat was stifling; the darkness 'like a pit'. A Scottish ship's chief officer approached with a light. He wanted to know why they had doors shut and was told they were under orders to close them.

'Then you'll droon if we go doon!' was his comforting reply.[4]

He and other officers were aware that a Morse code operator in the Cocos Islands had sent an SOS message that an enemy ship was in the vicinity of Direction Island. This was a major British communications crossroads with a concentration of underwater cables and a large wireless tower. The centre coordinated Australian, African and Indian telegraph messages.

Captain Mortimer ('Long John') Silver, the convoy's leader on the *Melbourne*, decided to send the *Sydney*, a fast, modern, light cruiser, to investigate.

The *Sydney* was about 80 kilometres and two hours away north of the Cocos Islands. It responded to the order, changed direction and steamed towards the targeted island ready to protect the centre.

Trooper Ellwood remembered the moment:

'All of a sudden . . . the *Sydney* on our left flank belched out huge volumes of black smoke and fell over the horizon. The *Melbourne* sailed smartly across and took up her [*Sydney's*] position.'[5]

Captain Silver warned the *Sydney* it would probably encounter the most predatory German ship in the Indian Ocean, the *Emden*, which was believed to be nearby. It had become the cannibal of the Pacific and Indian Oceans. When the Japanese, Russians and British destroyed or banned bases in the Pacific, the *Emden's* resourceful Captain von Müller and his crew captured ships for their needs of fuel, equipment, labour, food and even soap. So far it had travelled 50,000 kilometres and had done $12 million worth of damage. It had sunk or captured a cruiser, a destroyer, 16 merchant ships and 11 colliers. It had bombarded oil facilities in China and India, upsetting the British while disrupting transport. The *Emden* had caused the price of rice and insurance to rise in the Indian Ocean region. Four allied navies had sent 78 warships looking for her.

So far it had avoided them all, while picking its moments to attack others, and destroy British bases. Direction Island seemed an easy target. Instead of using its guns, the *Emden's* Captain von Müller decided to land a raiding party that would carry out the necessary destruction. It took longer than he anticipated.

At 9.15 a.m. on 10 November, the German captain was alerted to another British ship close by. He decided to leave his raiding party on the Direction Island beach and take on the intruder.

At last, after months of mayhem, the German boat met its match in the *Sydney* and was crippled then destroyed in a fierce battle. The *Sydney*, with a gaping hole in its side, rejoined the Australian convoy. The news spread worldwide and boosted Allied morale. The successful entry by Australia into the conflict coincided with the British army's capturing of Basra in the southern provinces of Iraq, also in November 1914. The British now set their sights on conquering Baghdad, the central province, and Mosul in the north. These three acquisitions, if successful, the British hoped, would give them access to big oil reserves, which were being explored as the war progressed.

The sinking of the *Emden* had drawn the Australians into the war a lot sooner than anyone expected. But events were yet to decide where their main participation would be. En route, they learned their destination would be Egypt, not England. After having French lessons on board with the prospect of fighting in France, they began thinking about seeing the pyramids before going on to Europe. Yet as the convoy cruised north across the Indian Ocean, the British were considering helping their Russian allies who were struggling against the Bulgarians and the Turks in the Caucasus—the mountain range in Russia's southwest. A diversion was needed to distract the Turks. British War Council member Churchill drew up a plan for the Navy to attack Turkey's Gallipoli Peninsula. The idea was for a convoy of warships to blast away the Turkish defenses on the Peninsula and sail up the Dardanelles, the 61 kilometre narrow strait between the Gallipoli Peninsula in Europe and the mainland of Asia Minor. The ultimate mission would be to take Constantinople, the Turkish capital.

Annexing Turkey seemed to Churchill as natural as any previous acquisition for the Empire, especially as since 1831 the British and French had been encroaching on areas of Ottoman domination, which for nearly 400 years had stretched from Algeria to the Persian Gulf and from Aleppo in Syria's north to the Indian Ocean. The French had been first to shake the Turkish ruling Sultans when they grabbed Algeria in 1831. They delivered a further blow 51 years later when they seized Tunisia. The British looked on anxiously and enviously at these French moves, which threatened their coaling stations on the Arabian seaboard and sea route to India. The British began increasing their footholds in the region from Aden to the Persian Gulf.

As the Ottoman Empire looked increasingly like an ageing lion struggling to hold its domain, the British in 1882 occupied Egypt and then the Sudan. The last of the absolute Turkish Sultans, Abdul Hamid, who had been on the throne six years, held on nominally to suzerainty or 'control' but it was no more than a sop to his prestige, which had been dented heavily by these other Empires. Into the 20th century, they had left the Sultan with real control over just Libya on the Northern African coast, which Turkey had previously dominated.

Now if Churchill had his way the last remnants of Ottoman power would be snuffed out. Apart from the fact that Turkey was siding with Germany, the British wished to keep the Suez Canal in their control and open. It was the main route to Britain's 'Jewell in the Crown', India. There was also the not insignificant matter of oil, which had been discovered at Mosul in the northern province of Iraq. This held the promise of an important development, especially now that shipping activity was already frenetic in the war and coal was not expected to meet demand. Iraq's potential wells encouraged Churchill. The country's strategic ports and railways had yet to be secured.

As the Australian convoy sailed on from Colombo, two divisions of the Turkish 4th Army were being assembled with nine batteries of field artillery and another of howitzers (short guns for high-angle firing of shells at low velocity) at Beersheba in Palestine (now southern Israel). The commander was the wild-eyed Djemal Pasha, Turkey's Minister of Marine and one of a triumvirate of 'Young Turks' ruling Turkey since a coup that overthrew the Sultan in 1909.

German General Friedrich Kress von Kressenstein (who signed himself 'Kress') was the strategist/adviser behind him. This Bavarian born artillery officer, 46, had been part of Liman von Sanders' military mission to Turkey since January 1914.

They planned to invade Egypt as a counter-measure to the build up of British and French forces. Their approach march was by the tracks from Beersheba to Ismailia, an arduous trek across 300 km of the Sinai Desert, made worse by the need to carry pontoons for crossing the Suez Canal. This way they hoped to avoid the British Navy and military stationed north of Ismailia.

8

Culture Clash

Postcard thoughts and clichés about the Eiffel Tower, French girls, the Folies Bergére, the Moulin Rouge, the cancan, strong cigarettes and berets were forgotten when the troopers had their first glimpse of the mighty pyramids of Giza near Cairo. In thousands of letters home, the men of the Australian Light Horse wondered about these pharaohs' tombs since spotting them for the first time after disembarking at Alexandria on 4 December 1914. The pyramids seemed unearthly as the men got closer on the 115-kilometre train ride to Cairo. How were they built? Were they astronomic observatories, places of cult worship, or constructed by extraterrestrials?

The troopers gathered together as a brigade for the first time at Maadi, a European suburb five kilometres from Cairo, where they met their commanding officer. Chauvel had arrived from London the night before. He and his men were eased into Egypt as if in some bizarre English county. Maadi was populated by English families, who tended their abodes and gardens of bougainvillea and wattle as if they were at home. They kindly set up recreation tents for the bemused yet grateful Australians. Concerts and plays were put on; soldiers were invited to tea in the manicured, shaded gardens. There was even a stall selling honey, jam, writing paper, recent English newspapers and tobacco. It was all very British and genteel.

Yet the arrival was not without its hardships. The men had to lead their horses through boggy land to a base camp on the outskirts of Maadi near the Pyramids, where they had to pitch tents in the rain. The weather was mild during the day, but bitterly cold at night. Promised huts had not been built. There was no water. The soldiers had to march a couple of kilometres to a prison for showers. Complaints filtered through to Chauvel, but he was not concerned after having seen Salisbury Plain where the unhappy Canadians were camped. Only Siberia, he suggested, could be worse than the miserable conditions in England's south in the winter of 1914.

Chauvel's brigade of about 1,560 men consisted of three regiments, each of about 520 men. He knew many of them and the 75 officers. He had trained some of them, including his second-in-command, Major William Glasgow, 40, who had an outstanding record in the Boer War, where he was mentioned in dispatches at the relief of Kimberley, and which earned him a DSO (Distinguished Service Order). There was also the outstanding Lieutenant Colonel R. M. Stodart. All his commanders and a dozen other officers had been in the Boer War. Chauvel was pleased with his charges. He wrote to Sibyl 11 days after arriving:

'I like my command immensely; they are a fine lot of men and horses.'[1]

His emphasis was nearly as much on the walers as on the men. About 5,000 of them were watered in local irrigation canals. The other nearly 3,000 were led to the Nile, two kilometres away. They had lost more than 220 of them en route, three times more than the anticipated attrition rate. The losses, mainly due to pneumonia, were put down to overcrowding and lack of ventilation in the lower decks.

The horses were not yet ready for mounted work, but were being exercised up to it daily. A problem arose when the fodder prescribed by Australian vets ran out. The horses had to remain discontent with Egyptian barley straw (tibbin) until new supplies of oats, bran and chaff arrived.

The troopers' first contacts with the locals began as shops of all kinds sprang up along the routes they were permitted to travel. They ranged from tobacconists, hairdressers and cleaners to newsagents, tailors and antique sellers. Food vendors, photographers and beggars of all ages were there to 'deal' with these strange, well-heeled and well-built antipodeans with their gruff but mainly friendly manner, and their magnificent, well-tended horses.

One point of interest in the Queenslanders was the emu plumes in their slouch hats. They appeared a feminine touch, which was so incongruous with the overall demeanour of the Australians, and added a certain splendour to the battered, yet distinctive headgear. Although they were amused, no Egyptian dared make fun of the look. Anyone among the Queenslanders' fellow countrymen, or other forces, who had the temerity or stupidity to ridicule the feathers would buy a fight. The adornment was worn with such fierce pride that within days of arrival every trooper from every state's Light Horse wished to adopt the feathers. From then on, they were the badge of the Australian Mounted Riflemen.

Every day near the troopers' camp a decrepit donkey-lorry would arrive laden with everything including rusty kitchen sinks, stove-pipes, tables, chairs, crockery, utensils and clothes. The locals would sit among them and call out to the troopers as they passed. It was part of the culture shock once the troopers ventured away from little England at Maadi and had a good look around crowded Cairo and the surrounding countryside.

One soldier, Major Coe, summed up the differences from their limited Australian experience, and the prejudices:

'The shops never closed. The natives won't work on Friday; they say their prayers in the open. Women are beasts of burden, child marriage, harems, high palaces, indescribably filthy stinking houses in which the donkeys, bison, fowls, sheep and goats all sleep together with the natives; camels, overloaded donkeys, Arab horses, motor cars, phaetons [four-wheeled horse-drawn carriages], pyramids, Sphinx, tents, desert, cultivation, electric trams, plough drawn by camel and donkey harnessed together, scorpions, huge beetles, mosquitoes, morning temperature 45 [degrees Fahrenheit], midday temperature 98, no rain, bell tents, marquees, the smell of the east, home memories; mix the lot and that is Egypt . . .'[2]

In Cairo, the locals adjusted to the new arrivals. One sign read: 'Don't go elsewhere to be cheated Australians. Come here!'

Another said: 'English and French spoken; Australian understood.'

The alleged reaction of the locals to the antipodean 'invaders' was reported by the Cairo correspondent of the London *Star* newspaper:

'Look in any direction you like and you will find that Australia has captured the town—captured, I said, not captivated. The remarkable physique and virility of the rank and file together with the phenomenal luxuriance of their language and the peculiarity of their manners have inspired among the native population the kind of affection that a tyrant is said to provoke occasionally in his victims. There is something almost Oriental too in their openhandness; they fling their money about like nabobs.'[3]

Most of the Australians and New Zealanders were not despotic, yet their aggression was always lurking. They hated cruelty to animals. This coloured their views towards Arabs who maltreated their horses and left them upright bags of bones. They would be abusive to locals who overloaded their donkeys; they might force a man off his animal and place his overburdened, trailing wife, on it. There might be physical response if the Australians felt they had been taken down in a deal. They were rowdy and feisty when drunk. Intoxicated or sober, they despised the servility of the working-class Egyptians as much as they reviled the air of superiority of British officers.

After hearing 'Australia very good very nice' and 'You very nice man' many times, the troopers' attitude changed from uncomfortable to irritated. Any bullies among the visitors tended to bully; the more benign lost their respect for the locals. This was balanced by the generous, genial nature of most of the Australians, which could not be changed by bad experiences in the market place whether buying a shirt or a 'sheila'.

In turn, the locals grew wary of the Australians, but they still attempted to cosy up to them. They had money and they were spending it.

Many of the Australians were impressed by the wealth they saw in the salubrious palaces, hotels, mosques and boulevards in the centre of Cairo. They were stunned by the city's outskirts, which harboured the squalor of the poorer classes. It was a shock compared to home, where there was nothing like the stark contrast between rich and poor.

Local hygiene, thieving, and prostitution in the Cairo streets soon became the talking points. The Australians were disgusted by the Arab habit of carrying food for sale in their soiled robes. It was not unusual for sellers to fondle their hair looking for lice and fleas as they haggled with the troopers. They also licked the fruit to give it a sheen before handing it to over. Pies, rissoles and stews were made in front of them, and it was noticed that yesterday's meat leftovers were added to the ingredients. The source of the meat itself was questionable. Rats were rumoured to be a strong possibility. The cities were infested with them.

The scantily clad prostitutes displaying their wares on the balconies, in the alleyways, lanes and streets in the red-light districts of Wagh el Birka and Wassa, appalled many of the visitors. Yet this did not stop them entering houses and watching a pornographic variation of the cancan.

Many of the same men would no longer be virgins after their stay in Egypt. The bolder 'lads' were soon encouraging and chiding the more prudent young troopers to take their chances with the alluring offerings. These experiences had their consequences. More than 3,000 of the Australian and New Zealand force contracted syphilis. This blighted the original pleasures and exacerbated the initial prejudices about 'filthy Arabs'. Without a cure for venereal diseases the problems and attitudes would remain and fester.

The third major irritant was the way the Arabs bargained and their propensity to steal. The Australians' dry humour was on show in the bazaars at first.

One dealer approached a Light Horse officer:

'Five pounds for one beautiful scarab!'

The officer laughed.

'Not ha! ha!' the dealer persisted, 'It is 3,000 years old! See that marking? It is from the time of the ancient Pharaohs—Rameses the Second in fact.'

'Too old,' the officer said with a shake of his head. 'Got any nice new ones.'[4]

After a short time many troopers thought the dealers were dishonest and grasping. Local tradesmen were as 'cunning as rats with gold teeth'. Petty thieving was common. In the troopers' collective mind, the rapacity was akin to theft, and they could occur simultaneously. While a vendor was bargaining up the cost of a dodgy watch, the buyer might have his wallet stolen by one of the myriad boys in the bazaars. Pickpockets annoyed the troopers. But the greatest ire was generated in brothels when belongings were stolen while they were busy with women.

Resentments about dirt and dishonesty built on a preconceived bias against Arabs, based on nothing or limited experience of Syrians in Australia, reinforced by attitudes that pervaded the visitors' thinking and utterances. The White Australia Policy, instituted since Federation in 1901, exacerbated the approach to dealing with racial differences. The use of the slang 'Gyppos' by officers and troopers to describe Egyptians represented a sense of superiority over the locals that did not help in relations with them.

A Light Horse private wrote a letter home that, while not a universal view among the Australians and New Zealanders, still reflected a pervasive attitude:

'There is something repellent about Eastern races,' he said with the certitude of the misinformed or uneducated. 'All places with large "native" coloured population are undesirable, but vice and depravity are more deeply ingrained in Cairo than elsewhere.' He attacked the 'complete absence of moral sense of nine-tenths of Egyptians of all classes'.[5]

A combination of boredom and lack of respect led the Australians to play practical jokes. Usually they perpetrated pranks on their mates, and that did not stop. But in Cairo, the locals become the butt of them. Some were crude; others were harsh. If a hawker's food was of suspect origin or simply designated 'bad', he would have his stall tipped over. Those carrying fruit in their upturned robes might have them slit with the swift use of a knife. Oranges, apples and lemons would spill out. Soldiers on a balcony would toss coins into the street. A crowd would form. People would fight on the ground for the money. They would have buckets of water tossed on them. The drenched scramblers would continue to struggle over a coin, much to the mirth of the jokers.

A major part of the problem was that many of the men had been stationed in Egypt for several months. The novelty was wearing thin. Insurmountable differences caused by the language barrier and the culture clash on many levels were causing distractions that were leading to problems.

Chauvel and the other commanders were working overtime at training, and bringing the discipline he so desired after the Boer War into the performance of his troops. When the horses were fit, he began mounted training, which reduced the time for his men being able to 'play up', although on many nights they were free to indulge themselves in Cairo.

9

Lawrence Shows His Hand

While Chauvel kept his restless troops from clashing with the locals, Thomas Edward (T.E.) Lawrence was embracing them while putting in 18 hours a day in Cairo building an intelligence network in the Middle East. Fairhaired, jut-jawed, puckish and short (at about 5 feet 4 inches or 166 centimetres), Lawrence was an aesthete and an Arabist with a growing comprehension of all aspects—military, political, historical and archaeological—of the region. The 26-year-old's knowledge already rivalled that of anyone in the British armed forces, the Foreign Office or academia. It began with him winning a scholarship to Jesus College, Oxford. He came under the influence of David George Hogarth, keeper of the Ashmolean Museum, and a political intelligence officer specialising in the Middle East. This mentor was the first to spark the impressionable young Lawrence's love for the region. Hogarth delivered a vision of a future in the Middle East in intelligence work. The academic eased him into studying military tactics and urged him to train his body to resist pain and exhaustion. After much fitness preparation, he went on a 1,600-kilometre tour through Syria.

After several summers in the area taking part in military surveys, archaeological digs and further treks, he had been recruited full-time for British military/political espionage with the outbreak of war. This experience added to an already unusual personality. Young Lawrence was the son of an Irish estate owner—Thomas Chapman—and heir to a baronetcy, who had left his wife for the governess of his four daughters, Sarah Maden. Chapman changed his surname to Lawrence, and T.E. was the second of their four sons born out of wedlock. This unconventional background and experience in a strictly religious environment in the UK in the 19th century, with the opprobrium of being 'born on the other side of the blanket', stuck with Lawrence for life. Coupled with this were his homosexual proclivities, latent or otherwise, in an era when such practices were illegal. It developed a certain caution, secretiveness and quirkiness in Lawrence's character. Perhaps because of it, he was well-suited to the paranoid profession of spying. Certainly this chosen trade added a complexity to his character (in much the way it did a generation later with homosexuals Anthony Blunt and Guy Burgess—members of the Cambridge University spy ring that was controlled by the KGB's forerunner in the 1930s and 1940s).

Lawrence was a cog in a unique British espionage outfit in Cairo, known innocuously as the Arab Bureau, which was working to bring down the Ottoman Empire. His role at first was to improve operational maps for the military. He also helped produce the *Handbook of the Turkish Army* (1915), which he had to update with new intelligence reports. His work expanded in several areas within months.

The bureau was the first modern intelligence gathering unit of the 20th century. Its uniqueness stemmed from it being two operations in one. One branch did the cryptography—the cracking of the codes intercepted from German and Turkish communications. Its operatives passed on intelligence to the Bureau's second branch, the field agents, including Lawrence, for action. The two departments formed part of one collegiate body in the one building in Cairo. They all knew each other well. And with one common cause of bringing down the Turks—a key ally of the Germans—they believed they were doing their job to win World War I and uphold the British Empire and its expansionist aims in the Middle East.

The equivalent would have been the better known Bletchley Park in England in World War II, which later did all the deciphering and breaking of German codes that gave the Allies such advantages over their enemies. The Bletchley Park scientists provided the data for their intelligence agents in London, other parts of the UK and the world. The difference in World War I was that the agents assigned to work against the Turks with the British military (and later the Arabs in the region) were all ensconced in the same Cairo bureau. The code-breakers were on close terms with the spies such as Lawrence. Because of their isolation, this developed a highly effective sense of teamwork among friends and acquaintances. Each arm comprehended and appreciated the work of the other. There were three areas of intelligence: signals intelligence (Sigint), photographic image intelligence (Imint—used for tracking enemy movements, especially by air, in which Lawrence developed a specialty), and agent-based intelligence (Humint). All had a concept of what each was doing. They would wander into each other's offices and chat every day.

The bureau was the brainchild of Brigadier General Gilbert ('Berty') Clayton, a veteran of the British-controlled Egyptian army. As soon as war looked likely in 1914, he put together unlikely bedfellows with one common link: they were all Arabists. They included people from various backgrounds: the House of Commons; British journalism; banking; Oxbridge; archaeology and the colonial service.

Among them (apart from author, archaeologist and orientalist Hogarth) were Brigadier Wyndham H. Deedes and Major Kinahan Cornwallis.

Their arrival in late 1914 and early 1915 coincided with huge technological breakthroughs, which aided their efforts. The bureau's boffin department had at its disposal wireless telegraphy linked to developments in aeronautics and improvement in photographic techniques.

By January 1915, they were already 'tracking' the movements of Turkish forces in Syria and the Hejaz.

These developments were already giving the bureau an edge in the war. Lawrence and others built networks and infiltrated agents throughout the Middle East, 'turned' deserting Ottoman officers and interrogated POWs.

Lawrence kept notes and diaries. He had more than a keen sense of history and his place in it, and he felt compelled to write in a fuller form when the opportunity came or the muse struck. For now, he had in mind living any adventure that came his way. He always had a sense of detachment. Whatever was happening was 'research' for a future torrent in narrative form.

He was not a daydreamer. No-one worked harder than Lawrence as he put himself across several areas in the job. Schooling at Oxford gave him important contacts and allowed his analysis to be read and heard in high places.

Lawrence was pushing hard for the British to take control of Alexandretta, a northern Syrian coastal port close to the border with Turkey. In early 1915, this was not because he feared the Turks so much, but more the French. He had a distrust of them and their rivalry with the British Empire that bordered on obsessive. He was not alone in Britain, where the political/military elite in which he was enmeshed were keen to keep the French limited in their influence in the Middle East, especially as oil had been discovered in the region.

'In the hands of France it [Alexandretta] will provide a sure base for naval attacks on Egypt,' he wrote to Hogarth, 'and remember, with her in Syria & compulsory military service there, she will be able to fling 100,000 men against the [Suez] Canal within 12 days of declaration of war (of France against the UK).'

In a follow-up letter on the same issue, Lawrence demonstrated his already considerable lobbying influence:

'The [British] High Commissioner [in Egypt] is of the same opinion, and General Maxwell [Commanding officer of the British forces in Egypt] also. K [Kitchener] has pressed it on us; can you get someone to suggest to Winston [Churchill] . . . and tell the FO [British Foreign Office] that it is vitally important that we hold it.'

He added:

'Please try to push it through, for I think it is our only chance in the face of a French Syria.'[1]

He was ambitious on behalf of the empire and had influence, even if he depended on Hogarth to push his views. He intended to have his own direct lines of communication to key decision-makers as soon as possible. His acute political instincts, already attuned to infighting, were telling him that in wartime all objectives could be accelerated.

On 14 January 1915, he wrote to Hogarth mentioning important agents and contacts. He told him of Germans he had met in Syria, who had been given appointments in the Turkish army.

'Musil,' he said, 'is head guide to the general [Turkish] Staff in Damascus. Moritz is out there, and Meisner is building railways.'

Lawrence knew in detail what was happening at Carchemish, on the frontier between Turkey and Syria, where he had supervised archaeological digs a few years earlier.

'The Germans have built a light [rail] line through the S [Syrian] Gate, and are taking some stone [for bridge building] from Kalaat at Jerablus. The bridge is pushed ahead.'[2]

Lawrence was stepping up his espionage networking aware that knowledge in this region of empire was a precious commodity. The stronger his sources and information, the more he would be heard in Whitehall where the ignorance on the Middle East countries was only matched by its imperial arrogance towards them.

IO

Invasion Preparation

The day Lawrence was showing his back-room, back-alley influence on paper, Trooper Bert Canning of 4th Light Horse Regiment, B Squadron, was penning his own diary. Training with Chauvel's Light Horse was about to begin at last. It inspired the laconic soldier to make his first succinct entry:

'Thursday 14th January 1915: Spent day getting kit together preparing for route march to take place on following day. Articles carried on man—bandolier [soldier's cartridge belt]; belt with four pouches; bayonet; wire cutters; 150 rounds of ammunition; Rifle; Water Bottle; Havasack containing 1 carryall, 1 soap, 1 towel and 1 meal; One [military 'universal'] saddle— Overcoat; waterproof groundsheet; blanket; Cap comforter; Horse brush pad; Mess tin; Rifle; [canvas] bucket; 1 horse feed; 1 Picketing Peg; 1 Heel rope; 1 Linking Rope; 1 [leather] shoe case [containing two horse shoes and nails]; and then the man. Poor horse.'

Thirteen days later, he was stimulated enough by events to write:

'We started out at 9.30 a.m. to pursue A Squadron who was acting as a beaten force on retreat.'

He had two roles as a signaller and then a 'galloper', and 'so had a good opportunity of seeing both sides of the [mock] fight.' Canning was not impressed:

'. . . In the end both squadrons got mixed up. It's a good job it was not in earnest. It would be interesting to know what the Colonel [Chauvel] thought of it. Day finished up with the worst dust storm we have had up to date.'[1]

The colonel was furious. Chauvel decided to make conditions tougher. Two days later, on 29 January, he moved his brigade from Maadi to Heliopolis in the desert. The men were unhappy. They lived now in what seemed a perpetual swirl of dust and sand.

In early February, Brigadier John Monash arrived on a second convoy of 19 ships with his 4th Brigade of infantry, which included Queensland's 15th Battalion, commanded by Chauvel's former military pupil, Lieutenant-Colonel James H. Cannan. The 4th Brigade would be aligned at least in structure for the moment with Chauvel's Light Horse and the New Zealand Brigade under the heading '2nd Division'. It was the original Anzac contingent. British Major General Sir Alexander Godley would command it. He had been running the New Zealand army, and his unpopularity preceded him. He was disliked for the way he treated the New Zealanders; his attitude was 'my way or the highway', which was not appreciated by the antipodeans.

The all-Australian 1st Division under Bridges, which for the moment was getting all the accolades, preferences and press attention, made up half of the combined Australian and New Zealand contingent. The two divisions were controlled by the popular General Birdwood. He was no less a disciplinarian than Godley, yet his manner was more friendly and less abrasive. It may have had something to do with their size. Godley was a towering 196 centimetres (6 feet 5 inches), and could well have been a prior incarnation of the English actor John Cleese. Birdwood, known as Birdie, was chirpy, short, wiry, nervous and encouraging. He was the more judgemental and acerbic in his observations. And his views had more weight with his superiors in the London

War Office. He didn't think Chauvel was much of an officer. He described him as 'slow', which was almost certainly because Kitchener's chief of staff George Kirkpatrick had put this on paper a year earlier. Birdwood added that Chauvel was 'lacking in decision'.[2] Hamilton didn't believe he would make a leader.[3]

He had a very high opinion of Monash, who was more of a mystery to the less erudite Birdwood because of his German/Jewish background and his experience in the Australian militia and not the regular army. Whereas Hamilton had no doubts about him, Birdwood had a few. Monash didn't get around much on horseback. He was always thinking, planning and preparing, and had little time for riding. He preferred studying maps and intelligence to roving around among the training troops. He was the same age as Chauvel (49 years), with a successful dual background as a building engineer and lawyer. Monash was now bringing his civilian skills to the armed forces and was, even before setting foot on a battleground, in preparation and knowledge, better equipped on paper at least for modern combat than anyone else. He was a gunner, and knew all there was to know about artillery. Monash had studied the new weaponry of planes, tanks and machine-guns. He could not wait for the chance to combine them with all the new technology and communications in conflict. In addition, he had spent two years in intelligence. He spoke German fluently, had travelled the country and knew the enemy and its fighting capacities.

But like the well-equipped and more war-experienced Chauvel he was not going to receive any favours. With the mindset and attitudes of the British High Command set firmly in the 19th century, with their emphasis on arcane fighting methods, there were no guarantees that these outstanding and ambitious characters would ever have a chance to display their skills. Not even the lugubrious Bridges, well known to the War Office, was given much credence as a rising star.

The British commanders such as Birdwood believed that they had a major advantage over their dominion counterparts, which they thought gave them actual and bluffing rights. They had commanded in battle in more than just the Boer War (Monash had not been there), and had been in command of forces in the far reaches of the empire. Until these former colonials were tested in this expected bigger conflict, there were few ways of judging their substance or capacities.

Plans being prepared in the British War Office were about to bring on that testing arena, but not in Europe.

Bert Canning was beginning to warm up to the training. If he touched his diary, he was inspired. On Saturday 13 February, he scribbled:

'Until 10 a.m. Bayonet fighting. From 10 a.m. holiday. Went into Cairo then out to Albesy-a to reinforcement camp. Saw Turkish prisoners that were captured during the fighting on the Canal.'

Earlier in February 1915 the Turks, led by Djemal Pasha and advised by Kress, had attempted to invade Egypt from the Sinai Desert. The aim was to capture or destroy Britain's vital artery to the east and Australia. The planning was poor. The Turks advanced across the Sinai in three columns that were well separated from each other. Each had been sighted from the air and bombed. The enemy launched a flotilla of pontoons on the Suez Canal but this was destroyed by artillery and machine-gun fire. Just one pontoon reached the far (western) bank. The Turks occupied forward trenches on the Sinai side of the canal, but were driven out.

'They [the captured Turks] are dirty looking wretches and half-starved,' Canning noted, 'I think they were only too glad to fall into the hands of the English. The 7th and 8th Victorian Infantry went to the Canal but arrived too late to take part in the fighting. The Turks were driven off about two hours before they arrived. The Indians stood the brunt of the fighting. They are fierce fellows and know no fear.'

A month later, Canning and four other troopers in his squadron were taught how to use explosives:

'We used both the fuse and electricity for firing the charges . . . The work of demolition is generally carried out by engineers. But on active service it often happens that a bridge or some such thing may have to be blown up at a moment's notice to stop the enemy.'[4]

The Light Horse was now well prepared for battle. But the type of conflict and the location were still unknown.

The British Minister for War, Lord Kitchener, leaned across his London Whitehall office desk and handed Sir Ian Hamilton two small travel guidebooks on Turkey. Always cool and implacable, Hamilton squinted at them. He opened the yellowing pages and found the publication date: 1887.

Kitchener was almost apologetic. He handed Hamilton another book: a text on the Turkish Army, which may have been translated from Turkish. Hamilton flipped through the chapter headings and index but found no reference to the Gallipoli Peninsula. The area seemed hardly a military or even tourist destination. Not even the Turks knew much about this remote and barren part of their empire 300 kilometres from Constantinople.

Churchill's grand plan to send the British Fleet to blast its way to Constantinople had flopped at the tip of the peninsula. Mines laid by the Turks stopped the mighty boats with their 15-inch (38.1-cm) guns. Minesweepers were harassed out of doing their job. Naval commanders told an irate Churchill to come up with plan B.

He was now a bulldog with a bone of contention. He suggested to Kitchener that a land invasion was necessary. Kitchener gave the command for that to Hamilton. He cobbled together a not altogether cohesive force of the British regular army's 29th Division, the two divisions of Australian and New Zealand troops stationed in Egypt, the Royal Naval Division and a French contingent. The 75,000-man force was far bigger than anything Hamilton had ever handled. Kitchener made Turkey's conquest look easy. Hamilton, wily, pragmatic and intelligent, knew full well that it would not be. Despite skills as a poet, writer and teacher, he was still a soldier. He would obey orders and get on with it, even if the intelligence on the unsurveyed

Gallipoli amounted to a few tatty, out-of-date and incomplete textbooks.[5]

The sizeable expedition would go ahead without maps or any real sense of the terrain. Hamilton only knew that the peninsula had ugly ridges and valleys. It was rugged and barely habitable. There were a handful of villages of fishermen and shepherds.

On 18 March, an allied British and French naval force was destroyed at the mouth of the Dardanelles. Seven hundred sailors were killed and nine ships disabled. Three battleships were sunk. This made it clear to Hamilton that he would have to control the peninsula before the British fleet could sail on to Constantinople. The long finger (61 kilometres) of land that he was targeting would be armed with howitzers and batteries along two coastlines. One faced the Aegean Sea; the other the straits.

Hamilton knew he was in for a bureaucratic fight with Kitchener for men, equipment, supplies and weapons. The war minister wanted most resources applied to the grim Western Front in Europe, not a doubtful sortie into the Middle East that was meant to distract the Turks from the Russian Front.

The Hamilton-led expedition was supposed to be a secret, but not for long. The Turks had their spies everywhere. Seventy thousand nationals lived in Cairo. Everyone in the major cities and ports along the Suez was aware that shipping was jammed with troop ships. There was a big build-up of military camps outside Cairo. Activity in the Aegean was increasing. The British had just tried and failed to sail up the Dardanelles. The Turks were preparing for more British attempts to invade their territory.

The triumvirate running Turkey was reluctantly allowing German help in the form of military commanders, advisers and equipment. They had been enemies in other times, but now they had a mutual opponent. Otto Liman von Sanders arrived to organise the defence of Gallipoli and the Dardanelles after the Enver Pasha-led Turkish disaster in southern Russia and a bungled attempt earlier in 1915 to invade Egypt.

The efficient, thorough, uninspired Liman von Sanders

moved into the former French consul's home in the Gallipoli township on the east coast and began garrisoning the peninsula. Trenches were built, barbed wire was laid out and guns were set up above the most likely landing points. Liman von Sanders worked towards a build-up of 60,000 defensive troops, with a reserve of another 60,000 close by.

By late March 1915, some of the Light Horse regiments were being eased into patrolling, which was the nearest thing to action. Bert Canning reached for his diary:

'Left camp at 4.30 p.m. for night operation; took up a line of outposts for about 3 miles [5 kilometres] across the [Sinai] desert. Had a very exciting time as scout to find out where the enemy convoy was placed; just dodged being captured on several occasions. Managed to get the required information and send back same to Outpost C.O.'[6]

Not all the troopers were like Canning. Most of Chauvel's men were becoming frustrated by the lack of action. Their basic training had been intensive for 11 weeks, but it was finished. Many of the men grumbled as they spent nights in the desert digging trenches. In daylight hours, they sweated out repetitive riding exercises to keep them and their mounts in condition. The men wanted to do what they had come half-way around the world for: fight. Like all the others in the two divisions, they had to await orders.

A buzz went through the troopers' camp when Hamilton turned up at Heliopolis on 29 March 1915 and reviewed the troops.

He gave nothing away to Chauvel or Monash when, on horseback, he reviewed their men. The two compared notes after this and concluded that an invasion was about to start somewhere in the Aegean.

The wait continued. Some troopers took the time to see the sights, including the pyramids, the pharaohs' tombs, and museums. Others found trouble. Chauvel and Monash fought to build the necessary esprit de corps, and succeeded. But inflexible

Bridges was not so fortunate. The main hell-raisers were in his 1st Division. He was furious with them and unforgiving. He sent 300 home to Australia for drunkenness, insubordination, desertion and attacks on locals. This was the ultimate humiliation for most, who wanted to be with their mates for whatever was to come.

The Australian officers hoped for some respite over Easter, when it was thought that most of the men would turn their minds to their faith and families.

It was not to be.

II

Wassa: a Very Different Battle

A group of Australians and New Zealanders had had enough. They were frustrated by the inaction. One in 10 of them had venereal disease; many had wallets, pens, keepsakes, clothes and watches stolen in the brothels in the Cairo red-light district of Haret el Wassa. On Good Friday, 2 April 1915, some decided to riot. Led by 12 ringleaders, including some from the Light Horse, a small mob arrived in Cairo late in the afternoon. After a few hours drinking, their disgruntlement grew over grievances in an alien, unsympathetic culture. After dark, they turned their anger towards a multi-storey brothel, determined to wreak havoc.

Although he did not take part, Robert Ellwood of the 2nd Light Horse witnessed the incident. Some mates from his regiment were involved.

'There were the good naughty girls and the bad naughty girls,' he said, 'and the bad naughty girls had the habit of taking the soldiers down. They would go through his pockets if he [a client] happened to be drunk or if he slept there [at the brothel] that night. This resulted in a feeling of resentment to some of the girls . . . Some of the boys went there with the intention of not doing any harm to the girls, but cleaning the place up . . .'

The incident led Bert Canning to make the longest entry in his diary:

'. . . something happened between the lower women and natives [and the Anzacs] which set up a free fight. Before long it swelled into a regular riot.'

The Anzacs grabbed the women and their Greek pimps or 'bullies' and dragged, pushed and hurled them into the street.

'Houses were ransacked,' Canning observed, 'and pianos, beds, and furniture were hurled from two, three and four stories into the street. These together with donkey carts and furniture from eating houses were piled together and set on fire.'[1]

The bonfire drew a crowd, including hundreds more Australians and New Zealanders who had been in the area. They joined in the bedlam.

The Cairo fire brigade appeared. The revellers blocked their attempt to douse the flames. The firemen pulled their hoses into position. The Anzacs manhandled the firemen, pushing and shoving them away from the conflagration. They cut their fire hoses. Fights broke out with the pimps, the firemen and spectators. The Anzacs seized some of the fire engines.

The (British) military police or 'provos' arrived on foot. The Australians and New Zealanders formed a solid phalanx in front of the brothel, parts of which were on fire. They threw bottles and rocks at them. The police were outnumbered. They retreated. The antipodeans then set alight a nearby Greek tavern where the pimps congregated. Shop windows in the street were smashed. Looting began. The wild mob was now out of control. One of its own members informed the military police that the only possible way to stop it was to ask the Lancashire Territorials in. The Anzacs liked and respected them. The Territorials were sent an SOS. At first they could not prevent the rioting, brawling and looting.

'The Australians were heaving jerry pots full of rubbish [from the brothel's balcony] on top of the Territorials,' Ellwood said, 'and a piano was also pushed over [the balcony].'[2]

That was the final straw for the Territorials. Their commander ordered them to fix bayonets and advance on the crowd, now a jumbled mix of Australians, New Zealanders and locals. Instead of the hostility shown towards the police, the rioters listened to the Territorials' commander's pleas. Many were drunk, but not stupid enough to take on their armed Lancashire 'chooms'. A few arrests were made. Soldiers began drifting away, their revenge exacted on the offending prostitutes and their pimps.

The Australians called the incident the Battle of Wozzer (Wassa).

Soon after this fiasco, troopers recalled a bar in the area where there was a large jar on a shelf. Preserved in it was a set of testicles and penis. The latter had been split from end to end and splayed apart. The story put about by local pimps and prostitutes was that it had belonged to an Australian who had wronged a local virgin. The item existed, but whether it belonged to a digger or trooper was unlikely. No-one reported such a loss on the tour of duty. Yet the message was clear.

'Some of us took it as an incentive to be good,' trooper Ray Hall of the 5th Light Horse Regiment noted.[3]

Wassa was the low point of the build-up to war for the two divisions. A court of inquiry was held a few days later. Fifty witnesses were questioned. The court 'judges', including commanders Bridges, Chauvel and Monash, inspected the brothel area and had to withstand abuse from prostitutes. Some women had been left with very little more than their reputations, a few thousand fewer clients for the moment, and nowhere to ply their trade. The court sat for four days but produced an inconclusive report. A few minor charges were laid, but no-one was sent home.

The divisional commanders were hoping more than ever for the directive to proceed to a war zone, where the soldiers' energies could be focused on their mission, whatever it might be.

The day after the end of the Wassa inquiry, the force learned it was about to go to war. Then the Light Horse brigades were informed they would not be going with the infantry. Despite little being known about the Gallipoli Peninsula, the limited reconnaissance made it clear that the tight, sharp ridges, narrow valleys and thick scrubby gullies would not be suitable for mounted riflemen.

A disappointed Chauvel informed his men. Before any sustained sour reaction could set in, he and his fellow New Zealand brigadiers held manoeuvres. They were in the middle of them when Chauvel had his 50th birthday on 16 April. He was in the desert and not in the mood for celebration. Besides, his sprightly ways and lean frame made him look far younger, and he wished to keep that image especially when surrounded by men half his age and younger.

On 23 April, they trekked for several days. Chauvel instigated exercises in crossing the Nile in local boats by having the horses swim across, 500 a time.

'You ask any bushman how to do that,' Robert Ellwood recalled, 'and he would be nonplussed. It was done by linking each horse to an endless rope stretched across the water from bank to bank. Each horse had on a headstall with a ring under the chin [for connection by a small rope to the 'endless' (very long) one].'

A trooper led the first horse in, followed by the rest.

'Only three or four men got wet,' Ellwood said, 'and we lost only one horse. He didn't seem to have any idea how to swim. He simply lost his head and bobbed up and down in the water . . .'[4]

Chauvel's aims were to toughen them up and work them harder than ever as a distraction from being held back while their mates from infantry headed in boats to Gallipoli. After a concentrated week of rugged, demanding desert activity, Chauvel led his men back to Heliopolis.

On 28 April, he began to receive information about the

landing at Gallipoli three days earlier. Any thoughts that the invasion of Turkey would lead easily to the objective of taking the peninsula and marching on Constantinople evaporated. The landings on the Aegean side of the peninsula and at its tip, Cape Helles, led to brutal battles and stalemate in both theatres in the next few days. Details of the bravery shown by the soldiers were tempered by the number of dead and wounded already filling the Australian hospital at Heliopolis. Chauvel visited the wards. He was sobered by the injuries to the soldiers, some of whom he knew well. Despite this or perhaps because of it, Chauvel reflected the attitudes of his patient troops when he wrote to his wife on 29 April:

'We have no news of our going yet, which is pretty sickening.'[5]

Far more sickening were growing reports from the cove where the invaders landed, and the hills above it. The attrition rate was so high and swift among the two divisions of antipodeans that Birdwood, after consultation with Hamilton, Godley, Bridges and Monash, asked for a thousand volunteers from among mounted brigades back in Egypt.

Chauvel bucked at this request. He had experienced what the break-up of Australian units did in the Boer War. He would lose control of his brigade, and his troopers would be tacked onto other forces wherever needed. Fragmentation would lead to disintegration. He feared that within weeks he would have no command at all. He wanted none of it; nor did his New Zealand counterpart H. A. Russell. They both pushed to keep their brigades intact. Chauvel contacted Lieutenant General Sir John Maxwell, overall commander of British forces in Egypt, and in charge of the mounted brigades left stranded while Hamilton and Co. invaded Gallipoli. The intercession worked. Maxwell countermanded Birdwood's directive. Chauvel and Russell kept their commands intact.

On 8 May, the Light Horse brigades were set to board a ship for the Greek island of Lemnos in the Aegean Sea before heading on to Gallipoli. Chauvel wrote to his wife, keeping his letters banal, as if everything was sweet and routine. He had bought her a 'frock' in Cairo.

'I am told it [the dress's material] is great for summer and washes well,' he said, with all the authority of the fashion unconscious, 'it may be rather a bright blue, but I think you will like it.' He avoided mention of the casualties at Gallipoli. He adhered to the required code of not writing about military matters. Even if he had been free to do so, he did not wish to alarm the young Sibyl in London. 'I am just off [to Gallipoli],' he said without mentioning Turkey, 'so cannot write any more [for now].' [6]

Chauvel ordered 50 of his men to stay behind with the horses. He also instructed that all the rubbish around the camp be set alight. The next day as the ship sailed he asked for a count of his men, and found that there were 30 more than his expected complement.

An inquiry found that more than half the men he had told to stay behind with the horses had slipped aboard to be with their comrades on this first venture into conflict. Chauvel demurred. He took no action, deciding that such troopers, who had acted in the knowledge of the upheaval and heavy casualties already on Gallipoli, were worth having aboard.

PART TWO

Gallipoli Siege

12

Baptism of Fire

The troopers could hear the boom of the big guns long before making out the coastline. As they sailed closer, evening set in. Hills above Anzac Cove became shadows, lit up as the heavy artillery fired into them from ships in the foreground. Closer still, the troopers absorbed the deafening crash as shells were fired off and shuddered at the dull thuds as the hills were struck. The ship carrying Chauvel and his first two regiments anchored off the coast. The big guns ceased after dark. Rifle fire punctuated the night, rising and falling in crescendos, accompanied inharmoniously by the harsher, spitting sounds of machine-guns.

Lights were out on the ship. Enemy submarines were prowling the area and had already done considerable damage. Early the next morning on 12 May, the artillery began again from nearby ships aiming at the hills where 40,000 Turks dominated the heights. When the sun was up Chauvel and his men had their first clear view of the battle area. They could see a small beach. Behind it rose cliffs that seemed to merge with steep peaks and ridges on dark, scrubby hills. A mist had descended on the heights but the cove was bathed in sunlight. Intermittent clouds of shrapnel—spherical bullets scattered by a bursting charge—hung over the beach.

Chauvel led his regiments into boats that ferried them past massive battleships to the shore with light showers of shrapnel coming down.

'Things were pretty warm,' he noted in a letter. '. . . the beach was an inferno—raked all along with shrapnel from the right flank; guns were everywhere and [there was] hot rifle fire all along the line.'[1]

It was 9 a.m. The battle above this cove, already designated 'ANZAC', had been going 17 days. The small beach was crowded. The siege in the valley a few hundred metres away meant that every square foot on the beach was being used. Tents, stacks of ammunition boxes, equipment, soldiers, stores and animals were squeezed into an area about 90 metres long and 25 metres wide.

Chauvel was taken straight to the 2nd Division's commander, Major General Godley, who informed him that he and his regiment would take over from Monash and his decimated 4th Brigade. It had taken the brunt of the fighting and had held the line in Monash Valley since 26 April, the day after the Australians had hit the beaches running. They were in severe need of a break. This was the first order or information Chauvel had been given.

Godley told him that the valley was a vital defence post. If that was penetrated by the Turks, they would haemorrhage down to the beach. What Godley didn't say was that this would lead to a massacre at the cove.

'Monash will explain the situation,' Godley informed him.

Monash's deputy, the heavy-set Lieutenant Colonel J.P. McGlinn, took him to meet Monash before he marched up the Light Horse troopers to relieve part of 4th Brigade infantry, and a battalion of British marines. Chauvel left the beach with an armed guard of troopers and strode along the scrubby track. Monash's engineers had buttressed it with sandbags two metres thick, placed intermittently along the twisting track on the left and right at points where the path was exposed to enemy snipers. Screens of brushwood to hide approaching Anzacs had been mounted on wires. With deafening sounds of artillery shells landing and clouds of shrapnel now bursting right near him, Chauvel was led through Shrapnel Gully to Monash Valley, an 800-metre narrow cleft. Its high walls were baked yellow and free of vegetation. The passage was marked with the debris of war, including dead mules with packs scattered. Coming the other way was the chilling reminder to Chauvel of the events since 25 April with a steady trickle of the dead and wounded being stretchered to the beach. The path curved around hills to the most treacherous part of the valley, which was more vulnerable to snipers than at any point along it. Monash's HQ was to the right of the valley. The actual construct was nothing more than a flimsy hut, which would not have withstood the blast from one well-directed grenade.

Monash, without his helmet, was sitting on a wooden plank at the front, poring over a map. He stood up to shake hands. Despite the chaos going on around them and lack of sleep for most of the past 17 days, he seemed calm. He was courteous and friendly. This provided a fleeting measure of reassurance to Chauvel, who was entering a type of war zone he had never experienced, and for which he was unprepared and untrained.

Apart from their precarious position, he was struck by the noise, which had intensified to a point of distraction as he reached the front line. Monash told him he would get used to it. Displaying an eccentric side, Monash had timed the biggest gap in the noise since he had arrived on 25 April. It was 10 seconds. Some of the men at the front were not coping. Others were already deaf. It was a test for the coolest of nerves. Even soldiers prepared to commit the bravest acts in battle were a jangled mess because of the constant, nagging, at times eardrum-splitting whines, crashes, thuds and explosions.

Nearly as offensive to the senses was the smell. In the Boer War, Chauvel had been close to human and animal corpses rotting in the intense heat on the veldt. But he had never experienced the hideous, concentrated, biting intensity of the odour at Gallipoli.

Monash showed him the terrain, first on the map. The Australian front-line trenches were 20 to 25 metres away. To the right (as they faced the heights) on the slope was Courtney's Post. Quinn's Post was further north about 80 metres away. To the left were the New Zealanders at a ridge called Russell's Top, and north of that, Walker's Ridge. To the right of Monash's hut were trenches manned by brigades of General Bridges' 1st Division.

The Turkish trenches began from just 15 metres in front of the twisted lines of Anzac positions. The Australians named the enemy trenches. Among them was the 'Chess Board' after viewing aerial photographs which displayed a system subdivided into irregular squares. Its complexity demonstrated a determination by the Turks and their German advisers to make any British advance impossible. There was also the 'Bloody Angle', which had such a turn that it ran at 60 degrees to the others, and 'German Officers' Trench', so named because some had been spotted there. Then there was the caustically labelled 'Dead Man's Ridge', set above and beyond the Turkish front lines. Many Anzacs had been hit by snipers from there.

Monash had survived and led with courage in those terrible first weeks. He passed on tips for Chauvel, which would test his leadership skills and survival instincts. He was told about officers bobbing their heads up in the trenches to show their men how fearless they were. They were either dead or wounded. Monash deplored this. The men needed leaders. They had to not wilt under pressure. Nor did they need to be foolhardy.

Chauvel brought up his regiments, who were briefed with the aim of relieving members of 4th Brigade and the British marines from their positions. Their arrival did not change much. The Light Horse took over Pope's Hill, allowing the 13th Battalion (of 4th Brigade) to become the section reserve. But the 14th still held Courtney's; the 15th and 16th continued to alternate at Quinn's. Most of the new arrivals were held back from taking over the toughest posts. They could not be expected to enter the 'hot' areas without any preparation.

This proved correct when the Turks stepped up their bombing and shelling as soon as the 2nd Light Horse regiment led by Lieutenant Colonel R. M. Stodart and his deputy Major William Glasgow entered the line. The enemy could see the change. It wished to make it as 'hot' as possible for the fresh troopers, who, almost to a man, had never been in battle. Predictably, they were rattled. Casualties were quick. Birdwood and Godley inspected the position of the 13th Battalion. They judged Stodart to be unsettled. This was no place for novices, especially those trained more in another form of warfare. They ordered all but one 2nd Light Horse squadron (128 men) out of the line and replaced them with Monash's 15th Battalion.

This left Monash with a dilemma. He had more than earned the right to retire to the beach. But most of the soldiers in the line were still under his command. On top of that, the new command needed constant advice and guidance.

'Chauvel is very fidgety and often calls me to consult in the night,' Monash wrote in his diary.[2] After no sleep for so long he was irritable when he finally had a chance for a slumber, still in his flimsy dugout HQ. Yet he understood and liked Chauvel. Monash decided to stay on duty for at least two more weeks. The new commander was most thankful.

Monash had gained experience, knowledge and comprehension in those 17 days that many officers could never learn in peacetime and many would not approach in years of war. He had learned much about the way British officers operated. Hamilton, for whom he had the utmost respect, was on a battleship directing the battles of the French and British contingents at Cape Tebe, and the British/Anzac forces at Anzac Cove. His command capabilities were hard to measure at that point and distance. More representative were Birdwood and Godley. Monash, the lightning-quick learning novice, did not pass on judgements on them to Chauvel, whom he knew had his own experiences with British command in South Africa. He simply explained what had happened and let his successor in the valley make his own mind up. Monash had been upset and frustrated by the way his men had been used as cannon fodder by Godley, and sent needlessly to their deaths in useless attacks. Monash, just a brigadier, could do nothing about these ill-planned, careless, inhumane plans and schemes unless he wished to resign his commission early. He was powerless but for one aspect. He could use his exceptional skills as an engineer, gunner and weapons expert (he had designed the Monash-Stanley gun, which could pop up and fire over parapets) to construct the best possible defensive trench system.

Apart from his offer to stay with the new commander in the valley, this was his most important legacy to Chauvel. Monash was convinced that his set-up of trench systems and positioning of machine-guns and artillery would stop any surge by the Turks from the hills above. But he added one caveat for Chauvel. The diggers at the front a few metres from them had been magnificent in the harshest of conditions. They would make the difference in the end.

The chances for survival did not seem good. At any one time a thousand diggers—now a mixed force of his 4th Brigade and the Light Horse—could be in position. The Turks, advised by the Germans, could direct a massive force of five to 15 times that in a rush down through the valley. This had not happened yet, but there was a build-up of Turkish forces in the hills above. Despite the odds, Monash was confident that they would be stopped, no matter what they threw at the Anzacs. This in turn bolstered Chauvel, who was pessimistic on arrival. He felt after the first day that he had been put in a hopeless situation. After two days he was certain of it. But by day three, Monash's optimism was helping Chauvel to settle in. Yet Chauvel conveyed his pessimism to Birdwood, who was not impressed.

'From the time of his arrival here,' Birdwood wrote, 'he has always struck me as taking the gloomiest view of everything connected with the Expedition and he never seems to put life into things as he might.'[3]

Birdwood, relying again on past testament concerning Chauvel, did not allow for the fact that he was a horseman. At Anzac Cove he and his troopers were being used purely as infantry, a factor that at first upset him and many of his men. There would be no field work on horseback on this godforsaken peninsula. There wouldn't even be many beloved walers but mainly pack-horses and mules. Chauvel's first reaction was that there had been a gross misuse of his skills.

He was secretly disdainful of the Australian infantry to begin with. Chauvel had not been impressed by what he had seen of his friend Bridges' 1st Division in Egypt. They had caused the most trouble, and he wondered about all the Australian infantry.

But he had a different view after those initial days of bewilderment at Gallipoli, especially with what he was experiencing with Monash's 4th Brigade. The soldiers of its 13th, 14th, 15th and 16th Battalions, some of whom had appeared wild and often undisciplined in Egypt, were very different under extreme pressure at Anzac Cove.

Monash showed Chauvel the entire Section 3 front and took him up to Courtney's Post at night, the second most dangerous trench in the valley, then Quinn's Post just north of them. It was the worst. Snipers on Dead Man's Ridge could hit targets in Quinn's from in front as well as behind.

Just before they arrived, trooper Ronnie MacDonald was shot in the hand by a sniper. His war was over for the moment. As he was being assisted down, Monash and Chauvel hauled themselves up ropes on a small ridge to Quinn's and dropped into the trenches. Chauvel was amazed to hear enemy voices making noises at the diggers, trying to frighten them with whispers about bullets, bombs and death. Some of the diggers were hard at work, making the most of the darkness to deepen the trench and tunnel further. Their spades moved easily into the topsoil-free, rocky brownish earth, but they laboured more when lifting it out. If they stopped digging and there was a few seconds abatement of rifle or machine-gun fire, they could hear the Turks doing the same, moving closer to mine tunnels, as the Anzacs were doing too.

This style of warfare could not have been further from the minds of Chauvel and his troopers. They had not been trained as infantry and now they were learning all there was to know about subterranean life in the trenches, the saps (tunnels dug to approach, undermine or invade the enemy territory), and the communications trenches that led to their bivouacs.

They naturally grumbled about the conditions.

'We had no tents or huts,' Trooper Raymond Hall said. 'Tents were too noticeable from the Turkish lines and their aeroplanes. They would have attracted shellfire . . . We had no large dugouts of the sort used in France and Belgium, subterranean rooms safe from shellfire. The soil was of a friable nature. Large excavations would have required timbering to make them safe, but there was no timber available for that purpose.'[4]

The Anzac dugouts were narrow slits on the edges of gullies. Their height depended on the slope's steepness. They were also on the sides of saps. These just-habitable holes were normally around 6 feet (183 centimetres) deep, and the width of an oil-sheet cover at about 2 feet (61 centimetres). Some were for two men; others four. When a soldier went on night shift to the trenches, he had to take his oil sheet with him for warmth. If it rained, he might return to a waterlogged dugout.

'The furthest any of us got from that was down to the beach,' Robert Ellwood, now a second lieutenant, noted, 'We collected water in rum jars and brought it up to the different units.'

The troopers' food issue was bully beef from the Argentine.

'It was terribly stringy stuff,' Ellwood recalled. 'There was also marmalade, tea, cheese and biscuits. The biscuits were at least 3/8 in. thick. You had to use a stone to break them, and they flaked.'

They would ram an entrenching tool handle into the biscuits inside an empty shell case until they were powder. This would then be mixed with the bully beef and fried in mess tins.

'We'd persuade ourselves we were making rissoles, or stew of it,' Ellwood added, 'We lived on that. There was no such thing as bread [available].'[5]

Birdwood, accompanied by Monash and Chauvel, climbed up to precarious Quinn's for the first time to have a look at the Turkish positions. It was 14 May. He too obeyed all the rules and kept his head down. Seventeen days earlier, British regular major F. D. Irvine from Bridges' 1st Division had stood up at Quinn's and argued with diggers in the trench who implored him to drop down. He was killed by a sniper. After this, diggers asked for periscopes to enable them to shoot without raising their heads above the parapet. The diggers had yet to be given them. But Birdwood was using one when a sniper fired and hit the periscope's mirror. A bullet fragment hit the top of his head.

Birdwood slumped back, bleeding from the scalp. He was helped by Monash and two diggers down into the valley and stretchered off, a bullet fragment lodged in his head.

The cutting down of the commander of the two divisions at Anzac Cove was the low point in the siege so far.

13

Assaults in the Valley

The hardy Birdwood had a headache the next day, Saturday 15 May, but was up and about. He was visited at breakfast by Bridges, who told him he was going up the valley himself to visit one of his few friends, Chauvel, and Monash.

Monash volunteered to meet Bridges and his staff three-quarters of the way up at the sandbag-barrier-protected dressing station run by Captain Clive Thompson. The time set was 9.15 a.m. Monash left his dugout HQ and made his way smartly below the trenches at the head of the valley.

Bridges, accompanied by two senior staff, Captain Dick Casey and Colonel Cyril White, strode up the valley at 9 a.m. They reached the dressing station below Steele's Post on the front line west of the Chauvel/Monash headquarters. Bridges wanted to have a cigarette. He lit one and moved from behind a barrier back to the path to smoke it. He was a tall man, and therefore an easier target for snipers on Dead Man's Ridge, high above him. He had a foolhardy reputation, and often rattled his staff by reckless behaviour, especially in taking risks moving near the trench posts. He chided White and Casey for their caution. This time they did not bother to say anything to him. They had been mocked enough. But Thompson was concerned.

He warned Bridges to be careful, telling him to come behind the barrier. Bridges ignored him.

Monash, glancing at his watch often, reached the path down to the dressing station a few seconds before the appointed time. He was not running but moving quickly nevertheless, aware that a mobile target was tougher for snipers than a stationary one. This was a place where several diggers had already been hit. He was 20 metres away from Bridges. Monash looked up. At that moment, a bullet struck Bridges in the thigh, splitting open his femoral artery.

Monash and Thompson carried Bridges behind the sandbags. Stretcher-bearers hurried him down to the beach and he was ferried to a hospital ship.

It was disturbing news for Chauvel. The day before, Birdwood, commanding the two Anzac divisions, had been struck down, and was lucky to have survived. Now the commander of 1st Division was incapacitated. Chauvel owed his appointment as commander of the 1st Light Horse Brigade to Bridges. He died three days later.

It was another needless waste of a leader when they were in short supply. (His body and his big charger, 'Sandy', were shipped back to Australia for a state funeral. Sandy, saddled and stirrups reversed in honour of a fallen division commander, led the parade down Melbourne's Collins Street, and became the only horse ever to return from abroad during or after World War I. The parade was a shock to the big, solemn crowd. Bridges was then the best-known Australian Gallipoli leader. The ceremony gave an unexpected sense of gravity to the situation on the peninsula, which was not being portrayed by reports on the campaign in the UK or Australia.)

Chauvel hardly had time to mourn his friend and benefactor. The Turks appeared to be preparing for an attack. They had not done so for more than a week, time enough for him and Monash to supervise the fortification of trenches from Pope's Hill to Courtney's Post. Monash insisted that machine-guns be set up offensively where possible. They deepened and widened the trenches, countermanding Birdwood's original directive to keep them shallow in order that men could jump quickly from them to meet at attack.

On 17 May, the sound of the Turks picking and digging their way closer to the Australian trenches, particularly at Quinn's, was audible, even with the continual din of weapons fire. This indicated that at the very least some sort of offensive was about to occur, even if it were restricted to underground. At midnight on 18 May, the Turks hit Courtney's and Quinn's with everything possible in the most intense fire yet experienced at these two vital defensive posts. The now battle-hardened 16th Battalion held firm despite many of them being deafened.

This was the softening-up for something bigger, which was the wrong tactic. The Turks had yet to learn the value of complete surprise. Monash predicted to Chauvel that a big offensive was coming. They would both be in for a long night. They alerted their officers. All the Anzacs were ordered to sleep with their boots and battle clothes on.

Enemy troop movement was noticed at 3 a.m. on 19 May. They hit at 4.20 a.m. in a long line from Russell's to Bolton's Ridge. The 14th (which included 22-year-old Albert Jacka and his companions from Bendigo) and 15th Battalions took the brunt at the head of Monash Valley. Machine-gun and rifle fire spat as wave after wave of Turkish soldiers descended, screaming their love of Allah, and inspired by a band behind them playing military marches.

Grenades were a constant worry as they were lobbed and thrown into the Anzac trenches. The soldiers did shifts on one of the deadliest jobs on Gallipoli or anywhere: smothering live bombs with blankets folded into eight or more thicknesses. There was a simple art to it.

'You had to be as quick as a cat and a bit braver,' Trooper Raymond Hall wrote, 'There was literally only a split second in it.'

If successful, the smotherer stopped the flying bomb fragments. If not, he might lose a limb, or his life.

'This was the sort of work that once earned Victoria Crosses,'

Hall said, 'but with us it was all part of daily work and earned no special mention.'[1]

At first in the 19 May attack, the Anzacs were preoccupied with defence. But after a few minutes, they realised that there was no supporting artillery to back the Turks. The pre-dawn light allowed the Anzacs to spot shadowy figures coming at them. The Anzacs climbed onto the parapets of their trenches and blasted the oncomers without being fearful of incoming shells. Machine-guns raked over the thousands of attackers.

By 5 a.m. the assault seemed to have collapsed. There was a lull, although firing continued. But then the Turks came again. Twelve of them broke into the line at Courtney's, threatening to run over the top and down the little slope to the HQ of 4th Brigade and the close by Light Horse HQ, where Monash and Chauvel were waiting, revolvers at the ready. They were prepared for the worst as they attended to a never-ending stream of inward and outward dispatches, orderlies and messengers.

The attackers hurled bombs, reaching a firing trench. They took cover, pinned down from in front and behind by 14th Battalion members. One soldier behind them was Albert Jacka. After some manoeuvring, Jacka charged the trench, bayoneting two Turks and shooting five. The other five made a run for their lines. This stopped a dangerous attack, which if successful would have opened up a hole in the line through which thousands would have followed in this biggest attempt yet to drive the Anzacs into the sea.

The battalion's commander Lieutenant K. G. W. Crabbe later told Monash of Jacka's superhuman effort. Monash told Crabbe that he would be recommending Jacka for the Victoria Cross, the highest battle bravery award in the British army.

After the initial failed attack, Monash was confident they had withstood the worst. The battle continued for another seven hours, during which a scythe of Anzac fire cut down 10,000 Turks by midday, when they stopped coming. Three thousand were dead; seven thousand were wounded. By contrast the Anzacs, including the Light Horse, had 160 dead and 600 wounded. The Turks had thrown a quarter of their entire force above the cove at the Anzacs, and had failed.

Monash took time to write in his diary:

'Everybody exhausted with want of sleep and mental strain.'[2]

He was now more optimistic than ever, believing the worst could be over in attempts to take the cove. His attitude was in the light of 24 days straight at the front with sleep amounting to the equivalent of two nights.

Chauvel was feeling better, more from relief than anything else. The success of the defence buoyed him a little, although after being in command a week he did not have Monash's prior experience with which to measure if they had had just weathered the worst.

The next day, Chauvel wrote to Sibyl with considerable understatement:

'Things have been a little strenuous lately and I have had only two or three hours sleep in the last forty-eight.'

His changed impressions of the infantry, especially 4th Brigade, from Cairo, were complete:

'They [the Light Horse] are simply magnificent, and so are Monash's men,' he wrote. 'I am living cheek by jowl with Monash here and find he is really a very fine soldier. He has been of very great assistance to me the last few days, and very willing indeed considering I have ousted him out of the command of the section.'[3]

Soon afterwards, Chauvel visited Quinn's Post, and was struck by the cheerfulness of South Australians and Tasmanians from his 3rd Light Horse Regiment, who were temporarily relieving the exhausted 16th and 13th Battalions. One machine-gunner, 22-year-old Sergeant Ross Smith from Adelaide, made an impression. His confidence was uplifting for all around him. This post was the Turks' first target in their recent assault and still the most treacherous position above Anzac Cove. This smiling trooper seemed to be enjoying the challenge of it. Smith was observing all the rules about keeping his head down in the trench, and of moving carefully to avoid the snipers. It was all done with jokes and chat that seemed to relax everyone. Chauvel knew it took gut-tightening courage just to be there, but thought Smith was genuine and not faking his bravado. No-one could relieve the dangers or avoid fear. Troopers like him were important for morale.

Chauvel kept his letters to Sibyl innocuous. Gallipoli was almost a lovely holiday location.

> I am writing in my dug-out which a most excellent batman has made very comfortable [he wrote on 23 May] but the smell of dead Turks, which lie in their hundreds, if not their thousands, in front of the lines is awful, especially at night. There is talk of an Armistice to bury them but I am doubtful it is coming off. The climate here is delightful. I am very fit. Rough hill climbing is giving me a waist again. My belt is back to its old hole.

The armistice did come off the next day. Chauvel and Monash were among the many soldiers who wandered between the lines. Three thousand Turks were buried. Chauvel wrote the next day that it was a 'Godsend to get them underground as the smell was unbearable.' He noted that the 'Turks were friendly to our fellows' and that 'there was no treachery of any sort.'[4]

He did not disapprove of fraternising with the enemy at these special moments of truce. The more ruthless Monash did not like it.

14

No Triumph

German submarine commander Otto Hersing on board *U21* gave the order: 'Fire!' A torpedo streaked its way towards the unsuspecting British battleship the *Triumph* just off Anzac Cove. It struck dead centre. The *Triumph* keeled over slowly. Sailors began diving into the sea. In the hills, Anzacs and Turks ceased fighting for a moment. They scrambled to higher ground for a better view. The Turks cheered. The Anzacs stopped eating lunch to watch in awe as the stricken vessel tipped onto its side. Small boats raced out from the shore to pick up the surviving sailors. Bigger ships belched smoke as they departed the area as fast as possible for fear of being another victim. As they slipped away, the *Triumph* turned over, and then floated upside down, water spouts of steam coughing from it. The Turks kept cheering.

'The Turks had wonderful targets as we massed on the hills and gazed down,' trooper Ion Idriess of the newly arrived New South Wales 5th Light Horse noted in his diary on 25 May. 'They did not fire. I don't know whether they were "sporty" or whether they were too excited gazing at their own triumph. Then she sank . . . the Turks tore the shrapnel at us and we ran for our burrows.'[1]

Monash, always alert to the psychology of the moment, had a conference with Chauvel and their mining engineers with the aim of bringing forward the timing on the blowing up of a Turkish underground listening post. The Turkish failure above ground in the massive assault of 19 May had caused them to step up their subterranean work. An increase in tunnelling was noted. This was the time, Monash suggested, to retaliate. He and Chauvel directed the engineers to detonate the targeted listening post, which collapsed the Turkish tunnel.

The crash and thunder of the tunnel collapsing mid-afternoon caused the Anzacs to cheer.

Monash and Chauvel ordered their own tunnelling to continue. The enemy, undeterred, was soon digging again. At 6 p.m. on 28 May, the engineers underground warned that the Turks were about to set off a mine explosion. They indicated the likely area of front-line trenches that would be blown up. This was cleared of soldiers.

*

A horrific explosion between the lines at 3.20 a.m. shattered the relative calm of 29 May and left a massive crater in the Anzac trenches. Chauvel and Monash, just back from his first two days off on corps commander Hamilton's boat, braced themselves. The Turks took advantage of the commotion to make their first concerted attack since the disaster of 10 days earlier. Backed by artillery this time, and throwing bombs (grenades), they tore down between the trenches either side of the crater before the dust and earth projectiles finished falling. They reached the Anzac communication trenches. The next stop was an open run into the valley. But the 13th Battalion machine-gunners at Pope's Hill cut them down with intense, accurate fire, finishing the attack in half an hour.

There was still some mopping up to do, as a group of Turks remained in a bombproof communications trench. They were trapped. Pre-dawn light would expose them if they tried to go further or retreat. Even though this strip of front-line trenches was empty, it was controlled by the Anzacs.

Godley, from his HQ on the beach, ordered that the Turks be captured immediately and the Anzac front trenches reoccupied. Chauvel arranged for a contingent made up of 13th, 15th and 16th Battalion diggers led by Colonel G. J. Burnage to a position just under Quinn's Post ready to do battle. Burnage was wounded. Monash ordered Colonel Pope from his position some distance away (at Pope's Hill) to take charge of the contingent. Monash and Chauvel thought there might be confusion when Pope arrived. Other senior officers may have felt compelled to lead in Burnage's absence. With the main danger of penetration past, Chauvel decided to put Monash in command in the valley and to follow Pope up to Quinn's to make sure the change of command went smoothly.

Monash, at the insistence of Godley, again urged a charge to drive out the remaining Turks, who were cornered in a bomb-proof trench. But, as predicted, there was confusion at Quinn's. Several officers disagreed with the necessity to charge over the maze of trenches to the bombproof trenches. Those who knew the terrain tried to persuade Chauvel to change his mind. They were concerned about Turkish bombs, machine-gun fire and artillery that was hitting the area forward of their trapped men. Monash, under continued pressure from Godley, kept sending messages to charge, as the debate below Quinn's continued. The unflappable Chauvel remained adamant there should be a charge. Major H. Quinn, who knew the area better than anyone, was hesitant. He thought the action superfluous, as did his adjutant and other officers. The Turks had nowhere to go. They would either be killed or forced to surrender in the next few hours. Chauvel stood firm.

Quinn was directed to reconnoitre. He was only away a few seconds when killed by machine-gun fire. The charge went ahead, its timing fortuitous. The Turks began another attack at the same time. Their machine-gunners, bomb throwers, snipers and artillery gunners stopped for fear of killing their own men. This gave the Australians just enough time to retake their empty front-line trenches and help fend off the advancing wave of Turks. Yet they could not dislodge the trapped Turks from the communications trench.

By 5.30 a.m. the attempts to break through ceased. At 8 a.m. the trapped Turks surrendered. The unlucky Quinn, who had made the post his own, his adjutant and the officers on the spot had been right to suggest that a charge was unnecessary. Similarly, Chauvel had done his job in directing the attack. They were not to know that the second assault would be brushed off with relative ease. His main concern was to mop up the Turks in the Anzac line. Godley, a long way from the action, had ordered the attack without any forethought. It was his way. Sometimes it worked. Usually it didn't.

Despite the avoidance of major penetration through Anzac lines, the assassins in the hills were deadlier than ever, as were the shrapnel bursts.

'Snipers shot fifteen Aussies this morning,' trooper Idriess wrote in his diary on 29 May, 'and shrapnel got four of our regimental men. It is heartbreaking to see so many men killed and maimed when they are not in the actual firing-line. No matter on what peaceful errand we go, death goes too. We never know whether we will wake up alive.'[2]

*

Chauvel's decision to go up to Quinn's impressed the men. He stayed there until 8 a.m. when it was clear that there would not be any more assaults that morning. Just as he was leaving the post, the Turkish prisoners were filing past. One of them broke from the ranks and tried to kiss Chauvel. He sidestepped the Turk, much to the mirth of the digger captors.

Chauvel had shown a cool demeanour under stress just as he had as a 26-year-old in 1891 during the shearers' strike.

Despite meeting this crisis, he remained forlorn about the Anzacs' chances of breaking the depressing siege on Gallipoli. He accepted Hamilton's invitation to join him aboard his HQ base on the battleship *Arcadian* at Imbros Harbour for some rest. Hamilton did this with all the commanders on Gallipoli to assess them, their morale and the situation. Chauvel, still worried about his Light Horse forces and their continuing losses, gave a frank, undiplomatic assessment of the conditions at the head of Monash Valley. The corps commander took this as pessimism. He expressed his annoyance to Godley, who responded by saying he hoped that Monash, who had rested on the *Arcadian* a few days earlier, had not given Hamilton 'anything like the same idea'.[3]

Monash had been much more upbeat, and pleased to have a chance to chat with Hamilton, which created a different atmosphere than with Chauvel. It was a matter of perspective. Monash appeared optimistic. He was forever planning and assessing, believing there was always a solution that would lead to a break out from Anzac Cove and victory. Monash's 30-year engineering background, legal work and extensive military training caused him to think there was always a way to win, just as he would in a court room or in successfully putting up a bridge. He never viewed a situation as hopeless. He had already spent a lifetime problem-solving. Mathematical puzzles had been his hobby since he was 10 years old. Yet on Gallipoli he was not privy to the battle plans or their design. There was no problem for him to solve. He had no say in them. He was powerless except in defensive tactics, which were successful but had nothing to do with overall tactics and strategy for actually taking the peninsula. He put up several plans to Birdwood for taking Turkish strongholds but they were ignored. The only way his ideas about winning could be tested would be if he were to take over as corps commander. There was no chance of that on this battlefield.

Given this limitation, Chauvel's 'pessimism' was closer to realism. He had fought in another kind of war, and knew what a siege mentality was. He saw no way out. Continual engagement was a waste of lives and time. But Chauvel was as impotent as Monash on Gallipoli. His honesty and negativity were unacceptable.

Hamilton's response was to suggest to Godley that Chauvel be relieved from his command at the head of Monash Valley. Godley, irritated as he was with Chauvel's lack of diplomacy, did nothing. Even with his unreflective mentality, he realised the Light Horse commander's assessments had validity. But it was not what the anxious corps commander wished to hear from one of his key officers.

If Chauvel was correct, the expedition to the Dardanelles would be a failure and blight on Hamilton's career, and that of its author Winston Churchill.

15

Counterattack

After 29 May, fighting settled down in the valley. The Turks stopped trying to destroy the Anzacs at the cove in one hit. For the moment it would be a battle of bombardment and attrition. Monash felt his first-up job had been done, given its restrictions. He and his fighting 4th Brigade, bearded, bedraggled and nearly exhausted, were taken out of the line, leaving Chauvel in total command. The New Zealand Infantry Brigade took over Quinn's and Courtney's.

The immediate crisis over, Chauvel took time to write to Sibyl at Queen's Gate Terrace, London. He put his address as 'in a dugout':

'. . . The Turkish papers describe us as the "White Cannibals". We've [the Anzacs overall] been at it for five weeks and it's almost like everyday routine . . . they shell us a lot and don't do much damage—if any—and loose off an awful lot of ammunition into the atmosphere, while we sit under cover and wait for them to come out.'[1]

The lull even gave Chauvel time to comment on the appointment by Australian Defence Minister George Pearce of Colonel J.G. Legge, who was to take over command of 1st Division after Bridges' demise. This was a major blunder. Legge was chief of the (Australian) general staff based in London and out of touch with the upheaval at Gallipoli.

Chauvel wrote he was 'shocked' at the decision and felt aggrieved that he had not been appointed himself. His exacting experience in the valley, he rightly thought, would give him a fair claim to this step-up in leadership. But he was not aware that he had upset Hamilton with his bleak outlook, which meant he had very little chance of an upgrade at that point. Monash too was justified in believing he had a claim. But he was overlooked and miffed about it also. (When Legge 'performed' on Gallipoli, he was judged as not equipped for the job. He lasted only a month before Birdwood shipped him off to Egypt. Pearce later admitted his bungle in making decisions about leadership on a far-off battlefield.)

Chauvel and Monash were both promoted to 'temporary' brigadier general, which to some extent eased their angst. Chauvel made his feelings clear to Birdwood, who told Hamilton. The commander-in-chief was prompted to write to Birdwood:

'I think Brigadier-General Chauvel may be quite reassured as to any apprehensions aroused by the appointment of Colonel

Legge in so far as it affects his own reputation and position. It is clear to me that the Australian government had predetermined to appoint Colonel Legge and that the claims of locally employed officers (at Gallipoli) were never seriously weighed in that connection. Otherwise some reference would first have been made to general Headquarters here.'[2]

Chauvel had made it clear that he was no shrinking violet. Hamilton may not have been enamoured with his assessments of the campaign; yet the commander-in-chief was very aware of his self-confidence and self-belief.

Chauvel, a religious man, who acted as a lay-preacher at his local Anglican church at home, brought a parson up to Monash Valley for the first Anglican communion service to be held in the Light Horse Brigade in the month it had been there. It was held in a narrow gully among the troopers' dugouts.

'The parson [wearing] a spotless surplice and dirty, old felt hat had two ammunition boxes for an altar and the dust in the bottom of the gully to kneel on . . . It was quite well-attended despite the discomfort.'[3]

On 13 June, Chauvel showed signs of boredom, writing:

'The Australian Light Horse are now cave dwellers and I am living the life of a rabbit.' But he was 'fit and having good rations'.[4]

Three days later, he contracted pleurisy. Doped up with morphine, he was placed on the hospital ship *Gascon* and taken away from Anzac Cove. He was hospitalised in Alexandria and took convalescence at Heliopolis over seven weeks.

Chauvel was pronounced fit to return to Anzac Cove early in August, just in time for the biggest counterattack in the battle. He travelled on the boat back to Anzac Cove with several other Australians who had recovered from wounds and illnesses. Among them was Ronnie MacDonald, his hand healed after being shot at Quinn's in his first week at Gallipoli. He had spent two months recuperating at Luna Park Hospital Cairo, from where he wrote often to Rania MacPhillamy in Sydney. She had completed her training with the voluntary arm of the nursing service, which was under the auspices of the Red Cross. He could not wait to return to his 1st Regiment. He was buoyed by the knowledge that his dark-eyed beauty with the sensual lips had already booked a boat for Egypt which would depart on 27 September.

Chauvel would be stationed at Quinn's with the view to attacking from there as part of a multi-pronged offensive. His absence meant his part in it would be minor. But his 1st Light Horse Brigade, along with the 3rd Brigade's 8th Regiment from Victoria and 10th from Western Australia, would be in the thick of it.

The Hamilton/Birdwood/Godley battle plan for a break-out from Anzac Cove looked impressive on paper. It had sweet logic, with plenty of pieces ready to fit like a jigsaw. First, there would be diversions by the British at the bottom of the peninsula at Cape Helles. Second, there would be a break-out to the left from Anzac Cove on the night of the 6th. This force (including Monash's 4th Brigade) would come around like a left hook through the rugged, dark ridges and spurs, supposedly to hit the strength of the Turks in the heights.

Third, a big British reinforcement would land a few kilometres north of the cove at Suvla Bay, another expected diversion. With 45,000 fresh soldiers it was hoped they would provide an impetus for breaking through the Turkish defences.

Fourth, Australia's 1st Division would attack to the right of Anzac Cove at Lone Pine.

All these actions were meant to distract, slow up and soften the Turks, while more direct attacks were made by the New Zealanders on the Turkish stronghold at Chunuk Bair (Hill); and then the Australian Light Horse regiments would swoop across Russell's Top to the Nek, a narrow ridge, and sweep up from Quinn's Post and Pope's Hill. They were all heading to the Turks' stronghold hill: Baby 700. This target was the focal point. The British command knew that if they took it, they would break out of the cove at last. The German officers and the Turks were also aware of this.

Chauvel arrived back on 3 August in time to witness a 'feint' by an attacking force from Pope's Hill.

'It drew such a perfect hurricane of machine-gun and rifle fire, supplemented by shells and bombs,' A. C. N. Olden of the 10th Light Horse noted, 'as to leave no doubt to the enemy's never-tiring vigilance.'[5]

The Turks were there in force, and waiting, aware from their spies at Anzac Cove that the big effort to burst through was coming.

This fierce response to the Anzac demonstration worried Chauvel. He was concerned too about the state of the men in his 1st Light Horse, and those also in the 3rd Brigade. Most were not fit. Many looked weakened and wasted. The intense heat of the summer, the constant nerve-jangling noise and the long front-line vigils had taxed the men too much. On top of that, the contaminated, fly-blown food with the attendant dysentery and diarrhoea, and the water shortages, had left their mark on hollowed faces. Chauvel felt that the youths he had seen and led in May and June had matured grimly well beyond their years in a few months. Like older men, they could not now do the cliff-climbing exercises ordered by Birdwood to 'harden them up'. Such fitness drills were abandoned.

Chauvel could see the deterioration. He had felt it himself with the debilitating pleurisy, which could be brought on by mental or physical strain, or a combination of both. Further worrying was the grand break-out project that he had no say in. Even for a private without any tactical pretensions, this plan had too many 'ifs'. All the forces fanning out had to win their battles if an overall victory was to come.

Chauvel, who was a good tactician, had serious reservations about success, simply based on what he knew about the command's approach before his illness. But he had returned to find the mood had changed at the cove. Being locked down for 14 weeks had built frustration in some and caused others to be 'stir crazy'. The monotony of war was having a major impact. Important issues included continual killing, destruction, disease, water, food and living conditions.

Chauvel now found a mix of grit and desperation.

Captain Vernon Piesse, who had been in hospital, insisted on returning to the cove.

'I want to be in it when the boys go over,' he said.[6]

Everyone, from the foot soldiers and troopers through officers to Hamilton, Birdwood and Godley, wanted to break out of the Gallipoli siege.

16

Insanity at the Nek

Chauvel used binoculars to scrutinise a point across Monash Valley. He could see movement at Russell's Top where other Light Horse troopers were waiting for the word to charge. It was approaching the pre-dawn time for them and 255 troopers from his 1st Brigade to strike; 55 from Quinn's and 200 from Pope's. There were 300 more troopers in reserve.

Birdwood said that these two direct lines of attack were to be 'diversions', which was the description too of the diggers' attack now in its 11th hour across to Chauvel's right at Lone Pine. This was a clever, if deceptive use of the language, almost as if the contact with the enemy would be minimal, even minor. But the Australian 1st Division, engaged at Lone Pine, was in a full-scale battle of the most brutal kind, with bayonet, bomb and bullets flying close in a tight labyrinth of trenches.

Chauvel was under orders to send his troopers north with the ultimate target being Baby 700 hill, where the men at Russell's Top would also be heading. The New Zealand infantry was coming from behind this Turkish stronghold.

The time ticked over to 4.23 a.m. on 7 August 1915. The artillery support by the navy and land batteries had been going 23 minutes when it stopped, seven minutes ahead of schedule. This was a blunder. It would give the Turkish defenders confidence they could break from cover to blast the Australians without fear of shrapnel. Chauvel felt uncomfortable for his own men and the main force of troopers on Russell's Top, who were now doubly on edge. The first line of 175 in the 90-metre-long trench facing the Turks was from the 8th Light Horse Regiment, mainly horsemen from Victoria's Western District. They gripped their bayoneted rifles, waiting for the call to climb out by wall pegs and charge the Turkish trenches at the Nek not much more than 70 metres away. They were cold in their shirt sleeves, shorts and English-style sun-helmets. Not even their second shot of rum had warmed them for long as their nerves geared up for action. The pre-dawn light allowed them to see what was in front of them: the narrow neck of land varying from 30 to 50 metres wide running to the Turkish lines.

A few seconds after the British naval artillery stopped, 'a fierce crackle of fire came out of the Turkish trenches,' Captain L. F. S. Hore wrote:

'We knew we were doomed. The bombardment had failed and simply advertised our attack. I was in charge of the right wing of the second line [of the 8th]. Under me [were] three subalterns and 175 men. We were to start our charge after the first line had gone about 50 yards.'[1]

They had little idea about the outcome of the battles elsewhere except that there had been 'success' in the fight at Lone Pine to their far right. This was conveyed to them to lift them for their own effort. The plan was simple. The first wave of men would take the Nek trenches by thrusted bayonets and hurled bombs. The second wave would sweep on to the objective up hill Baby 700 and the, until now, impenetrable Turkish trenches at the heart of the defence at the heights.

Behind the 8th Regiment were lines three and four (many from the Western Australia's wheat belt) representing the 10th Light Horse Regiment. Line three would push further up the hill as far as possible. The fourth line would carry picks and shovels, ready for entrenchment.

All the men would have had some sense of a fait accompli from what they were carrying: wire cutters, planks, empty sandbags, full water bottles, periscopes, scaling ladders and six biscuits each. This projected a breakthrough at the Nek and an occupation on Baby 700. Even the white patches on their shirts to stop the British artillery hitting them, and the red and white marker flags also at hand, indicated an expectation of 'mission accomplished' before they even sprinted forward. The ultimate aim was to dig in far into the heights—about 200 metres away up Baby 700.

This was Godley's plan, with Birdwood adding his thoughts. Chauvel had no say in it. This kind of bayonet attack was more relevant to the Napoleonic wars of a century ago and earlier. For some reason known only to Godley, he had decided to go back to the days before the rifle. One factor not questioned in the last minute directive was that the men would carry little ammunition. Their trusty rifles would be unloaded and just for skewering the enemy. The motive behind this was cruel. It would influence the troopers to keep running at the enemy trenches.

Trust was a vital thing; the officers had an idea, which had been put down on paper in strict orders. The troopers had been fired up by Jack Antill of the 3rd Light Horse Brigade, who had built a reputation in the Boer War. He left any capacity for articulation behind him in South Africa. He was brave then. Now he was shrill and bull-headed; an intimidator. He responded to Godley's logic without any comment; not even a query about being able to fire off a round of ammunition when the men reached the trenches. This plan appealed to Antill. It was not complex. It was what he saw as gutsy: a straightforward charge at the enemy, something, he reminded everyone who had not read Banjo Paterson's articles in the *Sydney Morning Herald* in 1900, he had done in the Boer War. Yet there were differences 15 years ago. He was then on horseback on an open plain. It took courage or madness or both to behave the way he did then. The Nek was a narrow, hemmed-in strip and far more treacherous. And he was not in the actual charge.

The troopers had been told often that the Turks would be distracted; a New Zealand infantry battalion was set (so the plan indicated) to hit them from the other side of the hill just as 8th Regiment charged. Yet no-one in the urging, inspiring, aggressive, bullying words had said anything about 'Plan B' if the Turks were not distracted; if their machine-guns in the pre-dawn, half-light of a mid-summer morning were trained straight down the narrow funnel at the 600 troopers.

This was the last thing on the minds of the spirited young men who had joined up with visions of mounted infantry work and cavalry charges. They had not expected to fight like this; in mainly subterranean conflict with the odd moment of close-in combat for which they were not trained or prepared. They had courage beyond what anyone could expect. Some of the troopers had faked recoveries from illness to be in this attempted 'break-out' from Anzac Cove. Others had tried to bribe their way into the front line. They did not want to let their mates down. They had all seen enough death and terror at Gallipoli to be excused for not wishing to buy into a fight where it was likely that they would be killed or wounded.

But they all wished to be there.

People from all states in the vast country had been drawn together on this remote finger of land. Unaware of it themselves, they were in the process of forging the character of a new nation. They were forming personal values about selflessness, mateship, love, friendship, courage, respect and self-discipline that would bind them and create principles that they hoped would help them through this conflict. All these features were fused into a desire to fight against huge odds in the face of a terrifying death. Bravado could not explain why they wished to be in the battle; nor could the shots of rum.

These men (there were no boys now) were on a level of endeavour reached and experienced by relatively few in history. Perhaps only the crucible of war could mature so many so quickly and profoundly.

As the seconds ticked down, the Turks ripped off a few more bursts of machine-gun fire. Some of the troopers at both Quinn's and Russell's Top let go expletives of despair or anger. The Turks had seen the build-up. They were ready. No matter how much courage the Anzacs had, it could be no match for hot flying lead. In the past 24 hours, the troopers had been led to believe the defence would be limited. But without the supportive artillery fire, many of the Anzacs felt suddenly more vulnerable.

Lieutenant Colonel Alexander White, with a bandaged head, could easily have avoided this combat. But he wanted to lead the charge. He shook hands with Antill in the trench. His eyes followed the second hand of his watch as he silently counted down to zero.

'Go!' he yelled. The troopers scrambled out, White in front. The noise was terrific, but not from the Anzacs. The steady crash of machine-guns drowned out everything else. The fire, coming from 30 machine-guns spitting hundreds of bullets a second, was powerful enough to sever limbs. Many troopers were hit climbing out of the trench. Some only managed a few paces. White was hit after about six paces and stumbled a few more. Most were slaughtered a long way from the Turkish trenches. The handful that did reach them was outnumbered by the enemy. The first line had been cut down in minutes.

At the same time, William Glasgow led the troopers out from Pope's and Major Bourne and his men moved off from Quinn's. Bourne's troops had a similar sudden, shocking fate as at Russell's Top. Only five of the men were not killed; the 50 victims were shredded within seconds. Some of Glasgow's men protected or hidden by rock and cliff wall for some of the approach, reached the third line of Turkish trenches. But most were mown down.

Bourne consulted Stodart, his commanding officer. He agreed that the next line at Quinn's should stay put. This battle, just 10 minutes old, was unwinnable. After Stodart received Chauvel's acquiescence, Bourne delivered the 'stop' order.

Over at Russell's Top, the irrational, inflexible Antill had no such misgivings, or second thoughts. He motioned the second line of 150 up and over. After climbing over their fallen cobbers, dead, dying and wounded in the trench, they too were facing the terror of the Nek.

'We saw our fate in front of us,' Hore noted, 'but we pledged to go. To their eternal credit . . . not a man in the second line stayed in the trench. As I jumped out I looked down the line and they were all jumping over the parapet. We bent low and ran as hard as we could. Ahead, we could see the trenches aflame with rifle fire. All around, smoke and dust were kicked up by the bullets. I felt a sting in my right shoulder. I thought it couldn't be a hit or it would have hurt more . . .'

Hore dashed on in the surreal dance with death. Seconds seemed like minutes; minutes were eternity.

'I passed our first line all dead or dying it seemed,' he said, 'and went on a bit further and flung myself down about 40 yards from the Turkish trenches. I was a bit ahead of my men having got a good start . . . I looked around and saw them all down, mostly hit.'

Hore was pinned, unsure what to do. He couldn't lead. There were no men to be led. Blood was oozing from his shoulder.

'The dirt was spurting up all around like rain from a pavement in a thunderstorm,' he added, 'some bigger spurts near me were either bombs or pom poms . . . the trench ahead was a living flame, the roar of musketry not a bit diminished.'

He was protected by a tiny fold in the ground and a Turk six weeks dead. Hore scanned behind him again. Six of his men signalled they were unhit. He faced a dilemma no captain ever wanted. He knew if he called them on and led the charge into the wall of bullets, they would follow. Should he send these loyal men to their deaths and valour, or back and another chance at life? Hore, for a second in time, was God with the ultimate power over six human beings and himself. He figured they had done far more than they should have in getting so close. He motioned for them to retreat if they could.

'I started to shove myself backwards on the flat of my stomach,' he said. After easing back a few metres he felt a sting in his right foot. It was his second hit. Blood now seeped from his boot too.

'As long as my arms and chest were right, I didn't mind.'

He crawled back for an hour through the slain troopers.

'There were no live men near me,' he recalled, 'except one who did the same as I did.'

Hore fell into an Anzac sap, and then managed to limp out into one of the back trenches. He removed his shirt and was relieved he had only a flesh wound. He was too stunned to remove his boot and look at his injured foot.

'I lay down wondering how on earth I got out of it,' he recalled, 'Our Colonel was killed; one Major gone and the other wounded; my three subalterns were dead, and about seventy percent of my men . . . so perished the 8th Light Horse.'[2]

This amounted to more like murder than mass suicide. But not by the Turks. They too, had been under orders on several occasions, particularly 19 and 29 May, which could easily be construed as manslaughter by their commanders. The excuse that it was war should not have been enough. Commanders like Chauvel and Monash would never have sanctioned, let alone dreamt up, such daft and deadly plans that put their charges in such danger, especially if there was no chance of victory. But no-one was likely to be brought to account for the disaster at the Nek, and forward of Pope's and Quinn's. More likely there would be a cover-up.

Unfairly, Antill's reputation would probably remain intact. The 3rd Light Horse's 59-year-old English commander Brigadier General F. G. Hughes, who could have stopped the butchery, would remain mute. Godley, on the beach and out of touch, was most culpable. Not even gross stupidity in war could be an excuse for what was happening at Anzac Cove on the early morning of 7 August 1915.

William Glasgow was in a former Turkish trench. There was no tougher soldier or commander at Anzac Cove. He would not stand for cowardice or insubordination. Yet his mind was quick and flexible. Unlike Antill, he had developed and matured since the Boer War. He adapted to the reality of what was happening in those vital first 10 minutes.

Looking left he could see the slaughter at the Nek 70 metres away. Ahead and above them there were more manned Turkish trenches, including those that had just destroyed the 8th Light Horse. Glasgow did a rough count. He was down to 40 or 50 men. About 150 were dead or wounded. He decided to withdraw.

'The air was hazy with lead,' one officer from the incoming 10th Regiment at Russell's Top noted. The Turks were still using at least 30 machine-guns to sweep down the funnel of the Nek. The troopers now knew what the enemy strength was. There was no way any attack into no-man's land could succeed, even in part, with say one trench being occupied. Disastrously for the 10th, making up lines three and four at Russell's Top, they did not have Chauvel commanding them. The third line did have Major Tom Todd and Lieutenant Colonel Noel Brazier.

'You've seen what happened to the 8th,' Todd said to Brazier, the Regiment's commander. 'We won't even make the [Turkish] trenches . . .'[3]

Brazier had no doubt Todd was correct. He hurried down a slope to brigade HQ. Brigadier General Hughes had left for an observation post. Only Antill was there. He and Brazier, as it happened, hated each other. Brazier told him he thought the 10th Light Horse should not be sent out. Antill disagreed vehemently.

'Push on!' he ordered.

Brazier was then compelled to follow the frigid directive. He did not think to find Hughes. Godley was at his HQ on the beach, and difficult to contact. But even if Brazier had managed to stall for 10 minutes to speak with Godley, it is unlikely he would have stopped the mass killing. He and Antill were like-minded.

Brazier returned to the trench at Russell's Top.

'I'm sorry lads,' he told his men, 'but the orders are to go.'[4]

Right along the line of 150 Western Australian troopers, mates shook hands, and grim-faced, wished each other luck, knowing that they were running into an impenetrable wall of lead, and death.

At 4.45 a.m. with the early morning sun already hot, the third line clambered out. Piesse, who had left hospital for this, was cut down within 10 metres of the Anzac trench, as were half the others. Two brothers, barrister Gresley and farmer Wilfred Harper, urged each other on as if in a sprint at a school sports event. They went further than anyone else but were killed on the parapet of the enemy trench. Ten troopers led by the ebullient, jovial Lieutenant Hugo Throssell were running on the left. Seeing the fate of a hundred comrades, he ordered that his men dive into a small fold of dead ground. They gathered close.

'A bob in and the winner shouts,' the 31-year-old farmer joked. Then he reassured his charges they would be 'right'. He ordered them to sit tight until dark when they would attempt to crawl back.[5]

Antill was again informed of the horrors at the Nek, but he insisted that the fourth line, led by Major Joe Scott, should attack. Many of these men, even more aware of what was in store than the previous three lines, disagreed with Brazier's attempt to stop them. Thirty of them on the far right of the trench were so concerned that his efforts might succeed that they beat the gun, dashing forward before an order was given either way. They were impeded by the bodies of the dead and wounded at the parapet and strewn along the short dash. Some found cover from piled bodies. Many went on. They could see the Turks two deep in the front trench. Machine-gun fire was still coming at them from both flanks.

Hundreds lay dead or wounded in the sweep from Russell's

Top to the Turkish trenches. The Anzac trench, where there were still scores of dead and wounded of the 8th and 10th Regiments, was now unmanned. Brazier, Major Love, Todd and Major McLaurin of the 8th had a hurried conference. They decided to visit 3rd Brigade HQ a third time to ask the command to withdraw the attacking lines, and not to send any more troopers along the Nek for more carnage. This time Hughes responded, overriding Antill's desire to 'push on'.[6]

The focus now was on retrieving the wounded in no-man's land. This was nearly impossible, given the Turkish defence. Through the day injured men were seen moving; crawling a few paces here; raising a hand for help there. As the hours crept on and the intense heat reached its zenith at about 3 p.m., less and less movement could be spotted even with binoculars. Most of the wounded out there were dead or would die. Stretcher-bearers and medics would have to wait until night to help the odd trooper who may still be alive.

Hugo Throssell and his wounded brother Ric were among those who managed to crawl back and live.

The insanity of the Nek was over.

17

More Slaughter at Hill 60

Attention in Monash Valley turned to defence with the 9th Light Horse Regiment moving up to take over Russell's Top. The real fear was a counterattack. If it had occurred earlier on 7 August, there is little doubt that the Turks would have made it right through to the beach for the first time since the Anzacs had landed on 25 April. But the enemy commanders decided not to come, or could not. They were stretched in all directions away from the cove: at Helles to the south, at Suvla Bay, Lone Pine and in the rugged hills to the north-west of Anzac Cove.

The combat at Lone Pine saw 2,000 Australians from 1st Division and 7,000 Turks killed. The attackers there had managed to reach the enemy trenches for some of the bloodiest fighting imaginable. But it was the only 'victory' for the invaders. The new British force at Suvla Bay dithered for days on the beach, sorting out, among other pressing matters, which officers would be served their meals first. This allowed the Turks to man the hills above them, as they had at Anzac Cove. The New Zealanders struggled and failed to come round the back of Baby 700. They too were slaughtered. Monash's 4th Brigade got lost at night in the rugged spurs and ridges, and moved on too far left to call it a left hook. It was more like a failed round-arm swing. It was stopped well short of its target.

The toll on the force of troopers was horrific. Chauvel's 1st and 2nd assault regiments suffered 204 casualties out of 255 men engaged, an 80 per cent loss rate. The 3rd Brigade's 8th and 10th Regiments lost 362 out of 400, a more than 90 per cent casualty rate.

On 9 August, Chauvel wrote to his wife, mentioning for the first time the toughness of battle and casualties:

'We are in the middle of a devil of a fight . . . I am sorry to say I have lost Moffat Reid of Tenterfield, and Nettleton . . . both of whom I liked enormously. We are pretty sure they are killed although we have not found their bodies yet. The censors will not let me tell you about the fight . . . it is still going strong on our left [the Nek]. My part in it took place two days ago and I believe we acquitted ourselves creditably.'

He moved from a damp to a dry dugout, fearing he might get pleurisy again.[1]

By 9 and 10 August it was clear that the multi-pronged attack on the peninsula had failed. The Anzac positions, and those of the British forces at Helles, were more or less the same as before the execution of the now not-so-grand plan. Overall there were 22,000 casualties for the gaining of a few acres of useless ground. Chauvel's brigade remained in its position around the head of Monash Valley. He applied for his spent and dilapidated force to be put in reserve, as did the command of 3rd Brigade.

His request was denied.

Chauvel and his 1st Brigade were promised an easier post, but for the moment they would stay in Monash Valley. The 9th Regiment (from Adelaide), which had been in reserve at the Nek, and the 10th were not so fortunate. They were wanted for combat duty at Hill 60, a knoll with a 60-metre slope held by the Turks. It was a small bit of territory in low country a few kilometres from the beach between Anzac Cove and Suvla Bay. The Turks, led by Lieutenant Colonel Mustafa Kemal, the officer most responsible for stopping any Anzac advance in late April and a British assault from Suvla earlier in the month, had his men well set up in the heights again on and above Hill 60. This kind of operation pleased the Turks. The battles were now confined to areas close to the sea. The invaders were locked down and still in a state of siege.

Early on the morning of 20 August, a Turkish officer ran down Hill 60 towards the British forces carrying a white flag. This happened occasionally when the Turks wished to bury their dead. But this officer kept running. He passed several dead Turks in no-man's land. British soldiers rushed and apprehended him. The officer, a vibrant 28-year-old Arab, Muhammad Sharif al-Faruqi, was deserting. This was not an uncommon event on the peninsula. But this man came offering something in return. In fluent French, he claimed with gusto and apparent sincerity that there was a sizeable Arab contingent within the Turkish army that was willing to revolt against the Ottoman Empire.

The well-educated Sharif al-Faruqi was found to be from a

prominent family in Mosul, northern Mesopotamia (Iraq). His looks and charm added to his conviction, which landed him in front of Hamilton on board his command ship. They spoke in French together for some time in what was a 'discussion', officer to officer.

'Nationalism is the principal drive for most Arabs,' he claimed.

He urged the British to support a revolt that would help overthrow the Turks. Deserters, and in this case, traitors were viewed with a sceptical eye. Hamilton, ever the gentleman, turned him over to his officers for interrogation, again in French. He passed on useful information concerning Turkish military manoeuvres in the fight against Russia, and in Mesopotamia, and also detail on the enemy reserve strengths at Gallipoli. He had some further information on troop movements and the reorganisation of the Turkish 4th Army in Syria. Some of this new data tallied with rumours and other information. Al-Faruqi began to look more and more credible. There were no holes in his tale.

Hamilton, an intelligent man who prided himself on being a good judge of character, was not easily duped. He wrote a report for the minister of war on the meeting and al-Faruqi. Lumped in with the useful intelligence was the less verifiable commentary on Arab nationalism. Hamilton did not query this even though he was aware that the concept of one Arab 'nation' was unusual. The Arabs tended to be tribal; the idea of nationhood was something alien. Nevertheless, it fitted what the British wanted to hear about undermining the Turks, by having the role of the Sultan usurped by another spiritual leader, who would be in their pocket.

Despite the Gallipoli campaign going poorly, Hamilton was held in high regard by all the decision-makers and influential people in the UK, from the War Office to the prime minister and the king. His imprimatur on al-Faruqi's credibility and intelligence meant that the concept of 'nationalism' as a goal by most Arabs could be a basis for undermining the Turks in the Middle East.

In less than two weeks, al-Faruqi was sent on a boat to Cairo for further questioning at the Arab Bureau by T.E. Lawrence and its director Berty Clayton. The two interrogators were further satisfied beyond Hamilton's report. They believed the time was right for revolt. All the British had to do was find a way to fire it up.

Money, gold and weapons were said to be the fuel.

On 21 August, Godley and Birdwood had come to the battle zone to supervise an attack on Hill 60 that tactically resembled the futility at the Nek. There was a difference in terrain; no artificial funnel would manifest at Hill 60. But attacking it over open, unprotected ground had the same effect. Fifteen hundred men from Monash's already hammered 4th Infantry Brigade, the novice British army coming up from Suvla, a depleted Indian Brigade, and the broken-down New Zealand Mounted Rifles (unmounted here) were in Godley's mixed force.

As at the Nek, Quinn's and Pope's, there were horrific losses. Part of the approach to the hill had been taken back. Now Godley was obsessed with retaking all of it. It was of little or no strategic importance. A lot of energy and lives would be lost in the effort. Yet he ordered another assault on 27 August. Monash's 4th Brigade 'shell' was lined up again, this time with the 5th Infantry Brigade, the New Zealand Mounteds once more, and the British 5th Connaught Rangers. Hill 60's summit was taken and its machine-gun nests wiped out.

Fresh troops were called up for support. But before they arrived, the Turks were well into a fierce counterattack using bombs (grenades). They soon drove out the Connaught Rangers from their shallow, 135-metre-long trenches on the left of the sector, facing the enemy.

Godley sent the 9th Light Horse Brigade in to have a go at taking over the same trenches. They 'made a very plucky effort' but were driven back.[2]

Now it was the turn of the 10th, who had suffered so much at the Nek.

*

There was a further imperative for these men. They knew the strength of the enemy, yet this was overridden by the desire to do something for their lost mates in the funnel from Russell's Top. Everyone kissed their bayonets for 'Mick', 'Pete', 'Huey', 'Dave', 'Bob' and several hundred others. Revenge, more than at any time at Anzac Cove was a unifying, powerful motivation. Officers didn't need to urge on the troopers as they moved single file from their bivouac at 10 p.m. on the night of 28 August and towards the position on the hill held by the New Zealanders. On the way up, every second NCO (non-commissioned officer) and private was handed a sandbag containing 10 cast-iron spherical bombs. All ranks carried two additional sandbags for barricade building. At least this was different from the Nek; some of their fellow Anzacs had managed to fight and entrench.

A shallow trench on the New Zealanders' left was allotted to the troopers. They were briefed. Their objective was to take 135 metres of trench about 70 metres from them. If captured, it would create a continuous line between Anzac forces and those from Suvla to their left.

The attack was to be in the now familiar two lines: the first line assaulting with bayonet and bomb, the second carrying picks and shovels.

It was just short of 1 a.m. on 29 August. The troopers shook hands with the men near them in the lines, usually their mates.

It was on again.

Hugo Throssell led a 70-metre dash. The machine-gun and rifle fire was deadly but indiscriminate and not focused. It was not as thick as at the Nek, yet he knew he would be lucky to reach the Turkish trenches. For some reason the Turks had not heard them coming. Noise interference was so common that it was possible that the crunch of boots on gravel and thud on grass had been drowned out. It was dark. The enemy could not see the troopers until they were almost on them.

Throssell and his men threw themselves at the enemy in hand-to-hand fighting. A battle that resembled Lone Pine ensued.

Many of the Turks were killed. Most fled to another nearby trench. The Australians dug in. They tore into the white, hard 'pipe' clay. Their sandbags were filled. A barricade began to emerge between the trenches. They were close: eight metres away at the narrowest and 16 metres at the most. The Australians removed their bayonets, loaded and fired. The two sides could lob rather than hurl bombs at each other. The combat continued to be vicious. The Turks, screaming their love of Allah, kept coming to replace their fallen comrades. Sandbags were folded and used to smother bombs. Some fizzled, others blew off limbs. Firing went on until ammunition ran out or rifles became too hot to hold. They would be tossed away and replaced by weapons of the dead and wounded. Throssell was reaching for a dead companion's rifle when he was hit in the neck and left shoulder. The force of one bullet drove his 'Australia' badge deep into the injured clavicle. He insisted a trooper stop the bleeding by applying a rough tourniquet, but no-one dared suggest he leave the trench. Throssell was determined to carry on until the little earth cavity in the middle of nowhere was secure.

Throssell, 'by his fiery valour and witty sallies heartened the thinning ranks', according to the regiment's historian, 'and inspired the troopers to resist with renewed vigour'.[3]

He found he could still heave a bomb with his uninjured right arm. He kept fighting alongside the cool-headed Lieutenant Tom Kidd, whose indifference to danger had earned him the nickname 'Bombproof'.

Syd Ferrier, a corporal, 10 metres from the two fighting lieutenants, hurled a bag on a bomb. He was a fraction late. His left arm took the full brunt of the explosion and was sheared off. He fell back, fighting to stem the blood flow. A stretcher-bearer was called. Ferrier was administered morphine. His wound was dressed. Refusing to leave the trench, he began lobbing bombs again. He kept doing it until he keeled over unconscious. Ferrier was stretchered to the beach, where a boat would hurry him to a hospital ship with scores of injured, some of them with even worse wounds.

After two hours the trench was held. Throssell left it to have a 'breather'. He found his shirt and trousers shredded with bomb fragments. A trooper lit him a cigarette. Throssell's hand was shaking. His injuries had seized up his muscles. He could not put the cigarette to his mouth. The trooper did it for him.

It took 15 minutes to have his wounds dressed. Instead of leaving with others for the makeshift jetty and the hospital ship, he ignored the medicos and made his way back to the trench and climbed in.

Replacement troops from the second line of the 10th had taken over. Their commander, Captain Horace Robertson, took one look at him and ordered him to leave.

'And don't come back!' were Robertson's parting words.

He had already decided to recommend Throssell for a VC.

The 10th threw more than 3,000 bombs through the night. Ferrier was said to have been responsible for about 500 of them. He paid the ultimate price, dying on the hospital ship at 5 a.m. just as the Turks were pushed back to distant trenches. At dawn, after four hours of blistering conflict, the counterattacks ceased. Hill 60 was in control of the British forces at dubious cost. Hamilton made much of the 400 acres that had been secured by the action. But it was near-worthless real estate despite the Aegean Sea views.

Kemal was unhappy to give up anything to the invaders; but in private he could smile. A big amount of manpower had been expended for no strategic gain.

The only advantage was in a lift in morale in a small section of the Anzac camp, where there was some sense of retribution.

Gallipoli End-Games

Monash Valley remained tense. As the days crawled by with searing heat at midday and freezing cold at night, the devastation there of 6 to 10 August sank in and took morale to its lowest point, the news of the 'success' at Hill 60 notwithstanding. Two depressing factors were at work. First and foremost was the loss of men and mates. Second was the sense of defeat. The Anzacs were a competitive lot. They often used sporting analogies to describe their battles.

Winning to these men was close to everything. They were haunted in the knowledge that they had been smashed in the break-out attempt. They took it hard. The spirit was still there. It had to be rekindled. Inspiring talks and 'congratulations' for 'gallant' efforts given by British commanders such as Birdwood would not do it now. They had become irritating to the troops. Godley, who was always disliked, would have been hated to the point of mutiny if the soldiers, all volunteers, had been privy to his attitudes, planning and comments. Occasionally the command's mentality slipped through to Australian officers and their staffs, and could not help but filter down to the men. When Monash oversaw the decimation of his 4th Brigade in the first few days of Anzac and asked Birdwood for replacements, he was told to 'produce more men' as if they could be grown on the walls in the valley. Godley thought that was funny. Monash was at first appalled; then angry. When that second emotion simmered, he realised he could do nothing to change things. He could either resign in disgust, or hang on in the hope that he just might one day be in a position to make an impact. This seemed remote for most officers in those black days at Gallipoli.

*

By early September, 'fire-up' speeches or words from the key commanders were like the utterances of football coaches who couldn't plan, connive or force a 'win', or whose message had become unheard because it had become repetitive, unconvincing and platitudinous.

Chauvel, laconic and measured, believed as much in deeds and actions as words, and in that way reflected the approach of his troopers. Birdwood at least, and Godley in a limited way, were beginning to comprehend his method of dealing with the Australians. They were a different breed to the British forces. In the month since his return to Gallipoli, Birdwood was beginning to see him differently. No more would Chauvel be described as 'slow'. He had proved his nerve in tight situations at Quinn's. Respect from the troops was noted.

He was dealing with the problem of his brigade being hemmed in, yet he was always looking for a way to get back at the Turks. Any small measure of revenge was appreciated by him and all his troopers. Any hit on the enemy was helpful to the collective mental state. If they had to rank targets, the ultimate pay-back for most of them would not be against the machine-gunners or bomb throwers, but the dreaded snipers. They had taken a big toll whether in the fierce moments of 19 and 29 May or the battles of 6 to 10 August, or on any day since the Anzacs had arrived. Every digger and trooper at the cove and in the valley knew someone well who had been killed by a bullet from the hills.

Chauvel would never forget the 'hit' on his benefactor Bridges 12 weeks earlier. With this in mind, he seized on a New Zealand idea of forming a special squad of marksmen from among the troopers. They were all good shots. The best would match any of the enemy. Many of these men had honed their skills shooting moving targets from rabbits to kangaroos since they were kids. At Chauvel's request, Subaltern T.M.P. Grace of the Wellington Battalion chose a party of 30 crack shots. He sent them to vantage points in the valley at night. They waited until morning and began to score hits against the Turkish snipers, who had terrorised Anzac Cove for 17 weeks. The trooper marksmen were successful to the point where Chauvel was able to write to Sibyl that they 'got the [Turkish] snipers down to such an extent that latterly we could actually get mule convoys up and down the Valley in broad daylight.'[1]

The continual worry about another major Turkish attack remained and caused his weary men to stay in the line. The Anzac command and force now discounted any further effort to break out in the next few months at least.

On 4 September, the 1st Light Horse Brigade was sent to take over a series of posts with seaward slopes further to the left (north) between Anzac Cove and Suvla Bay. This was a much safer area to patrol and control than Monash Valley. One position was at Destroyer Hill; another was in a valley called Sazli Dere. They were part of the 400 acres acquired after the victory at Hill 60 on 29 August, which meant the brigade was not in reserve. Yet the region was a relief when compared with where they had been.

'It was comparatively clean,' Chauvel noted. 'I am busy building my HQ and have acquired enough galvanised iron to have both my dugout and the office rain-proof, as well as shrapnel-proof. We have a most beautiful marine aspect and the bathing is much nearer.'

It was 'delightful' to have any view at all.

'We have been living all this time in the bottom of the [Monash Valley] gully. There are dead Turks however, all around us and the smell is not nice, but we are burying them as we find them . . . I dreamt last night of the cat I poisoned at Mornington, and found afterwards in the bush house after thinking I had buried it.'[2]

The men could light fires at night when it was bitterly cold; they could swim in the heat of the day. Some played cricket on the beach. The troopers were even afforded the luxury of taking their boots off at night, something not granted for the entire time at Monash Valley. The 1st Brigade had been at the cove from day one. The men deserved the less demanding posts.

There was a complete change of pace. Chauvel had time to

write more and fuller letters. He reverted to giving Sibyl a picture of a holiday atmosphere, describing the dispatch riders who galloped the seven kilometres from Suvla Bay to Anzac Cove and back again each day. It was turned into a macabre event. The Turks in the ridges and hills could snipe at the riders for the entire route.

'It [the mail delivery] had to be done at the gallop,' Chauvel said. 'The rider was fired at from the moment he left the shelter of Lala Baba until he reached the wide communications trench near Anzac.'

All the Australian light horsemen, New Zealand mounted riflemen, and the British Yeomanry (cavalry) 'were tumbling over each other to get the job'.

It was daily entertainment for the entire beachfront ride. The rattle of Turkish musketry heralded the departure each morning and continued for the entire course. No-one was hit for three months.

'There was always heavy wagering on whether the post would get through,' Chauvel said, 'and it is probable that Johnny Turk had his bit on as well.'[3]

The value of life on Gallipoli had become heavily discounted.

All lived with the thought that they could be killed any time. Wills were written, reviewed or adjusted by the men as they contemplated dependants and the fact that they might not make it back home. Chauvel was among those who made changes. Sibyl wrote asking for clarification over 'heirlooms' (china, clocks and other items). His concern was that he could not make 'decent provisions for her future' before he 'departed this life'.[4]

Legge, who had been in Egypt building up a new division, came back to Gallipoli with two brigades of his new command. Chauvel remained irritated by him, regarding him as a usurper who had not earned his position or power by the gruelling, dangerous experience on the peninsula.

'I have not seen him [Legge] yet,' he wrote to Sibyl, who remained his confidante for discussing worrying topics (except the war itself), 'and don't intend to if I can help it.'

A month later, he was further annoyed:

'Legge is picking the eyes out of our [Light Horse] Brigade simply by offering higher rank [to join his brigades].'

On 25 October he reported on the departure of Hamilton, the scapegoat for the Gallipoli failure.

'They say he looked awfully down in the mouth when he left,' Chauvel wrote. He remained concerned that Hamilton had 'turned dog on me' in the false belief that Chauvel had been pushing the Australian government for a higher appointment.

'A Melbourne pressman called Murdock [Keith Murdoch], the man who used to write up Legge in *Punch*, who had an interview with Sir Ian,' he wrote, 'told Brudenell [White] that Sir Ian made some very caustic remarks about Australian officers who were seeking high commands! It is rather rotten if Sir Ian thought it was me. I have taken steps however to see that Birdwood knows better.'

Chauvel's concern was based on the assumption that Hamilton had influence. But his axing meant he had none. Birdwood and Godley were now the two key commanders on Gallipoli no matter who replaced Hamilton. Chauvel got on well with Godley and was in favour with Birdwood. This became clear when Godley and Monash were on leave. Chauvel was given command of the Anzac Division for short bursts. On 6 November, 1st Division's commander H. B. Walker was wounded and Talbot Hobbs fell sick, allowing Chauvel to take over 1st Division.[5]

Five months after Hamilton had declared he should be removed from his command for his direct analysis of the siege at Anzac, Chauvel was now popular with the people that counted. His steadiness under pressure, cool leadership and respect from the troopers and officers had changed the appreciation of him.

'He strikes me as having become much more alert and resourceful of late,' Birdwood wrote to the Australian minister of defence Pearce. 'He is more ready to assert himself and come to a decision.'[6]

Chauvel took up his role controlling the 3rd Infantry and 2nd Light Horse Brigades with enthusiasm. There was always patrolling, underground mining, digging in for the winter and some minor skirmishes with the Turks to preside over until relieved by Monash's infantry brigade towards the end of November.

On 27 November, he reported that it was snowing for the first time, which did not augur well for a winter. This was sure to be as tough as anything yet experienced at Gallipoli.

'It was quite an alpine scene,' Chauvel wrote, 'but oh! so cold and frightfully muddy.'

He asked Sibyl to send some warmer socks.

Two weeks later he told her he wanted higher rank as 'some compensation for greater responsibility', and for 'leaving a mounted unit'.

He was pushing for the 'temporary' rank of major general, and had asked Godley to write to the Australian government to request it for him.[7]

Then came an unexpected shock. The British forces were to leave the peninsula in December 1915 and early January 1916. Chauvel was to depart with the main force at Anzac Cove.

His last instruction at Gallipoli was to Lieutenant Colonel L. C. 'Elsie' Maygar, temporarily in command of the 8th Light Horse.

'You are to hold the trenches at all costs,' he told him. 'At 2.30 a.m. you pull out.'

Forty-four-year-old Maygar, the 6-foot (183-centimetre) grazier from Euroa, Victoria, was the perfect selection for this last act at Anzac Cove. He had won a VC at Geelhoutboom, near Natal, on 23 November 1901 for a selfless act that typified the very best of the troopers and the Anzac mentality. One of his men was left stranded in the open when his horse was shot from under him. Maygar galloped forward under intense fire, dismounted and ordered the fellow Victorian to mount his horse and ride hard for the British lines. Maygar, rifle in hand, drew fire until his charge was clear and then dashed for cover himself.

Now at Russell's Top, the scene of the terrible destruction of a regiment that Maygar now commanded, he selected 40 volunteers from among the troopers who he knew would fight to the death in defence of the evacuation. Among them was Ronnie MacDonald.

Without a trace of cynicism, Maygar said:

'I had my usual good luck to be given command of the last party to pull out of the trenches, the post of honour for the 3rd Light Horse Brigade.'[8]

Maygar had lost plenty of his men killed and wounded at Gallipoli. They ranged from older veterans such as Sergeant David Crawford, 37, who had been decorated and mentioned in dispatches in the Boer War, only to be killed in action on Walker's Ridge on 23 June, to younger charges including one of Crawford's nephews, Frank Merritt, 19. He had been in the first charge at the Nek on 7 August. Hits by shrapnel to the stomach and gun shots to the arm saw him on his way home to Australia with severe wounds from which he would suffer for the rest of his life.[9]

Men like these, especially the thousands that would never leave the peninsula, were an inspiration for Maygar, MacDonald and Co. They would stay at their posts no matter what the Turks did. The stealthy departure, unlike the arrival and intervening eight months, was an unqualified success. Even the last to leave, Maygar and his men, all survived.

'We left Anzac in the dead of night [18th December],' Chauvel wrote, 'evacuation carried out without a casualty and without the Turks suspecting it . . . it is a very great achievement. Of course, we are all very sad at leaving the job unfinished but after the failure of the Suvla landing [when 45,000 fresh British troops arrived] in August it was really the only thing to be done.'

Once at the island of Mudros he wrote with some relief, and even joy:

'I slept in pyjamas last night; I woke up to the sound of a band; and I have seen a woman; several in fact, mostly Greek peasants, but one real Australian nurse riding, or should I say, "on a horse". In other words we are more or less in civilisation again.'[10]

He had little idea where he would be posted next, although he expected at last to be in charge of mounted riflemen in battle.

After the Gallipoli experience, Harry Chauvel felt ready for any command that would come his way.

19

Lawrence's Ambitious Blueprint

All men dream; but not equally. Those who dream by night in the dusty recesses of their minds, wake in the day to find that it was vanity; but the dreamers of the day are dangerous men, for they may act their dream with open eyes, to make it possible.

T. E. Lawrence

Second-Lieutenant T. E. Lawrence paced the polished floorboards of his office at Cairo's Arab Bureau as he dictated to an uninterested secretary, who tapped out his memorandum meant for the British High Command at the War Office, London. It was titled: 'The Conquest of Syria: if Complete'. Her boredom was from the persistent letter writing that her boss insisted on two, sometimes three hours a day. Had she understood the import of this letter of 10 January 1916, she may not have been so listless.

Lawrence was fully briefed on the British failure at Gallipoli, which had been saved from disaster by the brilliantly planned and executed evacuation just completed the day before by the removal of the force at Helles. He was also mindful of the recent (18 December 1915) call by the Sultan for a Jihad against the Infidels since the Turks had joined Germany as an ally in the war. In this case, 'infidels' meant all non-Muslims, particularly the British, who had established a protectorate in Egypt. This would 'legitimise' Britain's strong base in the Middle East from which to prosecute war.

Lawrence was amused by the scope of the sultan's jihad. He wondered if it encompassed Germans, who were mainly Christian and non-Muslim. But he was well aware of the seriousness of the situation if all Arabs and Egyptians took up the call to 'defeat' or 'kill' all the infidels. It was unlikely, but radical political factions in the Middle East could be induced into using the jihad as a pretext for subversive action.

To counter this, the precocious young intelligence officer, who had been in his job for 15 months, was suggesting a blueprint for victory against Turkey. There were other influences at play here. His brothers Frank and Will had been killed on the Western Front in 1915. Their deaths inspired Lawrence to take a more active role in helping Britain in its struggle to win.

He did not see himself as a battle commander. He wrote that he was different from a soldier and hated 'soldiering'. At Oxford Lawrence had studied the experts on war and battle such as Clausewitz, Jomini, Mahan and Foch. He understood the campaigns of Napoleon and Hannibal. He had more than a passing knowledge of the wars of Belisarius. Yet he believed he had no natural instinct or desire to command in or fight his own campaign. Nevertheless, his activity indicated he could lead through influence.

For the moment, Lawrence had put aside his paranoia about the French, having acknowledged the Turkish achievement at Gallipoli. With the tiptoeing away of the British troops, the Turkish revolutionary leaders would be ambitious to use their freed-up troops for other aims in the region in salvaging what they considered valuable of the Ottoman Empire.

The military option of defeating Turkey had been mismanaged at great cost of men and prestige in the mini-war on the peninsula. Lawrence was putting up a new plan that he knew at the very least would be read by the decision-makers in Whitehall. He had absorbed Hamilton's report, now embellished with other experts' views in Whitehall, and his own perceptions obtained from interrogating Sharif al-Faruqi in September 1915. It all seemed to make good sense to Lawrence, who had maintained a romanticised view of Arab aspirations, gleaned in his undergraduate days and vitalised by his travels, especially in Mesopotamia (Iraq) and Syria. He saw Arab nationalism as a useful vehicle for helping to overthrow the Turks, but was not enamoured with its grand ideas about development and modernisation. He loved the concept of the old Syria and ancient Hejaz. He despised change. Lawrence wished the mystical land he had first encountered as a youth in 1909 could be maintained. He wanted the layer of oppressive Turkish rule removed but did not wish this world to be a victim of 'progress' and 'technical advance' preached by nationalists, who were picking up radical ideas from other countries. He was infatuated with the Bedouins and the semi-nomadic or tribal peasants. Lawrence regarded them as the 'true' Arabs. He contrasted them with what he saw as 'fat, greasy' townsmen of Syria and Palestine. They spoke the same language and were of the same race, religion and culture. But Lawrence saw them as adulterated by city life and therefore different and inferior. He wanted self-determination for the traditional Arabs and even reactionary elements—the Bedouins, the conservatives, sheikhs and Islamic elders. They represented his own romantic ideal of how the Middle East should look and be organised if the Turks were removed. In many ways, it was an undemocratic vision. Lawrence's mind was steeped in history. Radical change that destroyed its romance was not on his radar. But the flaw in his prism was that it ignored reality. Most Arabs lived in the cities. It could be argued that they were the 'true' Arabs.

Al-Faruqi seemed to represent his misty vision at least in part. He appeared to present concrete evidence from the inside about intrinsic Arab ideals and aims to rid themselves of the Turkish 'yoke'.

Lore had become fact. A feverish Arab quest for 'nationalism' was just below the surface throughout the Middle East. It only needed a catalyst that would lead, literally, to a trigger.

Lawrence broadened the concept. He wished to use this as the way to bring down the Ottoman Empire, which for 300 years had rivalled the influence of the British. He may have been regarded as over-ambitious, even cheeky to be putting up plans for victory so soon after the High Command had stumbled and bungled in Gallipoli. But he would not stop, aware that the vacuum of failure would be filled by other plans for 'success'. He knew that his path to influence had been smoothed by Hogarth, and that his words would end up on the right desks. Whether his ideas would be acted on would be another matter. Yet he knew also that he was respected now after a stream of useful memorandums flowing from Cairo. He was now an Arabist with few peers. There were a handful of real 'experts' on the region within the military, and even fewer with his analytical skills and now solid, direct training as a spy. Bureau director Bertie Clayton relied on him.

A main plank of his blueprint was to take away for all time the religious supremacy in the Muslim world of the Sultan of Turkey. This celebrated ecclesiastical position had kept for centuries an authority and cohesion in the widespread Ottoman Empire. By changing this and passing the religious 'crown' to another non-Turkish Muslim leader, Lawrence suggested, the British could 'support' the new regime and so undermine the Turks from their religious heart. This was a radical departure from the 'military-only', sledgehammer approach. He would have the Muslim world split, and the British back an Arab group that would help overthrow the Turks in the region, particularly Arabia, Palestine and Syria.

Lawrence, working up a head of steam as he dictated to his secretary, said:

'England cannot make a new Khalifa [spiritual leader] as she has made a new Sultan of Egypt any more than the Japanese could impose a new Pope on the Roman Catholic Church. Nor can the Sultan of Egypt make himself Khalifa.'

He reckoned that an Egyptian Sultan's actions would be 'suspect' because of his relations with the British.

'The true Arab and even the Syrian has such a living contempt and dislike for the loose-mouthed Egyptian,' Lawrence noted, 'that this would entirely forbid him ever to recognise any spiritual overlordship assumed by one [an Egyptian puppet for the British] without the force to support him.'

Lawrence was definite that the new spiritual leader should be Hussein, Sharif of Mecca. He had been active since 1913 in Arabia and Syria, 'asserting himself as an arbiter of morals'. The Turks had been paying him well but Lawrence did not see this as a problem. The British could offer him more using Egypt or India as the conduit to send him money and gold.

Hussein was also kept under control by the Turkish army. The way to get rid of this was to cut the Hejaz railway line, which was built from 1894 to 1900 by the Turks, with German assistance, in order to maintain an Ottoman grip on the Arabian Empire. It was promoted as a 'religious' railway reaching from Damascus and Beirut into the Hejaz ('the barrier'). This region of Arabia's west was defined mostly by the Red Sea, extending from Haql on the Gulf of Aqaba to Jizan. Its main city was Jeddah, but it was better known for its Islamic holy cities of Mecca and Medina. The Turks used the railway for moving soldiers, arms, supplies and trading goods. The army was also paid via the line. If it were severed, Lawrence pointed out, 'We destroy the [Turkish-controlled] Hejaz civil government . . . and we resolve the [again, Turkish-gripped] Hejaz army into its elements—an assembly of peaceful Syrian peasants and incompetent alien officers.'

Lawrence was confident that once the railway was stopped the Turks would be left almost impotent in the region and that the Arab chiefs in the Hejaz would 'make their own play'.

The Bedouin tribes, he believed, would help the British cut it.

'They [the Bedouins] hate the railway,' Lawrence declared. 'It has reduced their annual tolls and way-leaves [demanded from those travelling the tracks through the desert region].'

He concluded the memo with:

'This cutting can be done by occupying Deraa if Damascus is neutralised; at Amman, if Jerusalem can be passed, by blowing up a viaduct; and at Maan by an occupation.'[1]

Lawrence was aware that his suggestion and scheme for a

revolt by the tribes in Arabia would not be viewed by his superiors as a major campaign. It would be the first important step in curtailing and disturbing Turkish control in the region. Driving them from Sinai, Palestine, Arabia and Syria altogether would need a full-scale military operation.

Two days after this analysis was sent to London, he dictated another memo, 'The Politics of Mecca' which went further:

'Hussein's activity seems beneficial to us, because it marches with our immediate aims, [which are] the break-up of the Islamic "bloc" and the defeat and disruption of the Ottoman Empire.'

Lawrence thought British aims would be helped also because 'the states that Hussein would set up to succeed the Turks would be as harmless to ourselves as Turkey was before she became a tool in German hands.'

He believed the Arabs were even less stable than the Turks.

'If [the Arabs were] properly handled,' he said, 'they would remain in a state of political mosaic, a tissue of small jealous principalities incapable of cohesion, and they would always be ready to combine against an outside force.'

Lawrence added that the alternative to the British connecting this way with the Arabs would be another European power, most likely the hated French, 'which would inevitably come into conflict with the interests we already possess in the Near East'.

He was well aware that these propositions to make the Arabs rebel meant he was deceiving them on the future of Arabia. The British, including Lawrence, had no intention at all of giving any Arab group freedom or independence. He would be lying, or giving them false hope, from the beginning. He would later admit this in his opus, *Seven Pillars of Wisdom*, as if he had a conscience over the duplicity:

'I could see that if we won the war, the promises to the Arabs were dead paper. Had I been an honourable adviser I would have sent my men [Arabs enlisted in his spy network in preparation for the revolt] home, and not let them risk their lives for such stuff.'[2]

But he saw that they would be important in clearing the Turks from Arabia, and looking ahead, in the main game of the political carve-up of the region (Sinai, Palestine and Syria) once the Turks were pushed out by the British.

Lawrence gambled that deceiving the Arabs was necessary for fast uncostly success in the Middle East. But he was convinced that a win could not be achieved without them. A British double cross, he felt, was worth the risk to ensure victory. He believed that Arab interests would only ever be substantial if they fitted in with British aims of increased dominance of the British Empire and keeping the French from power in the region. Lawrence had a further personal goal to defeat any rivals he had in Whitehall concerning Middle (or 'Near') East strategy and tactics, particularly over the fate of Syria. He would continue as long as possible to sell the Arabs the belief that the British were behind the push for their eventual taking of power in most of the Middle East.

The money and gold that would be promised to them were meant to be a strong sign of good faith.

20

Birdwood's Push

Lawrence's grand design for a new-look Middle East, Arab Revolt or not, would mean nothing if the Turks could not be defeated in a major British military effort in the region. The most vital part of that would be the Light Horse. An expedition would need mobility to scout, fight and be the 'shock troops' covering vast areas in Egypt, Sinai, Palestine and Arabia. Infantry were essential too, but in the scheme of things not as important as the horsemen. Set-piece trench battles using artillery such as those going on concurrently in the gentle fields of Belgium and

France, caused the horse, an easy target from long distances, to be superfluous in that kind of warfare. But the battles in the deserts and rough terrain of the Middle East were a mix of the ancient and modern. Artillery could be hauled across the dunes and along the rough tracks and valleys. But the big guns would not have the impact in time and space they were having on the Western Front.

Therein lay a dilemma for Chauvel when he moved from the Greek islands back to Egypt early in 1916. On the one hand, his ambitious side wanted to be in the big conflict in Europe with an Australian infantry division. On the other, he preferred to be with the horsemen, who seemed certain to be active at some point beyond patrolling, especially with the Turkish success on Gallipoli. Birdwood, now in charge of all Australian operations in Europe and Egypt, had more than hinted that he could have one of the five Australian divisions that were being formed post-Gallipoli. He was in favour in front of Monash, whom Birdwood was reluctant to promote because of lingering (false) doubts about his German background. Some rumours even suggested he was an enemy spy. Yes, he could fight Turks, but how would he go against armies from the nation of his parents' birthplace? He and Chauvel had emerged as two of the more competent Australian commanders at Gallipoli in the eyes of British command. Yet Chauvel's ambivalence caused Birdwood to act. He appointed him commander of the Mounted Division. It would not be going to Europe. He would be based in Egypt for the time being. This resolved Chauvel's dilemma. His war would be in the Middle East. He would command all the Australian units remaining in Egypt, including the newly arrived 1st Squadron Australian Flying Corps, and several medical and naval units. Once Birdwood had made his decision, Chauvel would have been relieved. He had the stomach for any kind of warfare, but he did not fancy close trench battles. The more he considered it, the more he felt comfortable with his immediate future. He would be on a mount (when he was not in a Rolls-Royce as a divisional commander) doing what he liked most and did best.

*

Another problem for him and the other commanders was the downtime in this period of hiatus early in 1916 when the fresh troops coming from Australia and the Gallipoli 'veterans' had to be reformed in old and new divisions, trained and re-equipped. The 60,000 Australians (half of them recruits just arriving) were causing more chaos in Cairo with some of them rioting and the brothels becoming targets again.

Chauvel and Monash, who both enjoyed female company, were more understanding than their British counterparts. They did all they could to keep the men active with drilling and patrols, but when they played up and caused trouble, they were more sympathetic and tended to turn a blind eye to excesses. This period—January and February 1916—further diminished the reputation of the Anzacs. They were seen as undisciplined. To the British in Cairo, their behaviour was intolerable. General Murray wrote strong letters of complaint to High Command in Whitehall. Birdwood did the same to Kitchener's military secretary. The British governor-general in Australia, Munro-Ferguson, was forced to respond and complain. Blistering missives crisscrossed the world. Their tone and commentary were more or less the same: wildness on leave led to poor form on the battlefield.

Chauvel, influenced by his experiences of the Boer War, also subscribed to the importance of discipline and training. But he and Monash made the distinction between the men letting off steam in bars and brothels and the capacity and desire to engage the enemy. They had witnessed the highly disciplined, courageous performances of their men under the worst conditions ever in war. They would defend them forever.

On top of that, these commanders were worldly men. Most of the veterans reacted like Chauvel did when they saw a woman for the first time in eight months; many could not resist the main option for female companionship of visiting bordellos. Very few had built any worthwhile relationships with partners in Egypt. There was no time or opportunity to meet women apart from prostitutes, where there would be practically no attachments beyond sex and carousing.

*

One trooper in a different situation was Ronnie MacDonald, who was the envy of all his mates and acquaintances. He would be meeting Rania MacPhillamy, who had travelled half-way round the world to be with him. He was luckier than most, if not all the servicemen. He had some regrets. One was easy to talk about. En route back to Gallipoli in late July, the binoculars that Rania had given him as a going-away gift were stolen at Heliopolis. How thoughtful those presents had been. The binoculars had made MacDonald feel a fraction safer. He used them often to note the positions of snipers in the hills above Anzac Cove. Their theft upset him nearly as much as the bullet in his hand. But at least he still had the other gift from her, the writing pen, which connected them through their letters in 1915.

Since arriving in Cairo in late November, Rania had a job as a nursing aide at No. 2 Australian General Hospital at Gezirah Palace Hotel outside Cairo. This was a former luxury hotel. Mounting Gallipoli casualties saw it converted into a hospital early in the year. Many Australians had already been nursed by her. Her warmth, innocence and natural good looks would have endeared her to every one of them, who fantasised over this angel from 'back home'.

In mid-January 1916, she and MacDonald were able to reunite after more than 15 months and copious letters of affection and love. But it was not all that both would have hoped for, or dreamt of. In Rania's eyes, MacDonald had changed. His stay in Egypt and active service on Gallipoli had created a man she was not quite sure about. He looked more mature. The 'Gallipoli stoop', that most of the men had from moving around in the trenches and dugouts, aged him. He was somehow harder, more on edge. He confessed he had been carrying a secret regret; one that had made him feel guilty for not mentioning it in his letters. He was no longer a virgin, and had had 'experience'. Their correspondence does not reveal the exact nature of his dalliance, but the tone and references in their letters made it likely that he confessed to having had a Cairo prostitute. His main opportunity for such affairs would have been in the extended wait five months before shipping off to Gallipoli in May 1915. He was not alone. Most of the Australians had such diversions in that time. Yet this would have been no excuse for Rania.

It was not something that the well-bred country lass of class wished to hear. She had led a sheltered life. Her background gave her no grounds for being broadminded over such a central issue as a partner having indiscriminate sex before marriage, especially if his desires were directed towards a cheap harlot from the backstreets of Cairo. Rania may have been a trainee nurse but she had not been exposed to life beyond the average girl in country New South Wales. It certainly did not run to a prospective husband, the love of her life, cavorting with an Egyptian whore. The news devastated her and caused an irreversible split, almost.

Her biographer Jennifer Horsfield wrote:

'Rania was wounded and shocked by this confession from the man she hoped to marry. Pained, hurtful letters passed between them, but she could not bear to lose touch with him completely.'

MacDonald's mother noticed a change in his correspondence, even though he did not let her know the problem between him and Rania. His letters had been cheerful even through the worst in Gallipoli. Now, in the desert sands of Egypt, 'between heat, dust and flies and paratyphoid injections he wrote as if he was down and out'.[1]

He was depressed. Despite his cheery letters, Gallipoli had disturbed him. Now the inaction in debilitating heat in the desert as he carried out patrol work in the Nile Delta irritated and frustrated him, as did the result of his opening up to Rania. He was bitter about his circumstances and stricken with guilt over letting her down. He wrote of leaving the Light Horse at the first opportunity he could and the hope of joining the diggers in France.

Yet MacDonald kept writing, and with the pen Rania had given him.

While there were words passing between them there was a faint hope of reconciliation.

21

Challenges to the Ottoman Empire

Just how strong any British military campaign in the Middle East would have to be was driven home in March 1916 when a British force attempting to take Iraq's central province was surrounded by the Turks at Kut on the left bank of the Tigris about 160 kilometres south-east of Baghdad.

This siege had come about a few months earlier after General Townshend, a regular officer of the Indian army, who was in charge of a mixed British and Indian force, had driven the Turks up the Tigris to Ctesiphon. Townshend and his troops ran into a tough force under Khalil Pasha, advised by Field Marshal von der Goltz, the veteran German commander who had reorganised the Turkish army. Townshend and his 10,000 soldiers were pushed back to Kut where they dug in surrounded by the Turks.

The British had put together a force to relieve the cornered troops, but it failed after repeated attempts.

In a desperate bid to break the stalemate, Lawrence was ordered by no less than the chief of the imperial general staff (CIGS), Sir William Robertson, to make contact with the commander-in-chief of the Turkish army and attempt to bribe him with a million pounds to let the British troops escape. This was an amazing directive. It overrode the general trying to relieve the besieged army, and Sir Percy Cox, the chief political officer for Mesopotamia (Iraq).

Lawrence, pleased that his status had taken a remarkable leap, left Cairo on 22 March on a boat to Kuwait. He stopped for a few hours at Basra, then reported at army headquarters on board a steamer moored in the Tigris.

None of the British officers were happy about this or the emissary sent with the authority to 'purchase' one of the Turkish leaders 'such as Khalil'. They told him that his mission was dishonourable from a soldier's point of view, which was a reminder to the intelligence officer that he was not a military man.

Lawrence countered by informing the British officers involved that he thought them incompetent, and went on with his mission. He lined up a meeting with Khalil, whom he described in the overwrought, breathless terms of the novice spy wishing to impress. Nevertheless, his masters were left in little doubt about the appearance and character of their target for bribery:

Khalil . . . strong clean built, flat-back broad shouldered, active man, about 35, in accordance with appearance hard and energetic, supple in physique and characteristic. Large straight mouth, thin lips and large hard brown eyes. Without appearing exceptionally clever seems to have good memory, keen alert brain, good general grip of affairs and above all personality and force of character. Polite and cordial, though slightly bored with details. Somewhat restless and impatient, which traits combined with his determination, and the fear of consequences which his relationship with Enver [Enver Pasha, leader of the Young Turks] confers upon him, might possibly impel him to rashness of action, which however would be whole-hearted and have strong driving power behind. He sets great store in personal bravery for which he himself is famed.[1]

Lawrence put the one million pound offer to Khalil. He rejected it, implying that the British could not buy him off with such a paltry sum. Lawrence doubled the offer. The Turk had much pleasure in deriding it and turning it down once more.

Late in April, Lord Kitchener at the War Office in Whitehall sent a cable to the commander of the Middle East Force British General Murray in Cairo: 'Little or no prospect of saving Kut . . . any success you can achieve during the next few days will be most valuable.'

There was to be no counterpoint to the failure in Mesopotamia. The Turks had begun their push towards the canal via the northern route over Sinai closest to the Mediterranean. They had just defeated the under-prepared and under-resourced British 5th Mounted (Yeomanry) Brigade at the posts of Katia and Oghratina 40 kilometres east of the canal into the Sinai, where they were massacred. The Yeomanry had been recruited almost entirely from the farmers of the English shires, and its officers mainly from the landed gentry. There was no doubting their courage, but the officers particularly tended to approach a fight as they did cricket on the village green. War was sport that would not take them too far from the way they lived in the local town. Many were from rich families. Their camels were laden down with good wine and food. When the Turks attacked, the yeomanry officers' camps were abandoned. They were found later to be stocked well enough for a banquet most nights. They and their men were prepared more for war on England's gentle moors and green fields, not the harsh desert of northern Sinai, which did not augur well for leadership. They were surprised at the fury and force of the Turkish thrust in conditions they knew well. The British landed gentry were playing away and not enjoying the fields of the host opponent.

Despite the shortcomings of their officers, the British Mounteds fought well with sword and rifle, but were outnumbered and outflanked. 2nd Brigade of the Anzac Mounted Division was rushed out to assist but too late. They encountered the battered and wounded yeomanry straggling back towards the canal. At their destination, they discovered the hundreds of English Mounted Infantry who would never struggle anywhere again. Corpses in their hundreds were left where they had been slain by Arabs, who had been left to guard them overnight.

The yeomanry who had escaped told of a Turkish attack in the early morning of 23 April under the cover of thick fog. They had opened fire from very close range with light guns, machine-guns and rifles. Survivors were certain that local Bedouins, who were allowed to roam through the lines, had pinpointed the exact British position. Otherwise the fog would have been a cover for them as well.

The assault had begun at 5.30 a.m. The yeomanry resisted

for two hours until they ran out of ammunition. Then the Turks had rushed them from all directions. Some of the British cavalry escaped. Those captured were left in the hands of the Bedouins, who proceeded to strip and torture them through the night.

The Australian Light Horse, who came across the result of the butchery were sickened and sobered by what they saw. No matter how long this war in the desert continued they would never trust the Bedouins again, regardless of directives from the British command about how to deal with local Arabs. If there was a chance they were in the pay of, or under the control of the Turks, all Arabs would be treated with suspicion.

The Anzacs were alert for any ambush when they reached the main town in the area, Romani. But the Turks and the Bedouins had done their worst and withdrawn further east.

The Turkish departure was certain to be temporary.

The Turks now seemed likely to have two coincident and clear 'wins' over the British in the Middle East in April following closely on the grand victory at Gallipoli.

One way or the other the British invaders would have to react strongly, or expect further setbacks.

Chauvel prepared to retaliate. The experience of desert patrols had reinforced what he already knew after decades in the saddle. The horses were going to be vital; the difference between winning and losing minor and major battles. The Sinai was too much for the infantry. Foot soldiers were not mobile enough in the harsh, vast terrain. Worse, they could not take the conditions. It was important to have a strong central remount depot. Many more horses were needed, and Chauvel chose someone to run it who he knew could be trusted to do a top job in difficult circumstances: his old acquaintance from school days, Banjo Paterson.

He had lost track of him early in 1915. Paterson's veterinary unit had not been in demand; the Gallipoli campaign had little use for them and he could not stand the idea of sitting in Egypt minding horses while war raged on the Gallipoli Peninsula and in Europe. He took a boat to England, pulled strings where he could and snared himself a job in France as an ambulance driver at an Australian-inspired hospital run by an austere Quaker, Lady Dudley. He ferried the wounded from the rail terminus at Boulogne-sur-Mer.

It was worthy work but would never hold Paterson for long. In March 1915, he heard about the recruitment of more mounted infantry in Australia. He returned home and applied to be put in 'remount service'. He was now 51 years old. Fearing rejection, Paterson put his age down to 49 on his application for a commission. By the stroke of a pen he was back in his 40s and eligible for service if he passed the medical. The doctor ignored his arm and checked for a hernia. He had not suffered from one and was so on his peripatetic way for another attempt to serve in this war, this time as a major.

Paterson wrote of his responsibilities in the remount unit, which included tens of thousands of horses and hardy mules in similar numbers:

'To take over the rough, uncivilised horses from all over the world by the army buyers; to quieten them and condition them and get them ready for being heel-roped; and finally to issue them in such a state of efficiency that a heavily accoutred trooper can get on and off under fire if need be.'[2]

Horses came in mobs of thousands. Breaking them in and perfecting their patience under stress would be the difference between life and death for every trooper at least once in battle, and in some cases, often. Paterson had 800 rider/trainers under his command. Many buck riders, who roamed Australia in the rodeo shows, had joined the mounted infantry after the outbreak of war had closed down their performance work.

There were some 'rough' horses in the continual intakes.

'I think everybody [horse sellers in several countries] that had an incorrigible brute in his possession must have sold it to the army,' Paterson noted. 'I usually only ride horses intended for Generals and thus I got the pick of the mounts.'[3]

He was not content with managing a bland depot—'a sort of parish outfit'. He wished it to become 'justly celebrated'. Egyptian notables, wandering English celebrities and aristocratic women, he said, all competed to secure invitations to see the unit's shows. Paterson injected some parochial assessments of his squadron of Queensland horse-breakers and New South Wales buckjumping show riders, compared with others from Victoria, Tasmania and South Australia. His riders were far superior, he claimed.

'We won five out of seven events open to all troops in Egypt at a show the other day,' he wrote. One event was wrestling on horseback.

'One of my Queenslanders, a big half-caste named Nev Kelly, pulled the English Tommies off their horses like picking apples off a tree.'

He said of his rough-riders: 'They dearly love to do a bit of "grandstand" work even though they risk their neck by it.'

But the gung-ho approach had its down-side. Writing to a friend, he noted he had two men with broken legs, one with a fractured shoulder blade, two with crushed ankles 'and about seven others more or less disabled'.

Nevertheless, Paterson boasted that he had never had to tell one of his riders twice to mount a horse, no matter how hostile it appeared.[4]

The importance of the Paterson-trained horses was soon apparent in the increased bombing raids by German planes—'taubes'—in May 1916 in daily runs over the desert. The Light Horse outposts would spot them and ring their regimental HQ. Once the alarm was raised, every trooper would rush to his horse and gallop straight into the desert. After a few hundred metres, the scattered troopers and their horses would stay as still as possible. The pilots and observers had trouble in differentiating between them and the scrub or palms.

'It is a curiously triumphant feeling,' Ion Idriess noted in his diary, 'a feeling with a delicious little scornful thrill, holding your horse motionless and gazing up at the ominous metal bird flying.'

The well-drilled mounts remained as still as their riders. The Germans flew so low that troopers could make out the hooded heads of pilot and observer gazing down unable to see up to 600 stationary troopers and their mounts on which to drop their bombs.

'So much for the aeroplane,' Idriess wrote. 'Modern vulture of war beaten by the instinct of ground things.'[5]

The troopers disliked listening-post work at night. The air was sweet and cool, the desert still. They were often surrounded by bush. There was usually strong moon and star light, which highlighted the sand, making it glitter yellow interspersed with black shadows. It would have been romantic in other circumstances. But those on duty feared the Bedouins, who had no love for any foreigners or invaders, as was seen by the way they mutilated the yeomanry on 23 April. Every so often one would creep up behind a trooper and slit his throat or push a knife into his back. The Australians treated them as hostile and nearly as much an enemy as the Turks. The Light Horse patrols regularly brought in small parties of Bedouins, mostly women, children and older men with their bony goats and scrawny camels. The younger men were either wandering the desert or fighting for the Turks, especially in the northern reaches of the Sinai. The troopers felt that these tribespeople were passing information to the Turks, which was not surprising, given that they were technically their rulers.

One thing that Paterson and his horse-whisperers could not do was train the mounts to be silent at all times. They could tame a wild horse or quieten down a noisy one. But they could not ensure an animal remained mute. Any sound carried far. The troopers on perilous night duty were concerned about their horses giving them away.

'A neddy would whinny companionably,' Idriess recalled. 'His mate a way back in the main body would answer; other cobbers would eagerly reply until the whole column was whinnying.'[6]

Another enemy was the sun. Some Anzacs were getting

sunstroke during the blistering days. There were plenty of instances of men becoming delirious or worse. The hot winds would carry the stench of the dead humans, horses and camels, victims of this scattered desert war. They had little to offer now except ugly reminders of their demise and abandonment to the jackals, birds of prey and flies, which outnumbered everything else and bothered the troopers as they had at Gallipoli.

Ronnie MacDonald was another trooper sick of the conditions after months of patrolling. The food was about the only thing improving after the sustained diet of bully-beef and rock-hard biscuits. There was little joy with the water. He was not allowed more than one full water bottle in 24 hours. It was sometimes brackish, and not made more palatable by chlorinated tablets, which the doctors attached to the Light Horse had issued for compulsory consumption. The dissolved chlorine was meant to kill bacteria. MacDonald and the other troopers used it for cleaning the rust off stirrup-irons.

He had seen enough sand dunes and even the scattered oases of date palms for a lifetime. The heat caused rifle-bolts to scald hands, and was made worse by sandstorms, which bit and burned exposed skin. The sand itself became an enemy cursed more than the Turks. It was so hot sometimes it would shrink boots.

The troopers and their horses were being stretched to new levels of monotony, which did nothing for MacDonald's ordeal over Rania. He could not see her unless he was granted rare leave for a break in Cairo. His letters reflected distress and frustration.

On 16 May 1916 he wrote:

'Very close to Hades. You feel that you never want to see me again let alone write. You can't feel any worse about me than I do about myself. I'm going for the Infantry or any old thing the first chance I get. One crowded hour in France will beat this rotten job. Have never known the heat the way it is today—all my candles have melted together.'

It was cold at night. Fog in the deep valleys would sometimes envelop the troopers like a silent ghost. It was so thick that men on patrol could not make out horses in front of them. The only positive was that it was less likely they would be picked off by snipers.

Like all the troopers, MacDonald was grateful for his horse. It would be his radar in the dark. Not a night patrol would pass without one of the mounts stopping dead a metre from the edge of a ravine of sand that presented a sheer drop of sometimes 100 metres into the fog soup. All the troopers would then spread out, their horses tentatively searching for a way down, which would see their saddle-girths deep in the sand.

On 18 May 1916, he wrote:

'Write and tell me about the case you nursed [a soldier with smallpox]. I would give anything Rania, to start over again and be good enough for you.'[7]

Lawrence, mission unaccomplished, was still in Basra in May for Townshend's inevitable unconditional surrender with his troops exhausted and ill, and the Kut 'garrison' out of ammunition, food and supplies.

He was busy dictating again, this time in a report back to the Arab Bureau. There was more than vindictive bite in his denunciation of the British officers for their running of the entire campaign to relieve Townshend. It was an indiscreet move, but invaluable for its sharp analysis, where there had been none before. Lawrence was now the diligent spy making the most of his first big assignment when no-one else was either equipped or willing to put their thoughts on paper so succinctly for consumption in Cairo and London.

The main reason for staying in Basra was more clandestine. He received a coded directive from Cairo to execute his plan for an Arab revolt. Clayton was sending him a group of nationalist leaders, many of whom Lawrence had already contacted, which was on its way to Basra. No promises were to be made by him except in general terms 'to do all we can to help Arab independence'.

All this had been driven by Sharif al-Faruqi's original information at Gallipoli. Nine months later this was a dress rehearsal rather than the start of an actual revolt. But it was drawing Lawrence in, willingly.

The British mentality was clear in the secret directive: money was the root of all support and action when 'we are getting in touch and buying people'.[8]

Lawrence carried out a small mission of his own to see if there was any local support in Basra for a potential revolt. He was disappointed, finding only a dozen in a 'Pan-Arab' party. In another report from there, he reiterated that the best way to foment revolt was to organise Hussein as spiritual leader in the region in place of the Sultan of Turkey.

The British had been promising much to Hussein in the months after al-Faruqi's defection. Even the British High Commissioner in Egypt, Arthur McMahon, had been putting enticements on paper. Hussein read certain commitments into them. But the experienced British diplomat kept his English vague, and with out-clauses. It was implied that almost all the Arabic-speaking countries of the Middle East would be free to choose their own political futures. The freeing of the religious centres from Turkish rule in the Hejaz would also cause a flood of Muslim pilgrims to the region.

On the basis of British backing, Hussein planned to install his four sons as the heads of four nations, with him the supreme governmental and spiritual leader of the Arab and Muslim world.

He had been convinced of the good intentions of his British political 'friends'.

Carve Up, Build Up

The Australians cannot be driven, but they might be led anywhere.

Colonel J. R. Royston

Any prospect of an Arab revolt would have been stalled in the days before it began had Hussein and his sons known about the secret 'Sykes–Picot' agreement signed in late May 1916 by the British and French, and given assent by the Russians. It had been drawn up by two senior government figures, Britain's 36-year-old Lieutenant Colonel Sir Mark Sykes, 6th Baronet, and France's Monsieur Francois Georges-Picot, 45, a diplomat of some standing. Both were Catholics and had first-hand knowledge of the Middle East. Their deal was a carve-up of the Middle East if the Allies (including Britain and France) won the current war and the Ottoman Empire was dismembered. They even produced a little map with colouring reminiscent of a junior school text book for their respective government and war cabinet heads to digest. The plan was approved, which was fine on paper for these two Western imperialists.

The Syrian coast (much of today's Lebanon), was to go to France, while Britain would take direct control over Iraq's central province around Baghdad, and the southern province around Basra. Palestine, always a 'problem' because of the interest of other Christian powers, especially Russia, would have an international administration. (When the Russians dropped out of the war, the British regretted the Palestine idea and would push for control.) This left great areas of land, including what is now Syria, Mosul in Iraq's north, and Jordan. The carve-up concept then was that these outstanding areas would have local Arab chiefs who would be supervised by the French in the north and the British in the south. (Not long after Sykes–Picot was agreed, the British also set their sights on Mosul, Iraq's northern province because of the oil discoveries. They had wanted the French in the north as a buffer against Russian expansionism. But later it became clear that the Russians would not be attempting moves in the area in the immediate future. There was no need for the extent of the French buffer. Potentially oil-rich Mosul was now more desirable.)

Plenty of the 12 Sykes–Picot clauses paid lip-service to 'the Arab State or the Confederation of Arab States'. A once over lightly reading may have fooled the uninitiated in the back alleys of the English language, especially when penned by lawyers who had the equivalent to PhDs in obfuscation.

Part of the deal was that Palestine was to be an international zone, in theory to be owned by no-one. This depiction would lead Zionists to believe that this would be the 'promised land' of historical meaning and a national home for Jews. In reality, there was strong objection in the British Foreign Office to allowing Jews into the Palestine for fear of upsetting many regimes in the Middle East that would not like to see a new 'interloper' state.

This blueprint again had plenty of out-clauses that could be argued several ways, but which would be interpreted by any neutral observer as being strictly in British and French interests. It was about empires, guns and money. They both had all three and the Arabs had little with which to challenge them. Clause 2 of the 12 in the agreement was dominant, unequivocal and clear:

'That in the blue area France, and in the red area Great Britain, shall be allowed to establish such direct or indirect administration or control as they desire and as they may think fit to arrange with the Arab State or Confederation of Arab States.'

It was remarkable that it was ever written in the first place. Britain and France, enemies for centuries, had agreed on a carve-up that appeared fair to them (and no-one else except the Russians) and their ongoing expansionist colonial ambitions. The main proponent was Sykes, an expert on the Ottoman Empire, who had travelled widely from Cairo to Baghdad. He was from a prominent family and wore several other professional hats as a Conservative MP. Sykes was a big, hearty Yorkshireman with a powerful personality. He was a Kitchener protégé, and even wore a similar moustache. He was used to getting his way. Yet he knew he could not bully or bluff his tall, conservative counterpart Georges-Picot. He was from a prominent French family of the old school, which produced many of his country's diplomats, colonial governors and high-ranking bureaucrats. He was the pompous and devout son of historian Georges Picot (and great uncle of Valery Giscard d'Estaing). The younger Georges-Picot was a graduate of the select Ecole des Sciences Politiques and of the Ecole de Droit. He was close to the powerful colonial lobby groups in France, while maintaining his own power and dignity, and that of his country.

Georges-Picot had been negotiating with the British since November 1915, before Sykes appeared at the table. He had displayed that typically French approach of starting undiplomatically from the position that there was no way but the French way, and then working backwards from there. Sykes was called in to help. He touched a positive nerve when he discovered that Georges-Picot was inherently an Anglophile, a near extinct breed among the French. He learned the English language properly in the manner the Germans did, but unlike the Germans managed to comprehend the nuances of British humour. He had even read all Sykes's books, two of which were parodies, and two of which were well-studied travel books: *The Home of Islam* and *Through Five Turkish Provinces*.

Sykes was a wealthy, aristocratic dilettante. He had the characteristics of those in the British ruling class who liked to flit around the fringes of British diplomacy. He was also a fun-loving ebullient type, which the Frenchman appreciated.

Sykes admired French culture but was not enamoured with the way they managed their empire. After visiting French North Africa, he said:

'They are incapable of commanding respect. They are not Sahibs [Hindu for "honoured friends"], they have no gentlemen. The officers have no horses, or guns or dogs.'[1]

Despite this attitude, he and Georges-Picot got on well. They enjoyed each other's company as they sat down together in London and Paris with maps and sharp knives in the attempt to dismember, on paper, an enemy empire.

They worked a diplomatic miracle, with terms apparently equitable for the British and French. But nowhere in sight was a serious accommodation for an Arab state run by Arabs.

Lawrence arrived back in Cairo in early June 1916, just before the true revolt of the Arabs against the ruling Turks began in earnest in the Hejaz at Medina, the second holy city of Islam. Two of Hussein's sons, Ali and Feisal, deserted the Turkish army and took 500 other Arabs with them. The brothers sent a jointly signed letter to the local Turkish commanding officer. It informed him that their father had ordered them to take this action. The communication was to be taken as a declaration of war by the Arabs against the Turks.

On 16 June, Hussein in Mecca, the birthplace of the prophet Mohammed, fired on the Turkish barracks, signifying the official beginning of the revolt.

While the revolt in the desert in the east was in foment, troopers in the Sinai were still doing the monotonous patrolling over endless dunes. Some, such as Ronnie MacDonald, were so disillusioned at the lack of action they were forever thinking about desertion. But in his case, a woman's love and apparent forgiveness changed his demeanour. In mid-June, Rania sent him a birthday gift of tobacco, and her best wishes. He took it as a sign that he had a chance to restore their relationship.

MacDonald wrote her a letter, elated that she seemed to be offering him a chance. He applied for leave. He was given three days in Cairo in July 1916. In that brief time, he and Rania patched up their relationship. It seemed that in the months since they had last seen each other she had learned more about the behaviour of soldiers on leave. The young woman would have had life lessons and experiences that changed and perhaps matured her outlook. She would have seen enough patients with venereal disease to understand that most of the soldiers had spent time in brothels; she may have heard stories at first hand about the demi-monde of Cairo. Whatever her change of heart over MacDonald's indiscretion, he referred to her in his next letter after their Cairo encounter as 'you dear broadminded little girl'.

'If you still think I am worth giving up everything for,' he wrote, 'help me to build up a strong chain of thoughts, that we will marry and it won't be long . . . I love you Rainbow. Your new Ronnie.'[2]

Their rapprochement had come just in time. All leave was cancelled a day after he returned to his squadron for more work in the desert. An army of Turks had been spotted marching east in the direction of Romani.

The war between them and the Anzacs was on again.

The first to sight the enemy was the New Zealand Mounteds Brigadier General Chaytor in the observer seat of an Australian Flying Corps 'Tac R' biplane. He had spotted Turkish forces about 20 kilometres east of Romani at Bayud. Chaytor's keen eye had estimated there were 3,000 enemy and 2,000 camels. He scribbled, noting that the contingent was attempting to hide in a valley. They were bringing big guns, probably 5.9-inch howitzers, which would impede their progress. The intrepid brigadier asked the pilot to check his fuel gauge. They had plenty in the tank, and time. It was 4 p.m., giving him at least two more hours in the air. They flew on to Bir Jameil, spotting about 2,000 more enemy infantry and 1,000 camels. He made notes again, directing the pilot towards Bir el Abd, where they could make out a further 3,500 Turks on the move, just. From the air, they seemed to be hardly animated, retarded by the fierce heat, water shortages and the need to haul those sizeable artillery pieces.

Chaytor had seen enough. He ordered the pilot to fly west until they were over the Australian 2nd Light Horse Brigade, and then dropped a message. That was on 19 July 1916. Daily from then on the Royal Flying Corps sent their pilots aloft to gauge more about the enemy advance. It was soon ascertained that there were 25,000 Turks with about 10,000 camels moving tardily from El Arish on the Mediterranean coast on an 80-kilometre trek towards the wide oasis area containing Romani. They had been travelling mainly at night to conserve energy and also to avoid aerial reconnaissance.

News that the enemy was on the march their way brought elation in the Light Horse camp. Turkish prisoners confirmed the troops were mainly from the Gallipoli battle, and included mainly Anatolians, among the best of the Ottoman Empire. If anything could electrify the Light Horse, this could. Any major encounter would be fought with maximum fervour by the Australians, who would be desperate for victory. This would be round two, on a different arena.

The Anzac Mounted Division was tired of endless patrolling, and only minor skirmishes with small bands of Turks, or in rounding up Bedouin tribesmen and their families in the area. The troopers wanted action. Those who had come from Gallipoli had been battle-starved for seven months. The rest, making up half the force, had not seen action apart from these occasional run-ins with Turkish raiding parties and patrols.

Until now the clashes had been fierce, but it had the feeling of a 'gentleman's war' about it as reflected in Chauvel's letter to Sibyl a week earlier. He left two prisoners taken in a desert 'stunt', as he called it, comfortable and with water and hoping that 'their mates will come for them'.

'We also rescued an aeroplane which had come down in the desert,' he wrote. 'That is the third we have helped in during the last few days. They have to take them to bits and pack the bits on camels.'[3]

This was a far cry from the Australians on the Somme in France and Flanders right then involved in fighting that was seeing thousands killed daily. Chauvel and his troopers wished to justify their travelling so far to fight for Australia, the empire, or even avenge the fallen at Gallipoli. There were few 'bragging rights' in Egypt or the Sinai so far, especially when it was widely known that the best infantry troops had been filched from Egypt for fighting in France.

The Cairo-based British commander-in-chief, General Murray, perhaps honourably, had been hand-picking the best battalions to be shipped off to the Western Front. He carried out his brief to defend the canal to the letter by building trenches near it in the northern Sinai and 'vigorously patrolling'. There was to be no expedition to Palestine or further. His only concession to that was the painfully slow building of a military railway from Kantara on the canal, heading north-east roughly towards Romani, and it was hoped, at some future date, El Arish. But with the Turks on the move, the situation seemed about to change. Turkish prisoners and spies were informing the British that the advancing enemy force was being commanded by Kress who had directed the failed attack on the canal early in 1915. He was now organising a second push to take it, this time with better planning and support.

Kress would have been encouraged by the recent defeat of the yeomanry in the oasis. If all the defending forces were that easily defeated, taking the canal was feasible, if not likely.

Before Chaytor's report, the Anzac troops had a high rate of sickness, with troopers calling in ill daily to the medical orderly. After it, the orderly had nothing to do. Every trooper wanted to engage the enemy.

The intensity of encounters and small battles increased as the Turks advanced until they were 10 to 12 kilometres from the line of posts manned by the British in front of Romani. It ran 10 kilometres south from Mahemdia at Lake Bardiwell on the Mediterranean and faced the lower foothills and Romani sand dunes.

The Anzac mounted brigades were moving out on patrol east towards the Turks near Oghratina, which had been taken from the yeomanry. Some patrols rode out every night to listen for the enemy and do nothing else but report back on the Turkish positions. 'Cossack posts', perhaps two or three sections (12 men) or more at a time, would often fire on the enemy, mount their horses and depart post haste. The enemy prepared ambushes, taking cover behind tufted hillocks and sand dunes. On one Cossack mission, part of a squadron of 7th Light Horse Regiment was surrounded by Turks three times their number, some of whom were close enough to snatch at their bridles. The Australians galloped clear under heavy but wild fire. No-one was struck. They dismounted 250 metres clear, took their horses out of the line of fire and defended as the Turks advanced. After 20 minutes they rode off again another 250 metres, and engaged the advancing Turks. This happened four times. On the fifth occasion, the Australians cheekily made a fire and boiled tea, making a point that even with superior numbers the enemy was no serious threat in these circumstances. The Australians reckoned the Turks were cautious, slow and poor shots.

These troopers, together for the first time in the Sinai, were boosted by the experience, believing they would win any engagement of similar numbers. But there weren't to be small Turkish forays once the main body of the 25,000 strong force drew closer.

'Nightly [from 20 July to early 1 August] the Turks advance a few miles across the desert,' Idriess noted in his diary, 'thousands of men in far-flung waves—the first wave sheer desert fighters and as noiseless. They seem to arise out of the very sand in overwhelming numbers. Some of the Cossack posts have been bayoneted as the men were springing on their horses.'[4]

Chauvel wrote on 25 July:

'We are having a strenuous time here . . . we have had a fight of some sort every day for the last week and have taken a few prisoners. We [Mounted Infantry] are the only troops in it so far. It is rather funny; the [British] Infantry have the greatest admiration for our men, but seem to think they are more or less savages. The latest rumour in their lines is that I have issued a Divisional Order to the effect that "all prisoners are to be brought in alive." '

Turkish prisoners, he claimed, were treated very well and given plenty of the troopers' own rations, cigarettes and water.

'They [troopers] put them [Turkish prisoners] up behind them on their horses, 'he added, 'to bring them in because they are footsore.'

The gentleman's phoney war was continuing despite the two forces—the Turks' 25,000 and Chauvel's contingent of about 1,500—drawing closer together.

A German plane dropped a message very close to Chauvel's 'front door' at his Romani HQ on the morning of 25 July. It thanked him for the courtesy of the Australian Flying Corps. It had pointed out that one of the enemy hospitals was in an exposed position.

The German note also asked Chauvel to have his own hospitals more distinctly marked.

'I hope they don't drop a bomb so accurately [as the message to his front door],' he remarked.[5]

Turkish scouts informed their commanders that the line of British infantry posts in front of Romani was impenetrable. This led to a big flanking movement that would travel south of the line.

Chauvel was disquieted by Murray in Cairo not allowing him 3rd Mounted Brigade (still run by tough Jack Antill, who was in defence of the canal further south) for the defence at Romani. Murray removed Chaytor's New Zealand Mounted Brigade and in its place gave Chauvel some yeomanry troopers, two batteries of horse artillery and a camel column. Chauvel wanted a stronger mounted force. He was not thrilled that Murray had given executive control of the Romani operation to British Major General H. A. Lawrence, who insisted on giving orders from either Kantara on the canal or nearby Hill 40. This was about 20 kilometres from the action, which was too far for informed and quick decision-making. Another irritating factor was the personality clash between Murray and General Lawrence. As a big action loomed, the tension between them increased. All staff worked hard to placate them. Lawrence reckoned that Murray interfered with battle-planning too much. This may have been the case, but Murray had a strong point when he suggested Lawrence should get closer to the front than Kantara, so he could make faster, better decisions.

Chauvel, who had respect from both men, stayed out of the feud. He agreed with Murray on Lawrence's remoteness at Kantara, but he did not intervene. This was his way. He was never confrontational. Even when Hamilton had little time for him at Gallipoli, Chauvel kept his own counsel. He never lost his steady demeanour, preferring like Monash at moments of crisis to put his personal thoughts on paper to his wife for later succour and understanding. Yet at times his aloofness from verbal spats was tested. He was angry at 2nd Brigade's commander Colonel Ryrie, an Australian member of parliament, for ducking off to London to attend an empire parliamentary conference. But Chauvel could not remain upset at Ryrie. He had known him since before the Boer War and liked and admired him. Chauvel could not understand how a military man with such a strong background could let a conflict of interest take him away from war, even if important issues of state and politics were involved. After Ryrie was struck in the neck at Gallipoli he returned to the front there in October. He was struck again by artillery shells in the last month of the Anzac stay on the peninsula.

Ryrie had been in charge of 2nd Brigade through the earlier battles of the desert campaign, but would now miss the next major encounter with the Turks.

Chauvel was disappointed, but again he preferred to vent his feelings on paper, writing to his old commander, Hutton. Colonel J. R. 'Galloping Jack' Royston took the diligent Ryrie's place for this conflict, to be known as the Battle of Romani. It may have been a blessing in disguise. The tall, heavy-set, 59-year-old South African was the most popular man in the Anzac Mounteds. When he had first been appointed commander of the 12th Light Horse Regiment, there had been resentment from some that he was not an Australian. But he already had a strong record with the Australians. In April 1901 during the Boer War, he was given command of the 5th and 6th contingents of the Western Australian Mounted Infantry. Royston had also led in the Zulu Rebellion of 1908, and the campaigns in south and west Africa in 1914–15.

He always began a connection to a new command with the words:

'Treat me right, and I'll treat you right.'

This 'treaty' worked well with the Australians. This ebullient man-mountain's cheerfulness soon won over all under him. And he knew his charges well.

'The Australians cannot be driven,' he said, 'but they might be led anywhere.'

The knowledgeable thought behind this comment expressed much about Royston's exceptional character. In typical style, he chose his aide-de-camp for his 'reckless riding', which meant he might just keep up with his commander.

'Jack was brave, magnificent, spectacular and imposing,' the aide-de-camp noted from his close proximity, 'a dashing man of quick decision, yet so humble, sincere and lovable.'

Banjo Paterson knew Royston well from Boer War days and dubbed him 'Hell-fire Jack'. He was, the balladeer said, one of the 'most picturesque personalities in the British Army', who was 'by instinct a bandit chief and by temperament a hero'.[6]

Chauvel had no hesitation in temporarily elevating him.

He had no choice in this operation but to accept the disjointed and unharmonious command from the distant General Lawrence. Chauvel had been through it at Gallipoli and had to make do with a less than satisfactory plan here.

Yet there was one aspect of his force's remoteness that did not bother him. The initial part of the battle would be left very much to his initiative.

23

Rumble at Romani

These Anzac troops are the keystone to the defence of Egypt.

*General Murray, commander of the British Egyptian Expeditionary
Force, World War I, until May 1917*

Chauvel and commanders under him, including 1st Brigade's Lieutenant Colonel Meredith, rode to the end of the line of Romani outposts after nightfall on 3 August 1916. Chauvel had to make a decision on the defence and consider options concerning withdrawal. With a force more than 10 times his own coming at him, there would be no chance of taking on the Turks in a direct battle. He had to calculate a compromise between defence and strategic backing away.

He trotted around for half an hour, then he used binoculars from high on a ridge of sand. The bright stars above and a low quarter moon allowed him to see enough. He ordered the 1st Light Horse there to form a line running east, giving the whole defence a curved 'hockey stick' look, with the top of the handle touching the sea coast and its bottom, made up of the Light Horse outposts, running east. The Turks were aiming to surround the entire British force, close on it, strangle it and take Romani. To do it now they would either have to make a wide sweep south and traverse the Sinai's heavy, steep dunes, where the sand would sink deep with each soldier's tread, or they would attempt to break through the Light Horse barrier. The first choice would prove just possible in the night, but when morning broke, the Turkish troops would be stranded in the killer heat of mid-summer without easy access to vital water supplies. The artillery would be immovable in these conditions.

Romani's close proximity to the canal (40 kilometres) made

this battle crucial. If the Turks took it, brought up their entire force and dug in, they would be hard to budge.

Chauvel's tactic had forced the enemy's hand. They would have to take the second option and smash through. He set up fixed battery positions. Telephone lines were laid between outposts, which covered five kilometres. His judgement on when and where the Turks would attack was crucial.

He reckoned from reports coming in that this would be during the night (of 3 August), or the next morning.

Fully aware from their intelligence that they were taking on Australian Gallipoli veteran brigades, the Turks had been following 2nd Light Horse squadrons returning from reconnaissance late in the evening. They planned to march in the gullies up to Wellington Ridge, a key strategic point close to the Romani camp. At dawn they would charge down from there and destroy it. They would then be behind the outposts held by the British 52nd Infantry Division, which would be the second target to overwhelm. This would put them in a strong position, and in control of the end of the railway Murray had built from Kantara. The Turkish aim was to have all this done by early morning before British reinforcements could come up from Kantara, Hill 40 and Hill 70.

Then the Turks would have achieved a major breakthrough.

This neat foray, masterminded by Kress, was upset before the battle began. They arrived at midnight to form up for the attack, only to find Light Horse waiting for them. Chauvel's choice of the defence line was perfect. The Turks had to hold back an hour while they adjusted their plans.

They hit hard at 1 a.m. on 4 August.

The silence of the night, with the moon setting, and the light less illuminating, was split by Turkish battle cries:

'Allah! Allah!' 'Finish Australia!' 'Death to Australia!' and other unintelligible yelling. It was familiar to the defenders, but no less nerve-wracking than at Gallipoli. The screaming was soon accompanied by rifle fire along the five-kilometre line. The Light Horse responded. The darkness limited the chances of either side striking many blows. Bullets caused sparks as they skimmed into the sand.

The Turks came in big numbers, and the fire was intense for an hour, forcing the troopers back. But they were not about to crack. After Gallipoli, nothing was too tough, not even the 10-to-1 ratio of the attacking force against them. Chauvel had complete faith in his brigades, especially this one. He had commanded them through the hell on the peninsula and knew that their lines might be broken, but their spirit would sustain them.

The troopers retreated squadron by squadron, with one covering the other, and found order out of the chaos. Chauvel wished their critics, who bitched about their lack of discipline from Cairo, could see them now. He was tempted to bring 2nd Brigade to support them, but he stuck to the plan to let the 1st take the brunt of the attack until dawn, still four hours away.

A problem was the brigade's western flank, where the line finished. The Turks were making an effort to pour round it in a wide sweep from where they could carry through with their plan of taking Wellington Ridge from behind, then Romani and the British outposts.

The battle became gruelling. Meredith was having trouble communicating with his Light Horse posts positioned on sand dunes, some of them so steep that detours of a kilometre had to be made to reach them. The situation for the defenders was made worse when communication lines were cut. Now the squadrons were isolated from each other.

By 2 a.m. the battle had become Gallipoli revisited. The two sides were just 35 metres apart, warring in the dark. The Australians were under orders to limit their hand-to-hand fighting, which took another level of discipline for them. But the order was understood. The alternative meant they would be outnumbered and overrun.

The right flank was under fierce assault. Outposts were being pulverised. One group of five troopers saw their horses shot or lost, except for one game beast known as Bastard Bill, a more than 16-hand chestnut. He was infamous for bucking and never having been fully broken in. Only the best riders would take him on. His spirit was evident in this crisis. He had not cut and run with the other horses. Bastard Bill had stood his ground, almost as if he knew he was this quintet's last hope of escape, which he was. Three troopers hurried across the sand and mounted him. They prayed he would not buck, which he always did when mounted by anyone. Instead of complaining about his load, he stood firm. The other two balanced on a stirrup either side of him and hung on as best they could. The mighty waler dug his hooves into the soft sand, snorted and sweated his way a kilometre under fire carrying a massive load of five troopers clear of immediate danger.

Any other horse would have collapsed. But not this Bastard. (The gallant favourite of the campaign was rewarded by never again having to put up with a trooper on his back. He had a much gentler time as an officer's packhorse from then on.)

The Turks were lifted by their breakthroughs and forcing the Light Horse back here and there. They were keen for further successes. Many removed their boots to move better in the sand. About 8,000 of them pushed past the Light Horse's western flank and headed for Mount Meredith, a huge dune that led to the first main target on Wellington Ridge.

Chauvel warned Royston of 2nd Light Horse to be ready, although he still held them back. The Turks made several screaming assaults on the nearly perpendicular Mount Meredith southern slope. About 20 men from 1st Light Horse, led by Lieutenant G. P. Edwards, defended stoutly. The attackers were sent tumbling down the sand. Realising that a frontal move up the steep wall was impossible, the Turks began moving around the dune and coming up the easier approaches at its sides. Fighting was so close in the dark that one trooper bent down to help a wounded comrade up onto the saddle behind him, only to find that he had reached for a Turk.

At 3 a.m. the Light Horse had to abandon their post on the

crest after suffering severely, with many men and officers killed and wounded. The Turks were relentless now as they continued their encircling movement. The Australians kept easing away, somehow still holding order in the graduated retreat.

The enemy took control of Mount Meredith. They set up a machine-gun nest and began sweeping the Light Horse's shrinking lines.

Dawn touched the cold dunes at 4.30 a.m. and the combatants could see each other for the first time. The troopers realised the extent of the numbers against them. Several thousand Turks were making their way still wider on the right flank. Their aim to encircle the Light Horse, including the waiting 2nd Brigade, seemed likely as the heat from the sun became apparent. The Turks could use their artillery now they had targets. They commenced sweeping the line of Wellington Ridge with shrapnel, while also aiming at the British infantry outposts. The noose was being tightened.

Chauvel hurried on horseback to the 2nd Light Horse's camp near Etmaler.

It was the moment to take the initiative.

24

Chauvel from the Front

Chauvel took up a position at the head of the 500-strong mounted infantry of the 2nd Light Horse, which was itching to join the battle. Directly behind him was the less graceful but also inspiring figure of the brigade's big commander, Jack Royston. They wound their way from the camp outside Etmaler in full view of the encircling Turks and the battling 1st Brigade. Its troopers began cheering. They were lifted by the very welcome and inspiring sight of Chauvel and the brigade commander trotting forward and the men, their rifles slung over their straight backs, clearly fresh and ready.

There was no point in the troopers charging over the sand. They and their mounts would be exhausted before a shot was fired. Yet the steady trot had its own menace. It spelt relief to their fellow countrymen. It meant the enemy would have to fight harder in the brutal conditions, which every Turk would have realised was impossible. They had given everything all night. They, like the Anzacs, needed relief and water, both of which were not coming.

The psychological impact of Chauvel's tactic on the enemy was huge. Thousands of Turks, dehydrated and already feeling the sun heralding another day of boiling conditions, watched the reinforcements, their appearance timed to perfection. There was no cheering from the ridges and valleys; no shrill cry of thanks to Allah; just a minute's shocked silence only punctuated by an odd shot or spit from a machine-gun.

Chauvel rode up to Colonel Meredith on Wellington Ridge, now the last bastion before Romani, as the shrapnel pumped over and around them. A Turkish infantry contingent reached a ridge in front of them.

This was Chauvel's most demanding challenge since the aborted break-out from Quinn's and Pope's at Gallipoli on 7 August 1915, a few days short of a year earlier. It was the same shrieking, fierce enemy, but this was an even more precipitous moment. If his heart-rate was up, he did not show it. Staying calm and measured, characteristics in non-combat situations that Birdwood and others had once misjudged as 'slow', he ordered Royston to send two regiments in on Colonel Meredith's right to meet the enemy onslaught.

To a lesser commander, the situation would look hopeless. But Chauvel had been banking on two factors that had nothing to do with weaponry or numbers. The sun's heat would begin to sap the energy of all the combatants.

The Turks did not have access to the wells at Romani. Their water supply was drying up; they had been fighting and rushing for more than four hours. The Australians would continue to slip back, and still without hand-to-hand combat where possible. The order was understood, and against the defenders' instinct. But Chauvel was ever mindful of the overwhelming Turkish numbers as they gathered on the ridge opposite and moved into the valley in front of Wellington Ridge. The Turks were now just 300 metres from the Light Horse line and 700 metres from Etmaler Camp. Despite the Anzacs' eagerness for close combat with bayonets, hands and boots, they knew that an organised pull-back was the disciplined, better route to survival.

The next few hours would be crucial. The Turks were gaining ground but it was taking time. Each 100-metre advance now was vital and brutally tough to achieve. They had to scrap for every bit of cover.

The Turks who had swept the widest and beyond Wellington Ridge were threatening Etmaler. Chauvel ordered a withdrawal from the Ridge, and part of the defence was sent to block the advance on Etmaler.

The Ridge was taken by the Turks just after 7 a.m. Chauvel took his 1st Brigade out of the line. It was retired to Etmaler. The brigade had fought to the limit of their or any force's abilities, losing ground by design but not the battle.

The 2nd Brigade was pushed to the front. Its 3rd, 6th and 7th Regiments and the Wellingtons attached to it took up the squadron-by-squadron fight and retreat. In the Anzac tradition, no wounded were left in the sands if they could be retrieved.

In this crucial hour, when many troopers would distinguish themselves with courage under fire, the 7th Regiment's 29-year-old Corporal F. P. Curran was outstanding. He single-handedly carried and rode in seven injured men. He worked methodically as shrapnel rained on him and machine-gun fire raked the sand in front of Wellington Ridge. Curran was not going to stop. The Turks had to end his work, and they did with a bullet in the back as he attempted to reach his eighth trooper. He lay in the sand, but no-one could reach him before he died.

Such acts of sacrifice, the ultimate Anzac ideal, inspired everyone who witnessed Curran's efforts and many others who would soon hear about it. This kind of individual effort squeezed that extra bit of resistance out of men stretched to the limit as the sun beat down.

Chauvel rode under fire from regiment to regiment, shoring up the confidence of their commanders and men, which in itself lifted the troopers, just as the Turks began to mass on the crest, stopping short of Wellington Ridge itself. There was no move to make the rush at the Anzac line. The Turks had taken six hours to reach this point. Their lines of communication were down. Their leaders were disorganised. They did not realise that part of their force was rounding Mount Royston and close to Etmaler on the wider approach. The attacking army was running out of water. It was nearly exhausted and the sun was still rising.

The 2nd Brigade readied itself for a Turkish onslaught. Royston rode along it. He had not stopped moving since his men went into battle. He was a big target, but he rode with complete disregard to dangers. In the first hour, Royston tired out two horses and was on his third as he roamed the front line, calling:

'Keep your heads down, lads. Stick to it! Stick to it!' and also:

'You are making history today! Write it now! Write it well!'[1]

The troopers were motivated whenever this huge figure and sweating horse pounded up to them. He stopped to speak to New Zealander Lieutenant Colonel Meldrum, in charge of the Wellingtons.

'You can give them no more ground,' Royston said, 'or we shall lose the camps [at Romani and Etmaler].'

'If they get through my line here,' Meldrum replied in a defiant Scottish brogue, 'they can have the damned camps!'

A short time later, he galloped up to a group of troopers.

'We are winning now!' he called, attempting to rally his men again, 'they are retreating in hundreds!'

A trooper poked his head over a parapet. He was shocked

to see no retreating Turks 'but the blighters coming on in their thousands!'[2]

It was 8 a.m. before Turkish riflemen crawled from the crest to the ridge. They began firing, but their delay had given Chauvel's Ayrshire and Leicester batteries a chance to position themselves. The British gunners attained their range and then pulverised Wellington Ridge, clearing it within minutes.

Eight hours on, the Turks had been brought to a bloody halt.

Chauvel sensed from the lacklustre performance of the enemy that this was the chance to counterattack. But he could not risk it without reinforcements. He tried to reach General Lawrence only to find the communication line to Kantara was down. Lawrence, the executive commander of the battle of Romani, could not be contacted. It emphasised the poor set-up in having the ultimate decision-maker so remote from the battle.

Chauvel was left with an anxious wait, knowing that at his last conversation with Lawrence an hour earlier he had established that Chaytor's New Zealand Mounted Infantry, Antill's 3rd Brigade, and English Major C. L. Smith's Camel Column should move to the battle area.

Only a squadron of yeomanry of the British 5th Brigade turned up in useful time. It defended the railway just beyond Etmaler and Romani to Chauvel's right. On his left, the British 52nd Infantry Division manning the line of posts running north–south from the Mediterranean had been under continual shell fire, which held its soldiers in position through the night. After dawn it moved a small contingent to take up some slack on the left of the Light Horse. This allowed Chauvel to extend his right across to Mount Royston, where the Turks were menacing Etmaler and the railway. The yeomanry horsemen were now in position. These three moves led to further stalemate.

The minutes slipped by. The heat became fierce. Chauvel's mood moved from anxiety to frustration as the chance for an effective counterattack diminished. He requested the 52nd Reserve Brigade take over his position so he could send his men at the Turks. But the reserve's commander refused. General Murray in Cairo had prescribed the timing for any counterattacks, no matter what the situation. Meanwhile Lawrence at Kantara was still not contactable. Chauvel was forced to thin his line and send first one regiment, then another, to prop up his wilting right flank.

The mobility of the Light Horse and the accuracy of their fire kept the Turks from further advance. They began digging in for a battle of attrition. But this was the wrong tactic. They had no water, whereas the Anzac brigades and the British infantry had a small source of it.

The Turkish entrenchment also bought Chauvel more time, especially with the confused communication that prevented assistance coming to the oasis.

Chaytor arrived with his New Zealand Mounted Infantry about 2 p.m. and Chauvel got a message to him to take Mount Royston. Meanwhile, Galloping Jack was punishing himself hard along the line, and continuing to fatigue horses. On his thirteenth steed, he gave Turkish riflemen the umpteenth chance to hit this sizeable moving object. He was struck in the calf. He retired to have it dressed, mounted his fourteenth horse and did what he had exhorted his men to do; he kept going.

Just before 3 p.m. Chauvel rang Royston's HQ to find out how Chaytor's attack was progressing, only to discover that Royston was wounded but was fighting on. He had gone to find yet another horse. Chauvel jumped on his own waler and galloped hard down to where the remounts had been gathered. He found Royston, his leg bandage trailing behind him, and ordered him back to a field ambulance to have his wound redressed. Royston had lost some blood. Chauvel advised him not to return to the battlefront until he had rested, but knew that it would be impossible to stop him.

Chaytor's force, aided by the yeomanry, who did not need

to guard the railway head any more, made a concerted attack on Mount Royston. But it was hard going. Chauvel negotiated again with the British infantry's reserve to attack Wellington Ridge. They at last agreed to do it. With support on his left from the British, and Chaytor pinning down the Turks to his right, Chauvel directed his fatigued 1st and 2nd Brigades to join the counterattack.

The Turks under siege on Mount Royston held on. At 6 p.m., they cracked. Two battalions surrendered. Chauvel wanted to know how the British Reserve Infantry Brigade was going and found that this force, which had done nothing all day, had yet to budge from its posts. Chauvel wished to know why.

The infantry moved out at 7 p.m. It was getting dark. The British brigade decided the rough ground and heavy Turkish fire coming from Wellington Ridge were too much. They broke off their action and retreated. This caused problems for Chauvel's Light Horse brigades, which despite their weakened condition and the lack of support on their left, were making good progress in the demanding conditions as the sun went down.

Chauvel called off the attack and sent some of the more deserving squadrons for watering at Romani and Etmaler. He could not feel satisfaction yet, but there was relief. The exhausted Turks would be unlikely to take Romani now. They were spread over two long arcs starting around Hill 110 east of the 52nd Infantry Division's line and running south of Mount Royston to the small oasis, Bir el Nuss. Chauvel retired at midnight for a few hours sleep with Turkish artillery lighting up the sky with star shells.

His only immediate recorded comment on the day's extraordinary events was in a letter to Sibyl:

'The fighting on the early morning of the 4th was the weirdest thing I ever took on. It was over rolling sand dunes; the enemy, who were in thousands, on foot, could see our horses before we could see them in the half light. It was awfully difficult to find cover for them [the horses] . . .'

Later he gave historian Henry Gullett a more considered analysis.

'It was the empty Turkish water bottle that won the battle,'

Chauvel said, 'Meredith and Royston put six hours on to it [the holding off of the enemy]. Meredith by his gallant stand in the night was chiefly responsible for the success of the delaying action; Royston, by his ceaseless activity and fearlessness [was responsible] for the holding of the line we gradually withdrew to. Chaytor carried out his part of the contract as soon as, and as efficiently as, it was in his power to do so.'

He saw Romani as the first decisive victory attained by the British Land Forces in the war except for campaigns in West Africa.

'It changed the whole face of the campaign in that [Sinai] theatre, wrestling the initiative from the enemy,' he said. 'It also made the clearing of his [the enemy's] troops from Egyptian territory a feasible proposition.'[3]

Against enormous odds, Chauvel's calm strategy and the courage of the force under him had been successful, so far. But there was still hard work ahead on day two of the battle.

25

Push West to Katia

The 2nd Light Horse Brigade supported by two battalions of Scottish Rifles hit Wellington Ridge before dawn on 5 August. The Turks, weakened by lack of water and exhausted by the effort of the previous 28 hours, collapsed under the assault of the Australians and Scots, who used their bayonets freely. More than 1,500 prisoners, many dehydrated and in need of quick medical attention, were taken. It was the biggest haul Chauvel had been involved in and a most gratifying feeling to have a comprehensive victory over the enemy. On 19 May the previous year, he had been in command when Monash's defence system and the Anzacs' determination had stopped the onslaught of 10,000 Turks, which caused their leader Mustafa Kemal never again to sanction such a huge blitz. Yet even though that too had been a rout, it did not enhance the Anzacs' position.

Chauvel's performance at Romani left open a chance for a major victory.

This combined action of Light Horse and Scots enhanced again a growing rapport between the Anzacs and the Highlanders. It had begun when Scottish artillerymen attached to the Australians asked if they could wear the now famed emu plumes in their hats. This was accepted by Chauvel and his troopers. They admired the Scots' fighting qualities, enjoyed their company and regarded the request as a compliment. But it was turned down by the British High Command.

At 6.30 a.m. Lawrence ordered Chauvel to take command of all mounted infantry (except the Camels Mobile Column) and pursue the enemy. It was far too late, but still a welcome step-up, which was recognition for his performance. His force in the main now encompassed the New Zealanders, the British Yeomanry and the three Australian brigades, which included Antill's 3rd. The 3rd had left Hill 70 and had marched 30 kilometres when Chauvel ordered it to go another 30 kilometres almost due west to the oasis at Hamisah. Antill's instructions were to cut off and engage the Turks stationed there or on the retreat from the main battle area.

Chauvel's plan was to pursue the Turks with his other four brigades. The Light Horse troopers were so scattered that he could not start until 10.30 a.m.

'It was sad,' trooper Idriess noted in his diary, 'many of the sections had vacant places, hurriedly made up to strength . . . each troop rode short of men and horses. A man would turn to speak to his mate, only to shut his mouth quickly, on remembering a new man rode there.'

There was a problem with the condition of the horses. They had been carrying up to 130 kilograms and had laboured for days in the hot, deep sand, many without water for long stretches. No amount of training at Paterson's depot could prepare them for this. Their 'chase' had to be slow.

This retarded pursuit allowed the depleted, dispirited Turks to fall back into the desert to the west. They had set up a rearguard with part of their force at Katia on the edge of a two-kilometre-wide, salt-water swamp. A line of machine-guns rimmed the west of the deep bog.

Chauvel's tired force plodded on. They were kept alert by Turks they encountered. But these men did not resist. They were demoralised and made no attempt to fight. The sun's rays had taken any remaining vigour out of them that the previous 36 hours battles had not. The desert that the four brigades passed through was littered with the debris of a retreating enemy: dead animals and men, arms, munitions and equipment.

The troopers knew how to conserve the energy of themselves and their horses. They had learnt in the previous eight months in the desert to avoid plundering their small rations of food and water.

The novice British division, the 52nd, which had only been in the desert a short time, was struggling on the march after manning the outposts at Romani. The British infantry's 42nd Division, which had been brought to the oasis as support, fared far worse. Its troops had been in the desert only a few weeks, and by noon its battalions were showing acute distress. About 800 men from one of its brigades had gone missing.

The Australian 5th Light Horse Regiment, which was coming to the action later than the rest of 2nd Brigade, came across some of these men.

'Many were already crazed with thirst,' Idriess noted. 'We prevented numbers of them from doing dreadful things.'[1]

Some were scratching in the salt pans for water. Others were vomiting from sunstroke. Not a few had discarded their equipment and were delirious, screaming and running across the burning sand. Pressure for them to go into action prematurely had come from the War Office in London.

Murray was forced to respond to its demands. The Romani victory had to be exploited. He had tried to explain the problems in the desert, especially for inexperienced foot soldiers, but had not received a sympathetic ear.

The vast oasis presented a different atmosphere than the previous day, which had been dominated by the sound of action. Now it was graveyard quiet. The troopers listened for warning sounds of Turkish ambushers. But there was none as they approached Katia.

Once there in the afternoon, some of the Anzac troopers and their horses had time for a quick watering; then they were rushed into position.

Chauvel was mindful of the time. Once the sun set, he did not wish to be stranded. He wanted a quick destruction of the Turkish defence, and even the capitulation of the entire force. Timing was everything to this measured commander. His sixth sense, about when to push and when to retreat, was working overtime. It was telling him that this was a moment to thrust forward.

Chauvel surveyed the area. In front of the swamp on his (east) side lay a narrow, bare salt pan, stretching for a few kilometres north and south. From his perspective there was no way of knowing that there was a bog beyond the salt pan. The Turks, though not entrenched, were well set up with a thick clump of palms (hod), which afforded a useful defence. They waited, well concealed individually, although Chauvel and his men knew they were there. The Turkish rifles and machine-guns would be supported by artillery to their rear.

Chauvel lined up his three Anzac brigades of 700 mounted infantry in three lines on the edge of the bare salt pan. The Light Horse made a formidable sight, their bayonets held high and glinting in the melting mid-afternoon sun. This would be the most electrifying moment for many of the troopers since the aborted, horrific charge on foot at the Nek. The prospects as they looked along the flat, concrete-like salt pan to the spread of palms harbouring the Turks were decidedly more to the Anzacs' liking than the funnel of death at the Nek. They expected machine-guns, artillery and rifles to blast at them. Fortified by their dependable horses under them and the fighting spirit of each cobber in the lines, they were ready.

Chauvel lowered his binoculars and looked at his watch. It was approaching 3 p.m. as he waited impatiently for the last of the third line to position itself. He was ordering a mounted charge, the first time in the desert campaign. This was close to the 'old-style' 19th century cavalry attack, the only real difference being that they carried bayonets rather than sabres. It was what he and his men wanted and dreamt of. The mental thrill of the prospect of it had helped influence many to volunteer to fight in the first place. This seemed a suitable opportunity. There were no complaints now about exhaustion. In anticipating what lay ahead they were revitalised as fighting troopers.

Chauvel raised his hand to the commanders. The Anzacs charged, yelling and waving their bayonets as they galloped full tilt across the salt pan's hard ground for about 1,500 metres. The Turks began firing but with little impact at that distance. Then after 1,000 metres the horses reached the bog. It stopped them, breaking the momentum of the charge, as all the troopers came to the same abrupt halt, nearly colliding with each other. Some of the mounts were up to their knees in the thick slime. The Turks adjusted the sights on the rifles, artillery and machine-guns and began a second wave of firing.

The commanders wasted not a second in ordering all troopers to dismount and carry the fight on foot. The horses were taken to safe ground, leaving their riders to their plight in the swamp.

Chauvel's force was literally bogged down in a fight in the cruel, debilitating heat. He knew that the chances for a smash-through and defeat of the Turkish force would evaporate with every hour as the sun moved lower.

*

Five kilometres south of the swamp battle, Antill marched on to Bir el Hamisah. The 3rd Brigade's 9th Regiment, in its first major engagement in the Sinai, fought with panache and took 425 prisoners and seven machine-guns. Even though the Turks turned their big 5.9-inch artillery guns on the brigade, it was spread enough to suffer little impact, and losses were few. Yet Antill, for reasons known only to him, decided to withdraw west to a small oasis, Bir Nagid, for the night.

This lost his brigade the initiative and the chance for it to cause an enemy capitulation, especially as further north the afternoon was drawing to a close with Chauvel's force in stalemate on the marsh battleground.

Keeping in touch with his commanders, Chauvel was aware that water was again perilously low for both man and horse. Many troopers of the 1st and 2nd Brigades had used just one water bottle in 36 hours. Each bottle carried just a quart of water, much less than required in the furnace-like heat. Their horses had gone further, most not having had a drink for 56 hours. A squadron of 2nd Brigade held the unenviable record of its horses going without water for 60 hours, some of them saddled the entire period. It was not unusual to see a trooper remove his slouch hat and give his mount a drink in it.

With no chance of a complete victory by nightfall, Chauvel called off the engagement, leaving him and his men discontented with a 'draw'.

He could do nothing about the hidden swamp, which the Turks had chosen well. That was the luck of war and everyone would have to surmount the bitter disappointment. Chauvel knew too that he would have had little support from the British infantry. They had arrived at Katia in shocking condition. Hundreds in every battalion (each held about 1,000 soldiers) had fallen out en route.

'Many lost their senses,' according to historian Henry Gullett, 'and dug madly with their hands in the burning sands for water. Still more fell unconscious, and not a few died.'[2]

This was without the Turks firing a shot at them. Inexperience in the desert was taking a toll, but even for the battle-hardened Anzacs the stress was more than they had encountered anywhere. Chauvel could do little about the conditions, but he could about tactics. He was dissatisfied with the running of the battle, especially at Romani, by remote control. But even worse in his mind was the display by Antill.

He would have questions to answer about his retiring his 3rd Brigade prematurely from the fight when it seemed to have the enemy down for the count.

The thirsty brigades made their way slowly back to Romani under bright stars. The horses refused food. They would not touch it if they had gone several hours without water. There had been 'orders to water' during the battle but sometimes it was impossible for the horses to be looked after. Some missed out. This weakened them to the point where some lay in the sand at each temporary halt. Many of the troopers were similarly worn out. Some slept in the saddle and relied on their steeds to lead them to their camp.

At about midnight at Romani and Etmaler, the horses had just enough strength to bolt for the troughs to consume the brackish water there. The men, against orders, joined their mounts in swallowing the unhealthy liquid.

For some, it was either that or severe cases of dehydration, or worse.

A Tragedy Inscribed in Sand

In the desert we have written our names.

Motto of the Desert Mounted Corps

The Turks had been pushed west of Katia, but their force, down to under 20,000, was still of concern. The War Office in London had been bellowing for a complete victory, which put pressure on Murray to make demands on the Light Horse and infantry. But this was where command from a distance was at a disadvantage. Chauvel and the other more sensible leaders in the field could not be bullied so easily, especially when they knew the real condition of their men and horses, and their chances against a well-assessed enemy.

He rested most of his force on 6 August and the next day sent Chaytor and his New Zealand brigade to rattle the Turks at Oghratina, where the yeomanry had been massacred four months earlier. Antill, now unpopular with Chauvel, was ordered with more precision than normal to help out by turning the left flank of the Turkish resistance, just five kilometres from the coast. The mission was to push them so far west that they would give up and retire the 80 kilometres to El Arish. But the two strong brigades could not persuade their opponents to go that far.

Murray was still being hectored from London about a more decisive victory than at Romani as if it were being played out on a village green in Kent. He communicated the urging to General Lawrence, although they were still not talking directly to each other. Lawrence in turn told Chauvel that this rearguard Turkish force should be broken and its guns captured. Then the rest of the force still had to be pursued. The burden would fall on the Light Horse. It was clear that the infantry divisions could not march that far.

Next morning, 8 August, the Turks were found to have abandoned Oghratina. The Light Horse forward patrols discovered them on the track to El Arish, dug in east of the well at Bir el Abd, 34 kilometres from Romani. Ronnie MacDonald and two other troopers were assigned to lead an advance guard regiment for Chauvel's main force to the new enemy stronghold. He wrote a rushed letter to Rania, aware now that the conflict could go on for some time and that he might not be able to communicate with her for weeks.

'Good bye till then my dear little girl,' he wrote.

The troopers entered a valley. A contingent of Turks, hidden on the crest of high sand dunes, waited in ambush. Snipers opened fire on the three troopers. MacDonald and the other two were shot in the head and killed instantly. Machine-gun fire followed and pushed the regiment back.

There was no chance for the bodies of the dead troopers to be recovered. They lay in the heat and sand, their mates keen to retrieve them. Trooper George Edwards, a close friend of MacDonald, was determined to return. The Bedouins, who prowled the edge of battlefields, stripped soldiers of every item on their bodies. In the desert, it seemed nothing was wasted, and there was no respect for dead foreigners.

At 2 p.m. on 8 August, Chauvel joined his force (without 1st and 2nd Brigades)—the New Zealand Mounteds, 3rd Brigade and yeomanry—and took overall command, this time setting up a base at Oghratina. He was feeling all of his 51 years. He had not changed his clothes for days and had slept when he could on the sand like all his weary troopers. In the evening, he prepared his battle order for the next day's attack on Bir el Abd. He managed to scribble a letter to Sibyl:

'We have fought and won a great battle [Romani] and my men have put up a performance which is beyond all precedent . . . Our losses have been heavy, of course, but absolutely nothing in comparison with what has been achieved . . .'[1]

He ordered his force to attack on the 9th but found the Turks at Bir el Abd even better set up than they were at Katia with a powerful artillery support. They had 6,000 soldiers opposed to Chauvel's 3,000. The Light Horse attack was soon blunted. The Turks then counterattacked. The Ayrshire Battery was targeted with the aim of destroying their horses, which would impede their movement. Thirty-nine horses were killed. The Turks wanted the guns. The New Zealand machine-gunners took the brunt of this assault, at one point firing at the advancing enemy from just 100 metres.

Chauvel ignored General Lawrence's order that he bivouac close to Bir el Abd and retreated to Oghratina in the same orderly manner achieved at Romani. It was a slow pull-back through country featuring countless sand hills of uniform height and scrubby patches, both of which were ideal for hiding and launching an ambush.

The Anzacs wished to take every single one of the 210 wounded away from the battlefield, leaving as few troopers as possible to the Turks. They and their Bedouin partners were brutal with prisoners, and every trooper feared capture. Many would prefer to fight to the death rather than be taken and starved or tortured. Other wounded made every effort to escape. Two men with bad leg breaks managed to haul themselves onto horses and gallop away 10 kilometres. One survived; the other died from multiple wounds.

At dawn on the 10th, George Edwards at some risk led a small burying party out to find their three fallen comrades. They prepared deep graves, aware that the Bedouins had been known to dig up the dead and take whatever was on them, particularly boots, which were coveted items. Edwards put on each grave a small wooden cross bearing the names.[2] These sites were a poignant reminder of the Desert Mounted Corps' insignia:

'In the desert we have written our names.'

Rania was devastated at the news of Ronnie MacDonald's demise. She wrote to Edwards asking for any reminder possible of her lost lover. She was further saddened by the paucity of items, particularly photographs. Edwards had been in Ronnie's section over nearly two years sharing living quarters from Egyptian camps to desert listening posts with him and two others. He sent Rania his spurs and badges. But she wanted something more personal; something of his essence, if it were possible. None of his friends had shots of Ronnie. Edwards had taken some, which had been sent back to his parents in Australia. He found a photo of Rania that Ronnie kept close in the breast pocket of his jacket. It was touching because it had been literally close to his heart. It was a fragment important to him, but not of him.

Edwards took a shot of Ronnie's grave, a rough plot in a remote valley of shifting sand dunes. This was more tangible to Rania. She found that picture poignant and something for her to cling to; the last piece of the jigsaw in a short, unfulfilled life, and relationship.

On 9 August, Chauvel's brigades had another fling at the enemy, but it held firm. At night Royston replaced Antill as commander of 3rd Brigade. Antill had been summoned to the Western Front in France for command there. Chauvel made no effort to retain him, and may well have been happy to see him go. The troopers of 3rd Brigade, who had suffered often under Antill's callous ways, were lifted by the change.

After 10 August the rearguard Turks did not wish to continue the fight. At night, they slipped back further along the track to El Arish following the main retreating body, this time holding up at Salmana. Chauvel sent the Light Horse after them again for more skirmishes. On the night of 12 August, the Turks decamped once more, this time all the way to El Arish.

The British may not have had their sought-after crushing victory, but the Turks had been cleared by Chauvel and his Light Horse Division from the oases close to the Suez Canal. There was satisfaction for the commander in knowing that his Anzac force had taken the brunt of the fighting. The British 52nd Division was shelled at Romani, with 195 casualties. The 42nd engaged little. There had been a cost to the Anzacs: 203 killed and 801 wounded. Yet it was light given the achievement of pushing back an original Turkish force of 25,000.

Chauvel and his troopers were more than pleased that they had clawed something back from the enemy that had held sway at Gallipoli. His fine leadership had made up for the distant confusion of his superiors.

Murray had been quite happy to give up any of the infantry for the Western Front, but after Romani he would use all his experience to hold onto the Anzacs. Birdwood, who knew how tough the Light Horse were on Gallipoli, now wanted them sent to France to fight as infantry. But Murray would have none of it. He wrote to the War Office saying:

'These Anzac troops are the keystone of the defence of Egypt.'[3]

This was fully understood by the War Office since Romani, but public recognition in the British press was welcomed. English correspondent W. T. Massey wrote in the London *Observer*:

'The brunt of the fighting was borne by the Anzac mounted troops. These magnificent horsemen had been anxious to follow their [Australian] Comrades to France, but they were retained in Egypt because they are ideal soldiery for work in front of our defences. And they acquitted themselves magnificently.'[4]

Such comment lifted the profile of the Light Horse and Chauvel's reputation.

The Anglo-Arabian

The Arab Revolt had stalled by September 1916. Hussein did not seem to know how to proceed. Nor did he have capacity to gain wide Arab support. The Arab Bureau and T.E. Lawrence had to shore up the organised challenge to the Ottoman Empire.

Despite the apparent lack of progress, Lawrence was inspired by Chauvel's success at Romani and the smashing rebuff to the Turks in the Sinai. It provided some hope that the British could remove the Turks from Palestine, then Syria. Meanwhile, to further stimulate the Bedouin forces in the Hejaz, he decided he should attach himself in some way to the force most potent and useful to the British in Hussein's family. Hussein himself was too stubborn and inflexible. His eldest son, the thin, doleful and consumptive Ali, 37, was too pious and dominated by Hussein. His poor physical condition left him edgy and easily fatigued. It gave gravitas and sadness to his large brown eyes, hooked nose and downturned mouth. Yet he kept a certain mannered dignity, which went with his intellect, interest in the law and an over-keen dwelling on religion.

Zeid, the fourth son and youngest, was only 19. Lawrence found him reticent with the flippancy of youth, and without the desire for the revolt. He had a Turkish mother and had been brought up in a harem, which limited his sensitivity to an Arab resurgence at the expense of the Turks.[1]

The second son Abdullah, who ruled the tribes of Arabia's interior, was more than capable, but he did not like or trust Lawrence. That left the third son, Feisal, who was suitable. The 31-year-old leader of the more worldly coastal tribes liked 'El Laurens', as he called him. The feeling was mutual.

Lawrence was fond of the tall, elegant Feisal. He even liked the way he walked and his regal bearing. The Prince's short fuse and occasional petulance was overridden by his apparent charm. His followers looked up to him despite his over-confident appearance, according to Lawrence, because at times he showed weakness.[2]

Lawrence believed he would be easy to manipulate if the wily Englishman reeled him in. Feisal loved to use his wealth for decorous objects, such as a bejewelled belt and dagger. The latter was gaudy and sparkling but hardly functional. It was all show, which said something about Feisal's character. Whereas Abdullah seemed to see through Lawrence, Feisal needed help and direction.

Lawrence noted his drive and ambition. Feisal was frustrated, at times angered, by the fact that he was the third son of a ruling Arab family. It meant he would inherit very little, despite his father's dream about controlling all Arab principalities (except in Lebanon). Once Hussein died, Feisal felt he would be beholden to his two elder brothers. The way around this was to take a kingdom and throne for himself. This was his promised land, dangled tantalisingly by the British. They were putting forward self-fulfilling prophecies about Arab nationalism, which were making even sharp individuals such as Feisal believe it was now a possibility.

Lawrence went to work on the relationship, showing great respect. He responded to Feisal's demands for gold, cash and weapons, and lent a sympathetic ear to his problems.

Lawrence began to wear Arab dress, which he believed made him more credible with Feisal and his tribesmen. He took on the mannerisms, ways and culture of a nomadic Arab, which he had studied at first hand for six years. He rode a camel with the panache and ease he showed in riding a motorbike on the back roads of England's rural counties. Lawrence sat cross-legged in true Arab fashion. He knew the etiquette of taking a meal with his hands. More importantly, he knew which foods he could cope with and which made him nauseous. Long before Feisal, he was an assimilated espionage agent, who adapted to a difficult job, with its intrigue and secretiveness in a culture in which he could relax more than in London or even Cairo. He claimed that homosexuality was not an issue in the nomadic environment

Harry Chauvel in August 1916

Brigadier-General Cox (*left*) and Major-General Chaytor

General Sir Edmund Allenby

Mustafa Kemal (*fourth from left*), the crucial Turkish commander at Gallipoli

Turks attacking Quinn's Post

Getting the mail from Suvla to Anzac Cove (under fire)

Troopers in Palestine after the weather has come in, and horses
were the only form of transport that could move

A German plane brought down in the Sinai Desert

Turkish troops manning the trenches

Harry Chauvel (*centre, with plumed hat*) before Beersheba,
with some of his top commanders

Harry Chauvel (*left*) with 'Galloping Jack' Royston,
El Arish, January 1917

Romani, looking north

Some Light Horsemen taking in the sights

Watering the horses

Trooper Cooper of the 8th Light Horse
– later in the Beersheba charge

where men wandered the desert sometimes for years without female company. This implied that he could indulge inclinations, latent or otherwise. It also implied that homosexuality was accepted by the Bedouins (a claim disputed by some historians, including Arabs).

'If you can wear Arab kit when with the tribes you will acquire their trust and intimacy to a degree impossible in uniform,' he said in his *Twenty-Seven Articles*, a manual written for political officers on how to handle the Arabs, 'it is however dangerous and difficult . . . You will be an actor in a foreign theatre, playing a part day and night, and for a dangerous stake. Complete success, which is when the Arabs forget your strangeness and speak naturally before you, counting you one of themselves, is perhaps only attainable in character.'

He would have been thinking of Feisal when he added:

'If you wear Arab things wear the best. Clothes are significant among the tribes . . .' Lawrence broadened the concept of 'wear', when he said:

'If you wear Arab things at all, go all the way. Leave your English friends and customs on the coast, and fall back on Arab habits entirely.'

He reasoned that once Europeans had the level playing field of culture and ways, they would beat the Arabs at their own game, 'for we have stronger motives for our actions, and put more heart into them than they'.

Despite the need to pull on thespian skills, Lawrence was still a spy living a lie. He noted in his elongated style how tough that was:

'. . . the strain of living and thinking in a foreign and half-understood language, the savage food, the strange clothes, and still stranger ways, with the complete loss of privacy and quiet, and the impossibility of ever relaxing your watchful imitation of the others for months on end, *provides such an added stress* to the ordinary difficulties of dealing with the Bedouins, the climate, and the Turks, *that this road should not be chosen without serious thought.*'[3]

Applying the secret agent's mentally arduous cloak of

subterfuge and deceit, he made himself a trusted adviser to Feisal and consultant extraordinaire. Lawrence influenced him to believe that he (Feisal) could use him to further Arab independence in the Middle East.

No spy in the British experience to that point had contrived a situation so well and so theatrically for the empire.

After the battles of Romani, Katia and Bir el Abd, there was a few weeks' lull except for the need of the Light Horse to 'screen' (patrol) in front of infantry troops moving on the road to El Arish. Chauvel decided on some house-cleaning. Concerned that the troopers, idle and on leave, might create more chaos in Cairo's red-light district, he encouraged Alice Chisholm, a 60-year-old Australian, to set up the Empire Soldiers Club, at Port Said, at the canal junction with the Mediterranean. This Goulburn-born daughter of a pastoralist married in 1877 and had five children. When one of them (son Bertram) was wounded at Gallipoli, Alice went to Egypt in July 1915 to be near him. She was shocked by the lack of amenities for soldiers and decided to set up a canteen for them near Heliopolis. This worked so well that she happily took up Chauvel's offer.

Rania MacPhillamy, who had known Alice in a Cairo hospital, joined her. Rania had been encouraged by her family and friends to return home after Ronnie's death. But her sister reminded her of bland country life and suggested she stay and do her good work on behalf of the troops. The link with Chisholm seemed to be the right move.

The women offered the resting warriors an atmosphere that was something akin to home, and among Australians. It was appreciated. Soon many preferred it to Cairo. Rania had found work, less stressful and demanding than at the hospitals, but with importance for the weary troopers.

The Turks had left one garrison of 2,200 soldiers 70 kilometres east of Romani at Bir el Mazar, the only place with a good

water well between Salmani and El Arish. They had four mountain guns, some anti-aircraft weapons and 10 machine-guns.
General Lawrence ordered Chauvel to move out his division of
four Light Horse brigades, and artillery support. They would be
backed by three companies of the Camel Corps dominated by
former Australian Light Horse Infantry and under the command
of English Major C. L. Smith, a VC winner.

There was almost no water en route. Seventy camels were
assigned to carry 20 gallons each to a point east of Salmani,
which would be there for the return of the Light Horse after the
battle.

Chauvel's force was to advance on this last Turkish bastion
before El Arish. The contingent typified the desert missions. A
big, sometimes huge, transport system was needed as well as a
suitable water supply. The camels could carry more than the
horses, but the walers were doing far better than expected in the
desert, and always covered territory faster, except in heavy sand.
There was no doubting the camel's endurance. It could go six
days without water. Yet earlier in the year the horse's capacities
in many facets of operations were established. The waler had
surprised the veterinarians by its capacity to go long distances
without water, although five gallons a day was 'ideal'.

The camel's other advantage was its carrying capacity. On
average it could carry loads of about 160 kilograms, which
was about 30 kilograms more than the average horse. It was
easy for a camel to load a man, five days' water and rations,
along with all the other paraphernalia. This included a generous amount of blankets and kit. The camel breed favoured by
the Australians was the big, white variety, plentiful between
the lower Sudan and the Indian Ocean. It was tough, and fast
when unburdened.

The camels smelt and could be cantankerous. But ever since
the Australian Camel Corps was formed in 1916 to help fight a
revolt by the Senussi Arabs in Egypt's Western Desert, the Australians adjusted to their moods and irritations, usually with
good humour. A disadvantage closer to battle was that they
could not be brought near to the action rapidly, or kept near

for a speedy escape if the enemy was found to be too strong, as experienced at Bir el Abd. Once a camel trooper dismounted he was then just an infantryman.

The Camel Column brought up the rear behind the Light Horse advance guard. Always in the background now 40 kilometres away, but becoming less, was Murray's railway being constructed along with a water pipeline.

Chauvel was ordered to raid Bir el Mazar, but bizarrely was directed not to become engaged in a strong effort to take the place. General Lawrence seemed to be hoping that Chauvel might just take it quickly, but if not he was to pull back. This made the Light Horse force disgruntled. After Romani and Katia they had wanted to take the Turks on again but this time with the numbers in the Light Horse's favour. The sluggish well-spread force, retarded by the Camel Column, was spotted by a German plane. It strafed them and flew off to report the advancing force to the Turks at the targeted oasis. Chauvel's night approach on 16 September would be no surprise. On top of that, the artillery became lost and did not show up. Chauvel always thought with cool logic. Despite his mounted riflemen's desire to engage the enemy, he decided that if a raid could not be successful quickly he would pull out of the operation.

The Turks were not about to capitulate after the first foray aimed at them. They stood firm. Chauvel did not want any casualties if he would have to pull out of a protracted battle anyway, which was what the Turks were promising. What was the point, he wondered, in seeing his men killed and wounded if there was to be no gain, no tangible reward for effort?

After a few hours, he aborted the mission. The light horsemen were not happy. But Chauvel, as commander, did not have to explain his decisions to the rank and file. Only his staff officers knew his basic thinking.

His move was vindicated on 18 September when the entire Turkish force at Bir el Mazar took off in the night and hastened back to El Arish. They believed that Chauvel's corps would return for a do-or-die attack, for which the Anzacs were now well known to the Turks.

Their decamping of the scene vindicated Chauvel's application of common sense. If he decided to strike hard, he would follow through. Yet if there were no gains to be had, he was not a 'gung-ho' type like, say, Godley or Antill, who wanted combat for combat's sake. He was concerned for his charges, even if they were less inclined to be worried about safety for themselves.

Another reason for not rushing into unnecessary battle was his concern for the horses. They had not been fed properly. Feed for some reason, possibly corruption, was not reaching the Romani base, and there were always concerns with lack of water. Some regiments would have access; others, due to operational involvement, might miss out, meaning horses would go without water and food for more than a day. The combination of nutritional shortfalls was taking its toll on the horses, especially those in the 1st and 2nd Brigades, which had seen the most action and covered the greater distances. There was also the problem of weight on the horses' backs. They had to be rested as much as possible. As the campaign into the desert progressed, the troopers had loaded up more and more. In addition to the basic accoutrements, saddle wallets were strapped over the front of the saddle, with a sausage bag of grain across them. There was an extra water bottle and nosebag attached to the saddle as the troopers anticipated longer rides. Greater distances meant the need for extra ammunition carried in a second bandolier slung across the horse's neck. A leather muzzle had been added to stop the waler being tempted to eat sand. Some troopers now preferred chains to the previous tethering head rope. Long sticks ('bivvy poles') were added to help put up makeshift shelters.

The saddles had become so heavy with attached gear that it often took two men to lift them.

One trooper wrote home saying that his mount looked like a Christmas tree. Once some horses were loaded up, it was often quite difficult to see where a man might fit. It was not unusual for bigger troopers to have trouble mounting. Yet the mighty walers did not complain, and therefore the troopers felt the load was manageable, which was what counted to them rather than a trim appearance.

But, along with the occasional hold-up with water and food on the longer trips, there were some problems. This was apparent on the ride back from Mazar. Chauvel came across a trooper whose horse had collapsed and seemed too weak to get up. The trooper had emptied his water bottle into a canvas bucket and was trying to entice the animal to drink. It had not had liquid for more than 35 hours. Chauvel tipped his own water into the bucket, which caused his staffers travelling with him to do the same. The waler at first did not respond, but after much cajoling it consumed the lot and struggled to its feet.

This caused Chauvel to make a decision. His 1st and 2nd Brigades would be retired to the canal until the troopers and horses were fully restored.

28

Time Out

During a meeting with Feisal on 23 October 1916, Lawrence was asked how he liked his camp in the Hejaz's Wadi Safra. He responded that he thought it was good, adding:

'But it is far from Damascus.'

It was an unsubtle reminder that the Arab capture of the Hejaz was just the beginning of the Arab Revolt. Damascus, the Syrian capital, was 500 kilometres north. Lawrence was emphasising that Syria should be the ultimate target. It was the state where the Arabs could make their first great national stand. What Lawrence did not tell Feisal was that if Damascus was not under Arab control by the end of the war, the nationalist Arab cause would be lost. More worrying for Lawrence was the possibility that if the Arabs did not have some force, even a token one, into Damascus first, then the French might be given control. (He was not yet aware of the secret Sykes–Picot agreement but he did know that something like it would emerge.) He knew the real force that was necessary to facilitate this (dominated by Chauvel's mobile Light Horse) was recuperating in the Sinai and Cairo, perhaps for the rest of 1916. Without it driving through Palestine and Syria, the Arab effort would be only window-dressing; a futile distraction for the enemy that would go nowhere and never challenge the might of the Young Turks now running the Ottoman Empire.

Lawrence was already forming a crude plan in private to install Hussein as leader in Syria. He would keep urging for a real British military push through Palestine, which he would monitor closely. If it came off, and if he had roused the Arabs sufficiently, he could deliver them control of Damascus just ahead of the British force. It would be a case of first in, best dressed—in flowing Arab robes, he hoped. At that point it might just be possible to keep the French out, which was always Lawrence's prime aim. Then some form of Arab government, either a puppet or something else under British control, could even be the outcome.

Yet he knew there were many hurdles to overcome before his dreams were to be fulfilled.

General Murray took his command from Ismailia back to Cairo and appointed Major General Sir Charles Dobell to control the forces in the Sinai and along the canal. He also requested a corps commander for the advanced troops, overlooking Chauvel. Murray's 'command by remote control' had caused him to underestimate Chauvel's proven abilities, and also to undervalue the performance of his troops. More attention to the battles from a closer position may have given him a better comprehension of the Anzacs. But he was now distancing himself further by retreating to the comforts of Cairo and club life there. He had made the excuse, legitimate enough, that the political problems of his command demanded the relocation. Yet he demonstrated by this move that he regarded the politics of command as more important than the operations.

On 25 October, Chauvel took off on a well-earned leave, with a stop at Marseilles, then a train to Paris and on to the Somme to rendezvous with Birdwood. The meeting was cordial. Birdwood was pleased with his successes in the Sinai but did not seem to have been fully or accurately briefed on them. 'Birdie' was his ebullient self. Chauvel was uncomfortable with Murray and General Lawrence running the campaign from so far, but said nothing about it. He had learnt from Gallipoli that it was right to put his case, but not let it spill into complaint. The hierarchy of the British command was sensitive to negative comment, especially from dominion leaders.

After four days in France, Chauvel left Paris for London. On the train trip, he was able to focus on seeing his beautiful young wife and children for the first time in two years. He feared the life he had been living on the front line at Gallipoli and the Sinai had etched itself into his appearance, including a receding hairline brought on by the pleurisy.

He had warned Sibyl to expect a much older, thinner and weather-beaten man. But she did not care. She had matured, if not in looks in her outlook, bringing up the three children on her own and being nagged by the perpetual worry that she would never see her husband again. Sibyl had been his confidante on paper, and knew the trials he had been under both physical and mental on various fronts. His courage as a leader made her both proud and fearful, especially as almost daily she learned that someone she knew had been killed or wounded.

The reunion refreshed both of them. Chauvel got to know his children again, especially young, bright Elyne, now three. The boys, Ian and Edward, were at school. Chauvel marvelled at their growth, and it made his heart sink to think about what he had missed. He would have appeared like an old man to them, and they would have been in awe of him. But his natural warmth and manner soon restored lost bonds.

T. E. Lawrence went first to Khartoum on his return journey to Cairo and consulted the influential Sir Reginald Wingate, the governor-general of the Anglo-Egyptian Sudan, who controlled the 70,000-strong, locally raised Egyptian army. Lawrence sought support for the Arabs being given more advisers, equipment and supplies. Wingate preferred landing a British force in the Hejaz if the current military deadlock between the Arabs and the Turks in that region could not be broken. Lawrence knew the Arabs would dislike this form of intervention, and once more he was certain it would lead to the French sending in troops as well.

Back in Cairo in November, he summarised the situation in the Hejaz for his superiors at the bureau and in the military, pointing out that Feisal's roughly 3,000-strong tribal army for five months had held up the Turks' advance to Medina and Rabegh.

'Rabegh,' (on the Red Sea between Yenbo and Jeddah, 320 kilometres south-west of Medina) he wrote, 'is not or ever has been, defensible with Arab forces.'

The Turks had not arrived there, he added, because Feisal's hill tribes had stopped them. But if the Turks got past they could not be prevented from a march 'until near Mecca itself' unless the Arabs were given increased arms. He emphasised the need for weapons such as three batteries of mountain guns they had been promised several months ago. Lawrence urged that if these weapons were delivered they would be able to hold up the Turks indefinitely.

'Their morale is excellent,' he added, 'their tactics and manner of fighting admirably adapted to the very difficult [mountainous] country they are defending.'

Lawrence claimed their leaders realised that provoking a 'serious issue' (that is, sending in foreign troops, especially white, non-Muslims) in the Hejaz now would lose the local war.

Instead he wanted the current guerilla-style battle to continue. It would lead, he suggested, to the Turks being worn down. They would be forced back 'on a passive defence of Medina and its railway communications'.[1]

This was a modification from his earlier views, and more subtle. He now feared that the 25,000 Turks at Medina might break out and recapture Mecca. There was little chance the Arabs could defeat the enemy at Medina, where it had a strong garrison. If any attempt was made to take it, there was a backup of another 25,000 Turkish soldiers guarding points along the railway, and they would be drawn into a battle, which would still confine the Arabs to the Hejaz.

If the Turks took Mecca again, it would mean the collapse of the revolt. The enemy would use it as a base for Turkish-inspired Pan-Islamic movements against Egypt and the Sudan. There was another worry that the Turks would use their railway line to move the garrison to reinforce the Turkish main army in Palestine and Syria. An Arab Bureau intelligence report from radio intercepts said that the Medina commander had received such orders. But the Turkish minister of war, Enver Pasha, had countermanded it.

It all went to Lawrence's argument that the Turks should be bottled up at Medina. Yet they should not be threatened to the point where they would break out.

'Our ideal is to keep his railway working,' Lawrence told General Murray, 'but only just with the maximum of loss and discomfit.'

He suggested the line should be blown up here and there. This would keep soldiers and repair gangs active. These numbers then could not be used elsewhere, such as in Gaza.

Lawrence had been studying ideas on guerilla warfare.

'Most wars were wars of contact,' he said, 'Ours should be a war of detachment.'

The goal was to contain the enemy by the silent threat of a 'vast, unknown desert, not disclosing ourselves till we attacked'.

The Arabs liked the concept. They preferred hit-and-run raids to face-to-face battle. They knew they would lose out to the better equipped and trained Turks in man-to-man fighting. But the Turks were also less mobile in pursuit. Lawrence realised that the Bedouin tribesmen did not like to sustain casualties. Family and tribal relationships were strong. Losses meant a weakening of their numerical strengths. 'Smash and dash' and looting for good measure was their way.

Lawrence was pleased to learn that General Murray agreed with him and happy not to be asked to commit British troops elsewhere. He was stretched anyway. He endorsed Lawrence's guerilla tactics. Murray was under at times confused orders from the War Office. He had originally been told to avoid any major sweep east towards Palestine. Yet after Romani he was urged to push his troops for even more victories. The thought of part of his army slipping down the canal to fight the Turks in the Hejaz seemed a stretch too far. The matter was settled when Hussein refused to accept British troops anyway. Instead, after Lawrence's urging, the British military began sending more instructors and supplies.

By mid-November, Hussein's forces were receiving more gold. Massive amounts of rice, flour, coffee and barley had arrived. They had nearly 4,000 rifles, 32 Maxim machine-guns, an Egyptian battery of field artillery, four 5-inch howitzers, eight 10-pounder guns, and 18 million rounds of small arms ammunition. The Hejaz reverberated to the sound of small arms being tested and played with, not always to the joy of the British instructors moving into the region.

Hussein, Feisal, British instructors and advisers, and Lawrence combined to increase the size of the Arab force and improve the quality of its leadership. But it was still a little rag-tag. Desertions of officers and soldiers from the Turkish army provided sources, but they were not substantial or comforting. More would come from the Arab Legion. This was made up of former prisoners of war in Egypt and India, and they were all volunteers.

More instructors and advisers began to arrive in the desert. But it was still Lawrence himself who was dominant in guiding the revolt's leaders. He returned to the Hejaz after only a few days back in Cairo.

He was fast becoming indispensable to the cause.

The 39-day break gave Chauvel time to restore his strength and he was in a good frame of mind when he boarded a train in Paris on 3 December for the return trip to Marseilles. He had bought the French edition of the London *Daily Mail* and he settled down to read it on the train. It carried Murray's dispatch concerning the Romani battle, now four months old. This spoiled Chauvel's relaxed demeanour. There was hardly a word about him or his troopers. He was not mentioned in the lengthy list of honours. Furious, he let off steam as he had done for two years by penning a letter to Sibyl.

'I cannot understand why the old man [Murray] cannot do justice to those to whom he owed so much. The whole thing is so absolutely inconsistent with what he had already cabled . . . I am afraid my men will be very angry when they see it [the *Daily Mail* report].'[2]

The writing was cathartic. But he remained unhappy with this insult to him and his men, both living and killed in action.

29

On Firmer Ground

Light horse must have all the features of fighting infantry, cavalry and the raider. They must have both terrifying force and capacity to fade like ghosts.

General Sir Harry Chauvel

It was a seminal moment for the Light Horse riflemen. After most of 1916 enduring the heat, flies, storms and soft sand, they stepped off the dunes onto the expansive, flat, firm ground that flanked the Wadi El Arish on the extreme fringe of southern Palestine. The date was 20 December and it was at night, although the bright stars made the way clear. A muted murmur ran through the advance 1st Brigade of the Anzac Mounted Division the moment the horses' hooves struck solid earth. The Sinai was behind them, and although they would return there to bases and on other missions, that part of the campaign, they all hoped and expected, was in the past.

Palestine was small, about the size of Wales. Yet it offered the varieties of soil and climate of a continent. It was a country of mountain and plain; of desert and pleasant valleys. It had lakes and seaboard. It had barren hills and desolate areas yet also broad stretches of deep, fertile soil. The 'invaders' were sensitive to the water problem after the trials in Sinai. The rainfall equalled that of London, and, if captured, was enough to sustain armies. But Chauvel was aware it was not a question of quantity in this first move into South Palestine. It was a matter of storage, of pumping and distribution.

He had in mind taking the region one battle at a time. For the moment, thoughts were on acquiring El Arish. As the grand column approached the Mediterranean town, the concern about water came into focus. Weeks earlier, night patrols of engineers had put down bores on the dry Wadi bed, but could not find any of the precious liquid. Chauvel had no choice but to secure the southern approach to El Arish, an ancient village of mud-brick houses, with three kilometres of palms between it and the sea.

The pressure eased with confirmation of rumours that the Turks had fled the town. Yet Chauvel, the level-headed commander, treated it as if it might be garrisoned still.

When dawn broke, the entire force ringed the town, a magnificent, inspiring sight for every trooper. There was no reaction in the town but for the first stirrings of people going about their daily business. Some stopped to stare at the motionless ring of troopers on their mounts. A 1st Brigade staff captain led a small party into the village. They were embraced by the townspeople. Elders in multi-coloured robes; children milling; women swarming and reaching up with food offerings; men kissing their boots and stirrups. All the villagers looked into the faces of these languid, slouch-hatted foreigners, with their unshaven, rough-hewn features, and easy manner in the saddle. Were they brutal as they Turks had said? Were they the alleged savages that everyone in the region had heard stories about?

'Can you tell me where the nearest pub is, cobber?' one of the horsemen said to a confused elder. The look on his face made the troopers grin. The villagers relaxed. They laughed and encircled the Anzacs.[1]

They decided they were very different 'conquerors' from the Turks. The chief sheikh then formally surrendered El Arish. He handed over one unfortunate Turk and a few alleged espionage agents as the Australians prepared to take over the town.

The beach became a popular destination. Two 1st Brigade troopers, both Gallipoli veterans, had just finished a swim when they noticed a mine near the water's edge. One of them bent to examine it.

Both men were blown to pieces.

Chauvel did not know where the Turks had gone, but a few hours after the occupation learned from air reconnaissance that a major part of their force was fortifying at the village of Magdhaba, 40 kilometres south-south-east of El Arish. He responded by pushing out patrols towards the new target, and other routes where the Turks may have also bunkered down.

The next day, Old Etonian Sir Philip Chetwode, 7th Baronet, who had taken over General Lawrence's job of commander of the advanced Light Horse and the 'Desert Column' camel force, dropped in to El Arish. His arrival befitted the cliché of an English baronet and Old Etonian of the era. The spruce 48-year-old had a certain careless style from his stiff-backed method of riding to his ivory cigarette holder. His nasal drawl added to the upper class image but belied his character, which was far from snobbish. He kept to Edwardian standards but was popular with the troops.

There would be no moving rough over the desert if he could arrive in comfort by ship from Port Said. The small fleet of grey boats that accompanied him, more than Chetwode himself, was a welcome sight for the troopers. They brought mail, supplies and food rations. The mine-sweepers began doing their job, just too late for the two Gallipoli veterans who had been killed on the beach.

In the retreat from Mons on the Western Front in Europe, Chetwode had commanded the 5th Cavalry Brigade under General Allenby. His main claim to military capability had occurred in the Boer War. He was a popular personality who had met Chauvel in South Africa. They picked up where they had left off. Chetwode decided on an immediate operation to pursue the Turks at Magdhaba.

Soon after arriving, he and two of his orderlies were riding past a section of troopers on the edge of the palm area. The Australians had just begun eating their well-earned rations of the usual—bully beef and biscuits—and made no effort to salute him or his orderlies. One of the orderlies broke away and rode up to the troopers.

'You are supposed to salute your superiors!' he said, with a lisp.

The Australians looked at each other and burst out laughing. The orderly went red, but before he could admonish them, one of the troopers asked:

'Where did you learn to ride like that, mate?'

'What do you mean?'

'Nothing; just that you and your horse look like you've got broomsticks up your bums.'

The orderly rode off in disgust with scoffing laughter ringing in his ears. He complained to Chetwode. He in turn wrote a letter to Chauvel.

'Not only do your men fail to salute me when I ride through your camps,' he said, 'but they laugh aloud at my orderlies.'

Chetwode also criticised the slovenly appearance of the Anzacs. Chauvel pointed out that they had had a tough night's ride and at the time were about to go out again.[2]

Soon after his arrival, a trooper arrived at Chetwode's tent, telling an orderly he wished to trade a bottle of whisky. He was sent away. Chetwode added the incident in the letter to Chauvel.

'Nothing wrong with the idea,' Chauvel wrote to his wife, '[The trooper] just picked the wrong tent.'[3]

He had heard variations of the same complaints before on Gallipoli, in Cairo and in the desert. On first encounter with troopers, this kind of insubordination and rudeness was often the first, sometimes lasting impression given to British commanders, brought up in the disciplined world of military life, where the rank and file were subservient and were meant to display it at all times. They had no concept of the Australian way or life or mores and values. Most British commanders did not have the flexibility to allow for the difference between regular soldiers, conscripts or the Anzacs, who were all volunteers.

Chauvel wrote the 'insulted' Chetwode a sympathetic letter but conceded nothing. Like all British commanders, he would witness, or learn of the troopers' deeds as fighting men. Then, depending on his character, he would either keep his prejudices, or he would relax his fixations, but never completely. The Anzac insouciance in British officers' eyes had more to do with different cultures and class systems than anything else. The British upper classes were never about to put the lower ranks and classes on an equal footing. The Australians lived in a far more egalitarian society where, in theory, and often in practice, people in all walks of life advanced on merit. Under no circumstances could British NCOs, for instance, become officers.

Monash, in particular, but Chauvel too, supported such promotions.

*

The column began at night after a delay caused by entanglement of camels and incoming infantry brigades. The mission was to reach Magdhaba before dawn on 23 December 1916 moving on a flat plain with the El Arish valley and Sinai sand hills on the right and on the left some distance away but in view, the fertile, far more inviting country of southern Palestine. The troopers were shrouded in fine dust from the dry plain as they bounced along, their horses enjoying the firmer ground and sometimes tripping from the renewed experience.

The troopers would have loved a smoke en route, or even a whispered chat, but light and noise travelled far in the desert night and were forbidden. They could not stop the sound from the horses, as the hooves beat a ghostly rhythm through the cold night air in their 50-minute ride every hour followed by a 10-minute break. There was also the hollow clunk and jingle of the 'Christmas billies' distributed to them by representatives of the Australian Comforts Fund before the march. They contained Christmas pudding, chocolate bars, tins of milk, biscuits and cakes. The troopers had tied the billies to their saddles to ensure extra food on top of their limited, monotonous rations.

The 10-minute breaks in each hour gave the freezing men a break from the saddle and freshened up their mounts.

Chauvel learnt at 1 a.m. that the water situation was precarious. Suitable wells had not been found. This limited the commander's scope and added urgency to any possible battle.

The forward 'screen' spotted huge fires at 4 a.m., which were at Magdhaba. Chauvel halted the advance on an open plain, ordered the men and horses to be fed, and then led a reconnaissance as dawn's first thin rays appeared.

The reason for the Turks' bonfires became apparent. It concealed their position and made Chauvel's decision-making tricky. He waited until action from planes from the Australian Flying Corps (AFC), including one flown by Ross Smith, the cheerful trooper who had impressed so much at the dangerous Quinn's Post and later Romani. They were under orders at 6.30 a.m. to fly low and bomb the Turkish positions they could spot through the haze. As the planes buzzed overhead and the bombs were rolled out, Chauvel and his staff, with much finger-pointing and lifting of binoculars, made notes of the positioning and the strong defensive fire from machine-gunners and riflemen. The airmen dropped messages about Turk locations and movements. The AFC pilots sometimes landed to take messages direct to Chauvel.

Enemy fortifications were now exposed.

Chauvel moved his headquarters to a high hill above the plain about four kilometres from Magdhaba, giving him a wonderful balcony view of battle proceedings, except for those of his 1st Brigade, commanded by Charles F. Cox. It was following up a report about Turks on the retreat in the south. His brigade had galloped into a strong enemy fortification thick with machine-guns. Cox had ordered his men to dismount 1,800 metres away and to continue the battle on foot.

The fast gallop caused many of the food billies to break loose, hurling them and their food contents on the approach to the proposed battlefield. Gradually Chauvel's forces encir-cled the embattled Turks with regiments of Anzac brigades and the artillery batteries under his personal control moving closer. A three-pronged dashing bayonet attack on two redoubts by Chaytor's New Zealanders, companies of the Camel Brigade and Cox's men from the 3rd Regiment met stiff resistance. But the yelling attacks were too much for the Turks as each part of the force tried to be first into the trenches of one redoubt.

They all stood up together and surrendered. It turned the engagement Chauvel's way. Yet even from his vantage point, he was unaware of the closeness to victory. It was approaching 3 p.m. He was thinking of pulling out. As ever, the problem was water supply. He consulted Chaytor, and Smith of the Camel Brigade, and then made moves to contact Chetwode, just as he (Chetwode) sent out orders to all his force:

'As enemy is still holding out and the horses must be watered, the action will be broken off. Each brigade will be responsible for its own protection during the withdrawal.'

Cox was handed the message just as his men, on foot and a

few hundred metres from enemy trenches, were about to attack a second or fortified position.

'Take that damn thing away!' Cox told the courier. 'And let me see it for the first time in half an hour.'[4]

The battle now had its own momentum. Even as this 'stop and withdraw' command was coming to Chauvel, the various parts of his force were close to victory.

To the south, the 10th Light Horse led by Major Robertson, eager as ever for contact with the Turks after its experiences at the Nek, was caught in a prolonged encounter. Breaking the shackles, Robertson led an old-fashioned charge straight at the Turks and by chance hit a column of 300 enemy soldiers retreating. They surrendered without any resistance. Continuing on, Robertson swung north and enveloped the enemy's right flank and advanced on the rear of their redoubts. It was an aggressive attack on an enemy that had a far bigger force. The swiftness of the swoop around ridges and grassy knolls gave good cover. The 10th was supported well by machine- and Lewis gunners, riding with them. The rapid encroachment meant dashing to cover, dismounting, engaging the enemy, mounting and rushing forward again.

On the left of the attacking line, 35 advancing light horsemen took on a trench of 400 with ferocity, galloping straight at them. Some horses and troopers were felled, but despite this, the others trampled through. To dismount when in the thick of the Turkish defence would have meant certain death. Instead the troopers crashed on. Lieutenant A. U. Martin felt his horse collapse under him when 30 metres clear of the trenches. He fell, hit his head and was dazed. He struggled to his feet as the Turks turned fire in his direction. His mate Lieutenant F. W. Cox, accompanied by Sergeant Spencer Gwynne, rode back. The fire intensified as they spotted Martin. Cox swooped close. He hauled Martin up behind him with Gwynne's assistance and then the two horses galloped clear.

The 8th Light Horse, another hardened set of Gallipoli veterans, which had taken on the hardest pocket of resistance, captured its

second Turkish entrenchment by 3.45 p.m., snaring 250 prisoners. At the same time irrepressible Royston, accompanied only
by his orderly, who by necessity would have to be a brave man,
rode up and down in the thick of the action urging on his 2nd
Brigade regiments. At one point, as the tide was turning, he rode
right up to a trench. Five Turkish rifles took aim. Royston raised
his cane and let go a blood-curdling roar in Zulu, the language
other than English that he knew. The Turks dropped their rifles
and raised their hands. They were not about to take on a huge
madman who yelled with such ferocity in a strange tongue.

At 4.05 p.m. all the enemy positions had capitulated. Chauvel's troops converged from the circle around the Turks' camp.
There was confusion as night fell, with the mingling of troopers,
cameleers and artillerymen. The competition to secure prisoners
brought some spirited exchanges between regiments. This was
the moment when the numbers were added up to see who had
'won' most; war became sport. A French military attaché, unable to make himself understood, was thrown in with the Turks
and counted by the accosting troopers' regiments as one more
enemy acquisition.

Casualties among Chauvel's forces were relatively light. He
lost only 22 men, which was the way he wanted it. He measured
success by the preservation of his men as much as the taking
of prisoners, the grim tally of enemy dead, and the winning of
'prizes', which at Magdhaba were large. Mountain guns, copious amounts of rifles and plentiful ammunition were taken. But
the impressive figure was 1,282 prisoners.

As military missions went, most observers could not imagine
a better campaign. In one day, the light horsemen and cameleers had ridden 80 kilometres to surprise and defeat an enemy.
Chetwode and his orderlies, fretting about minor disciplines
over saluting and dress code straight after an exercise, may have
noted a few pertinent factors. The controlled manner of their
night ride, the dash of the officers and the courageous yet sensible use of cover in approaching the Turkish positions would

impress the harshest of critics. But what should have dissolved all doubts about disciplines that mattered was the way these troopers fought. The cold efficiency of their use of Lewis and machine-guns, and the confident, brutal use of the bayonet would have to at least have engendered respect. It certainly created feelings beyond that in the minds of the enemy.

Chauvel and the Australians and New Zealanders would have had some measure of satisfaction as 1916 drew to a close. Those who had served on Gallipoli would have felt the scale was beginning to tip in their favour in encounters with the Turks, who had held sway the year before on the peninsula.

The troopers knew there was some way to go to exact the measure of revenge they felt was necessary to compensate in a small way for the loss of fallen mates. The eagerness of the Australians to attack the enemy was testimony to this.

On a broader scale, the Magdhaba annihilation would not receive much attention in the press in the UK and Australia, where all the focus was on the big battles in Europe, where, if anything, the German army just held sway. Yet Allied forces on the Western Front would have been very happy and surprised by such a big take of the opposition for so little loss in any battle.

While High Command's eyes had hardly diverted to events in the desert in the Middle East, increasingly during the year they read reports about victories there.

If nothing else, the British accomplishments in Sinai and now close to southern Palestine were becoming important from a point of view of prestige and propaganda when successes of any note in the war in Europe were few and far between.

PART THREE

1917

Armies are like plants, immobile, firm-rooted, nourished through long stems to the head. Guerillas are like a vapour.

T. E. Lawrence

30

Feisal on the Move

Feisal rode out front in flowing white robes. Lawrence, now an honorary Bedouin, was on his left, if anything more resplendent in white and scarlet. Behind them three banners of faded crimson silk with gilt spikes, then drummers thumping out a steady marching beat, and following on, the bodyguard's 1,200 bobbing camels. The men seemed to be attempting to outdo each other in the brightness of their coloured clothes, and in singing praise to Feisal and his family.[1]

It was 4 January 1917. The loose, unstructured contingent wandered its way slowly, in a traditional nomadic fashion, but still with some intent. Lawrence had managed to restart the stagnated Arab Revolt after much work.

The news that 160 kilometres to the north-west, not far from the Palestine border with Sinai, Chauvel's column had secured a swift and impressive victory at Magdhaba 16 days earlier, was inspirational. This so soon after taking El Arish, and only a few months after domination of the Turks at Romani and holding sway in its aftermath.

It was too early to be definitive, but Lawrence believed trends against the Turks were developing. Their invincibility after the aborted Gallipoli campaign had already been consigned to the dustbin of myth. While the Desert Column to the west was doing such damage, Turkish resources were being stretched, which would make them less likely to assign armies even deeper into hostile territory such as the Hejaz. This gave confidence to

Lawrence and kept his reveries about the possibilities for the Arabs alive. The revitalised revolt, so promising in the middle of 1916, was now to be extended to the northern Hejaz, with the main aim of capturing the Red Sea port of Wejh, 320 kilometres north of the village of Yenbo, which was held by a modest Turkish garrison. One aim was to use Wejh as a base for a prolonged harassment against the Turks' Hejaz railway, which was the lifeblood for their force in the area. The railway ran 160 kilometres to the east of Wejh and parallel to the coast. Its beginning was in Damascus. It was militarised in every direction. There were more than 200 fortified posts on the entire line.

Lawrence believed that the Arab hit-and-run raids on the railway would force the Turks to push their troops towards the north and Wejh and away from another port, Rabegh, which in turn would force them to abandon plans to advance on Mecca.

As usual, Lawrence, who was underrated as a military strategist by himself and his fellow British officers, had a complex, interlocking concept in mind. A second prong in his plan was to disrupt the Hejaz railway nearer to Medina in the south. He suggested that Abdullah (Feisal's brother) should move his force to a valley closer to the Medina line. From there he could attack the line and prevent a further Turkish advance on Yenbo or Mecca.

Lawrence's overall aim then was to have the armies of Feisal and Abdullah control a 320-kilometre stretch of the railway. Once supplies were cut, the Turkish garrison at Medina would be under Arab threat.

That was the immediate mission. The bigger, all-embracing project to him was still to defy the odds and head for Damascus. But in moments of euphoria he sometimes let slip even greater fantasies—his for the Arabs—about a great Arab army conquering the Turkish capital Constantinople (Istanbul) and by inference the entire Ottoman Empire.

This infuriated other British advisers, including Colonels Vickery and Boyle. Half-way to Wejh, Lawrence heard that Abdullah had almost reached the valley destination, Wadi Ais, without any problem with the Turks. Both armies had come so far without enemy interference. Over an evening meal inside

Feisal's tent, with the Arab leaders there, and Vickery also in attendance, Lawrence was excited.

'In a year we will be tapping on the gate of Damascus!' he exclaimed.

His words were met with a chilly silence. Vickery later told Colonel Boyle that Lawrence was a braggart and a 'visionary', the latter having the connotation of a lunatic. Not only did the British not want this, they did not believe it possible. Yet Lawrence believed his own rhetoric; he also had faith in his dreams. His 'views' were at cross-purposes to those of the other advisers. They saw rebellion as war; he saw it, naively, as more 'the nature of "peace"—a national strike perhaps'.

He was advocating something stronger than a national 'stop-work' movement; it was more like a niggling, nagging style of guerilla war. The Turks had power over the desert tribes, but on tribal territory. The Arabs were planning to make use of their huge knowledge of every ridge, cave, water-well, path, valley, sand dune and knoll. Yet Lawrence's scheme was more comprehensive than even that. He foresaw, or desired, a steady, relentless drive north rather than a sitting and holding pattern of hit-and-hide military tactics.

Perhaps over-optimistically, Lawrence believed that in skilled hands, preferably his own, the ultimate destination would be Constantinople.[2]

Chauvel's column force cleared the outskirts of the desert on the evening of 8 January 1917 on another mission, this time to reach Rafa, 40 kilometres from El Arish in the beautiful rolling country of the Negib (south land). They moved into excellent pastoral territory, similar to that experienced by the troopers coming from parts of Australia with good, regular rainfall.

En route, the New Zealand Brigade swooped on a Bedouin camp and collected 30 prisoners, with the column hardly losing step. Lawrence in the Hejaz was embracing Bedouins, but their brethren to the north-west were not trusted by the column. They were seen as controlled by the Turks, for whom they spied.

Chauvel ordered his now familiar encirclement manoeuvre when they reached Magruntein, the Turkish post several kilometres short of Rafa. The New Zealanders rode wide of the post just before dawn and were positioned to the east, or Palestine side. The other brigades took up their positions as dawn broke to reveal something that warmed the hearts of the troopers and cameleers.

They were in a rolling expanse of tender pasture 'splashed with patches of young barley', according to historian Henry Gullett, 'and sprinkled brilliantly with poppies, anemones, iris and a wealth of other wild flowers'.

The land was even more attractive to the walers, who had to be kept moving to stop them from grazing on the first green grass they had seen since leaving the Nile Delta. From another angle, it was deadly. The beautiful ground had no cover. Chetwode despaired that the 'dismounted cavalry' would not break through.

When the action began, the locals again carried on as if it was business as usual, ploughing their fields, sometimes moving between Chauvel's attacking batteries and the defending forces in the trenches.

As the battle progressed, the roughly circular column did not seem to be making headway. The machine-gun and rifle fire was too intense from the 2,000-strong Turkish 'fort'. But the column's casualties were light because it was well spread. Chauvel stood near his red divisional flag, which fluttered from a lance driven into the soft soil. He watched through binoculars from rising ground where he had a good view of the entire battle. Behind him were the horses, one trooper holding four at a time. Nearby his staff busied themselves over maps and at telephones, occasionally hurrying to their commander, who would be glacial in his concentration. Few, and only pertinent words were exchanged in these more tense moments. Further back and unobtrusive was Chetwode himself, viewing both Chauvel and the battleground. Overhead, British and Australian pilots (including the ubiquitous Ross Smith) flew about. For the first time in the Middle East conflict they used radio communication to direct the batteries' fire.

Chetwode's expectations given the terrain, the entrenchment of the Turks and their apparent determination were not
high, and his pessimism was well founded when Chauvel was
forced to throw in all his reserves. There was even a threat of
a complete reverse when the Inverness batteries and the New
Zealand machine-gunners ran out of ammunition. Then there
was the dreaded water situation. Only the camels had enough
for a prolonged engagement. The pilots reported big Turkish
reinforcements—at least 2,500 soldiers—coming in from three
different positions.

Chetwode, withdrawing to safer ground, conferred by phone
with Chauvel. The situation seemed hopeless. Chetwode was
inclined to withdraw; Chauvel concurred. Moments later, he
could see the New Zealanders making a bold move. Covered by
machine- and Lewis guns, they twice charged up a 700-metre
slope, careering with their bayonets bared towards the enemy
trenches. The audacity of the moves over open ground still in
fair daylight was too much for the Turks. They surrendered.
Inspired, the cameleers also charged another group of defences
and forced a further mass capitulation. The New Zealanders
took the rest of the trenches. Turkish resistance collapsed, with
just a handful making off as night fell.

Chauvel could add Rafa as another notch on his belt of
victories.

Turkish reinforcements were already engaging Chauvel's
troops a fair distance away when he ordered that two regiments
of 3rd Brigade, led by Lieutenant Colonel L. C. Maygar, stay
behind. After Gallipoli he seemed to specialise in holding a precarious position. Although nearly all the British wounded had
been taken from the battlefield during the fight, a field ambulance also stayed for any troopers who had been missed.

Chauvel led the rest of the weary force trailing sand-carts
with the wounded, including Turks, back to water and supplies
held half-way to El Arish. He feared the Turkish reinforcements would attempt to reoccupy Rafa, but he was overjoyed to
learn from air reconnaissance they had decided to retreat after
encountering Turks fleeing the battleground.

Rafa had been yet another strong victory. Losses had been heavier than at Magdhaba, with 71 killed and 415 wounded, but this was light compared to the Turks. Again, a sizeable haul of prisoners—1,635—was taken.

Chetwode had taken it all in, even the reaction of his 52nd Infantry Division, which cheered in the weary mobile column and helped water the horses. After this, he would be loath to raise the question of discipline concerning Australian or New Zealand forces. In two battles two weeks apart, he had witnessed the most professional, courageous and skilful mounted forces in his experience.

Like Generals Lawrence and Murray (and Birdwood earlier), he now had full confidence in the capacity and intelligence of Chauvel. Chetwode went to the extent of recommending him for a high chivalry decoration—a KCMG (Knight Commander of St Michael and St George). Only a week after Rafa, Murray informed Chauvel he had been awarded it for 'your services and the gallantry of your Division at El Arish, Magdhaba, and Rafa'. For some reason, unexplained and inexplicable, there had still been no mention of Romani. In the arcane world of military awards, this was an oversight by Murray that again displeased Chauvel and caused some tension between them.

But the KCMG placated the Australian's sense of a slight for him and his troopers that had seen him omitted from the New Year's honours list announced throughout the empire on New Year's Day.

General Lawrence, Chauvel's former commander by remote, vague control, summed up his embarrassment by later telling him that he (General Lawrence) was ashamed to find himself with a KCB when Chauvel had been ignored over the New Year.

The day after Rafa, Chauvel sent back troopers with vehicles to salvage equipment. They had to compete with Bedouin scavengers who came in numbers at dawn to grab what they could, from discarded weaponry to clothes and boots on the Turkish dead.

Historian Henry Gullett, who reflected the attitudes of the column, wrote scathingly of the desert dwellers, especially when they again tore uniforms and footwear from the Turkish wounded, and later dug up graves for the same purpose. He noted what he and the diggers saw as repulsive habits, with lice in their hair and the way they relieved themselves in their camps and left their excrement in the open for the benefit and attraction of flies.

By contrast, T.E. Lawrence embraced the Bedouins. He endorsed looting (as did Chauvel, tacitly with his troops in the Boer War, and this one). It had been a battle tradition among the Arabs for centuries. The scavenging he saw as a part of that, even from the dead and wounded. Lawrence did not mind things such as hair lice.

Gullett was critical of British policy, which 'pandered to these degenerate roaming Arabs of Western Palestine'. He suggested 'punishment' early in the conflict would have saved many Australian and British lives. The (British) Foreign Office, he said, insisted that the army leaders treat the Bedouins as 'respectable practising Moslems, kin to the Arabs in the Hejaz and of the same faith as the Moslems of the Indian Empire'. Instructions were given that 'special care must be taken not to offend their susceptibilities'.[3]

Clearly Gullett, and senior members of the column's command, were not privy to the plans of Lawrence, who had most to do with the Foreign Office's attitude to the Bedouins and how they were being used for British interests.

Lawrence's immediate task was the taking of the Turkish garrison at Wejh on the Red Sea. On 16 January 1917, he, Feisal and British military and naval representatives met to finalise details for the attack. Feisal's Arab force would approach the town from the south, while a smaller group of 550 would be shipped by the Royal Navy to the north, blocking any Turks attempting to escape.

Two days later, all those neat decisions were thrown out when

Abdullah's army captured a prominent Turkish commander, Eshref Bey, 'a notorious adventurer in the lower levels of Turkish politics' and a henchman of the Young Turks.[4] Feisal was wildly excited by the news and decided it was time for a celebration. Lawrence, Feisal and his men partied through the night until dawn. Feisal was meant to meet the Royal Navy's Admiral Wemyss to synchronise their combined attack, but did not show up. The 550 Arabs on board were becoming restless. The gun ship would run out of food if it did not sail for Wejh, so the admiral decided not to wait for Feisal.

On 23 January 1917, the force of six ships, accompanied by the two British officers, Boyle and Vickery, sailed as planned, from just north of the town. The admiral trained all his weapons on the town and bombarded it. This softened up the 1,200-strong Turkish force, and the Arabs had no trouble in rapidly taking the garrison, losing 20 men in the action. Lawrence, Feisal and his 5,100 camel-riders and 5,300 men on foot wandered in well after Wejh had been secured in Arab hands.

They had already rioted through the town, looting everything. Lawrence was appalled and for the first time realised the enormity of engendering any sense of discipline in the Bedouins.

He wanted Wejh as a base from which to attack the railway, 160 kilometres inland to the east. But he was unhappy with the Arab destruction and indiscriminate killing.[5]

Lawrence at first fretted over the 20 Arab deaths. He thought that if Boyle and Vickery had waited for Feisal's force, a war of attrition would have seen the garrisoned Turks run out of food and supplies. They might have surrendered without a fight. He felt indirectly that he had blood on his hands. The incident made him face the realities of his inspired notions about the revolt. It could not be the wishy-washy 'peace movement' or 'national strike' that he suggested feebly was the way forward. The uprising was going to mean men would be killed, possibly in big numbers. It was the beginning of the hardening of T. E. Lawrence.

He very soon rationalised the deaths and the mob looting that followed the battle, turning more to the result, which was the capture of an important base on the Red Sea.

31

The Turning

Lawrence hoped that the strategic acquisition of Wejh marked a turning point in the revolt. The Hejaz for the first time was essentially under Arab control. He felt a momentum building. Tribes that had sat on the fence until now began thinking about joining the swelling Arab force. The Turks were on the defensive to the west (in southern Palestine) and in the Hejaz in a sudden turn of events inside a few weeks into 1917. They had to deploy more troops to the railway, some of them coming north from the Turkish garrison at Medina (at the end of the railway line). More troops were taken from the 7th Division. A new garrison sprang up at Maan, about 850 kilometres up the line from Medina. Another was established closer at Tebuk, 500 kilometres away.

The Turkish threats to Rabegh 250 kilometres from Medina on the Red Sea coast, and Mecca another 200 kilometres south, evaporated. The Arab army, under British guidance and with their support on all levels, effectively had blocked the enemy.

Gradually the Turkish outposts were sucked back to Medina, and they would become increasingly isolated as the Arabs pushed north.

The lingering euphoria over the taking of Wejh and the Turkish flight emboldened Lawrence. He had drawn close to Feisal. A mutual respect had built up. Feisal demanded that he stay with him as his permanent liaison officer.

Rumours of the Sykes–Picot agreement reached the Arabs. Feisal quizzed Lawrence about stories emanating from Turkey that the British and French had decided on some sort of carve-up. Lawrence claimed he knew nothing about any such colonial power agreement but he knew that if the British won the war any pacts with the Arabs would be worthless. Yet he kept up the façade and deception of cooperation assuring Feisal that his superiors would keep their word.

Lawrence was a committed agent, simultaneously dedicated to the British Empire and future Arab states, which were almost certain at some point to be at odds with each other. He was slipping into the classic double-agent's dilemma, yet he was intoxicated with the possibilities for both, especially the Arab cause now it was active and he was a physical part of it. There was excitement in seeing his written ideas, some of them wild, others brilliant, being acted on. His imagination was overriding his pragmatism. All around him the less imaginative, such as Boyle and Vickery (himself a notable Arabist, who spoke the language with greater fluency than Lawrence, and was more adept at the colloquial) were acting strictly within War Office guidelines. They had comprehension of the Arabs, but no deep affection for them, their ideals or aims. They thought in terms of containment on every level and using them for British ends. Increasingly, Lawrence dreamt of letting them loose.

Part of his strategy was to influence Feisal not to trust or deal with the French. They had a plan to land an Allied force at the Turkish garrison at Aqaba, 500 kilometres north of Wejh at the tip of the small Gulf of Aqaba, a body of water that stretched well into the Sinai. Feisal had been under pressure to accept this.

Lawrence told him that the real French motive was to use the capture of Aqaba to restrict the Arab Revolt to the Hejaz. The Allied force—French and British—would then advance inland. This push would be presented to the Arabs and the world as 'an exercise in imperial conquest'. Arab leaders—Feisal particularly—would have their reputations damaged in the eyes of all tribes that might be thinking of joining the revolt for a northward thrust to Syria. This way the uprising would be diffused. It would fizzle out.

Feisal's response was to resist the French overtures.

Lawrence emphasised the possibilities for the Arabs if they

could be first to Damascus and other cities in Syria—Aleppo, Hama and Homs. The British, Lawrence said, would have to fulfil obligations to them. He again warned that the French, who wanted Lebanon and Syria, would act duplicitously. Lawrence could help manipulate the British side, he told Feisal, but being first into the region and the major cities would go a long way towards deciding Arab claims to run any proposed new state.

Lawrence emphasised that the Arabs had to extend the revolt north. They had to demonstrate they wanted at least a new state of Syria (a large territory east of Jordan) by being there and fighting for it.

In February 1917, 'reliable' reports (which it was unlikely either Vickery, Boyle or Lawrence would have sent) for consumption at the Arab Bureau and military headquarters suggested that the Turks would abandon southern Arabia (the Hejaz) to Hussein and Feisal. The Turks in that region were said to be joining the enemy force under Kress in Palestine. This put commander-in-chief Murray and all the military command under pressure. Until now, sitting in Cairo, he had a simple overview of what he was meant to do: clear Sinai and make sure the railway and pipeline kept extending. Now they were all the way to El Arish. He had supplies from the sea. Communications seemed to be satisfactory. Everything was set up for something bigger, which induced him to break from the 'politics' of Cairo and the Officers' Club and visit the moveable front.

Murray was not the most ambitious military commander. Perhaps that was why he had been sent to the Middle East. But now he had to consider a campaign that would push him into a different league: the invasion of Palestine. The collective wisdom of Murray, Dobell and their staffs was that a strike should be made against the Turks in southern Palestine before the expected (Turkish) reinforcements should arrive.

Another factor likely to lead to precipitate action was the alleged dispute (and therefore indecision) between the Germans and Turks over where a stand should be made against the encroaching British force, so well placed at El Arish for another surge. The Germans favoured maintaining a solid line of defence running from the most vital city of Gaza on the Mediterranean Coast inland to Beersheba, about 70 kilometres almost due east. The Turks wanted to pull back about 60 kilometres.

On a more fundamental level, there was a further internecine Turkish dispute in Damascus. Mustafa Kemal, the Anzacs' nemesis on Gallipoli, was there attempting to work out how to contain the Arabs' Hejaz revolt. He was appalled to learn that other commanders were thinking of abandoning Medina. It was difficult, Kemal was told, to keep the trains running and supplying that garrison. Troops, equipment and supplies would be better sent to the main Turkish front in southern Palestine. He was presented with a compelling logic. If the Turks lost Palestine they would lose Medina anyway. Better to give away that remote garrison and move the forces to Palestine. But this was a rationale for lesser men; commanders without his great capacity to inspire soldiers. Kemal refused to go south to supervise the dumping of Medina.

He waited until General von Falkenhayn arrived in Damascus to take command. The German had a complex plan, which seemed at best ambivalent about Medina. Kemal did not think it could work. He resigned and headed back to Constantinople, where he had the sympathetic ear of the Sultan. The Muslim spiritual leader cried at the thought of the holy city of Medina being lost to his influence.

Hussein, Feisal, Abdullah, Lawrence and the ill-disciplined Arab force would have been no match for Kemal mustering his army in the Hejaz. But he would not be there. Nor would he be in southern Palestine taking on the British and Anzac forces once more. The best Turkish commander was sidelined at a critical time.

Murray's spies had picked up fragments of these various disputes within the enemy camp and he was influenced to act on the conclusions from them. His military intelligence informed him that Gaza was lightly held. No more than 4,000 Turkish soldiers were said to be there. But his sources were not telling of another 11,000 in the immediate vicinity. Included were 2,000 Turks at Beersheba. That made 15,000 Turkish rifles all up, and those outside the city could be moved up in defence.

Murray was unaware that German and Austrian engineers had improved the water supply in Beersheba and other nearby areas, which allowed the Turks to spread their force well across the Gaza-to-Beersheba defence strip. This would be a critical factor in any conflict. The British infantry would be restricted. It was imperative that the Camel Brigade and two rearranged divisions of mounted infantry (Anzac Mounted Division run by Chauvel; the new Imperial Mounted Division under British General Hodgson) made their inland raids work fast. They had to take the Turkish wells. If not, any prolonged encounter would go the way of the enemy.

The essential factor in any battle lasting more than 48 hours was water. All other things being more or less equal, the controller of it would win.

Oblivious of the strength of the Turks in this respect, Murray returned to his Egyptian base convinced this was the moment to strike. The Turks could be easing away (while not withdrawing); in a few weeks they might well be reinforced. It was the time— between indecision and the Turkish reinforcements arriving—to send his force to take Gaza, the gateway to Palestine.

The Arabs called Gaza Dehliz el Moulk, 'Threshold to the Kingdom', and you could take your pick of which one it referred to. Its conquest for a few thousand years had been the first step for the invasion of Egypt from the north or the taking of Palestine from the Nile. Long before the modest Murray had thought about it, Alexander, Pompey and Napoleon had dwelt long on its military significance. Before them it had been important to the Hebrews, Pharaohs and Assyrians.

The religious link and mythology was not lost on the troopers. 'It is Samson's city,' Ion Idriess wrote, 'the strong man of Israel who when his foes were upon him tore down the city gates and carried them up the hill of Ali Muntar. At Gaza, when chained to the pillars of the Temple of Dagon, he pulled the roof down on top of 3,000 Philistines. Delilah was his girl.'[1]

The objective of the ancients' desires lay close to the sea. The main town had 40,000 inhabitants in 1917, but the Turks thought they would be in the way during a battle. They forced most of the inhabitants to evacuate. When the people were reluctant to leave, the Turks used whips and other bullying methods to hurry them out of their homes and shops.

Gaza was three kilometres inland, set on a low hill at the inner edge of coastal sand dunes. Covering five square kilometres, tall cactus hedges—plants nearly three metres high and up to five metres wide—made it a prickly problem for attacking troops. It was not only hard to get through; it was largely impenetrable to machine-gun and rifle fire.

Yet it was a superb natural defence. The Turks could wait for the advancing troopers coming across an outer rim of olive groves to the east and south. Artillery could be directed from high ground behind the wall of cactus. If Gaza was attacked from the sea, there was a further edifice of steep sand dunes.

There was no stronger natural fort in Palestine.

32

The Executioner's Malady

Lawrence had a terrible dilemma early in March 1917 in his campaign against the Turks and the Hejaz railway. He was regarded as an 'elder' of the revolt and thus above disputes among the various Bedouin tribes. From this precarious yet lofty position he was called upon to adjudicate on a blood feud between the Agayl and the Moroccans. This was on a visit to Abdullah's army in the Wadi Ais. A Moroccan—Hamed the Moor—had killed an Agayl member, and the Agayl tribe was demanding an 'eye for an eye'. It was desert law. The murderer had to be killed. Other elders seemed to have made themselves scarce, which left Lawrence to act as judge, jury and executioner. Hamed happened to be one of his servants, which added to the dilemma. The thought of slaying anyone like this did not sit easily with Lawrence (indeed, any of the elders). It put him under the microscope. If he refused, he would lose much credibility, for although he was highly regarded, such a backdown would draw into question his commitment to the revolt. On balance, Lawrence could not afford that at this moment. If he were to play a leading and guiding role in the push north, he had to have uncritical support. He made the decision to execute Hamed.

With great reluctance, but making sure not to show it, he asked that the Moroccan be taken to a sandy gully near the army camp. The situation was even worse when Hamed lay blubbering on the ground, with six Agayl looking on.

'Stand up,' Lawrence said, feeling his own body shaking. Hamed got to his feet. Lawrence levelled his pistol and pulled the trigger. The bullet hit him in the chest. Hamed fell to his knees coughing up blood. Lawrence took a step forward, aimed the gun, and with a trembling hand fired again. The bullet shattered Hamed's wrist. He screamed in agony. Lawrence took three paces to him, placed the pistol's barrel under his chin and fired a third time. The bullet came out the top of his head. Hamed's body gave one last shiver of life and he was dead.

Lawrence, in shock, called for Agayl tribe members to bury the victim. They dug him a deep grave, satisfied with their perception of justice.

Lawrence returned to his tent and collapsed. His diary entry for 12 March 1917 is cryptic and poignant. He sketched the valley in which he had carried out the shooting. An arrow pointed to something he called 'deathcrack'. In a shaky hand, he had scribbled: 'Slept here. Terrible night. Shot.'[1]

Lawrence was suffering from malaria and dysentery. Exhausted as much from his illnesses as his first killing in cold blood, he did not leave his tent for 11 days.

Still ill, he felt just able to lead a reconnaissance by a team of 30 Arabs on the Hejaz railway at an isolated and guarded station lying opposite Wadi Ais. He summoned his limited strength for a two-day camel ride before making camp amid some great tamarisk trees near a rocky outcrop. At dawn, Lawrence climbed a 200-metre ridge to view the station six kilometres away. The proposed target was a fort surrounded by three buildings and close to a multi-arched bridge that had been blown up by the Arabs earlier but was now repaired.

Lawrence and his squad waited until the afternoon for the attack party led by Abdullah's deputy, Sharif Shakir, a lean 27-year-old. Lawrence was attracted to him. In contrast to Abdullah, he was refined. He wore his hair in plaits, Bedouin-style and cultivated head-lice. He dressed in the brim—a girdle of thorns supposed to help hold in the stomach. Lawrence could manipulate this young man of his own age, as he could Feisal and others, whereas the strongly independent and intellectual Abdullah was a tougher proposition for bending to his will.

Shakir arrived with 300 men on camels. Lawrence had asked for 1,000. He was displeased and had to change his plans. There could not be direct assault on the station with that number. Instead it was decided the station would be hit by an artillery barrage. This would pin down the Turkish force while a group of Shakir's men travelled north through the night to dynamite the rails and cut the telegraph lines at dawn the next morning.

Lawrence led another group to mine the track at the next station to the south. He insisted that the Arabs did not talk or sing, which was quite a demand for them, as their camels loped along under bright stars. Arriving at 11.15 p.m. Lawrence alighted from his camel and approached the line with some reverence.

It excited him. He had never been so close to the Hejaz track, which was symbolic of so much in the region. He touched its steel. It was cold. Lawrence knelt and put his ear to it. Although no train was due, he imagined he heard different things, which he assumed were the normal sounds of minuscule contractions as the heat generated in the day dissipated. He ordered a 20-pound Garland-Martini mine be placed under a rail. Then he set up a pressure switch. It would detonate when the metals were depressed by the weight of the train. Next he scoured the area looking for a place to site a machine-gun. The most suitable spot was 500 metres away near a watercourse and hidden by bushes.

Lawrence directed the machine-gun crew of four to stay put while he led the rest of the group of thirty 200 metres north up the track to snip the telegraph lines. He directed one of his men to shinny up the pole to do the job. He managed to reach a couple of metres and fell back. Lawrence soon found that none of the Arabs could climb the pole. He dismounted, called on his experience climbing trees as a child, and eased himself up. Once at the top, he cut three wires. He was reaching for the fourth, when he overbalanced and fell. His guide broke the fall, bruising himself but preventing serious injury to Lawrence.

The plan was straightforward enough. Shakir's artillery at the first station would open up at dawn. The Turks would attempt to call for reinforcements but would not get through because the telegraph lines were down. This would force them to send a train south to Medina to alert troops. In turn, an attempt would be made to blow it up. When the train crew jumped out to fix it, they would be hit by the machine-gun.

Lawrence led his party back to their camp before dawn, in time for Shakir's 6.30 a.m. artillery blast. The boom of the big guns echoed through the valley. The first three salvos collapsed the top levels of the fort and the station building. Some shells struck a water tank, denting it and sending water out like a giant sprinkler. It flowed down the walls. A further volley from the artillery saw the fort catch fire and it spread to the wood pile used to refuel the train. Within minutes its wagons were ablaze.

The Turks scrambled to uncouple the locomotive and it chugged off south towards Medina.

Lawrence hurried to higher ground. He used binoculars to follow the train's short journey. He could feel his heart thumping as the train approached the next station. There was an explosion. Dust flew high and the train halted. It had not been thrown completely off the track. Lawrence realised that the mine had detonated late. Only the train's front wheels had come off the line. He watched in disappointment as the Turkish crew jumped out and began manoeuvring a jack under the wheels. They worked fast and unhindered. After two minutes, Lawrence wondered aloud what had happened to the machine-gun crew hidden in good range. Why weren't they firing?

He stormed into the camp and found the crew. A quick interrogation found that they had become bored with waiting. They had disassembled the weapon and returned to camp. Lawrence was apoplectic and vented his anger at the men. Then he returned to his vantage point to watch the Turkish train crew hoisting the locomotive back on the track. There was nothing to stop it rumbling off to Medina.

Shakir's entire force now was engaged in attacking the fort. Camouflaged by smoke, the Arabs made their assault, adeptly using any cover as they advanced. The Turks in one building were outnumbered but they would not surrender. A bloody battle ensued and every defender was killed. The Turks in the second building had seen the destruction of the first. They gave up. Shakir's men then closed in on the station and captured more than 20 Syrians who were working for the Turks. The fort was a tougher proposition, and the intense smoke made it near-impossible to storm.

At the height of the battle, Lawrence hurried to the other train station to examine the failed results of the mine explosion. The Turks had uncoupled and left a brake van. Lawrence climbed in and found it lined with cement, which meant only a direct artillery hit would destroy it. He left convinced that he had to improve his mining skills to ensure future attempts to derail trains would come off.

The Turks in the fort were putting up a solid stand. Lawrence and Shakir consulted and decided to break off the engagement having conducted more of a raid than a complete destruction of the fort complex and the station. Still it had killed and wounded more than 70 Turks. The Arabs retreated for the two-day ride back to Abdullah's camp.

Once there, Lawrence wasted no time in interrogating the captured Syrians to glean as much as he could about the Turks' strengths and weaknesses in Syria and the region. He was still suffering the after-effects of his malaria, but the experience of the raid had exhilarated him.

It had also delayed the psychological impact of his execution of Hamed.

General Murray pushed the button on Gaza on 25 March 1917. The battle was to go ahead. A decisive win at that pivotal place could well see the Turks on the run in Palestine and the region delivered to the British. That was the hope and expectation of the attackers, and the dream for Murray. It would be his bid for, if not immortality like T. E. Lawrence, then the reputation of having played a major part in turning the tide in the Middle East, which would have a marked effect on the entire war.

33

Blunder at Gaza

'It is believed that Gaza is not strongly held,' Chetwode told his Desert Column generals, 'It is therefore intended to push the attack with great vigour.'

The force being sent on the mission to take the town included two British infantry divisions (16,000 soldiers); Anzac Mounted less the resting 1st Brigade (2,400 dismounted troopers); the Imperial Mounted Division, including the Australian 3rd Brigade, but not the 4th, which was also resting (2,400 dismounted troopers); and about 1,200 rifles in the Camel Brigade. This made 22,000 rifles in all, a clear superiority over the Turks, at least in numbers on paper.

The 16,000 foot soldiers marched towards Gaza with much fanfare. They had the mounted troopers taking up positions on the small hills en route to watch them come as dusk settled on 25 March. The dust the infantry stirred up filtered towards the sunset. The troopers were surprised to hear bands accompanying the army as it spread wide across the barley fields, yet still in tight ranks, crunching its way forward, the steady tramp of boots making a formidable sound.

It was riveting for the Anzac onlookers because of its size at least. British Yeomanry and the camels formed long, flanking columns. There were also the transport columns, the white-hooded ambulance carts featuring red crosses. What impressed most were the guns.

'Battery after battery, limber after limber, swinging past,' Idriess recorded, 'we gazed down on the guns! What numbers! What calibres. We thrilled as we watched those guns. What things we could do with them! I smiled at the thought of our own precious little guns that had stood by us through the Desert Campaign. But these—why these are GUNS!'[1]

After the awe of it, all the troopers wondered what the future was for the Desert Column. Were they to lose their individuality in this bigger army?

They had been professional, at times beyond that and brilliant under Chauvel, with the more mobile force dominant in the desert conflict. But now they were into the southern Palestine region and away from the endless sand dunes, the Anzacs were concerned they might become marginalised. They were enjoying the small period of 'rest' and feasting on the local luxuriant figs, almonds and lemons. Their horses loved the forage in the Wadi Ghuzze region. But the troopers had come to fight. They wished to maintain the prominence they had in the last half of 1916.

Chetwode's plans seemed to give weight to fears that they would play a secondary role to the infantry. He aimed to send in his 53rd Infantry Division on a frontal attack from the south-east. Chauvel's force would envelop the town on the north-east and north. Hodgson's contingent would be east and north-east and join part of the envelopment of Gaza with the camels.

The horsemen had led the way so far. It now seemed the soldiers would be the front-line force.

The Anzacs approached Gaza at 2.30 a.m. on 26 March in thick fog, which had an element of treachery, but would provide cover until dawn.

Just before first light, the Australian 7th Light Horse Regiment, acting as an advance 'screen', emerged out of the lifting fog and appeared like ghost-riders to an enemy patrol. It panicked and opened fire. The horsemen scattered. German airmen and mechanics were awakened in a nearby field. They scrambled for their planes. A dozen troopers noticed them and galloped their way. The German hurried to start their engines. They wobbled the planes along the makeshift airfield. The troopers dismounted and fired as the planes struggled to get airborne.

Within seconds they were turning their machine-guns on any pocket of troopers they could find. The horsemen were too quick. They scattered and became tough targets for the spray-gun efforts of the airmen. No trooper or horse was hit but two of 2nd Brigade commander Major General Ryrie's best horses, which had been hand-picked by Banjo Paterson for him, were startled by the planes. They broke away and disappeared towards Gaza.[2]

There was chaos in the olive groves as the yelling troopers came across waking Turks, who had been surprised by the attack. The Australians crossed the road linking Gaza to Beersheba and cut all communication lines between the two towns. A squadron of the 5th Light Horse charged down a convoy of 10 wagons of supplies and shot the horses. Another contingent captured 30 German pioneers laden down with digging gear. The Australians ordered them to march at the double. The Germans wouldn't budge. They glared at their captors. The captain of the contingent ordered his troopers to fix bayonets. The very deliberate and intimidating acts of reaching for the sharp weapons and attaching them to rifles had the desired effect. The Germans moved at an impressive double.

Through the olive groves and along the roads, the troopers chased down little groups of Turks, who were unprepared and not ready to fight. They hurried for the town and the horsemen galloped after them to the outskirts. Here they came across a small mounted patrol escorting several gharries (horsedrawn vehicles shaped like large baths). They contained a diminutive Turkish general and his staff. The troopers galloped up, yelling and firing their revolvers. The shocked patrol escort fled with the Australians in hot pursuit. Four troopers trotted up to the general crouched in his gharry. He was flustered. They laughed at his predicament.

'Going somewhere mate?' one of the amused troopers said, training his weapon on the general. The Turk reached for a gold case, and nervously offered them each a cigarette. They declined. One of the troopers reached into a pocket. He pulled out a half-smoked stub of his own and solemnly handed it to the general. He looked at first querulous, then aggrieved. The troopers chuckled.[3]

The general, realising he was unlikely to be eaten alive, began to bluster about his importance, telling his new escort in Turkish that he was the new senior commander at Gaza on his way to take over the garrison. The troopers didn't understand a word. They continued to chuckle as he became more agitated.

Along a nearby road still on Gaza's outskirts, more troopers came across Turkish soldiers with two fine looking walers in their possession. They were found to be the ones Ryrie had lost when the planes startled them earlier in the morning. He was just showing his pleasure at having them returned when the troopers who had snared the new garrison commander wheeled him up. Through an interpreter and faulty English, the general complained about the troopers, who had shown him no respect.

'They laughed at me!' he said. 'They are common soldiers!'

'Yes, I guess they are,' Ryrie replied, 'but you've got to admit it was damned funny.'

Ryrie apologised for being busy and left the general with other prisoners under guard, which added insult to insult. A little later the Turk was taken to Chauvel, where he maintained his indignation, telling the Australian of his shabby treatment.

'I insist that you escort me to the rear of the battle area!' he exclaimed.

'I'm sorry I can't do that,' Chauvel said, deadpan. 'I am the only British Divisional Commander east of Gaza. Like me, my brigadiers are quite busy at the moment.'

Chauvel ordered a staff major to escort the Turkish commander to the prison. He was more than miffed at what he perceived as discourtesy.[4]

Chauvel's Anzac Mounted Infantry, aided by cover from a lingering fog, were making some headway under instruction to attack the Turks wherever they found them in hit-and-move-on raids that unsettled the enemy in the outskirts to the north and east. Smith's Camels and Hodgson's Imperial Mounteds horsemen were doing much the same, although they had been retarded by heavier fog in their vicinity.

By 10 a.m. the town was locked down and partly surrounded.

A planned frontal assault was needed by the British Infantry's 53rd Division, with the 54th in reserve. This would make or break the attack overall. But the fog impeded far more than the horsemen. Its commander, Major General Dallas, feared that when the mist lifted they would be most vulnerable, especially as his artillery support could not fire until it could see targets in and around the still-shrouded Gaza.

Chetwode and Dobell at their headquarters nine kilometres from the battlefield waited patiently for Dallas to make his move. They sent out the directive for an assault. No response. They tried another. Again nothing. The hours crept by with all the other mounted divisions in place and waiting to support the infantry. Chetwode then sent a terse six-part order. Dallas still did not respond.

At noon Chetwode became concerned. Half the daylight hours needed for taking the town had gone. Soon the water supply would become the determining factor as to the success or failure of the mission. The commander reasoned that if the 53rd met fierce resistance once it did in fact move, it would be nightfall before Gaza was invaded. At 1 p.m. Dallas responded with confused yet legitimate excuses about darkness, fog, lethargic artillery and a little resistance from the enemy. Now his troops faced a tougher task than at dawn. The mist had evaporated. The infantry had four kilometres of open ground to negotiate. The long, regular lines in open formation were a healthy target for Turkish artillery.

The British showed discipline and courage as they advanced in tough conditions. They pushed forward three kilometres checked by the incoming shells, and the failure of their own artillery to hit targets and give decent support.

The hours were slipping by.

*

Their progress was not fast enough for Chetwode. He decided on a modified plan. There had to be an assault by the well-placed mounted divisions. He put Chauvel in charge of the two divisions and ordered them to attack dismounted. Methodical as ever, Chauvel began to organise his scattered force of cameleers and horsemen, a sizeable task. It took time. Chetwode urged him to attack. It was 3 p.m. before Chauvel moved his headquarters to a hill with a useful view of the coming conflict. Chetwode put the pressure on.

'The success of the operation of Gaza,' he wired, 'depends largely on the vigour of your attack. It is imperative that the position should be ours before dark.'[5]

Chauvel would not be rushed. His brigades were set to go at 4 p.m.

The British infantry had struggled well under heavy shelling to reach a point about a kilometre from a central force of Turks placed on the fabled ridge, Ali Muntar, and protected by cactus. The enemy had waited until the British were in range. They opened up with machine-guns and rifles. The air, which had been split intermittently by the thumping artillery, was dominated by the steady, relentless ring of the rapid-fire weapons. The soldiers were vulnerable on the plain to the east and the bare slopes in the south. The artillery intensified.

The first impact of this barrage was to pin down the battalions. Yet their leaders did not panic or order retreat. They called for their men to rush the defence.

The brave move led to more punishment.

The Turks' commander at Gaza, Tala Bey, reacted by calling for reinforcements from Huj to the north-east and Beersheba to the east. He sent urgent radio messages saying that his defence was about to collapse as the British force closed in. But the responses were not good for the defenders. Incoming Turkish forces would not reach the city's outskirts until after dark.

The garrison's commanders prepared for the worst. Given the recent battles against the Light Horse, they expected to be swamped before nightfall. Surrender would be the only option.

The Light Horse troopers moved through the olive and orange groves on foot to the north and east of Gaza and reached its outskirts. The 2nd Light Horse Brigade in the north faced little resistance until they hit the cactus wall. Chaytor's New Zealanders in the east also encountered opposition. The defence became fierce. The troopers used their bayonets to hack through the cactus, but the Turks were there in big numbers.

By 4.30 p.m. the town was almost surrounded. The troopers were battling hard, tightening the noose. They believed, as did Dallas and his infantry, that they would break through and take the garrison.

The commanders in the field could not communicate their confidence to Chetwode and Dobell, and even if they could, these two felt that reinforcing Turkish troops on the march would cut off the Light Horse from behind. Dusk crept over the area. Chetwode and Dobell decided to pull out. They informed Chauvel, who was closer to the action. His commanders were confident. So was Dallas with the infantry.

'But we have Gaza!' Chauvel responded to the telephone directive.

'Yes, but the Turkish reinforcements are all over you.'

Chauvel did not believe this. The town was in his grasp.

'I strongly advise you to not order this withdrawal . . .!' he said.[6]

But minds were made up. Chauvel was ordered again to stop the action of the Light Horse. He protested once more, and contemplated letting his division fight on. But Dobell remained firm. The action had to be called off.

*

At 6 p.m. the garrison chiefs were ready to throw down their arms. They transmitted this to the reinforcements. Kress, who had ordered the extra Turkish forces to aid the garrison, decided that Gaza was lost to the British. He ordered the incoming troops to stop for the night well short of the besieged town.

At 6.20 p.m. Ryrie and Chaytor received Chauvel's directive to withdraw. They were incredulous. Their regiments were almost through the cactus. Their casualties were light: three killed and 34 wounded in the entire division. They were finding the Turks' resistance was falling away. The enemy was demoralised and disinclined to fight.

'I want that in writing!' a dismayed Chaytor told the dispatch messenger. An embittered Ryrie told his staff officers:

'There will be no withdrawal until every trooper has been collected. Not a man is to be left behind.'[7]

The order filtered down from brigade to regiment to squadrons and sections. Along the chain it was either disbelieved or ignored. When the order was confirmed, the troopers were angry. They could see into streets as light faded. They were empty. Resistance was almost non-existent.

Troopers, particularly Gallipoli veterans, were disgruntled. They were certain they were in for a walkover and they wished to crush the opposition at every chance. Just over two years ago they had arrived on the peninsula. Memories of that hell were fresh. Now they had to concede a 'draw'. It was not taken well.

As the Light Horse made their moves to break off the engagement and leave, no Turk inside the town or the close defensive perimeter made any effort to pursue them.

Dallas and his infantry, who had the toughest time on the open plain, were also disgusted with the decision. They had done the hard yards and were certain of a frontal breakthrough. The most important forward Turkish defensive position—Ali Muntar—was within their grasp. Dallas sent the message out to stop, unsure when it would reach his infantry. Whether the soldiers received it or not, they fought on in the dark. At 7 p.m. the British 53rd Infantry Division took Ali Muntar.

Forty-five minutes later, the garrison's top commander, Tala Bey, sent a message to Kress:

'Position [Ali Muntar] lost.'

The Turks did not realise that the entire British force had now stopped fighting and was retreating. Nor did Kress, who had held up the reinforcements. He sent Tala Bey a radio message:

'Having regard to the disposition of Turkish troops and leaders, can an attack [against the British] be successful at early dawn? I beg you to do your utmost to hold out that long.'

'Your telegram received. Please attack,' a desperate Tala Bey responded, 'at all costs, at 2 a.m.'[8]

The Turkish commander had fought the Anzacs at Gallipoli. He was certain that the garrison would face a bayonet attack at first light.

At 11.45 p.m. Ryrie's 2nd Light Horse Brigade and Chaytor's New Zealand Mounteds were intact and assembled. The exhausted troopers, pumped up after the battle, and then let down by the lack of action, were overcome by exhaustion. Those who had any strength chatted. Most men lit up a cigarette or pipe as they trotted along in the dark. The column, which would normally be noiseless and unseen, was conspicuous in the dark for the sprinkling of lights that dotted the blackness. Yet no officer worried. Everyone knew that the Turks had been down for the count.

There would be no pursuit of the withdrawing force that night.

Demolition Man

The consequence of the decision to withdraw from the Gaza operation had its impact at dawn on 27 March 1917. Kress had managed to push a big contingent of troops well up the line from Beersheba, and they were in pursuit of Royston's 3rd Brigade. The South African was relieved to come across an Australian Light Car Patrol, which itself was decamping the scene with Turks on the march towards Gaza.

Jack Royston galloped up to the leader of the car convoy, Lieutenant Mackenzie.

'Could you cover us?' Royston asked.

'Just what we're here for,' an ebullient Mackenzie replied. He motored up to a ridge overlooking the advancing Turks. The five cars lined up beside each other. They primed their five machine-guns and waited. When the enemy was within a kilometre, they opened fire. The impact was immediate. The Turks came to a halt. The troops at the front broke ranks and ran for cover.

Royston charged up onto the ridge.

'Splendid, lieutenant!' he yelled. 'Do you want a squadron to cover your retreat, or support you?'

'No, we're fine,' Mackenzie called, 'we've a bit to do yet.'

'Good luck!' Royston called, and thundered off to his troops.[1]

Mackenzie scattered his cars along the ridge and kept firing as the several-thousand-strong enemy force faltered, then came again. He was forced to move cars back along the ridges in a steady retreat until 3rd Brigade was clear of a deep valley and safe.

Mackenzie felt this was his little patrol's moment. He was not about to retire the cars. On one ridge they found Smith's Camel Brigade relaxed and having breakfast, oblivious of the advancing Turks. The brigadier didn't believe it. He asked Mackenzie to go back and see if they were still coming. Mackenzie obliged, only to run into artillery fire from the enemy, which lobbed perilously close. His patrol accelerated up to the ridge harbouring the cameleers. The brigadier ordered his dismounted riflemen to take up positions. He decided to hold the position for the day.

Mackenzie's patrol retired and reported to Chetwode, who was relieved to see the drivers safe.

Congratulating the lieutenant and his men, he ordered them an exceptional lunch of cold beef and tomatoes.[2]

Soon after dawn on 27 March Dobell ordered Dallas to reoccupy Ali Muntar. After all the effort the previous day to take it, then the abandonment, this was the most infuriating order Dallas ever received. The Turks were now back and reinforced. Dallas's troops had no sooner moved onto the ground they once held than a large body of Turks was upon them. The engagement was already a failure. Dallas's two divisions (the 53rd and 54th) were outnumbered and outflanked, as were two mounted brigades left in the vicinity: the yeomanry and the Camels. They all had to fight through the day and retreat after nightfall. Infantrymen were still withdrawing at dawn on 28 March.

At the time, and on reflection, the original decision to abandon the Gaza operation was the worst of the Middle East war to that point. It demoralised the fighting men, and delivered the Turks an undeserved sense of 'victory'. After the steady run of 'wins' for the Desert Column, this reversal outweighed everything so far achieved. The mission disclosed British intentions in southern Palestine and caused the Turks to make redispositions and plans to cope.

Chetwode and Dobell, over-cautious and let down by poor communications, had managed to turn a certain, important victory at Gaza into a humiliating 'defeat' for the British force. Dobell's report would attempt to finesse the loss, blaming the fog and claiming that the Desert Column had been successful in 'bringing the enemy to battle'.

He added that the Turks would now 'undoubtedly stand with all his available force, in order to fight us when we are prepared to attack . . . so far as all ranks of the troops engaged were concerned, it was a brilliant victory, and had the early part of the day been normal, victory would have been secured'.

Dobell assured Murray that two more hours of daylight was all that was needed. This was incredible 'spin' on the events that would make a leg-spin bowler of the time such as Arthur Mailey appear straight up and down by comparison. Murray took up the line in his report to the War Office, which was transparent and misleading. He estimated the Turkish casualties as twice those of the British when the reverse was the case.

This false, glossy report backfired on Murray. The War Office, either accepting the analysis, or calling his bluff, urged him to renew his offensive, especially in the light of new British successes in Iraq. He was instructed to make his objective the defeat of the Turks and the taking of Jerusalem. The British War Office and Prime Minister Lloyd George saw the propaganda value in taking the holy city, with the undertones of the old crusade battles, in which Christians fought Muslims. It would be a press distraction from the horrors on the Western Front in France and Belgium. The daily bulletins on death, injury and destruction had cast a pall over the mood of the British public. Yet despite the push from the prime minister and some in the War Cabinet, they were opposed by those (mainly the generals) who believed all energies should go into the Western Front, where in the end, the war would be won or lost. Diverting funds and troops to the Middle East seemed illogical to them. But Lloyd George had a different agenda to the military. He needed support to stay in power. The generals wanted more men, machines and everything to throw at the Germans.

The result was a firm directive to take Palestine, but with limited extra resources.

Murray prevaricated, having backed himself into a corner. He replied that he needed more infantry, five divisions in all. Unless he received them, he wrote, he could not advance. He needed a lot of luck to secure a big battle win. That would not happen, Murray advised, without huge losses. The Turks were already strengthening the entire line east from Gaza to Beersheba. Behind it the line from Jerusalem to Jaffa on the Mediterranean coast was being shored up.

The response from the War Cabinet was swift and demanding. It wanted him to pursue the Turks immediately with the force he already had. The underlying rationale was that if he was claiming a virtual 'victory' on the first attempt at Gaza, he should be able to secure the town with another mission using the same numbers. The cabinet was in the process of reviewing strategy after the British capture of Baghdad on 11 March 1917 and the beginning of revolution in Russia, which had triggered the Tsar's resignation. The British would push harder to throw the Turks out of Iraq. Their General Maude was continuing his offensive north. There were more than vague hopes in the cabinet that the 'new' Russian government would attack Mosul in Iraq, putting a double pressure on the Turks that may force their ejection.

With those pressures in the background, a breakthrough in Palestine was required. The cabinet was about to authorise an invasion of that country. British Prime Minister Lloyd George was the main protagonist for defeating the Turks and taking the holy city of Jerusalem.

Murray and Dobell had no choice but to resign or scramble to reorganise another attack on Gaza.

They chose to make a second attempt to take this vital town.

In reaction to the British failure at Gaza, Lawrence felt a greater than normal gesture had to be made on the Hejaz railway, such as decommissioning it, at least temporarily. He had to attempt to blow up a train. His first effort had failed, yet he was determined to become proficient at laying mines. Lawrence saw it as an important instrument in his terrorist activities.

He set off again for the Hejaz railway on 2 April with a party of 30, a machine-gun crew and a section of Syrian infantrymen. They ran into torrential rain on the first night and a heat so extreme the next morning that Lawrence could not emulate the Bedouins by walking on the burning sand. Worse was a storm that generated ragged yellow-and-blue sulphurous clouds. They settled on the heights. Then dust clouds blew up and rose 300 metres. They grew deadly in the form of a double vortex that swirled over the valley in which the little party was travelling. It hit hard, tearing at their clothes and eyes. The whirlwind was strong enough to cause chaos among the camels, causing collisions and stumbles. It passed in less than 20 minutes but was followed by rain that sheeted down and drenched everyone.

The party climbed a steep ridge in the afternoon in the hope of viewing the railway, but found it covered by the misty after-effects of the rain storm. On the way down a Bedouin slipped on the wet rocks and fell 15 metres to his death.

Lawrence was unsettled, wondering if the gods were against his mission, yet his diary entries showed he was determined to follow through. The party camped in the heights. At nightfall, he took al-Qadis, a senior Bedouin law-giver and a sheikh, across the plain to the railway towards a station—Mudahrij—to the north of his earlier attempted sabotage. It lay behind a steep escarpment. En route they heard the Turkish bugle call in a fort announcing dinner. This reinforced their need to move quietly.

They reached the railway at 10 p.m. and rode along the track searching for a suitable machine-gun position and place to lay the mine. Visibility was poor, which was useful for cover, but not reconnoitring. Lawrence became impatient and decided on a place at random. The three men alighted from their camels. Lawrence laid down the mine, with its hair-trigger igniter. It made him nervous. He placed two charges about 25 metres apart on the rail-cutting with the pressure-switch equidistant between them. Then he connected the switch to each charge. The two charges were his insurance against failure, whichever way a train was moving. At least one charge was likely to ignite as the train pressed over the tracks.

Light rain fell as Lawrence worked. It impeded his progress. The gravel and sand rail embankment became soggy. He noticed that every step he made now left an imprint. After the nerve-wracking job was completed in two hours, he signalled for the others to mount their camels. With rain still filtering down, he led them in a march up and down the line about 100 metres either side of the charges. This way, Turkish patrols, which always roamed the line before a train appeared, would find it impossible to find his footprints near the charges. He then led the others into the plain beyond the tracks with the idea the Turkish patrols would think that the camel tracks were merely those of Bedouins passing along and over the line.

The three saboteurs then retired to a ridge to spend the rest of the night in the freezing cold. At dawn, they were grateful for the sun's heat, which coincided with the arrival of a 30-strong force of Bedouins, including Juhayna tribesmen, themselves experienced dynamiters. There was also a machine-gun crew with the weapon strapped onto a mule.

At 7.30 a.m. a Turkish patrol of 11 emerged from the station. Lawrence crawled up to the top of the ridge to watch them. They began a thorough search along the line with much gesticulating and pointing at the camel footprints along the track. They prodded and even pushed a shovel deep around the line.

Lawrence watched and hoped. He was relieved to see them trot on towards the next station where they met another patrol. An hour later, the steady chugging of a train could be heard. Lawrence trained his binoculars on it as it emerged from the south through a light mist. He focused on the nine carriages. To his horror, he saw they were filled with women and children, most likely the families of soldiers at Medina. If the detonation was successful, he would be responsible for slaughtering perhaps 300 innocents. He held his breath as the train reached the charges. It rolled on over them, without ignition.

Lawrence was stunned, first at the relief of not having so many deaths of women and children on his conscience, and second at the failure of his demolition skills.

Just as he had thoughts of rejigging the mine charges, Turkish sentries five kilometres away spotted the Bedouins accompanying the machine-gun crew, although from that distance they could not have ascertained their intent. They opened fire knowing that they were unlikely to do damage. This was normal practice for the Turks when they spotted nomads, but the coincidence of the passing train and the crouching party may have aroused suspicions.

Lawrence feared the 1,000-strong Turkish contingent manning the forts at the two stations might be sent out after them. He ordered a hasty retreat. When well clear, the camels were walked slowly so as not to kill the poor mule labouring under the weight of the machine-gun.

They were forced to wait in a gully until late afternoon. Lawrence, well experienced in living with the Arabs of the desert, took time in what shade he could find under the blinding sun to write in his diary. He was a compulsive scribbler, and his notes would be useful as a base for a later report to Cairo.

'Travelling with them is unsatisfactory for an Englishman,' he wrote, 'unless he had patience as deep and as wide as the sea.' This was quaint code for telling the bureau that only he himself had this gift and knew how to handle them. Looking around him, he observed them eating and drinking. They did not seem to know how to stop downing coffee, which kept them alert when they should have been resting. They consumed milk as if it were water, and water as if were plentiful. They tore into the mutton rations with no regard for what would happen when it ran out. They smoked whenever it was allowed, which was usually in the daylight hours. There was no sense of discipline over anything that would sustain them for a long guerilla campaign. He described them as having 'no stamina of mind'.

'They dreamt constantly about sex,' he noted, and excited each other with lewd stories. The Bedouins would be perpetual hedonists if it were not for their tough existence.

These comments captured the way he thought mid-mission. They were useful for his own propaganda. They were meant to show his superiors that he understood them better than anyone else, while at the same time putting off other British agents from dealing with them. For this purpose he painted an unattractive picture of the desert Arab, especially in areas of self-discipline, which he knew was anathema to the mentality of the British military and its offshoots in intelligence.

'If they suspected one of driving them,' he wrote, 'they would resist or run away, but if one had the patience to present things from their own point of view, they would do one's pleasure.'

Lawrence observed further that their minds were similar to 'ours . . . they will follow us, if we can endure with them, and play their game'.[3]

Late on the afternoon of 3 April, Lawrence and the raiders made a bold return to the scene of their near-crime the night before. The Turks fired on them as a matter of course again, but no bullets seemed to come near. The enemy were having their sport as usual. When the party reached the tracks this time, al-Qadis suggested cleverly they hold a prayer session with himself acting as the imam in front. It was approaching dusk, a time for prayers. Although none of the party, including Lawrence, was religious, they went through the rituals, bowing, dropping to their knees and placing their foreheads on the ground.

It had the desired effect. The Turks stopped firing. The sun set. Darkness came. Lawrence began the unenviable task of scrabbling around in the blackness looking for the buried trigger. His job was made even more nail-biting when all the Juhayna dynamiters with him—about 20 men in all—pressed close for moral support. If he triggered the weapon now, he would kill the lot of them.

After pushing his hands into the sand for an hour, he located it. The trigger had been dislodged a fraction, which accounted for its non-ignition. He reset the mechanism.

The dynamiters then dashed off to lay charges north at a four-arched culvert and on the rails. Lawrence did his shinnying act up a telegraph pole to cut the wires, with two men at the foot to break his fall if he tumbled down again. This time he managed a more graceful descent.

Lawrence and the rest of the raiders had just mounted their camels when thunder-like explosions sounded up the line. The charges had gone off as planned, ripping up sections of the line and collapsing the bridge's top. This was the signal for the party to hurry back to their camp. They came so quickly in the dark that their own people at the base opened up with machine-guns thinking it was Turkish attack. But luck was with the guerillas. No-one was hit.

Lawrence, still feeling the after-effects of his illnesses, slept through the night. He had asked to be woken at dawn but was left to sleep on.

He was woken at 7.30 a.m. by the muted roar of his mines at last working, but not quite with the success he hoped for. A train carrying 300 troops from the Turkish repair battalions, and weighed down with tonnes of replacement rails for the section of line destroyed the night before, had triggered both charges. The double blast had battered carriages and caused casualties, but the train itself would run again, despite the damage done. The Hejaz section of the Turkish railway and lifeline to the Medina garrison was shut down.

Lawrence, still unsure of his demolition skills, was satisfied with his progress as a provocateur, especially at this moment when the Turks further west on the coast at Gaza seemed to have the initiative.

His efforts in several areas from shinnying up telegraph poles and laying mines to his tactics and determination had lifted his status in the eyes of the Bedouins. This was on top of his dutiful shooting of Hamed, which everyone knew was an awful responsibility. He was now more than an honorary sharif, and honoured elder. T. E. Lawrence was a serious leader of the revolt.

His reputation would precede him.

35

Gaza: Take Two

Gaza looked like a battle zone on the Western Front as the days slipped by after the stalemate of the first conflict. The 18,000 Turks dug in with trenches and fortifications, building on the city's natural defences and extending them to Beersheba. They had 101 artillery guns and 86 machine-guns, making victory for the British at best much tougher and more costly in terms of likely casualty numbers, and at worst, unlikely. Murray brought in eight tanks, making the assumption they would be effective in this different theatre, and that scourge of all soldiers, gas. There would be also much more heavy artillery (bringing the numbers up to 170 guns). Support would come from the French battleship *Requin* and two British 'monitors' anchored offshore.

The second Battle of Gaza would be a set-piece infantry battle primarily with the attack made by three infantry divisions (52nd, 53rd and 54th), the Imperial Mounted Division and the Camels. Chauvel and his Anzac brigades were marginalised. They would cover the operation's right flank towards Beersheba.

Chauvel was disgruntled at the disregard for the Light Horse but could do nothing but complain to his wife on paper. He and his troopers had been annoyed about the first battle and he had to work on keeping them concentrated on the job and being prepared. To brighten them up, he organised a race meeting on 5 April, with the main event being the Gaza Cup. Horses and camels were entered in various races and there was heavy betting on the results. It took the troopers' minds off the tedium of waiting for battle. The next day they began training in the use of gas helmets. The British, not the Turks, planned to introduce this ugly weapon. If they attacked after the gas shells had been fired, there was a possibility that they could be asphyxiated. After this, the troopers learned about the new Hotchkiss light machine-gun. They were not all certain about these weapons. Some found them cumbersome. Others thought they were the best weapon they had handled. Love it or loathe it, each troop was to be issued with one, which was to replace the Lewis gun. (Only the Cameleers were reluctant to use it. They preferred the Lewis gun.) Before the Hotchkiss was introduced, there was just one Lewis gun for each squadron.

This new order meant a step-up in fire power to four machine-guns in every squadron.

The land and sea bombardment began at 5.30 a.m. on 19 April 1917. This included six howitzers, which fired all the 350 British gas shells in half an hour. They had no impact and evaporated harmlessly. The Turks did not even notice. The first 'edge' that Murray thought would bring him victory had failed. The second advantage, allegedly delivered by the tanks, also did not have any major impact. Half of them broke down or moved unreliably; the other half except for one moving slow enough to take several artillery hits each, were destroyed by shells. It was up to the British infantry, which made its full frontal attack at 7.15 a.m. after the artillery had let go its barrage. First out was the 53rd Division, which had been keen to get back at the Turks. The 52nd and 54th followed up. On the right, the Imperial Mounteds made their move forward, while Chauvel's horsemen turned their eyes to the east to meet any reinforcing Turkish force.

The 53rd continued where it left off late in March and went in with courage. But this time the enemy was better prepared. Its artillery was accurate and its machine-guns more efficiently placed. The British did not make much ground. They had support from the artillery, which hit a few Turkish guns, but not enough. The British guns were too thinly spread over the too great a distance of seven kilometres.

*

Chauvel's Anzacs and the Camels (mainly Australian troopers) were protecting the right of the advancing 54th Division from Turkish infantry attempting to aid those in the city defences. The 3rd and 4th Brigades and the Camels pushed through the scattered yellow barley, the colour veil broken by red splashes of poppies. The fields provided cover, but also hid forward enemy posts and snipers. The mounteds were reinforced by a brigade from the 54th Division.

On the first-wave attack, a tank led the way on a path between the infantry and the Australians. The appearance of it scything and flattening its way forward seemed to encourage and draw a massive amount of enemy fire. The men instinctively falling in behind it, were caught in a fierce barrage, which was added to by machine-gun and rifle blasts. Troopers and cameleers—all dismounted—were hit in numbers. The already thin ranks of the attackers were beginning to show gaps. Big, broad-shouldered 32-year-old Captain A. E. C. Campbell, a Queenslander in No. 2 Company, and his cameleers, were among those that made it to about 400 metres from their target of a big Turkish redoubt. They were encouraged by the sight of the tank ploughing on, shells bouncing off it, in the same direction.

There was incentive to go on, if only by virtue of how close they were to their target of an entrenched hill protected by barbed wire. It ran for 200 metres in front of the main line of Turkish trenches extending towards the village of Atawineh.

The tank captain seemed hell-bent on crushing the redoubt. It moved like a huge armadillo but faltered in a patch of broken ground. Now pock-marked and covered in scorches, its crew lost direction, veering off to the right on the top of a ridge. Then it seemed to learn its error and navigated hard left, cutting across in front of the cameleers, who were in the process of fixing bayonets as they closed to within 350 metres of the enemy.

Turkish fire intensified by the minute. Many Australians were hit, forcing the rest to go to ground.

The Camels' No. 3 Company joined their fellow Anzacs on the ridge and suffered the same fate. One hundred men in the two companies were killed or wounded. Undaunted, Campbell, keeping pace with the rogue tank, called up six Lewis gunners and pushed them 50 metres ahead of his dwindling numbers. They took aim at the Turks, who poked their heads above the parapet, offering targets like watermelons.

Under cover of the Lewis gunners, the troopers made their run just as the tank pitched forward. It received a tremendous pounding and seemed almost to suspend concentration on anything else as it rumbled on. The brave crew kept it moving despite it being red-hot and coughing black smoke.

The tank crashed through barriers and the barbed wire, opening a passage for about 300 Australians and British infantry, who joined the dash. The lumbering monster mesmerised the Turks, who either ran for cover or tried to destroy it. But the closer it came, the more nerves frayed. The tank rolled over the front trenches in a cloud of smoke and dust, a crippled monster out of control. The 600 Turks had never seen such a terrifying weapon. They were preoccupied with the machine, worried that it would lurch in their direction.

All their gunners turned on the smouldering vehicle and brought it to a halt. Seconds after breaking down, it caught fire and exploded.

In the minutes this happened, a group of 30 Australians led by the bull-like Campbell were among the Turks, followed by 20 British soldiers. The 50 used their bayonets freely, and none more than the captain. He was hit by bullets but his equipment, clothing and an extraordinary amount of luck saved him. The astonished Turks, having been stunned by the tank's onslaught, lost their collective nerve. They climbed out of their trenches. About 500 dropped their weapons and rushed for their main line of trenches.

Swathed in blood, the unstoppable Campbell directed his following Lewis gunners into the open. They were ordered to cut down the escaping Turks in an Australian ritual. If they surrendered, they were spared. If they did not, whether they would fight or take flight, every attempt would be made to obliterate them as the Lewis gunners did this time. It was callous, but the

Australians saw it as 'sporting'. Those who had been at Gallipoli had no second thoughts about slaughtering the enemy, for whom in general they had respect and admiration for their fighting qualities. 'New' troopers, who had not been on the peninsula, knew what was expected. They too spared no bullets for escapees or fighters. But those Turks who gave up were not cut down. There would be mistakes and the odd exception, but the rule, both by strict convention and inclination, was to be fair to those who threw down their arms.

Campbell assembled 40 prisoners taken in the redoubt. He marched them to the British side and ordered them to stop. Then pointing to the Turkish trenches, the big man roared:

'Run!'

The Turks needed no further invitation. Campbell walked briskly back to his newly acquired redoubt, just as Turkish artillery and gun-fire swept over the area. He had just stepped close to the trenches when a German officer confronted him and aimed his revolver. Campbell reached for his holstered pistol just as a Turkish shell careered into the ground between them, killing the German before he could pull the trigger.[1]

He led the Anglo-Australian band over the next two hours as they fought to hold this unforgiving knoll. They were soon outnumbered by the Turks in the trenches 300 metres away. A German was urging them to counterattack, as machine-guns, rifles and artillery pumped into the redoubt. But the Turks, having seen what they were in for, hesitated.

By midday, there was a state of siege. The soldiers and troopers in the captured redoubt were being picked off. Campbell sent six messages for help. Four of the runners were killed. Two stumbled back wounded. No-one would learn of their plight. The Lewis guns would run out of ammunition within a couple of hours; then the diminishing numbers would be in deep trouble.

They could see a battalion-strong force of Turks forming up, ready for an attack.

Campbell ordered the 20 remaining men to retreat to a valley on the right, if they could. He weaved his way forward to tell the Lewis gunners out in front of the redoubt that they had to fall back too. He found them all at their weapons. Five were dead. The sixth, 24-year-old air-mechanic W. J. Barry, was wounded in the right arm.

Campbell told him to fall back if he could.

'What about my gun, sir?' the schoolteacher from Yass, New South Wales, called.

'Leave it! Save yourself!'

But Barry was attached to his weapon. It gave him strength. He had enough left to hoist the gun onto his left shoulder and stagger towards the valley. Campbell ducked his way back to the redoubt, where he found a quartermaster-sergeant, 26-year-old H. L. D. Malcolm, who should have been at the rear. Instead, he was working overtime to both tend the wounded and use a rifle to help in the defence as the attempt to leave was carried out.[2]

At 3 p.m. all the Australians had been evacuated except for Campbell, Malcolm and 37-year-old Lieutenant E. J. Aylwin. They were all former members of the 14th Light Horse Regiment, who had joined the Camels and were united now as they never had been.

Campbell ordered Malcolm to go first. At first he didn't hear. Campbell knew he had a hearing problem. He moved close and with sign language told him a second time to leave. Malcolm refused. Campbell pulled rank and was firm. Malcolm sprinted off over the 70 metres to safety in the valley. Campbell watched him, then ducked over to his good friend Aylwin. They had enlisted together at Toowoomba in late 1914.

'I'm going last, cobber,' Campbell said. 'You gotta go. I'll follow.'

Aylwin sprinted for the sanctuary. He had gone 50 metres when he was killed. Campbell was luckier and made it across the treacherous strip. He was one of five of the 102 men in 2nd Company who were not dead or wounded after this vicious engagement.

The battle was at a place that would from then on be known as Tank Redoubt in honour of the fearless British crew that had died leading the way.[3]

36

An Enemy Boosted

The Turkish big guns were proving the difference at Second Gaza. They kept the British infantry and batteries under bombardment and made it tough for the mounted riflemen, giving the horsemen a greater sense of the battles being fought on the Western Front.

As always in adversity, the most fearless came to the fore. The 8th Light Horse, led by Lieutenant Colonel Maygar, was fighting just to the east of the Gaza–Beersheba road. He cantered about the battleground on a grey horse in front of his firing line. Major H.J. Shannon, a 43-year-old grazier from Wangaratta, Victoria, was always the first man to push forward. Man-mountain Jack Royston, leading the 2nd Brigade again, thundered around where the action was at his height. It was his way. It would take, his men said, a direct hit with a shell from a big gun, plus a spray from a machine-gun at close range just to knock him off his horse.

He was not alone in his apparent indestructibility. Twenty-four-year-old trooper F.J. Manuell of the 11th Regiment, a stockman from Pine Hill, Queensland, was pleased to be leading two horses forward carrying new Hotchkiss machine-guns. He walked into heavy artillery fire. A shell landed close and severed his left foot. The horses reared up, terrified. Manuell managed to keep control of them until he could hand them to another trooper 40 metres away. Then he collapsed, his war ended, his foot lost, but his life saved.

Battle conditions broke some men, and made others. Some had their fingers shot off by deliberately raising their hands above the parapet. The wounds would see them invalided out of the war. Others, such as Bourke, New South Wales farmer Major P. A. Chambers, 41, of the 12th Regiment, received their lucky break but ignored it. He was hit in the shoulder. It was a deep enough wound to see him on his way to hospital. But it was the last thing on his mind. He had it dressed then hastened back to the front. Inside half an hour, he was so badly wounded in the torso that he was this time carried off the battlefield. Chambers was forced to accept his second chance at life.

The 8th Light Horse was pushed back at one point around noon on 19 April. Later when they went forward again, they came across the body of trooper W. G. Duguid. He had been bayoneted and stripped of his clothes and boots. It disgusted his mates. They expected it from the Bedouins, but not the Turks. They were ready to accept that the Turks were short of decent uniforms, belts and boots. But what did they need his wallet, neck chain and pay book for? Souvenirs? (Nearly six months later, when the 3rd Brigade entered Huj in the great drive up the Palestine Plain, they found Duguid's pay book in one of the enemy camps.)

The Anzacs were not above taking souvenirs themselves, but in the perverse manner of the way wars were fought, they could brutally kill a man, but leave the dead body clothed and with a modicum of dignity, or if possible bury it. Desert nomads were different. They wasted little and had less. They took what they could. Some Turks, perhaps only the odd one or two, thought this way too. Poverty was their lot. The war had given them a subsistence living of sorts, but there were shortages in everything and many more than the British fighters endured.

Courage in these battles was never restricted to the bold ones with weapons. The stretcher-bearers had as much if not more guts. They had no guns with which to defend themselves. As they crouched and bustled around retrieving wounded men from the field, they knew that their lives could be over in a flash. A sniper, perhaps annoyed because he had missed a target, might take a pot shot. When fighting was intense, the stretcher-bearers knew that the enemy could not be expected to spare them as they tended the fallen, even if they wished to. The Turks could not direct every bullet from a machine-gun, or an artillery shell exactly the way they wished. The lottery of life was in play as these humane operatives darted everywhere, finding cover where they could, but unable to avoid being stranded as easy targets as they rolled a wounded man onto a stretcher and hurried him away.

A clerk from Glebe Point, Sydney, 33-year-old Albert 'Tibby' Cotter of the 12th Regiment, a famous Test-cricket fast bowler with a fearsome slinging action, was among the stretcher-bearers. He used his strong chest and shoulders, once to heave leather missiles, now to lift injured men to safety. He and 25-year-old Captain W. Evans worked flat out all day with three others, dodging bullets and stepping around shells pitching near them as they tended to 240 fallen troopers. Two men they helped were Gallipoli survivors, Hugo Throssell, who was wounded, and his brother Ric, who died.

The conflict was similar in size and scope to those in France and Belgium, including the dogfights in the sky. Scraps went on close and low in full view of the terrestrial battlers, who looked up and urged on their side, or the plane they thought was on their side. It was always an urgent spectacle for the British. Their planes were inferior. The German machines bombed the horses, batteries and any HQ or camp they could. They were a menace. Any 'kill' of one brought joy to onlookers.

One fight on the afternoon of 19 April almost caused a lull in proceedings on the ground. The British pilot manoeuvred with skill but the German adversary seemed to have him lined up for a strike. He dived and fired his weapons but missed. The British plane now had the ascendancy. He careered towards the German, but the stress on his machine twisting and turning to avoid being hit had strained one of his flimsy wings. It flapped helplessly. The plane went into a spin. The pilot stood. He gripped one of the struts as if he could somehow defy gravity. The plane crashed, much to the horror and disappointment of British force onlookers, killing the pilot.

All the mounteds, both horses and camels, were set to swoop in if the British infantry could open any breach in the enemy lines. But it didn't seem to be coming. The left of the 54th was hopeful. It forced itself as far as the Turkish front line, but was hit by fire from Ali Muntar. Further to the left, and closer to the Mediterranean, the 52nd took Outpost Hill half-way to Ali Muntar. But that division too reached no further. It was forced back and lost the outpost. Further left still on the coast, the 53rd reached a ridge three kilometres from Gaza township. Yet its now hardened fighters could not edge beyond it. They too were countered.

The lack of a breakthrough had Dobell sweating and Murray nervous in his 'bunker' in Cairo. The major worries were apparent. The British force was running out of ammunition. The attack had been predicated on a swift victory. But when the Turks returned better than they received there was stalemate. Guns had to keep firing. The bullet and bomb piles diminished. There was also the perennial problem with water. Fresh supplies could not be gained east of Beersheba where all the wells were locked up by the Turks. Replenishment meant retreat.

The British action was called off in the evening. They did not know it but the Turks and their own ammunition were on the verge of exhaustion. Enemy commander Kress was not about to counterattack. The British fell back to their original positions. Murray frothed in dispatches that 'all ground gained must be held'. Dobell, near the battle zone, made a different, more pragmatic appraisal. He postponed the British operation for a day and in that time, in conference with Murray, suggested there was nothing to gain from carrying on.

Murray, disappointed and stunned, had little choice but to agree to abandon Gaza a second time.

The two battles of Gaza had gone to the Turks. They were buoyed by the success after being on the defensive and sometimes on the run for the last nine months. Their confidence was high. They began to dig in, reinforcing the entire Gaza-to-Beersheba line in the logical belief that if they could hold off two vigorous thrusts, then stronger defences and better trenches would make the line impregnable. Palestine in April 1917 seemed very much in Turkish hands. It was a welcome, almost surprising moment for the shaky Ottoman Empire and their German supporters after the setbacks in Sinai, Iraq and in the Hejaz.

By contrast, the second loss stunned the British. Dobell tallied up 5,900 casualties (compared with about one third that for the enemy), with the bulk of them (4,920) sustained by the infantry. The Camels had lost 345 and the Imperial Mounteds 547. The Anzacs had just 105 casualties, which mirrored their part in the campaign. In hindsight, Chauvel and his troopers may well have been relieved to be bit players in such a disaster.

The big overall total would have seemed in London like another battle result from the Western Front. There would be no more talk for the moment at Number 10 Downing Street about 'liberating' the holy city.

The commanders at Gaza ordered an urgent entrenchment. There would be no fall-back to the desert, but there was no talk of a third attempt at taking this now elusive city. The region was in fixed-position stalemate. It had fallen the way of the Western Front and Gallipoli. The depressing point for the British was that there seemed no alternative.

Murray did what some leaders do when responsibility rests with them: he sacked his number two, General Dobell, on 21 April, the day after the engagement ceased. Chetwode replaced Dobell in control of 'Eastern Force'. Chauvel took over as commander of the Desert Column, making him the first Australian and the first officer of a dominion force to command a corps. It was a wonderful boost for him. He felt he was fit and capable for such responsibility. He now had control over the biggest mounted force (cavalry or otherwise) in modern history and probably of all time. At full strength, he would have more than 30,000 mounted riflemen and cavalry under him. While the mounteds and cavalry had played a limited and decreasing role on the Western Front, despite all the efforts of the High Command, who mainly had a cavalry background and loved the use of the horse in battle, it was a different proposition in the Middle East. Mobility in the relatively wide spaces was vital, and while the automobile was developing fast, it would not be as important as the horse and camel in the region.

Chauvel recommended that New Zealand's Edward Chaytor be promoted to control Anzac Mounted. The dapper, lean 49-year-old, with the trimmed moustache and stiff upper lip, deserved his step-up. They called him 'Fiery Fred' because of a grumpy manner brought on by severe wounds in battle. In the Boer War, Chaytor suffered a bullet in the thigh, which caused an injury similar to the one that killed Colonel Bridges at Anzac Cove. Chaytor, with typical understatement, said the only lingering problem was that he was left 'slightly lame'. He could have added 'short-tempered'. He first saw action as an HQ staff officer on Gallipoli in May 1915, where he was injured again. It didn't help his demeanour, but if anything he was an even tougher commander in the desert campaign, always ready to lead. The Anzacs put up with his curmudgeonly manner. They respected him as a 'game old beggar', his courage and limp rounding off this image.

Murray reorganised the Desert Column, after consultation with Chauvel, into a corps of three divisions. After much politicking and administrative manoeuvring, Chauvel secured the divisional composition and nomenclature he wanted: Anzac Mounted, Australian Mounted (formerly Imperial Mounted) and a yeomanry division. This reflected its true nature with two-thirds of the Light Horse part of the column being Australians and New Zealanders (one brigade).

During the weeks of tedious yet important reorganisation, Chauvel was planning and plotting the way his new responsibility for the right flank leading into the desert should be handled. This was within the scope of Chetwode's clever scheme to smash through the Gaza–Beersheba line. He wanted a feint against Gaza, followed by a terrific thrust using infantry and Light Horse against Beersheba. It had to be swift. A day was all they would have. If the attack did not succeed in that time, lack of water more than the Turks would defeat the plans. The enemy controlled all the vital wells in and around the town except one. If they destroyed them, Chauvel calculated a loss for his force was certain. He would be forced to retreat.

His thoughts were influenced by the distance over empty plains past dry wells he would have to travel to position his force for a strike against Beersheba. He consulted his chief engineer, British Brigadier General R. E. M. Russell, over his assessment. Diligent research by him in files in Cairo over historic exploration of Palestine discovered that Khalasa, 22 kilometres south-west of Beersheba, and Asluj, 25 kilometres south, had been big towns until the previous century. This indicated they had good wells. With luck, water supplies could be resuscitated. This would give Chauvel a fall-back option and reserves for his troopers. Russell made discreet enquiries with friendly Arabs in the area. They told him that both wells were operating, but not efficiently. Engineers would be needed to achieve an abundant supply. Learning this, Chauvel directed a thorough search for any additional supplies in the vicinity.

Once this was done, he was anxious to carry out a mission in preparation for the Beersheba attack, whenever that might occur. Murray had given no signal that he would allow it, and there were rumours that he would soon be replaced. Chauvel, like all the commanders, loathed periods of inertia, which were caused often when command was constipated at the top. There was a limit to the number of times troopers could be directed over the area of light clay soil with the ever-attendant mist of dust. Sooner or later they would become distressed by the monotony as much as the conditions. Boredom overtook the collective mind, while dust seeped into their hair, clothes and lungs.

Without water the dust was far more problematic than the enemy, which had not threatened them since the Second Battle of Gaza. The season of the desert storm (khamsin) was with them in May and exacerbated the problem. At night the stars were blocked out by the grey, choking wall.

The diet didn't help the troopers' collective mood or condition. Bully beef and biscuits were unrelenting. The lack of vegetables helped cause septic sores that affected every man and rank. Bandages were rife.

Chauvel, as ever, worried about the horses. Despite the limited influence of the Light Horse at Second Gaza, Chetwode assured him that they would be as important in Palestine as they were in Sinai. The mounts had to be kept in good condition, which was not easy given the 19 kilometres travelled just to water them twice each day. At least he could rely on each individual trooper looking after his mount with grooming, feeding and watering.

The further the troopers went into the campaign, the stronger their bonds developed with their horses.

By early May, Chauvel was ready for an important military project that would also assist in focusing his troopers. The Turkish railway running south of Asluj was a concern. The Turks had not used it in the month since Gaza but it was always there and a potential menace for ferrying troops from Beersheba. Now that Chauvel had his eyes on the wells at Asluj and Khalasa, he wanted the railway, bridges and culverts destroyed. Apart from its use when the Beersheba battle began, the enemy was very keen to uproot the steel rails for military lines elsewhere. The

Turks had already done this on the old railway from Jaffa north up the Mediterranean coast inland to Ramleh.

With these factors in mind, Chauvel sat down with his engineers and plotted a massive demolition job after Chetwode approved it.

Neither man needed to consult Murray, whose record was under review at the War Office. His overall performance in charge in the Middle East over 18 months had been impressive. He had subdued the difficult Senussi (a religious sect from the Sahara Desert) inside Egypt and had calmed affairs in the Sudan. He had kept the pipeline and railway growing through the Sinai. He had reinforced the British on the Western Front with several divisions without complaint, which had endeared him to the War Office.

Murray's handling of the Bedouins in the Hejaz was less defined. He was not a cheerleader for the revolt or the Arabs taking the initiative, which he saw as reducing British influence. Yet he had endorsed support in money, gold and supplies by the military and the Arab Bureau to Hussein and his family in drawing them into the war against the Turks. That seemed to be having an effect.

Murray was a skilful negotiator, a good diplomat and a well-respected man of empire. He would receive fair marks for his main job of defending the Suez Canal and Egypt. But he had failed on the most ambitious assignment, which meant a change from a defensive mind to an offensive one in taking Palestine. He was not a commander with thrust. Murray's leadership by remote control had not worked at Gaza, and could not work in any dreams about taking Palestine from the Turks.

His failures would rest heavily on the War Cabinet, who now knew that Murray had been fudging his reports.

The hard-heads began to be cool in their correspondence with him.

37

Feints in the Desert

And King Solomon made a navy of ships in Ezion-Geber [Aqaba], which is beside Eloth [Eliat], on the shore of the Red Sea, in the Land of Edom.

1 Kings 9: 26

Lawrence saw the British failure in southern Palestine as the moment to attempt to take the Turkish-held town of Aqaba at the tip of the narrow 160-kilometre waterway offshoot to the north-east of the Red Sea, the Gulf of Aqaba. This town of warm climate, ringed by high desert mountains, was one of the most important strategic points in the entire struggle for control of the Middle East. Gaza was just 155 kilometres away to the west; Damascus was 350 kilometres. The Turks had kept Aqaba as an insignificant fishing village for 400 years but World War I had changed all that. Control of Aqaba, Lawrence believed, would put pressure on the Turks on the Gaza–Beersheba defence line. They would have to decide if they could spare men and resources to retake Aqaba. There would always be Turkish concern that they could be attacked on their left flank south of Beersheba.

Aqaba would also be the launching pad for the Arabs' direct thrust to Syria. Taking the port was a nice idea on paper. It was trickier, even outlandish in practice. Almost all thought centred on invading it from the sea, with a naval bombardment and infantry landing. This concept had been around for a year. But there had been no force behind it. Clayton was sounded out on the question by Charles Vickery, now the senior adviser to Hussein and the leaders of the Arab Revolt. Clayton questioned the need to stir up the Arabs in that region at this stage. Better to wait for a more opportune time, he suggested, which meant the issue was shelved. In May 1917, he poured more cold water on the idea. Clayton worried that the Arabs would claim the town as theirs, and that this would not do post-war for the British in the defence of Egypt. When tested, the real British strategy was becoming transparent regardless of the Sykes–Picot agreement. They would use the Arabs where they could, keep them under control and doublecross them concerning Syria when and if the Turks were defeated in Damascus. Lawrence's conflict of interest was growing with every advance by the Arabs. In the end, he knew he would have to accept the British position, but in this audacious plan for Aqaba he was in essence supporting the Arabs. Without that town in their grasp, they were contained by the British in the Hejaz region. If, by a remote chance, it fell to the Arabs in a purely Arab initiative, the entire dynamics of their relationship with the British would change. They would be presented with a fait accompli.

Lawrence was aware that he would never be allowed officially or unofficially to carry through any scheme for Aqaba. He would have to move in secret.

In Wejh, he met with Feisal, who was angry and frustrated about the lack of action in his push north. There were unconfirmed rumours that the French were about to land 60,000 troops in Syria. Feisal knew that Aqaba was essential as the next Arab move. He too believed in a seaborne attack, but Lawrence told him this would not be supported by the British. This heightened Feisal's gloom.

Lawrence ruminated on the alternatives. He had excellent intelligence from the Arab Bureau. The cryptologists continued to crack German and Turkish codes. It knew where enemy forces were. By contrast the Turks would not know—unless by fluke in the vast desert—where he and his force were. He examined the new, high-quality photographic maps from the bureau, consulted Arab leaders and thought long and hard about the only other way to attack the town: from the desert behind it. He knew that maps were deceptive. Aqaba was 400 kilometres north-north-west from Wejh. But the circuitous route suggested by those familiar with the terrain would be closer to 900 kilometres. Yet that wasn't even the issue. The force would have to negotiate the most inhospitable region on earth, including a stretch of desert known as al-Houl ('The Terror'). The good news was that there no flies there. The bad news was that not even they could survive it. The toughness of this trek meant travelling as light as possible, without artillery and machine-guns. Camels would have to be preserved. Without them there would be no chance of reaching the destination. If they collapsed, the would-be invaders would all perish.

The logistics were even more difficult when Lawrence considered the composition of any proposed contingent. It would be purely an Arab operation, but choosing the right people would be paramount. The Hejaz Bedouins would not travel outside their tribal areas. At least a group of about 17 of Feisal's Agayl would be in it. The raiding party knew how tough they were from the blowing-up of the railway. Besides, they were mercenaries and Feisal would have enough money to back them. The proposed attack force would start modestly with about 50 men, including some teenage servants.

Lawrence needed the toughest of men to go with him, and someone who had influence over the Howeitat tribe. Its members roamed the Aqaba desert region, and would be needed to swell the numbers for the final assault on the coastal city. This led him to approach its leader, the tall, straight-backed 52-year-old Sheikh Auda Abu Tayi, a brutal man who in essence was a psychopath. Some fitting this description did not look the part, but Auda did. His dark hair, streaked with grey, aquiline nose and ungenerous eyes gave him a mature, eagle-like appearance that made many nervous, and he played on it with his bullying mien. His rages were legendary. Those who crossed him in those moments were said never to survive. He had taken his blows and was wounded 13 times in fights. There were apocryphal stories about him tearing out victims' hearts and eating them. Tribesmen who fought alongside him swore by his ferocity. He boasted having killed 75 Arabs in close combat. No-one challenged the number for fear of being number 76. (No-one had kept count of how many Turks he had slaughtered.)

Yet he was quite the ladies man. He married 28 times.

Lawrence noted his dress style of white cotton with a red Mosul head-cloth. He admired his lean facial contours, big, expressive, dark eyes and big, mobile mouth. His beard and moustache were trimmed in his tribe's style and shaven under the jaw.

Lawrence had to have Auda on side if he were to have a chance of influencing the Howeitat tribes from Aqaba to Maan, needed for an attack on Aqaba.

It took nerve to approach him, but Lawrence's confidence in any situation had been elevated. His self-esteem had gone up after his railway attacks, and after shooting his servant Hamed. His stocks were high in the eyes of most Arabs in the region, Auda among them. At worst, he expected the idea of attacking from the desert to receive scorn, even ridicule from Auda, who had a foul mouth. To Lawrence's surprise, Auda liked the plan, and the challenge. He even began suggesting ideas, and the unlikely team worked together on a strategy to take Aqaba.

If Lawrence did not believe in the old adage 'Fortune favours the brave', he perhaps would now.

Lawrence deceived Clayton and the Bureau, telling them that he might be accompanying Auda and the Howeitat to demolish the railway at Maan, 170 kilometres north-east of Aqaba, an unlikely mission if he had been quizzed on it. But this young master of deception knew how to fudge things when required. He never mentioned Aqaba. The operation he 'perhaps' could be going on was not authorised by the British, but he could draw on funds already allocated to Feisal. They took with them £25,000 worth of gold coins (that would help pay, among many things, Bedouin levies on the other side of the Hejaz). Lawrence gave revolvers to Auda, the Howeitat strategist Mohammad el Dheilan, and Nasir, reputed to be a most accomplished guerilla fighter in the Hejaz. The 27-year-old Nasir came from one of the most influential families in the region. He had the respect of everyone, including Lawrence. While describing him as chinless with a weak mouth, he nevertheless recognised a certain aura about him. Nasir had led the revolt in Medina, firing the first shot. He had done much to initiate the movement of Feisal, a man not afraid to lead from the front.

On 9 May, Lawrence and his modest force loaded up with food, water and as much ammunition as possible and took off on their camels on the tough assignment. This was his greatest physical and mental challenge so far. At 28, he was ready for it and any test that came with it. Overriding this would be his quiet moments in which he would put down those immediate thoughts in his notebook; those precious minutes when he was the writer he wished to be, and was already in his own mind. The author in him dominated his inner thoughts and his future hopes. And this was an adventure that had to be recorded for him, a future audience and, he believed, posterity.

Not long into the march he was writing about an ordeal. Day two began in heat that seemed to devour oxygen. By 11 a.m. he was struggling. It was a relief that the other leaders, except for the impatient, scowling Auda, wanted to stop. The next day the heat reactivated his recent illness. He felt feverish. His face broke out in boils. Despite his years in archaeological digs in other deserts he had never encountered anything like this. And this was day three of about 30. Lawrence had always felt physically inadequate, but he believed he had a strong mind. Now in this godforsaken country he would find out.

It was even too much for the camels. They did not wish to continue in the searing conditions that seemed to bring the sun much closer than its 147 million kilometres. Everyone had to dismount and pull the camels by their head-ropes. Sometimes help was needed to push them from behind.

Four days in, he wrote in his pocket diary:

'Pain and agony today.'

His entries showed the frustration of not moving fast enough. But the desert dwellers with him knew better. They had learned to stretch time and expend little energy. 'Getting there' was not in their thoughts. Arriving alive was their aim.

On the fifth day the party reached Abu Ragha where there was a small pool, which allowed everyone to refresh. More Agayl there joined the mission. Among them were two young teenage boys, who amused Lawrence and took his mind off the suffocating heat. He made them his servants.

The bigger party moved off again on 16 May and was soon into a volcanic (harra) landscape that was unearthly. Basalt outcroppings standing at different angles narrowed the valleys through which they passed, forcing the party to move as a column. It emerged from this surreal, threatening environment into the sandy Wadi Aish, with its welcome waterholes and scrub. It was the obvious place to rest and let the camels feed.

It was also perfect for an ambush. Camel-mounted raiders from the Turkish-supporting Shammar tribe materialised in the heat haze as large quivering balls of dust. They swooped in on the weary patrol but were met by a swift reaction. The Agayl either propped and fired their rifles or ran at the invaders. Realising the size of their intended quarry, the raiders turned and fled.

Soon after the attempted raid, Lawrence, his pulse racing and his mind taken from the conditions, sat under a blanket and scribbled.

On 19 May—day 10 of the trek—the patrol crossed the Hejaz railway at ad-Dizard. After checking that a nearby Turkish fort was empty, Lawrence directed Agayl dynamiters to carry out the first sabotage of the mission. Using a relay of guncotton and gelatine charges, they detonated in sequence, causing long reverberations in the valleys that would be heard for 50 kilometres.

Lawrence did his now well-practised shinny up a telegraph pole and cut the wires. Two poles were tied by rope to six camels. They were thumped on the rump and galloped off, pulling down the poles.

Eight kilometres on, the party set up camp at dusk on a ridge. Lawrence, fatigued, yet with his fever subsiding and the boils disappearing, took notes again. He could hear Turkish soldiers at forts along the line shouting and firing at something or perhaps nothing. The Shammar would have warned them of the patrol, its fire power, size and aggression. The Turks would be aware of the disruption on the railway. Any strange shapes in the night would have them reacting.

Lawrence managed five hours sleep, his best for the trip, but was awakened in the middle of the night by Auda, who was to be the guide out of the area that was now infested with hostile enemy patrols. Best to travel at night, he advised. While the darkness harboured only enemies in Arabia, it was better to risk encounters than suffer under the hellish sun. They broke camp and moved on around hills and sand dunes for several hours until dawn. It revealed they were on the verge of a never-ending plain of sand and stone. It seemed devoid of grass, trees or shrubs. The vastness was already beginning to shimmer in the first heat of the morning. No-one would follow or attack them here, Auda informed him with a twisted grin.

It was al-Houl, 'The Terror'.

Coincident with Lawrence's daring and high-risk operation, Chauvel had taken the initiative south of Beersheba, which he hoped would push in a subtle way his British superiors into more action against the Turks. Once the enemy was disabled on their left flank leading deep into the inhospitable desert, there was a strong reason for the British to carry out Chetwode's daring yet plausible plan to smash through the Gaza–Beersheba line.

Chauvel had settled on the destruction of 32 kilometres of railway, including bridges and culverts in the biggest sabotage operation in the Middle East conflict to that point. He set up two columns of 100 men and four officers in total. One column was made of Australian engineers from his mounted divisions escorted by 1st Light Horse Brigade. It would move south to the railway line at Asluj. The second column, of the Camel Brigade, would march east from Rafa to another village on the line, Auja. The Camels would be supported by a squadron of Light Horse. To cover and divert attention, there would be minor feints and demonstrations by the British Infantry around Gaza, and by the Light Horse just south of Beersheba. The troopers and engineers had combined their practical ingenuity to pack the four tonnes of explosives in kerosene tins. Clips for attaching the charges to the rails were made from steel bands used to hold hay for the horses.

The two columns set out at dusk on 22 May. The engineers and Light Horse travelled from Shellal village in silence along a stretch of limestone ridge with sharp, jagged edges, which were not easy to negotiate in the blackness. At around midnight, the 6th Light Horse Regiment broke off 32 kilometres into the 48-kilometre march, and surrounded the village of Khalasa. No-one in it would be going anywhere that night or in the morning, especially if they intended to inform the Turks about seeing this strong force moving towards the railway.

The rest of the first column rolled on into much tougher terrain than anticipated and was delayed, arriving at 6 a.m., two hours later than scheduled. The Camels had the same problem with rough country. They arrived at 7 a.m.

Chauvel had wanted the whole operation over by 10 a.m. The late arrivals meant he had to change priorities. The main aim was to smash as much of the railway as possible. If that worked well, the two columns could attempt to knock down bridges and culverts.

The engineers fanned out down the line from Asluj. It was daylight when they began carrying the tins of explosives to the track. Locals spotted them in the distance near the village, but went about their business watched by a long line of mounted troopers, rifles on their laps, unfazed but alert.

Sixty kilometres away, the Light Horse reached a railway bridge eight kilometres to Beersheba's north. The engineers rushed to it, affixed explosives in a well-rehearsed drill and hurried clear. The Turks, awake now to a disturbance, began artillery shelling forward of the bridge, but too late. It collapsed in a growl of falling rock and blast of dust skywards. Two brigades of Turks jumped into action, galloping towards the bridge.

The Light Horse troopers made a wide sweep south and away from the destruction, their job of distraction carried out to the letter of Chauvel's directive.

Back at Asluj, the engineers heard the muffled roar of the bridge's demise seconds before they set their own charges at 8 a.m. The rail snapped and tore for several kilometres. That mission too was accomplished. Chauvel permitted the more daring raids on the bridges. There was just enough time, he judged, especially as no-one had yet spotted even a light Turkish patrol.

The engineers scrambled to a 24-arch bridge, attached explosives all over its stone and concrete pillars, and set the charges. The rumble was sustained for 45 seconds as each arch was damaged or fell, leaving a dust-shrouded uneven heap of rock and stones.

Down the track, General Smith's camel engineers, aware of the success to the north, began their end of the operation on the rail at Auja. The subsequent explosions shredded another 12 kilometres of steel rail. The engineers at both points now swarmed over culverts and bridges up and down the mangled line.

Turkish patrols began appearing near Asluj but they were soon frightened off by troopers only too pleased to have something to do other than watch the engineers carry out their handiwork.[1]

By 10 a.m. three demolition parties had ruined 22 kilometres of steel rail that would never again be usable. They had blown up bridges of 24, 18, 12, 6, 5, 3 and 2 arches; a viaduct; four arched culverts, a number of railway points and switches; station buildings; telegraph poles and plenty of Turkish property. (How Lawrence, who laboured long over a fraction of this level of destruction, would have envied Chauvel's management of so many skilled engineers.)

By just after noon on 23 May, the two columns were on their way back to Rafa and Shellal. The two Turkish brigades that had rushed to the broken bridge north of Beersheba arrived in the vicinity of the real destruction by 2 p.m., far too late to take on the Australian raiders.

Chauvel was well satisfied with his first operation as a corps commander. The Turks would not be able to bring troops by train south of Beersheba. This left the way open for a concerted attack.

There was now no obstacle to Chetwode's plan, except for the approval from General Murray.

He was now impotent and waiting for the War Cabinet to confirm or deny that he would hold onto his position.

38

Meeting the Terror

Auda was not joking about the lifelessness of al-Houl. The stifling sun did not allow a hiding place in the vast, trembling emptiness. Burning sand-storms dried skin and throats of every drop of moisture. Even he, the hard man of Arabia, was anxious over the conditions. Auda would now only move between dawn and dusk for fear of becoming lost at night.

Lawrence wilted to the point of collapse. Many times he nearly toppled from his camel. His concern for hurrying evaporated. Everything seemed futile. The party did not appear to make progress. The scenery did not shift. There were few sounds: the squeak of leather; the steady clip of camels' feet on stone; the swish of water in goatskin bags. The laughter of the boys was muted. Hardly anything was said for hours on end as every individual preserved the limited energy used for inhaling and expelling air that accompanied speaking.

The sand-storms caused the Agayl to cover their mouths with head-cloths to prevent sand parching lips and throat. Lawrence refused to follow suit. He was always testing himself against the elements, and himself, to extremes. The result was a throat so damaged that he could not speak properly or eat at all for three days. Was it worth it? No diary entry gives a clue, except that he did not complain.

Not even a lizard had been spotted on the hideous trek. On 24 May after five days in the 'devil's anvil', there were the first signs of life, both past and present. The Bedouins in this region had once worked grain from the wild grass (samh). The remnants of threshing pits were small pools of sand that left camels' imprints for days. More uplifting was the sight of two ostriches seen darting across the plain. This sent several Agayl off in search of eggs, which were found and devoured by Lawrence and the other leaders.

After noon it was discovered that one of his servants, Gasim, a grumbling, gap-toothed Maan peasant, was missing. His riderless camel was wandering with the main bunch. Lawrence made enquiries. There was no concern from the others. He must have fallen asleep in the night, they said. There was no use going back for him. He would be lost and dead. Lawrence wanted to make a search. They tried to dissuade him. It would be a waste of time, water and most probably life. But Lawrence was determined. He begged extra water from others and turned around. Twenty minutes later he looked back at his caravan. It had dissolved into the flickering horizon. This was another test, an even more perverse one than damaging his throat. Even if he found Gasim, would he find his way back? This may have been the loneliest moment of a loner's life.

Despite his masochistic streak, Lawrence was still logical and rational. He had a compass, which he used every day and was proficient at it. He walked his camel back through the threshing pits' sand pools, leaving a trace of his movement and the only real hope of finding his way back to the party.

After two hours, there was no sign of Gasim. Just at the point of despair, Lawrence saw more than the usual ghosts in a mirage. There was more disturbance. He galloped his camel forward. The movement was not an optical illusion. It was Gasim, distressed and hallucinating.

Lawrence gave him the water. He spilled some in his desperation to drink. Lawrence helped him onto the camel and directed it to the prints in the sand. The danger was not over. He was using the compass but after an hour he could not find the party.

He searched the horizon, praying for something extra in the shaking, dancing light. Then he thought he saw extra movement, not of a caravan of more than a hundred camels, but smaller. This grew black and split and merged until he could make out three camels coming his way.

Lawrence's hand trembled to his revolver. Were they Turks? He stopped. The riders did not seem hostile. Soon he realised it was Auda with two Agayl. They had come in search of him.

In his relief, Lawrence rebuked Auda for leaving a man to rot in the heat. The blubbering Gasim was transferred to another camel.

Auda proferred that Gasim was not worth the price of a camel. The animals were valued more than a lowly servant in al-Houl.

Lawrence valued him at less than half a crown.[1] Auda thought this English cliché hilarious. He sidled up to Gasim and belted him across the back of the head, repeating Lawrence's price assessment several times with a throaty laugh.

Though he gave no thanks to the three men for coming to search for him and Gasim, Lawrence realised this was more than an indication of the respect he now had from the Arab leaders. Auda was the test. If he now valued him this much, many Bedouins in the region in a short space of time would treat him almost like a brother and true leader. This brave act of rescue would again enhance the image of 'El Laurens'.

His on-the-edge mad streak, or exhibitionism or masochism, or a combination of all three, along with him being the architect of the plan to drive the Turks out, were creating a legendary status. Lawrence not only drew up grand ideas on paper. He carried them through in the desert, enduring pain and showing courage and leadership. All this was important in uniting the Arabs in the region, especially now when they were almost out of the Hejaz and into the southern Syria region.

The night of 24 May was Lawrence's worst. There was no water in the camp. Everyone spent a restless time, not managing the pangs that came without nature's lubricant and presaged death. At dawn the troubled caravan moved on to the vast Wadi Sirhan, and there was a sense of hope. This enormous valley marked the end of al-Houl. The terror had passed. A few hours later they were at the well of Arfaja. It went down six metres and contained a stinking, creamy sludge. But no-one cared. They drank until nearly ill. The camels were sent out to graze, and the men relaxed.

But leaving the horrors of al-Houl also left behind the natural protection of its desolation. Arab raiders prowled its fringes. Mid-afternoon, they invaded the area on swift camels and carrying rifles. The Agayl again reacted fast, running at them or propping and firing. These bandits fled also.

At night, Lawrence was sitting at a camp fire being served coffee when the raiders returned, firing wildly. The man serving the coffee was struck and killed. The fire was smothered. Lawrence's bodyguards and servants, along with several Agayl quickly on the scene, took up positions on the dunes and aimed in the direction of the bandits' rifle flashes. Within a minute, 30 rifles were firing at the invaders. They turned and thundered off again, this time more aware of the strength and purpose of the 'foreign' caravan.

Lawrence remained three days at the camp of a Howeitat chief gorging on mutton from the tribe's abundant sheep (sometimes against his will, but to please his hosts). Auda went into northern Syria to engage the chief of the powerful Rwalla, who had to be enlisted before there was a real chance to take Aqaba.

The caravan moved on through this giant valley deeper into Turkish-held territory, which made Lawrence nervous. Al-Houl was replaced by threats of a different kind. There was life here in the form of snakes and scorpions. The waterless region had been replaced by uninviting brackish wells, and there was uncertainty about what had been thrown down them. The interminable emptiness made way for stunted palms, salt marsh and occasional scrub.

Despite the hardships in the Hejaz, he now had to face the sharp end of problems, especially in explaining his mission to bands of Bedouins that appeared at their camp each night to swear allegiance to Feisal. They were all aware of British and French imperial interests in the region, although not the Sykes–Picot agreement. He heard himself, day after day, lying to them about this mission being entirely about Arab independence and nothing at all to do with Allied imperial aims. It was easier dealing with all the key people who set out on the mission with him such as Feisal, who had Lawrence's sugar-coated version of what British and French intentions were in Syria, or Auda, Nasir and the others. They had witnessed his dedication and determination. Those Bedouins meeting him en route took more convincing. They were tougher minded and shrewd. They had spent time in the major cities. Some were sceptical when they engaged this pasty-skinned, lantern-jawed strange little 'English' for the first time. Why would he be interested in doing things for the Arabs especially in light of British expansion in the Middle East? Lawrence projected the line that defeating and driving out the Turks would help the Allies in the war against Germany. It was accepted, but the deception was nagging him, especially when he had to ask for levies from them to keep the expanding caravan moving.

Auda re-joined Lawrence at Agayla, and brought with him a troop of Rwalla, indicating that they were in support. The mission was working too well. Some of the elders were becoming overly ambitious. They wanted to bypass Aqaba and go straight for Damascus, now. Lawrence argued against this. Going on to Damascus had too many imponderables. They could not be sure about garnering support from other tribes of northern Syria. If Damascus was taken, the Arabs would be isolated and, almost certainly, the Turks would take it back. The British were stuck south of the Gaza–Beersheba line. They needed to have forced the Turks back in Palestine and to be in support of the Arabs in Damascus to achieve a lasting control over that city and Syria.

The whole business of revolt had become unwieldy. It was drifting from his plan. He believed Aqaba had to be taken. He could not move ahead of the British force and it had yet to break through Gaza–Beersheba. Timing was crucial. Lawrence knew he had to stay in harmony with his British masters and the movement of the military.

Now he was up against the nationalists he despised. They did not want the British involved. They wished to take Damascus and Syria and set their own agenda without imperial influence. Lawrence had to be at his political, diplomatic and duplicitous best to get his way. First, he took Auda aside and told him if they struck at Damascus north through Rwalla territory, and not at Aqaba through Howeitat country, then the Rwalla would take the credit and most of the British gold. This swung Auda his way. Second, he worked hard on the tribal leaders, especially Nasir, whose strength among the Hashemites (the main Bedouin tribe) of the Hejaz meant he had to be swayed. So did Nasib, the leader of the Hejaz's al-Bakris. He was a fervent nationalist, who distrusted British motives. Lawrence persuaded Nasib to take his men to the Druse Mountains to prepare for the later march on Damascus. This removed a key nationalist supporter for the time being.

Lawrence also pulled out an argument that placated all the leaders concerning their fervour for taking Damascus. He made out that there were not enough funds in the kitty at the moment for such a costly push north.

Much of his angst and fear would be alleviated by a breakthrough on the Gaza-to-Beersheba line. But so far he had heard nothing from any visitor to the camps that would suggest this was about to happen. The inertia west of Gaza and that in the Wadi Sirhan began to take a toll on Lawrence. He became frustrated to the point of recklessness.

'Can't stand it another day,' he wrote in his pocket diary of 5 June. 'Will ride N[orth] and chuck it.'[2]

39

Corruption and Salvation

I f Lawrence had been aware of the situation in Cairo in early June 1917, he would have been even more depressed. General Murray was still hanging on but was never going to direct another attempt to take Gaza no matter how clever Chetwode's plan using Beersheba as the breakthrough point.

'The army was at a standstill,' Banjo Paterson observed from his privileged base at the remount depot outside the Egyptian capital, 'and an army never stands still. It either goes forward or backward.'

Paterson, wearing his two hats as a professional observer and the man who doled out the horses to everyone from generals to privates, met all the key figures. He took notes on what he saw in Cairo. It was not encouraging from the perspective of the British ever moving further than the Gaza–Beersheba line.

Paterson wrote about the 90 British generals who were living very well at Shepheard's Hotel and the Savoy, where Murray had his headquarters.

'They either just existed beautifully or they made themselves busy about such jobs as reporting upon the waste of jam tins,' he wrote. 'Others became town commandants, or examiners of an army diet.'[1]

Junior officers on leave from the front struggled to obtain a room at the big hotels. The rank and file had no hope. They were forbidden to enter them, even to buy a drink or meet a friend. This created friction. Soldiers and troopers rioted outside the Savoy one night, forcing officers out of their salubrious dining area to attempt to restore order. The rot had set in from the top. Murray himself enjoyed the privileges at the Savoy and rarely ventured out, and certainly not to the front more than once. He could hardly stomp around telling other generals to sharpen up. Matters were not helped by a large number of awards being given for 'gallant service' to the big Cairo staff, many of whom had never been to the front. They were more corrupt than any other group in the city, obtaining goods illegally and using their rank to ensure luxury. The most sought after item apart from French champagne was the automobile. The supply of bubbly kept coming but the number of cars reached its limit early in 1917. An order was issued that all privately owned vehicles were to be 'requisitioned', which was army-speak for confiscated, and in effect stolen.

Paterson wrote of an Australian lieutenant who brought over an expensive car from Europe for his even more expensive wife to use in Cairo. It was seized by the authorities on the day the order came out. His wife was most unhappy. She demanded that her husband retrieve it. He had to use cunning and daring to steal it back from a garage. The lieutenant shrewdly loaned it at times to the Red Cross to avoid it being taken again.

There were other problems. Desertion was one. Inaction had more to do with soldiers and troopers running away than action. They were streaming back to Cairo, and at best were absent without leave. Drunkenness, petty crime and further trouble in the brothels were on the increase.

The collective mind of the military's top brass was certainly not on the front where there was no action and apparent resignation to the stalemate common to the Western Front.

One of the few exceptions was Chauvel, who made only a couple of brief stops in Cairo. He remained close to his troopers on the Gaza–Beersheba line and in touch with his areas of responsibility. He covered thousands of kilometres checking on all aspects of the conditions and preparedness for the proposed, undated attack.

He was adapting to his Ford car. Chauvel would always be more comfortable in the saddle than the seat. Rare was the day in his entire life that he did not ride a horse. But he bowed in this long lull between battles to the facility of the vehicle as he trundled from south-west of Beersheba right up to the Mediterranean coast at Marrakeb. Chauvel was the quiet diplomat, appearing for appearance's sake, but also to check on all the brigades and the new yeomanry division under him, the training schools, hospitals and rest camps. He also visited the canteen at Kantara, where the selfless Rania MacPhillamy had joined the indefatigable Alice Chisholm, who had opened her rest place in defiance of the British army leaders. They were concerned among other things about the possibility that it could lead to some form of prostitution. None, of course, had met the formidable and puritanical Chisholm, or the dedicated Rania.

The canteen was an immediate success. Soon they were employing a hundred Egyptians and supplying meals and refreshments to thousands of troops daily. The British soldiers heard about it from Aussie mates and pleaded to be allowed to use it. The women did not discriminate. An infantry division availed itself of the 'home' cooking. More than 60,000 eggs were fried each day.

Chauvel met Murray in Cairo to judge for himself the intransigence at the top, and came away with assurances that there would be an attempt to break through using Chetwode's plan. But Murray would not put a date on it. Chauvel was unconvinced about the commander's commitment. He returned to the front to learn that since the demolition operation of 22–24 May his engineers were satisfied that after nearly two weeks work they could generate enough water at Khalasa and Asluj to support two divisions for an attack on Beersheba from the east.

Chauvel judged that all the logistics were ready. A firm directive was needed from headquarters, but he was pessimistic about

Murray's attitude. Chauvel's spirits were lifted by a letter from Sibyl. She had heard a strong rumour in London that Murray was about to be replaced.

General Allenby was said to be the new man for Cairo.[2]

Lawrence took off with two bodyguards on his trip north to Damascus on 5 June into enemy territory. He left Clayton a note in a journal:

'I've decided to go off alone to Damascus, hoping to get killed on the way: for all sakes try and clear this show up before it goes further. We are calling them to fight for us on a lie, and I can't stand it.'

With Shakespearean flourish, he wrote:

'. . . a bodily wound would have been a grateful vent for my internal complexities, a mouth through which my troubles might have found relief.'[3]

This was written by Lawrence the drama queen rather than the desert king. If he were to die, he wished to be remembered for the agonising emotion over what he was doing; an epitaph of sorts. The comments about death and his intention to 'chuck it' reflected his fear. He was galloping off for the first time into terrain festooned with enemy forts, barracks and patrols. There was a real chance he would be killed or captured. He had the mind not so much to confront his fears but to run at them. When pondering the courage of VC winners, he judged they were the same as cowards, who lost control and did suicidal things through a fear that at once froze and unfroze a victim of it. It was a generalisation. He may never have met characters such as Australian VC winners Albert Jacka and 'Mad Dog' Murray, who always seemed in control in battle, the latter being the gentlest of gentleman farmers away from the battlefield. (No doubt Lawrence would judge them as psychopaths.) Yet the overindulgent self-analysis worked for him, and as he travelled north in the darkness he felt he was pitching headlong at his phobia.

Despite the histrionic notes, he was on the job. Lawrence did not trust Nasib. He seemed to have been mollified over his desire to revolt in Damascus when he went to the Druse Mountains. Yet Lawrence worried that Nasib would meet Arab leaders in the city and incite them into a premature uprising.

Lawrence set a hot pace for four days, covering 255 kilometres, which fatigued his camel, but sated his perpetual desire to reach a destination as fast as possible. It alleviated the dreadful memory of the snail-pace drag through al-Houl. He arrived on 9 June at a camp at the foot of the Tadmor hills where he met an ardent pro-Hashemite, Sheikh Dhami, of the Kawakiba. Dhami promised to meet him and a force of his tribesmen, later at the little village of Bair, which would be the base for an assault on Aqaba. In the meantime, Dhami was kind enough to replace his camel. He also gave him 35 men for an attack on the railway north-west of Damascus at Raas Baalbek.

Lawrence was always conscious of putting his words into action in front of prospective followers. He took off with them. They skirted the white-peaked mountains of the Anti-Lebanon mountain range.

The operation took Lawrence's mind off his fears and onto other concerns he considered more prosaic and manageable, such as handling dynamite. He was now the experienced saboteur doing his job as he concentrated on finding a suitable place to cause a disturbance. A plate-girder bridge seemed right. Two months earlier he would have been unsure about his skills. But he appeared confident as he taped less than two kilograms of explosives under the bridge, stepped away and pumped the detonator. Much to the delight of the watching Bedouin party, it blew and twisted a girder, enough to disrupt traffic, although not dramatically.

Lawrence took off again riding south with an escort of four towards the village of al-Qabban, just five kilometres outside the oasis that was Damascus, the ultimate target. It lay to the east of the Anti-Lebanon Range's desert slopes. There were rolling plains east, north and south, which at this time of the year were dry and dusty. Further east was the vast Arabian desert, home to the nomadic Arabs.

The Turks overreacted to the minor destruction believing this might be the beginning of an uprising. They sent six battalions (about 6,000 soldiers) out of the Gaza front to the area, which would have to rank as the most profitable return from such a tiny amount of explosive.

Lawrence had an important and clandestine meeting at al-Qabban with Damascus's lord mayor Ali Riza ar-Rikabi, a covert Arab nationalist whom he had met before. The mayor agreed not to organise an uprising prematurely, although he didn't think he could anyway. Lawrence brought up the possibility of Rikabi taking over as governor of Damascus when the uprising eventuated. This Baghdad Arab came from an elite family. He was educated at the Turkish Military Academy and had a lifetime career in the Ottoman army. Rikabi was a lieutenant general (Chauvel's current rank) at the beginning of the war. He commanded an army corps against the British in Mesopotamia (Iraq). He was inspired by the Arab Revolt and was suspected by the Turks of secretly pledging his support to it. His substantial background helped him avoid prosecution, even execution, and he was 'demoted' to command a Damascus garrison in 1917 when no-one in the German or Turkish military hierarchy believed it was ever in danger.

Rikabi brought continuity as a key figure in the city's Turkish government, and change as a secret Arab nationalist. He was agreeable to the plan to put him in charge of Damascus in the event of the Arabs taking over, and this pleased Lawrence. He also found support to form clandestine Arab committees in every centre in and around the city as he sowed the seeds of sedition with promises of gold and weaponry. Many swore to rise and act at the declared moment.

Lawrence was able to leave the Damascus area feeling satisfied that he had gone a long way towards solving the volatile problems of takeover and transition once the Turks were thrown out. Such organisation was a precursor to the overthrow of the long-time oppressive ruler, first to assist in making it happen and second to consolidate the chances of the new regime surviving.

Lawrence headed south for a meeting with two other tribal leaders of the Leja and the Druse, who put their terms for joining an uprising. Finally he hurried to Azraq, an oasis near a lake where the Wadi Sirhan widened out to the Syrian desert, for a meeting with a key Emir in the Rwalla, Nuri Shaalan. He ranked only behind Feisal, Ibn Saud and Ibn Rashid as princes of the desert. Nuri was elderly. In his case, wisdom had come with maturity. He had ruled his tribe (the Anazeh) for 30 years, a long time in the desert, where old men, like ageing lions, were pushed aside by younger aspirants. That sagacity and his forceful manner had brought him command. Whereas Auda's battle record and reputation as a killer in conflict was second to none, Nuri Shaalan had been more restrained in his methods of holding power. Instead of Auda's homicidal propensities, the older man went in for fratricide, killing two of his brothers who stood in his way.

Nuri Shaalan was no diplomat. If opposed, a nod or a wink to his supporters would lead to silence from the opponent, or a quick liquidation. Lawrence needed his backing to use his roads. The old man was wary, shrewd and naturally suspicious. He suspected Lawrence of being what he was, an English spy. He called for a meeting in his tent.

Nuri Shaalan thrust a file into Lawrence's hand. It contained the Sykes–Picot agreement and analysis of it. This had been leaked by Russia's Bolsheviks to the world to demonstrate the duplicity of the British and French in dealing with the Arabs.

Lawrence was now face to face with his demons. He clung to a sliver of comfort in the knowledge that he had finessed Feisal on the issue months ago. Yet it was tough. Nuri was not to be trifled with. If a convincing argument was not provided, this man could destroy the Aqaba and later Damascus operations. He could also assassinate Lawrence, a thought very much on the Arab's mind.

Lawrence cited Feisal as much as possible. It was his first and last argument as to his bona fides. Nuri, eyes darting, listened to every nuance of his explanation as Lawrence, agonising internally, reached his bluffing best. Nuri half-bought the explanation, which was enough to keep both the Hashemite cause and Lawrence himself alive. But the shrewd Nuri would not commit himself to support, preferring to wait and see whether the Hashemites or the Turks would win.

Lawrence judged that he had Rwalla backing in all but the fight itself, and even then some of the tribes were committing men to an attack regardless of Nuri's reaction. Fence-sitting was not commitment, but Lawrence took comfort in the fact that it was not adversarial either.

He arrived back at the caravan's base at Nabk on 17 June, after a 12-day whirlwind journey covering 900 kilometres. The ride began in what he made out was mental depression brought on by fear and guilt, but ended with achievement. The rushed trek was both cathartic and successful. He had inspired the Syrian tribes for a revolt but on British terms and timing. They would not push ahead of the army stuck at Gaza–Beersheba. Lawrence sat down to write a detailed report on the various tribes and factions: how he had tempered blood-feuds in the interests of defeating the Turks; how the Syrian Arabs were ready to join the Hashemites for a strike.

Lawrence hoped his document would assist in obtaining the funds and resources from Cairo to achieve his eventual aims in Damascus.

The attack on Aqaba was imminent. By 20 June, a contingent of more than 700 men from Syria and the Hejaz had been raised. Yet still Lawrence and the Arab leaders had first to secure water and food before any concerted effort to take the city.

With that in mind, Lawrence detached 200 to guard the camp base in the Wadi Sirhan. A force of 500 then saddled up camels and horses, with Lawrence, Auda, Nasir, Nasib and Dhami leading. They turned south-west on a mission to salvage wells that had been sabotaged by the Turks and their Arab supporters.

Lawrence had the tricky job of extracting some poorly laid charges.

'I took out two sets on the end of a rope,' he noted in his diary. 'Nasty job, for all well-lining was very loose.'[4]

The force occupied the small village of Bair with its ancient wells set in a stony wasteland.

A small party was sent to Tafilah in the hills of Adorn to buy flour, staple food that would underpin nourishment for the time needed to take Aqaba.

Coincident with this sweep by the force, more blood feuds were settled in the hope of securing more Arab supporters. Lawrence kept talking up the revolt with other leaders en route. He broke away with a small party to make his point with an aggressive gesture by attempting to blow up a bridge, this time near Minifir in the Yarmuk Valley. It didn't work, but it was the thought and action that counted. The Arabs could see he was committed. Dissatisfied with this failed demonstration, he led a raid on an isolated Turkish outpost at Atwi on 27 June. They killed three Turks, which was an important step for him. Lawrence was whipping himself up. He did not murder here himself, but he had blood on his hands for directing the attack.

It was a brutal and gratuitous act but one he found necessary to build and maintain his image, and legend, as a committed Arab supporter and leader.

Bull Loose, Aqaba Taken

Geneneral Sir Edmund Allenby was upset and depressed. He was being dumped from command of the 3rd Army and relegated to an 'unimportant command' in the Middle East. At least that was his first reaction. The Battle of Arras against the Germans in northern France had ended on 16 May 1917. It also involved the 1st Army under General Horne and the 5th Army under General Gough. The British troops, including Australians and Canadians, had made significant advances but could not achieve the much sought-after major breakthrough. There had not been one in the nearly three years of the war. The fact that Arras had not worked for the British and it had been Allenby's plan were points against him. More importantly, Field Marshal Haig saw him as a strong rival and he (Allenby) was always at odds with Gough. He had plenty of 'enemies' within and this new appointment was opportune for them. They would be pleased to be rid of him. Haig would endorse his leaving. There would be no effort to keep him.

The rivalry, as much as the apparent downgrade, rankled with Allenby. It didn't help that he wasn't even first choice to replace Murray. British prime minister Lloyd George had wanted South African General Jan Smuts, who was in London for the Imperial Conference. Ever since taking office in December 1916, Lloyd George had pushed for a stronger commitment in the Middle East. He believed the enemy was weakest there and wanted to shake the Turks from power and control in the region, which the PM hoped would hinder the German campaign on the Western Front. He had come to office in a period of extreme public gloom and was under pressure to try a new tack to boost the nation's morale and his own position.

Smuts didn't want the job. It was too much of an insignificant campaign for his talents, he thought. Lloyd George's second choice, on advice from the chief of the imperial general staff Sir William Robertson, was Allenby.

He travelled to London to meet them, still feeling down. Yet the prime minister's attitude gave him some solace. Lloyd George appeared genuine in his congratulations. The most important character in the empire next to the king viewed the position in Cairo as more important than his part as a general on the Western Front.

Lloyd George wrote of his meeting with Allenby:

'I told him in the presence of Sir William Robertson that he was to ask us for such reinforcements and supplies as he found necessary, and we would do our best to provide them. "If you do not ask it will be your fault. If you do ask and do not get what you want it will be ours". I said the cabinet expected "Jerusalem before Christmas".'[1]

Allenby would have a fair amount of freedom. The war cabinet, Robertson assured him, would not decide on policy until he (Allenby) had analysed the Middle East theatre.

Lloyd George presented him with *The Historical Geography of the Holy Land*, by George Adam Smith. This included a detailed geographic survey, which Allenby would use for bedtime study. He appreciated the gift. He loved reading and collected books.

The prime minister's weight as a so-called 'Easterner' (a believer in taking the battle to the enemy in the Middle East, attacking where it was more vulnerable) helped the press view the appointment as an upgrade. No paper or journalist wrote Allenby down. The *Daily Telegraph* was fulsome, saying:

'Allenby is a man of almost giant strength and size . . .' Another paper touched nerves with: 'A man of his character has been badly wanted in Egypt for some time past. Gaza ought to have been in our hands at the end of last March . . .'[2]

The prime minister impressed on the importance of his mission. Allenby felt he would never overcome the 'demotion'. Yet he was a soldier. He would do his duty.

And that had been spelt out to him.

*

Allenby travelled to Italy, then a cruiser ferried him to Egypt where he arrived on 28 June. The trip took nearly two weeks. In that time he relaxed. He put all the intrigues, internecine squabbles and rivalries of the Western Front behind him. There would be no Haig to block him; no Gough to snipe at him behind his back. Yes, he was a bigger general in a smaller battle zone. But success and prestige could be his if he applied himself and had luck in the new theatre. There was no doubt about the prime minister's goodwill towards his mission. In fact, there was much more hinging on it than a sweet send-off. Lloyd George wanted a win for himself, his politics and the psyche of the UK and the empire.

Allenby was the vehicle.

The same day, Lawrence arrived back in Bair. To his satisfaction, a week's supply of flour had come in from Tafilah. It put a time pressure on the bid to take Aqaba. It had to be captured by 5 July or the food would run out. Bedouin scouts were still searching for more wells in the region. It was agreed that they were close to having enough sources to support an assault, but again for no longer than six or seven days. Funds, in the way of gold coins, were drying up, causing a further worry. Nasir was paying the Bedouins in promissory notes drawn on the British government and with Lawrence's imprimatur.

Another pressure bothered him. A force of 400 Turkish cavalry, which included four machine-guns, was thundering through the Wadi Sirhan looking for them. The Bedouins had spies planted as guides with the Turks to take them away from the scent. Yet it was a matter of time before they stumbled on the revolt army, if it remained static. With this in mind, the 500-strong Arab force broke camp at Bair. It was the last incentive to move on Aqaba.

They reached Auda's headquarters at the thorn-tree oasis of Jefer, east of Maan, on 30 June. Many of his family, if not moving around the country, often camped here. He had plans to build a massive home compound at Jefer even before the desert war was over. It would be funded by British gold and built, he vowed, by Turkish soldier-slaves.

The railway station at Maan, Lawrence's official destination for sabotage, 170 kilometres north-west of Aqaba, could be seen across a mud-cracked plain. The Turks had destroyed all the wells at Jefer but one, which they had filled with earth. It was a sign that although the enemy was a long way south searching for them, it was taking no chances and was now fully aware that something was afoot, perhaps concerning Aqaba. The well was Auda's property. He ordered his men to remove the earth. The force needed every possible well operating.

During this excavation in the boiling sun, Nasir consulted Lawrence, Auda and the other leaders. It was decided that he should order the Dumaniyyah Howeitat to attack a Turkish fort at the entrance to the huge pass at Nagb ash-Shtar. This led down to Aqaba.

If the fort was smashed, the battle for that port city would go ahead.

Allenby stamped his authority on the Middle East campaign inside 48 hours of arriving by declaring that his headquarters would not be at the Savoy but Kelab, a few kilometres north of Rafa, and much closer to the front. He would be a short car ride from every trench running from the coast to south of Beersheba. The luxurious, hedonistic Cairo days for a squadron-size list of officers in the Great War would be over within weeks. Wives and families would be left to carry on without the men in the city's playground at Ghezireh.

The sheer presence of the man was enough to make men run and cringe. Troop inspections were arbitrary but thorough as he swept through hot, dusty camps like a human whirlwind. He would roll up in his car, often unannounced if the words 'Bull loose' had not preceded him over the radio transmissions. There would be a quick, perfunctory shake of officers' hands, then a look at the troopers and horses.

The sight of this stiff-backed man moving towards a line of soldiers, pecking like an angry bantam cock if he spotted something out of order, such as an unshined boot or dirty rifle, was a shock after nothing from Murray for nearly two years. The ruddy-faced Allenby used all his height and massiveness if he needed to intimidate. There was no pushing through a line here to snap at a trooper, but the glint of his narrowed eyes jammed under his cap and above his large beak was enough to put everyone on edge.

Allenby may have been unpopular with some, but he was a leader and soldier, and he had every man's respect. Banjo Paterson had assessed him close up in South Africa, and now 17 years later, he met him again, this time at an inspection of the remount depot. Allenby was 'a great, lonely figure of a man', Paterson observed, 'riding [in a Rolls-Royce] silently in front of an obviously terrified staff. He seemed quite glad to recognise a friend in me. For a remount officer is like a Field Marshal: he has no hope of promotion and no friends whatever in the army.'

'Being a full-fleshed man,' Paterson further noted, 'the heat of Egypt tried him severely, and made him harder than ever. Where he had been granite before he was steel now.'

Allenby relaxed a fraction with the poet/horse whisperer. They chatted about their time in the Boer War.

Paterson asked him how he was feeling and was told frankly in an unguarded moment:

'I am afraid I am becoming very hard to get on with. I want to get this war over and if anything goes wrong I lose my temper and cut loose on them [staff and troops].'

He had yet to fault the remount depot, but he did criticise the walers. He reckoned they were 'a common hairy lot, compared to the horses that your Lancers brought to South Africa'.

Paterson pointed out that the Lancers' horses were a select group of fully trained police mounts in superb condition. It would not be possible to acquire enough of this special bunch to make any difference in the war.

Allenby poked his head in the cook-house and chatted to the chief cook, a South African. Noting the man's ribbon, Allenby asked about his war service, and his family. Then came the mandatory query:

'What are you serving to the troops?'

'They get stoo, sir, and plum puddin',' the cook replied, 'and any amount of tinned fruit. The chow in this war, sir, is Guv'ment 'Ouse compared with what we got in South Africa.'

This was said, Paterson observed, for the benefit of any potential complainers within earshot.

The cook-house inspection completed, Allenby turned to his cowering staff of 10 and said he now wanted to scrutinise the infantry's 10th Division. He received blinks, blank looks and diffident coughs. A brave staffer piped up that it was on its way from India. No-one was certain if it had arrived in camp. The Bull snorted. An even more courageous staff man stepped forward.

'If you please, sir . . .'

Allenby cut him off.

'I don't want to hear you talk!' he snapped, 'I've enough men following me around to staff the whole British army and you can't find me a division!'

Another officer, more foolhardy than brave, began with:

'Just at present, sir . . .'

'I don't want to hear you talk either!' Allenby barked. 'I want to get on with this inspection. Where is this division?'

The moment was saved by an orderly hurrying in with a phone message. The division had been located. Allenby said goodbye to Paterson and the cook, and the convoy rumbled off.

'That's the sort of general for me,' the cook said in admiration, 'a bloke that knows his own mind. My word, he did roar up them staff officers a treat. Do 'em good. Take some of the flashness out of 'em.'[3]

Paterson said that the troops would not write 'Allenby's own volunteers' on their hats. Yet, without an order being given, every soldier in Cairo and on the front knew there would be less rioting in the streets or brothels, and very little disobeying of orders. Slackers and fools among the officers and all ranks were on notice.

So were the Turks.

*

Lawrence, Nasir and Auda received the news at 6 p.m. that the Turkish fort at the pass had been taken. The forts' defenders had been massacred after one of its patrols had come across a Howeitat camp and killed women, children and an old man. Lawrence and the main force now headed for the railway at the closest point to the fort to cut the lines and blow bridges to ensure that enemy troops could not be brought in. That done, the 400-strong guerilla column then deployed to the Shirah plateau eight kilometres away. They had just started preparing the evening meals when three horsemen arrived to warn them that a Turkish battalion of the 178th Regiment had marched from Maan and recaptured the fort. The pass down to Aqaba was blocked again.

The cooking fires were put out; the meal was forgotten. The column could not afford to wait. It moved on through the night on the plateau, arriving at its edge at dawn. The light opened up the sight of a natural amphitheatre with the walls of the plateau and two others surrounding the plain thousands of feet below. Nasir, Lawrence and Auda trotted on to meet the Howeitat chiefs who had engaged the Turks at the fort. They learned that the Turkish battalion was encamped and resting in a gully on the plain less than a kilometre away.

There were vantage points for Arab snipers to fire down into the camp. They crept down to these points, almost encircling the Turks, and opened fire. The enemy camp stirred. After a lull it responded with artillery and rifle fire into the emerging sun and shadows, making it hard to judge range. This gave the Arabs advantages as the battle raged for hours. At noon the stinging sun beat down on the plateau. Its surface made it at first uncomfortable, then unbearable for the attackers. The water ran out.

By 4 p.m. there were heated verbal exchanges between the column's leaders about what should be done. An angry Auda decided to break the stalemate. He called for 50 of his Howeitat fighters to saddle up horses. He then led a charge downhill at the Turks. The momentum carried most of them fast and straight at the enemy. Auda's horse was shot from under him. He got to his feet and ran to where about 45 of his horsemen had crashed through the Turks, who had been caught by surprise after the 10-hour fixed-position fire exchange.

The enemy battalion broke up and retreated.

Lawrence and Nasir had watched the charge from a hill top to the east. They decided to cut off the enemy, leading their 400-strong camelry down the hill to meet the retreating soldiers. Lawrence was in the vanguard of the attack and for the first time right in the middle of a fierce battle. As his camel hurtled on, surrounded by frenzied Bedouins, he did not have time to consider the danger he now faced as they ran headlong at the enemy. The running Turks were stunned at the horrific sight of the huge wedge of cameleers coming at them, firing their guns. Some Turks propped and returned fire, but they were run over. In the huge melee that ensued, Lawrence, caught up in the fury, fired his revolver wildly. After all the sabotage blowing up railway lines and bridges, this was a real battle at close quarters. He was trapped in a surreal moment. In the excitement and pandemonium, he shot his camel in the back of the head. Down it went, knees hitting the sandy ground first. Lawrence was catapulted over the dead animal's head and knocked out. When he came to, the battle was over.

The Arabs were chasing the last small group of Turks across the plain.

Nearly half of the 300-strong battalion had been slaughtered. About 160 had surrendered. The Arabs had lost just two men in an astonishing victory in the most important battle of the revolt to that point. Auda, his blood-lust up, was laughing maniacally, showing everyone the bullet holes in his clothes, scabbard and pistol-holder. Perhaps inside he was crying at his good fortune. It was his initiative that had created the fury and won the battle. He was celebrating the luck of surviving it. Another Howeitat chief was kissing a miniature Koran on a necklace, which he claimed was a powerful charm that had carried him through the battle unscathed. Lawrence examined it.

It carried the tiny imprint of a Glasgow novelty company.

*

Lawrence was not a natural-born killer like Auda. The event, inevitable as the Arab Revolt built, traumatised him. He wandered alone over the battlefield that evening admiring the 'beautiful', young Turkish dead. But the asymmetric heaps of bodies offended him. Lawrence was compelled to line them up in neat rows. He spent hours arranging the corpses in the moonlight. While he toiled, he could hear the raucous Howeitat victors, boasting and yelling about their kills, speed and strength.

Their boisterousness prompted him to wish he was one of the dead.

Auda sent messages with terms of surrender to the remaining manned Turkish outposts on the approach to Aqaba. They all accepted. The 300 or so who abandoned their posts had retreated to the port city. These soldiers, unaware of the massacre in the valley, at first refused to give in. But they had doubts when they realised that help would not be coming. The railway approaches from the north and south had been destroyed. No relief battalions could reach them.

Lawrence's column pushed on past post after post, all empty. The following night, hundreds of Howeitat and other tribesmen joined the Hashemites, lifting the size of the force to more than 1,000 men. They found Aqaba ruined by shelling from British gunboats a few weeks earlier. The city was deserted. It was taken without a shot being fired.

On 6 July 1917, after the long circular journey from Wejh, Lawrence, Auda and Nasir entered Aqaba. Unless the Turks rallied and made a massive, concerted effort to take back the port, the day marked the end of the Hejaz war. Feisal would dominate the region. The British Navy would have access to every Red Sea port.

Lawrence's conflicting plans and dreams for the Arabs and the British, which had been threatened by the possibility of fragmented, premature attempts to take Damascus, were still alive.

41

Measuring Up

I was one of Allenby's officers, and in his confidence in return, he expected me to do the best I could for him. I was Feisal's adviser, and Feisal relied upon the honesty and competence of this advice so far as to take it without argument. Yet I could not explain to Allenby the whole Arab situation, nor explain the full British plan to Feisal.

T. E. Lawrence

Allenby had met his key officers by 6 July 1917. He knew and liked his second-in-command Chetwode. No problem there. He wasn't acquainted with the head of Anzac Mounted, Chaytor, but the New Zealander had a strong record in the campaign, and a reputation for thoroughness and reliability. Hodgson, commanding the Australian Mounted, had not put a foot wrong. The reports on him from Murray and Chetwode highlighted that he could be trusted to carry out all asked of him. Allenby also knew General Barrow, the head of the new Yeomanry Mounted, an officer of the old school, formerly of the Indian regular army.

Chauvel was an enigma. Neat, tanned and lean, but haggard-looking after more than two years on fronts from Gallipoli to Beersheba, he appeared to the new chief as unprepossessing, even shy. It was a confrontation of contrasts. Allenby was brusque and restless. He stood up from his desk to shake hands, sat down again, and then bounced from his chair to look briefly out of the window. Chauvel remained standing and still, calm in himself. Allenby found him agreeable enough in manner but laconic. At first glance, the 'Bull' liked officers to speak up and be confident in his presence. He hated waffle and small talk, but he felt comfortable with officers opening up to him. He could take their measure more easily. Yet this compact general kept his nerve and counsel when eyeballed. He responded only when a query was put to him. There were long pauses. Chauvel made no attempt to fill the vacuum.

Allenby had read his record. It was by far the best of all in his new command. In every situation from Gallipoli on, he had excelled. Everyone spoke highly of him but without pinning the Australian down by even a trite description. Chauvel had won every battle he had commanded in the Middle East. There was no blotting of the copybook, not even at Second Gaza, where his role had been marginalised for some reason Allenby did not quite understand. Chauvel's two brigades on the right flank there had fought two sharp actions against the Turkish 3rd Cavalry and had gained the ascendancy with relative ease. The total record was nothing short of brilliant.

Allenby decided on a little bluff and bluster to draw him out. He showed his displeasure at Chauvel's chief of staff being a field gunner, and his adjutant quartermaster being a Royal Marine. Allenby wanted to know why they weren't cavalrymen. Chauvel, precise and firm, defended them and said they had done very well, pointing out their strengths. For a moment or two, Allenby had nowhere to go. He was the new captain of the first XI, seconded from another school. Chauvel had big scores on the board and had not been dismissed all season. He wanted his winning team intact. Allenby blustered less and tried compromise. He could keep his adjutant quartermaster but it was imperative that his chief of staff should be a cavalryman. Chauvel wanted to keep the tried and tested one he had. Allenby slipped into cajolery. He promised he would obtain him the best staff officer in the British army. Chauvel demurred. The battle for the chief of staff position would carry forward on paper.

Allenby did not like Chauvel, a corps commander, remaining under Birdwood's command for Australian Imperial Force (AIF) issues. It had to end, Allenby demanded. He sent his military secretary Lord Delmeny, to attempt to persuade Chauvel to agree to cut the link, which Allenby saw as a hangover from Gallipoli. Chauvel did not say it, but he was holding onto vestiges of Australian independence from British control. Even though Birdwood was English, he was answerable to the Australian government, and always seemed to have Australian interests at heart.

Chauvel saw the benefit of Allenby himself having a direct line to Prime Minister Billy Hughes and the rest of the government. Issues and problems would be settled faster than the current arrangement where Birdwood seemed remote and preoccupied with the rest of the AIF's activities scattered along the Western Front. But Birdwood had always been loyal, Chauvel told Delmeny. He refused to endorse the change, which would mean Birdwood would be jettisoned from his link to the Australian force in the Middle East. Allenby was furious. Delmeny passed on a sense of his fury. Chauvel shrugged and said Allenby would have to make the change through the War Office in London. He then informed Birdwood, who acted swiftly to cut Allenby off. The War Office would not even discuss the issue with Allenby, who gave up.

He was not happy with Chauvel but at last had some sense of what made him tick. He had integrity and could not be bullied. He was loyal and was tactically clever yet honest. He was cool under pressure and stood his ground without bluster.

These characteristics, Allenby knew well, were most useful, in fact, essential in battle. He would monitor Chauvel's progress. The commander of the Mounted Corps would be the most critical role in Palestine and Syria.

He would be leading Allenby's shock troops.

The taking of Aqaba brought the problems of how it was to be managed and defended. Feeding everyone was the first problem. Auda's force, their 600 Turkish prisoners and the townspeople were almost out of food. Auda's men were butchering their own camels for meat. The second problem was keeping Auda's force together. There had to be rewards and support, or the Howeitat would lose interest and disperse into the desert, which meant Aqaba would be vulnerable to a Turkish counterattack. Lawrence had no way of communicating with Feisal at Wejh or the

British in Cairo. A message had to be sent. He decided to do it himself. There was only one direct route to Cairo and one means of transport: across the Sinai by camel. He wasted no time, taking eight tribesmen with him on the 240-kilometre journey that would be negotiated with the aid of a map from the Royal Geographical Society archives.

The little party left Aqaba on the afternoon of Friday 6 July, just a few hours after capturing the town, and arrived at the head of the pass, Nagb Akaba, at nightfall. They spent the night there and took off next day, never running their camels for fear of exhaustion after the energy spent in the days leading up to taking Aqaba. They arrived just before sunset on Saturday at a watering hole in the Wadi Themed just short of Bir (Mountain) Mohammad. On the Sunday, they reached Medifeh, and on Monday 9 July found the Suez Canal. It had been a steady trip, given they did not run the camels, of about 72 hours.

Lawrence found a phone. He got through to Inland Water Transport but was cut off twice in his explanation. Just when he was near despair, a British operator from the military exchange came on the line and helped him find someone in authority.[1] A launch was sent for him and he was ferried to Suez HQ, where he took a train to Ismailia. Lawrence had to change trains for Cairo. Another train pulled in while he waited. He could see into the salubrious saloon car. In it were British Admiral Wemyss and Allenby. Lawrence watched as the two men stepped onto the platform. They paced up and down in deep discussion, oblivious of the comical and repetitious saluting going on around them. An officer, suspicious of the slight, robed onlooker, approached Lawrence, wanting to know who he was. The officer's demeanour changed rapidly with Lawrence's story about Aqaba. Lawrence asked that the Admiral send a store-ship there, and that it bring back the prisoners. The officer said he would do it himself without interrupting the admiral and the general, who were still deep in conversation.

Lawrence learned from the officer of Allenby's appointment and Murray's departure. Lawrence wondered if Allenby was a typically cautious and intransigent general with a staff to match.

Would it take half a year to 'train' them on Arab politics and ambitions?

He was about to find out. He padded up the quiet Savoy Hotel corridors to see Clayton, who was working hard in his lunch-hour as ever. He entered the office. Clayton dismissed him, hardly looking up and saying in Arabic that he was busy. Lawrence announced himself. Clayton, stunned but pleased to see him, accepted a brief report Lawrence had written the night before. During the meeting, Admiral Wemyss rang to say the *Dufferin* was loading up with flour and other food for the emergency trip to Aqaba. Lawrence told Clayton of the unsatisfactory promissory notes that had been used to pay some of the Bedouin fighters. Clayton ordered £16,000 worth of gold coins, which he had rushed to the ship.

Clayton passed on Lawrence's report to Allenby, who wanted to see him. Lawrence guessed he had been attracted by the remarks stressing the help that the general could receive from the eastern tribes of Syria and how they could be used to destroy the communications of Jerusalem.

Lawrence's sandals flip-flopped on the marble floor as he entered the Bull's office. Allenby had been hurriedly briefed on Lawrence's extraordinary claims of achievement and would have been intrigued to meet this strange, sun-scorched little fellow. He carried a more detailed report concerning the secret 900-kilometre journey and the culmination of Aqaba's acquisition. He maintained he could call on seven groups of Arabs in key positions in Syria. Lawrence reiterated that they could, in less than six weeks, threaten the lines of communication of the Turkish army in Palestine, especially with Jerusalem. Lawrence spoke of the real potential for a general uprising in Syria, including the capture of Damascus.

Allenby sat in his chair looking at him sideways. He seemed puzzled as he listened with hardly even a grunt one way or the other to this surprising information.

While Lawrence let go a lather of explanation, he could see

the difficulty Allenby would have in adjusting to a very different war theatre. In Europe he had been a cog in the machine of war grinding against the enemy. Lawrence assumed his brain was dominated by thoughts of having more men and fire power, which was the wrong approach in the desert. Yet the one conduit through which Lawrence could force his ideas was Allenby's cavalry background. He would be at least disposed to comprehend what horsemen and cameleers could achieve with mobility in this region. Foot soldiers and artillery would be used, but the conflict would be won or lost on British manoeuvrability. This was emphasised by reference to the maps and the distances that had to be covered. Lawrence's example here was the fact that he had sapped the Turkish strength by attacking the Medina railway. Its forces had to be deployed to defend it.

All the time he was speaking, Lawrence was looking for a flicker from the Bull, whom he guessed was unsure how much of him was real and how much imposter.[2] Yet Allenby, known for his curt manner, would never have let the chat go on as long as it did if he had major doubts. As commander-in-chief, he had to absorb this amazing development, straight from the leading activist, even if he was having trouble adjusting to his 'littleness' and silk skirt.

Allenby let the intelligence officer say his piece without interruption, demonstrating that he was keeping an open mind. Lawrence, for his part, quickly warmed to the leader, pleased to be not removed as a crackpot, and thrilled to be able to relay the huge success, at least in his eyes, and perhaps Allenby's. He felt he was being looked on by a benign uncle, or maybe even a 'master' for him to serve, something he longed for.

'What an idol the man was to us,' Lawrence wrote, 'prismatic with the unmixed self-standing quality of greatness, instinct and compact with it.'

He ended with a long string of requests for funds (£200,000 in gold coins), supplies, weaponry and sundry items for continuing the guerilla war. Lawrence urged Allenby to take command of Feisal's forces, which would soon be transferred to Aqaba, and could be used to operate on his right flank.

Allenby kept listening. Lawrence placed more maps on the desk and went on. At no point did the general hold up a hand and say, 'Now, hang on!' or 'That's too much!' or even 'We can't do that!'

When Lawrence finished, the Bull simply said:

'Well, I will do for you what I can.'[3]

That was good enough for Lawrence, who paddled his way out of the office smiling to himself.

Allenby's mind was on the Gaza–Beersheba line and smashing through the enemy at the appropriate time. Lawrence's operations had added another dimension to the Middle East campaign. Allenby saw its value far more than Murray did. He had a rare flexibility of mind among the British generals, which when applied to Lawrence was tolerant. Where others found Lawrence overbearing and cocky, Allenby thought him unassuming. Whether he could deliver on all the possibilities and promises expressed, the harassment of the Turks on his right flank could do no harm.

Lawrence's efforts deserved recognition. The second-lieutenant was made a major. Allenby later recommended him for the Order of the Bath. He had made a bigger impression on the general than he thought.

Allenby had been in his new position just two weeks and was beginning to have a sense of more than hope about his prospects. He had Chetwode's fine plan, the best mobile force in the war, which for an old cavalry man was a blessing, and now this unexpected bonus of the Arabs on his right flank. His lingering ruminations on perceived 'failure' on the Western Front, whether by him, his personal enemies or his peers, were dissipating as he began to realise the possibilities of the new command.

There just might be a chance for restored glory after all.

By 11 July the flagship of the British Red Sea fleet *Euryalus* was anchored off Aqaba. Two days later another ship was unloading arms and supplies at the port. The Howeitat stopped drifting off or returned. No more camels had to be slaughtered. Feisal's forces began moving from Wejh to Aqaba. Arab regular battalions under the command of Jaffa Pasha were shipped by sea. Lawrence had convinced Feisal that his force should be under Allenby's command and based at Aqaba, which was just 160 kilometres from the main British force's base.

Lawrence's grand dreams suddenly seemed vivid and real. Yet his reveries did not last long. The British intelligence network with spies among the Turks informed him by telegram that Auda and another leader of the Howeitat, Mohammad el Dheilan, were negotiating to betray Feisal's cause and sell out to the Turks. Lawrence hurried to Aqaba and took a guide and camel to find the would-be turncoats. Instead of confronting them, which may easily have seen Lawrence assassinated, he made light of the detailed exchanges with the Turks, which he was able to relay verbatim. They were stunned, but because there had been no accusations, only questions from Lawrence to help him understand their reasons and plight, they opened up about their grievances.

Using tact, guile and humour, Lawrence ascertained that Auda and Mohammad were annoyed that they had not been rewarded for taking Aqaba. The Turks were offering big inducements. They agreed to give a down payment of gold, which was sent from Maan. Knowing of the deal, Auda had held up the messenger bringing the gold and had robbed him. This was told to Lawrence with great merriment, but he believed that there was more to their double-dealing than they were letting on. Lawrence emphasised to Auda that Feisal's army was on the way to Aqaba. So was a big cache of guns, ammunition and explosives. Just when this would have seemed intimidating to Auda, which it was meant to be, Lawrence added a sweetener, which was more alluring than threatening. Feisal was also coming with rewards. Lawrence offered to advance Auda some of it. He accepted.

This way, a Howeitat switch of sides to the Turks was avoided, for the moment.

42

Aid to the Arabs: Lewis and Stokes

There was extra pep in Allenby's step after his meeting with Lawrence. He was able to add a dash of surprise in his analysis of the situation in the Middle East. The potential on his far right flank, even if the Turks were merely hindered in their activities, or diverted with troops and supplies, added to the positives he could put in his report to the prime minister, who had expressed his interest, based on a fascination, in the Middle East. Allenby, like all good manipulators, put a persuasive case on paper concerning his plans to win this campaign. He was in a far more useful position now to test the prime minister's offer than he ever expected after such a short period. On 12 July, the day after Lawrence supplied his startling information, he outlined his plan and requirements and sent them off to London.

Lloyd George and the War Cabinet responded. Fresh troops would be sent, along with guns. Most useful of all were the new Bristol fighter planes, which promised, if not superiority in the air, then parity after years of German dominance.

On 16 July, Allenby wrote to the War Office that 'the advantages offered by Arab cooperation on lines proposed by Lawrence are, in my opinion, of such importance that no effort should be spared to reap full benefit'. If the plan worked, he added, 'it could bring about the collapse of Turkish campaigns in the Hejaz and Syria'.

Allenby couched Lawrence's efforts in terms of dependence on local rather than British manpower, which was now a key trigger word in the British army. The massive number of casualties on the Western Front had made the government and public conscious of continued losses and the need to conscript soldiers. There were manpower shortages just when Haig was building up to attempt for the third time to take the small, German-held ridge at Passchendaele near Ypres, Belgium, which observers were predicting would lead to further depletion of the force. Any offer to lessen that pressure in any theatre would be given a hearing.

Allenby requested that Lawrence come directly under his command. His maverick efforts, begun early in May, in influencing the Arab Revolt were now official. He was ordered to serve with 'Bedouin troops and advise on . . . direct operations'.[1]

Lawrence would have access to a plane, designated 'X Flight'. His long-distance travel by camel to meetings was over. The connection to Allenby changed all that. But with this sanctioned link to the main British force would come a modification in the nature of the battles in the desert. Allenby would insist on future railway raids having mobile specialist detachments and better aircraft backup. There would be extra fire power. These additions would move away from the exclusively Arab operations, which Lawrence would be able to accept if they were not too blatant.

Allenby began his movement of headquarters from Cairo to north of Rafa. He reorganised the command, dropping a bombshell by downgrading Chetwode, who would run the 20th Army Corps, one of two infantry corps in the new set-up, with Major General Edward Bulfin taking over the other, 21st Corps.

The Desert Mounted Column became the Desert Mounted Corps. Chauvel was chosen to run it, in the most prestigious battle command post in the Middle East. It was a shock, especially among the British officers. They all knew that he was the best 'cavalry' (as they would always call it) leader on the Eastern Front. But he was an Australian, and this was a British command. He was to take over a staff that had been Chetwode's. It was at that time the biggest mounted force in history with 34,000 mounted riflemen and cavalry. Chauvel was in impressive company. He was ahead of France's Marshal Jean Baptiste Bessieres, who in Napoleon's Grande Armee against the Austrians in 1809 had 29,000 cavalry. Napoleon's brother-in-law Joachim Murat had 22,000 under him in the same army in 1805.

But Chauvel had far more fire power than his counterparts a century earlier, and this at just the beginning of the Palestine campaign. Apart from the rifles being superior, each squadron had either machine- or Lewis guns. Added to this was the powerful artillery, which was mainly in British hands, except for Hong Kong and Singapore Mounted Battery, whose gunners were Indian. These would support the nine brigades of horsemen— four Australian, one New Zealand and four British. There were also three camel battalions; two were Anzac, one was British.

Ever the diplomat, Chauvel wrote a generous letter to Chetwode thanking him for his help and cooperation. Chetwode responded, showing that he had changed his mind, at least in general terms, about the Anzac troops, with whom he had not been enamoured at first. He wrote:

'I shall always be very proud of having had such a fine body of men under my command, as your Anzac mounted troops and grateful to you of the able way in which you have led them. I cannot say how much I envy you the command of the largest body of mounted men ever under one hand—it is my own trade—but Fate has willed it otherwise . . .'[2]

Chauvel's upgrade made him better disposed to his new chief of staff, which Allenby had insisted on. Tall, English 34-year-old Brigadier General R.G.H. Howard-Vyse, nicknamed 'Wombat', had an uneasy relationship with Chauvel at first, but they warmed to each other in the build-up towards the next major battle.

Allenby was dealt a personal blow when he learnt that his only son Michael, Military Cross winner and a fine gunner, had been killed in action near Nieuport, France on 29 July. The only consolation was a handwritten letter from Haig, expressing his condolences. It was an honest, generous communication, and ended the bad feeling between the two since the Somme and Arras battles.

Allenby carried on his command with typical stoicism, though he was in pain over the loss. He set the Gaza–Beersheba attack for September but his infantry, many of them fresh troops, were not prepared. He put the attack on Gaza–Beersheba off until the end of October, giving him nearly three months to get everything right.

His main objective now was an intelligence one. He had to deceive the Turks into believing that the British would throw everything at the massively guarded Gaza when Beersheba would be his secret first target.

Early in September 1917, Lawrence began his campaign against the northern part of the Hejaz line in keeping with his promises to Allenby. In return, Lawrence received two specialists: an English Lewis-gun instructor, and an Australian who handled the Stokes mortar. He was also given explosives. If and when the campaign advanced, Lawrence would be sent more and bigger detachments, which ran counter to his earlier dreams of a purely Arab 'uprising'. Yet he was not about to reject planes, Rolls-Royce armoured cars, and motorised field artillery batteries if they came his way as part of the deal with Allenby.

After Auda's near defection, Lawrence wanted to keep an eye on him and make sure that he and his tribesmen were kept busy for the Arab cause and not tempted to join the enemy. If he and his men received gold and food from the British, there was less chance that they would switch sides. But travelling with these desert mercenaries had its challenges. Lawrence could have done with a few psychologists. He first mission with Auda and 116 Bedouins from a dozen tribes, predominantly Howeitat, provoked tests he could do without. The members of the party argued and fought. Auda abrogated his responsibilities, hiding behind the excuse of possible bias. Lawrence was left as chief judge and jury on issues that he often knew little about. They included pay disputes, feuds and 'division of spoils' after raids. The cantankerous Howeitat, who seemed never fulfilled unless they were in dispute, took up much of his time when he had to worry about supplies, transport, tribal pay and the planning of operations. On his first trip alone, Lawrence had to settle 14 tribal disputes, a dozen assaults, four camel thefts, a row over a marriage settlement, and one case of bewitchment. The toughest of all were two cases of the 'evil eye', which Lawrence found impossible to adjudicate on. He thought it should be banned but Auda would not support any change to such tribal customs. Giving an enemy the 'evil eye', a mesmerising stare that seemed to do psychological damage to the victim, had been used in arguments for thousands of years.

The squabbling led to Lawrence not attacking a station on the line at Mudowwarah. Reconnaissance from a ridge 300 metres away indicated that about 200 Turks were in the block houses next to the station. The Australian mortar expert, Sergeant Brooks, thought it doubtful his shells could smash the solid basalt walls. Lawrence considered his force. Could the Bedouins, who had been acting like a disputatious rabble all trip, be trusted to attack and support each other like a normal military force fighting another? He thought the answer was 'no' at that moment. He decided on Plan B: to blow up a bridge further up the line. If this was done as a train passed, it would give the Bedouins a chance to indulge in their most coveted endeavour: looting.

Lawrence in this case took most of the risk in a five-hour operation by placing a detonating mine under a double-arched bridge and covering his tracks. The next morning, 16 September, a train was seen steaming up from the south to the station. Lawrence sent 30 Arabs off to distract Turkish patrols that were already moving out from the block houses to protect the train when it plodded north out of Mudowwarah on its journey to Maan. He then hurried to position himself at the detonator on a ridge about 200 metres from the bridge.

The 12-carriage passenger train pulled by two engines chugged towards the bridge.

Bedouin eyes flicked to Lawrence on the ridge as they waited for the train to reach the bridge. He plunged the detonator. A discordant sound of ripping steel accompanied the sight of black dirt shooting 30 metres into the air and the 'boom' of the second carriage's destruction. Other carriages slipped, slid and toppled along the line on and off the bridge. Lawrence signalled for the Lewis guns to fire. Brooks sent off his mortars, which slammed into another carriage. Seventy Turks and Austrians were killed mainly by Sergeant Yells, the Lewis gunner, and Brooks' mortars, making the action of the Bedouins easy. The Arabs opened fire on the dwindling numbers on the train who were resisting. Then they charged down to the train, whipping themselves into a frenzy of slaughter and plunder. Ninety prisoners were taken, including Austrian officers and NCOs. Soon all resistance from male passengers was overcome. The Bedouins got down to unsystematic and hysterical looting of anything and everything.

Lawrence joined them at the train, which was found to be carrying families of Turkish officers returning to Damascus, volunteers for boat service on the Euphrates, refugees, and ill patients being sent to hospital. Carpets, mattresses, quilts, clothes, clocks, cooking pots, food, ornaments and weapons were among the scores of items fought over and scrounged by the booty seekers. Lawrence let them go. He had long ago accepted this scavenging mentality as part of the Bedouin make-up. By doing nothing, he was tacitly encouraging the activity.

Women and children surrounded him, begging his protection from the plunderers.

Lawrence kicked them off with his feet, seemingly unconcerned at their distress.[3]

Lawrence was focused on doing what he could to destroy the train. It was a military operation for him, no more, no less.

The Austrian prisoners objected to some of the looting. A shot was fired at one of the Arabs. They retaliated, killing some of the prisoners. Again undistracted, Lawrence turned his attention to the best way of disabling the train so it could not be used again by the Turks. He climbed on the locomotive engine and placed a fuse and detonator on a cylinder. He lit the fuse, yelled for the looters to move away, jumped off and watched as the cylinder and axle were blown to pieces.

This explosion and the fire from converging Turkish patrols stopped the mayhem and led to a hasty retreat by the raiders.

A second rail destruction, this time on a goods train, took place a few days later near a station known as Kilo (Kilometre) 475. Lawrence was joined by a French officer, Captain Pisani, whose bravery in the venture earned him a recommendation for a Military Cross. During the attack, a Turkish officer realised that Lawrence and Pisani, despite their Arab gear, were Europeans. He made a point of trying to shoot them. Lawrence was hit only a glancing blow to the hip, which was dressed and caused him little discomfort.

The lesson Lawrence learned more than ever before was that he needed weaponry and professionals such as Yells and Brooks as the intensity of encounters like these increased. They were the difference between success and failure, especially when the marauding Arabs lost any sense of discipline in their frenzy to pillage. This meant intertwining even more with Allenby and his plans, and reliance on the support he was providing. Yet despite this development, Lawrence wished to keep the Arab identity of the revolt. He saw it as better for the British cause. It had to remain essentially a tribal affair. Otherwise, the Bedouins would object to the foreign intervention and fade back into the desert. As quickly as the desert sands covered their footprints, the revolt in the desert would disappear.

After these missions, Lawrence returned to Aqaba in early October and then travelled to Ismailia on the Suez Canal in an X Flight plane. It was then on to Allenby's new headquarters on the front near Gaza, where he received his orders in relation to the imminent large scale military attack. He also discussed his plans with Clayton and Hogarth.

All was in readiness for a final ruse in an attempt to fool the Germans and Turks.

43

The Prankster's Ruse

The outstanding officer on Allenby's staff in devising deception schemes was 39-year-old Colonel Richard Meinertzhagen, head of military intelligence. Lawrence described him as an idealist so possessed with his convictions that he was willing 'to harness evil to the chariot of the good'. He loved deceiving enemy or friend with scruple-free jokes.

Meinertzhagen had arrived in Cairo in May 1917 to join the Arab Bureau and had not been impressed with Murray, whom he found too much of a 'society soldier'. Allenby was more to his liking, mainly because he listened to Meinertzhagen's ideas, which had been successful in East Africa and Egypt. The most prominent so far was his installation of a radio-receiver station on the Great Pyramid, which intercepted and decoded enemy messages. Meinertzhagen discovered a key Arab spy at Beersheba. He sent him a letter thanking him for the information he had 'given' the British, along with payment in Turkish currency. Both were intercepted by the Turks. The Arab agent could not convince his masters of his innocence. He was executed.

Allenby, like a modern TV comedy host being presented with ideas by gag writers, heard suggestions from his staff and rejected all of them without a second thought, except for the two proffered by Meinertzhagen. The first was that it should be put about that Allenby would return from the front to Cairo from 29 October to 4 November. This was to make the enemy think that nothing could happen in that time. The commander-in-chief liked that one. The Arab Bureau's modern communications and espionage radio-taps, along with newspapers, had made this misleading information possible to disseminate and likely to be picked up by the enemy. Meinertzhagen's second scheme was for British planes every evening to drop packets of cigarettes with propaganda leaflets behind enemy lines. So far, so good. Then came the punchline. On the night of the attack the cigarettes would be laced with opium. He had tested the cigarettes himself.

'They were indeed strong,' Meinertzhagen noted, 'The effect was sublime, complete abandonment, all energy gone, lovely dreams and completely inability to act and think.'[1]

He had visions of the entire Turkish force breaking for a smoke and being serenely incapacitated while the British army enacted a walkover.

But Allenby did not like it at all. He vetoed it. For one thing, he thought using a drug was too much like employing poison, and he was not in favour of using either this or gas. For another, the commander-in-chief was looking for a more subtle deception.

Meinertzhagen was miffed. He was sure it would work, but kept his counsel. He would carry out the opium cigarette project in secret anyway.

After the rebuff from Allenby (who was 'brusque', the intelligence officer found, 'almost to the point of rudeness'), he was motivated to come up with something the chief would like. Meinertzhagen explained a simple ruse to him. A staff officer, ostensibly on reconnaissance, would get himself chased by a Turkish patrol and pretend to be wounded. He would drop a haversack stained with blood, containing papers, letters, maps and money. The papers had been prepared cunningly and skilfully. They were communications on strategy regarding the proposed Gaza attack, making clear that it was set for late November and that Beersheba would not be the main target. The point was made about the water shortages short of and beyond that village being an impediment for a concerted attack. One letter, which Meinertzhagen took great care over, was to a lover in England. There would even be a cut lunch in the bag.

Allenby, whose reactions to issues were quick and decisive, liked this deception. It appealed to his more hidden, subtle side. He imagined German officers poring over everything, and hopefully not debating the 'authenticity' of anything in the haversack. Allenby sanctioned this one.

Meinertzhagen went to work. He sent an officer out into

no-man's land near the Turkish front. He was chased by a mounted patrol and dropped the haversack on an open stretch. The Turks thundered past without noticing it. A second officer was tried. He galloped close to the front line and more enemy troopers but no-one took up the chase. Exasperated, Meinertzhagen, a big man and more easily noticed, took off himself with the magical cavalry bag, which had fresh blood from his horse on it. He found a Turkish patrol. It gave chase. He galloped for about two kilometres. The Turks pulled up. Meinertzhagen stopped, 600 metres away. He dismounted and fired his rifle at them. Annoyed, the Turks resumed the chase, firing in his direction. In the action of mounting up, he dropped the haversack and his rifle, pretending he was hit. Meinertzhagen took off, slumped over his horse's neck and weaving uncertainly. He looked back to see one of the Turks stop and pick up the haversack and rifle. Satisfied, Meinertzhagen bolted for the British line.

He wondered if the enemy would act on the contents beyond devouring his better-than-average officer's lunch.

German and Turkish officers ignored the food but digested the documents, and were in no doubt about their integrity. They regarded them as vital. They were so taken in that they put out a warning to all officers not to go near the front carrying secret papers. The enemy command now believed that the main attack would be at Gaza, combining the assault with a landing from the sea north of the city. The Germans and Turks thought the British aim would be to take the Turks from the rear and threaten their communications. They moved all their reserves up to Gaza. Thinking they had time to spare, the German advisers began reorganising their divisional structures.

Chetwode planned to leave tents erected in dummy camps. At nightfall, fires were kindled. Hurricane lamps were left burning. Small squads of horsemen rode back and forth on the banks of the Guzze. The dust raised gave the impression of troop concentration. The sham was not confined to land. Naval boats slipped into the mouth of the Wadi Hesi a few kilometres north of Gaza.

They took soundings as if they were intending an invasion from the sea. At the same time, another bluff was carried out on the island of Cyprus to prevent the enemy sending reinforcements from Syria to the Palestine Front. A camp was traced out on Cyprus. Buoys were set up as if they were for directing transport in the harbour. Enquiries were made through local contractors to create the impression that supplies were needed for a division. Whispers began on the island that were sure to reach enemy agents.

On the right flank of the British camp near Gaza, mounted patrols continued in front of Beersheba to accustom the enemy to their presence.

The proposal was that Chetwode's 20th Corps would creep off after dark towards Beersheba ready for the assault on the town.

The success of the deception was apparent from a Turkish commander's dispatch late in October from Gaza, where he was based, to the High Command at Jerusalem:

'An enemy out-flanking movement on Beersheba, with about one infantry and one cavalry division is indicated but the main attack, as before, must be expected on the Gaza Front.'[2]

Allenby issued his battle order on 22 October. It was essentially Chetwode's plan from June. He was to strike with 20th Corps at Beersheba from the south-west, while Chauvel, with two brigades of Mounted Corps, was to begin with an assault on the town from the east and north-east. The date set for the combined attack was 31 October.

Chauvel would stick with two veteran brigades, the 3rd and 4th, but there were changes at the top. Meredith had returned to Australia because of ill health. Royston was on his way home to South Africa to sort out 'private family problems'. At least, this was the force's public relations line. In reality, Galloping Royston's vigorous career in World War I had a most peculiar end when he deliberately inhaled poison gas before battle so he could recognise it in combat. He was hospitalised in October 1917 and sent home. Royston's act was not a strange attempt to avoid more combat. On the contrary, it was the folly of a man who genuinely wanted more. He was too ill to resume his post leading the 3rd Light Horse Brigade. Lachlan Chisholm Wilson, in charge of 5th Regiment, was promoted to take over from Royston at 3rd Brigade. Chauvel was also quick to put commander William Grant of the 11th Regiment in to lead 4th Brigade in place of Meredith. Chauvel had trained both in Queensland and had complete faith in them as strong, competent commanders. Similar to him, they were also superb horsemen who never looked like stiffly trained cavalry, but more like bush stockmen or show-ring riders.

Wiry, 194 centimetres (6 feet 4 inches), 47-year-old Grant was the son of a miner (later mine owner and grazier) originally from Stawell, Victoria. Soon after gaining a degree in civil engineering, his father died and Grant used his inheritance to buy the Bowenville Station on the Darling Downs in 1896. He also worked as a surveyor. Chauvel knew his background well, and his mentality, especially since Gallipoli, where he proved to be impetuous and spontaneous. His great Light Horse skills as a guide on night marches over sand dunes in Sinai had been honed on the wide plains of his home territory, where survival depended on bushcraft. At the end of the Sinai campaign earlier in the year, he had led his regiment over 240 kilometres of steep, rocky mountains in a week. All his troopers would go anywhere with him knowing his courage and the fact that he never got lost. Grant was not the reflective type. Given an order, he carried it out without thinking twice before or after he executed it.

Forty-six-year-old Wilson was the opposite to Grant both physically and in many aspects of character. He was short, rotund, quiet and shy. Wilson was born at Logan River and became a leading Brisbane lawyer. He had fought in the Boer War. On Gallipoli he made his name after a successful raid against Bird Trenches near Gaba Tepe. After repulsing a Turkish attack, he seized positions known thereafter as Wilson's Lookout. He had led his regiment in all the major engagements since

Romani 14 months earlier. No better horseman graced the battlefields, yet he was known also as an innovator. He introduced
the Queensland portable spear-point pump to obtain water in
the desert, a valuable asset as the campaign progressed.

In the week from 22 October, all commanders concentrated
on making sure the water supply was adequate. In the north,
Chetwode's advance brigades and rail construction companies
brought the ever-extending railway and water supply forward.
In the south, Chauvel ordered Ryrie's 2nd Brigade to work on
the wells at Khalasa and Asluj. They were both capable of delivering good-quality and abundant water. But the masonry in
them had been broken a long way down. Earth and concrete had
been dumped into them. By 29 October, the wells were clear, the
pumps were installed and the flow was strong.

A detachment of a new, surprising 'ally' appeared at the wells
while the troopers and engineers worked. They were Hejaz
Arabs based at the recently conquered Aqaba. The Australians had long been wary of Sinai Bedouins, and had restrained
themselves from taking action after a spate of incidents with
them over the past 18 months. The Anzacs had been ordered
to avoid tangling with them because they were 'potential' allies
against the Turks. This detachment of 70 camels was the first
proof of that. It had been with Lawrence fighting the Turks.
Allenby had asked him to be part of the coming battle for Gaza,
but he had declined the offer. Lawrence claimed (to one of his
biographers, Liddell Hart) that it went against his principle of
keeping a clear line between Arab and British forces. This Arab
party had then come under the command of Lawrence's colleague, Lieutenant Colonel S. F. Newcombe, a Royal Engineer
and one of the men involved in Allenby's stepped-up 'association' with Prince Feisal's force. Where Lawrence was building
his experience in demolition, Newcombe was an expert. He was
also adept at leading the Bedouins as raiders. The Arabs with
Newcombe claimed he slept with his head on the railway line so
that he could pick up the earliest vibrations of oncoming trains.

It indicated an unusual dedication to his penchant for demolition. He too was a legend among the Bedouins. He was obsessed with hurting the enemy. Over time, he kept many Turkish battalions on the defensive reconstructing culverts and relaying lines that he had destroyed.

The mission of the Arabs and their British advisers was to protect Chauvel's right flank east of Beersheba. If and when Beersheba was taken, Newcombe planned to slip around behind enemy lines and harass the retreating Turks on the road to Jerusalem.

Bulfin's artillery had been hitting Gaza for 72 hours by 30 October. The big guns from British and French ships had joined in. Their intermittent boom could be heard at Asluj. The noise signalled the beginning of the effort to smash through the line that had held up the desert campaign for half a year.

Chauvel reached Asluj with Desert Mounted Corps HQ on 30 October. A moonlight ride through a sultry night over 40 kilometres of rough country brought six brigades within striking distance of Beersheba just before dawn. Water was a priority. Some of the Light Horse filled their bottles at Khalasa. Then they made the night ride, which was hot and oppressive. Huge billows of heavy dust swept through the horse formations. It clung to columns in a dense cloud moving slowly across the lowlands south of Beersheba.

By midnight both men and horses were restless for the limited water they carried. The Khalasa wells were now far behind them. The nearest wells lay behind the defences of Beersheba in the heart of the town. Officers were finding unique ways to keep their charges going. The 11th Light Horse Regiment's Colonel Parsons trotted among his troops, delivering an encouraging word here and there. One Section of men of C Squadron was cursing the lack of water. Parsons interrupted them.

'You fellows should copy my example,' he said. 'For the

past 10 miles, I have carried a small pebble in my mouth, and I haven't felt the need for a drink.'

The men were left stunned by this advice. Parsons began to ride off to another squadron. Then a trooper observed wryly:

'If the Colonel travel 10 miles without a drink on a small pebble, how far will he go on a brick?'

Parsons heard the remark and joined the troopers in the ensuing laughter.[3]

Allenby's orders were simple and clear. Before the day was out, the town and its wells had to be taken. Logic told Chauvel that this had to be adhered to. If the town was not taken by nightfall, the Light Horse and infantry would be out of water and forced to withdraw. The third attack on the Gaza line would be a failure.

Chetwode moved 20th Corps into position south-west of Beersheba. At 5.55 a.m. the Muezzin heralded the new day of 31 October 1917 from the minarets of the town.

The infantry began its assault.

44

Charge of the 4th Light Brigade

Chauvel placed his headquarters on a high hill, Khashim Zanna, six kilometres south-west of the town. A mounted orderly carrying a lance with a red-and-white flag—Desert Mounted's insignia—stood close by as the commander used his binoculars to scan the basin in which Beersheba sat. He had 'a dress circle view of the show', the best he had yet had to command a major battle. He could see most of the regiments advancing on the town and had a good sense of how the battle was progressing through the morning.

Chauvel was confident. Beersheba was well defended by the Turks in numbers but did not seem to offer facilities for a prolonged defence. It lay in a shallow saucer at the foot of the Judean Hills, which rose abruptly from its northern outskirts, with high ground also to the east and south-east. Before the war it had been an ordinary trading centre linking the hinterland with Gaza's port. Beersheba's main activity seemed to have been as a camel distribution centre. The Turks had used it as a base for its operations in Sinai, putting up new temporary buildings. The Germans, in a good public relations act, had built a new mosque in the city's north. Apart from that religious centre, it appeared to the troopers from the distance just like an impoverished outback town. There would be no glory in conquering it as such, except for one commodity: the water.

Everyone—infantry and Light Horse—had begun well. But there was no wind. Artillery barrages left smoke that did not clear, making further shelling less accurate. Enemy cavalry, guns and transport were scurrying to meet the assault. The return salvos of artillery began to have an impact. The Turks had seen a deal of movement around Chauvel's HQ. His 10-minute break for breakfast had been interrupted by a rude German pilot, with no heed for rank, an officer's need for sustenance or potential indigestion. He flew low and strafed the hill. Chauvel and his staff had to duck and weave away. Soon afterwards it returned to roll out bombs. They exploded at the point where Chauvel had been standing, but he was well clear. When the plane disappeared into the clouds, he and his staff returned, unshaken and unscathed.

At noon, enemy artillery too decided it was an important position. Khashim Zanna was hit with heavy shelling. This time Chauvel had to abandon his lunch and dive for cover with the rest of his staff. After a second shelling, Chauvel mounted his horse and returned to his original position, unperturbed by being a hot target on his prominent hill with its best possible view of the ensuing battles.

He could see Chetwode's infantry was progressing. But the Light Horse from Anzac Mounted to the east of the town was being held up by a line of well-concealed machine-guns at a small outpost mound called Tell es Sabe. Troopers were being forced to dismount and inch their way forward. Heavy fire raked the plain. Shrapnel rained down.

A further problem was caused by ever-nagging German aircraft. They had been checked over Gaza by British planes, but Beersheba was not defended in the air. The German planes began wreaking havoc, killing horses and men, despite attempts to fan out and be less of a major target.

By 1 p.m. Chetwode's infantry had carried out a concerted, strong manoeuvre, driving the Turks from their trenches to the south-west and west of the town. But they had not overrun the enemy, which was holding its lines closer to Beersheba. Half an hour later, Chaytor's New Zealand Brigade had committed all its regiments in the east. Noting this, Chauvel, although reluctant, was quick to bring in another of Hodgson's Anzac Mounted Brigades: the 3rd led by Wilson.

Another plan, a contingency at this stage, was forming in Chauvel's flexible mind. He ordered the Victorian 8th Light Horse Regiment to report to him. It lined up in close formation and headed for the chief's HQ. This was just what the German pilots were looking for. Two planes swooped low, bombing and machine-gunning. They hit several men and horses, including one of the great Anzac legends, VC winner Lieutenant Colonel 'Elsie' Maygar, and his big grey waler. The horse bolted. Troopers dashed off after them. They caught the bloodied horse, but Maygar was missing.

At 2.45 p.m. Chauvel, with one eye on the clock, reassessed the state of battle. The Turks seemed to be weakening in the east. Chaytor's New Zealanders and Cox's 1st Light Horse Brigade had nearly surrounded the troublesome line of machine-gunners at Tell es Sabe. At 2.50 p.m., the New Zealanders had crawled to a line near the bottom of a slope about 150 metres from the Turkish trenches. The signal was given to charge. The troopers careered up the slope, yelling as they went and waving their bayonets. It was enough for 132 Turks. They threw down their weapons and surrendered. The rest fled north-west towards Beersheba. The four machine-guns that had caused so much havoc were taken.

Chauvel had an idea of what was happening from his vantage point. It was confirmed by the silencing of the guns. Seizing the moment without waiting for official confirmation, he ordered Wilson to take his 3rd Light Horse Brigade and strike north of the town for a line between two hills: 970 and 1,020. The 1st Brigade, moving on the left of the 3rd, was to make for a line between Hill 970 and the mosque. But the Turks were strong in those hills to the town's north and would be tough to dislodge.

The enemy had been pushed off Tell es Sabe, yet it was still in force to the south of the town.

Chauvel said he had learnt a major lesson at Magdhaba and Rafa: 'patience', and not to expect things to happen quickly. He had faced 'deadly pauses' there, which was 'so disconcerting to a commander'. But there had been none at Beersheba. Yet still, there was more of a time constraint in this battle.

As the sun moved lower, he realised he would have to make a decision. The wells had to be taken. There could not be a charge after dark. It had to be done now. He had faith in Grant as a commander of steady courage. His 4th Brigade had been starved of action. They would be full of dash. The horses would go hard, despite their dehydrated condition. They would smell the wells as they drew close to the Turkish trenches and this would drive them on.

Chauvel gave the green light to a grateful Grant.

In Beersheba itself there was a problem of uniformity of thought, tactics and defence. The Turkish commander Ismet Bey had 4,400 men and 28 artillery field guns to hold off the Light Horse after the British infantry's push in the morning. Ismet had been aware much earlier than his German commander Kress that this was no mere feint by a couple of brigades. But when he informed Kress of this by phone the German stubbornly responded that Ismet was wrong: there were only two brigades.

Ismet Bey was furious but could do nothing. Kress was not going to attempt to bring in reinforcements. He and his German staff had been conned weeks ago by the Meinertzhagen documents that said Beersheba was not the main target. This created a strange mood in the town with German officers convinced that there would be no attack, and Turks under them feeling sure there would be.

The Germans behind the Turkish trenches watched the build-up to what was going on at a ridge still with a sceptical eye. The officers insisted it was an elaborate manoeuvre; just another British ruse, a mere demonstration.

'We did not believe,' one German officer said, 'that the charge would be pushed home. That seemed an impossible intention. I have heard a great deal of the fighting qualities of the Australian soldiers. They are not soldiers at all; they are madmen.'[1]

Some observers now had second thoughts. Two regiments had disappeared out of view. Surely, the Germans thought, the Australian Light Horse could not be serious about an assault at this late stage in the afternoon. Only 'madmen' would attempt such an attack. Then again, some had heard stories (German propaganda) that the Australians were indeed insane and 'wild animals', untamed British colonial stock from a remote, primitive country in the Pacific.

From the enemy's view, the first squadron emerged in a line 1,100 metres long over the top of the ridge, then three kilometres south-east from the trenches and six kilometres from Beersheba itself. The Germans wondered what they were playing at. It was 4.30 p.m. The sun was setting and would be out of sight by 4.50 p.m. Light was already fading fast.

The sight of the vanguard coming over the crest of the ridge alerted the Germans and Turks. They still thought it could not be an all-out charge, but they weren't certain. Orders were run and barked to the artillery men. Wheels were spun and the big gun barrels lowered. The gunners were given the order:

'Fire!'

It seemed more of a nervous reaction than a serious attempt to stop the onslaught. The field in the Beersheba Stakes was too spread for the shrapnel to have an impact. The shells scattered hot metal from air bursts or hit the ground in dust explosions. Two horses went down fast, but in the waves of the 800 this was negligible as the horsemen bent lower and closer to the necks of their walers for more protection.

Enemy commanders scrambled to alert their machine-gunners on their right placed on Hill 1,180. When the charge's lead squadrons had come 1.5 kilometres—about half-way to the trenches—they were to rake the plain with machine-gun fire. The German advisers, getting twitchy, believed this would destroy the oncoming front squadrons. The rest would be forced to dismount in the traditional fashion, which would lead to a successful Turkish defence.

One horseman was hit in the eye. He could feel it hanging by a ligament on his cheek, but could do nothing as his horse hurtled on another 200 metres before the injured rider slipped off. He was one of a few struck down. The three lines were sweeping on undaunted by fallen mates. Shells were hitting the ground behind them now.

The charge was under the guns' set range. No matter how fast the Turkish gunners spun their trunnion wheels, the artillery fire would have limited impact from now on.

The German advisers were still confident that the Light Horse would stop any moment, park their horses and proceed on foot. They knew from the slouch hats and type of horses that the attackers were Australian riflemen. They were brandishing bay-onets, but they were mounted riflemen, not cavalry.

When the front of the charge was within 400 metres, a chill ran through the command and the Turks in the trenches.

The horses were not stopping. They could smell the water now and were coming straight at them. They could hear the blood-curdling cries from the Australians over the evening air in the brief lulls of artillery and machine-gun fire. They would have been unintelligible to the enemy—mainly bush calls and cooees. Some of the Turks had heard them before at Gallipoli. They were lunatics, demons, only stoppable with a phalanx of 30 machine-guns, as at the narrow, tight target range at the Nek.

But those weapons were fewer; the target provided by the Australians more diffuse. Ismet Bey and German officers made a decision. They were getting out, if they could. One officer was ordered to throw switches that would demolish several targets, including the all-important wells.

As the first line of horsemen thundered closer across the rock-strewn ground and were closer than 70 metres away, the bullets that had been flying over their heads due to wrong rifle calibrations now cut down some of the men and horses.

'We could feel the concussion of the fire in our faces,' Trooper Phil Moon said. 'I got my head down on old Jerry's neck and was doing some mighty deep thinking. Next to me, Johnson's horse gets it through the head; Johnson takes a tumble.'[2]

It was now a game of Russian roulette for that front line. About 40 were charging at a strongly held small fort. Nine of the horses were hit. The men fell clear on the broken ground, collected themselves and began firing. Another 20 swerved to the left, trying to avoid the thick fire from the fort, and aiming at a gap in the defences. Fourteen of them were stopped. The remainder squeezed through. Trooper Fowler, stranded right in front of the trenches and fortunate not be struck down, followed the dust of the others.

'I turned my horse and raced along the trench,' he recounted. 'I had a bird's eye view of the Turks below me throwing hand grenades . . .'[3]

In a flash, he was past the immediate danger, weaving through the shallower trenches and charging around scattered rifle pits and dugouts. Within seconds he was on his way to Beersheba.

To the right of the attacking line the leading squadron was commanded by Major James Lawson, who led the way with Lieutenant Colonel Bourchier on the left. They hurtled through crack Turkish Yilderim storm troops, brushing them aside almost with disdain, such was the momentum built as the horses' nostrils were now quivering with the scent of water.

There were casualties. A flurry of stick grenades were hurled at the horsemen, collecting about 14 horses and killing six troopers. But this in no way slowed the barging line, which crashed on past tents, redoubts and dugouts, and jumped a wide, deep trench. Some of the Turks, fortified by knowing they were well-protected, poked up their bayonets at the horses' underbellies as they straddled the trench.

Many Turks threw up their hands in surrender as the horses were upon them. But then, seeing the horses reined in well clear of them, they changed their minds, picked up their rifles and fired at the dismounting troopers.

Chaos set in as horse handlers struggled to move their assigned mounts aside and out of the line of fire. The other troopers charged on foot for the trench. They engaged the Turks in the most vicious encounter of this kind since the battle of Lone Pine on Gallipoli 22 months earlier.

Bourchier, favouring his revolver, and in his element in the close-in fighting, shot six Turks in quick succession from within five paces.

Lawson too was electrified by the charge. He dashed on foot at a small fort holding 100 Turks. Ignoring machine-guns, rifles and grenades, he led the attack, killing about half and accepting the surrender of the rest. (This would later gain Lawson a VC recommendation.)

The Anzacs were at their most unforgiving, especially after several incidents where troopers were killed by Turks who had previously surrendered. In one, Tibby Cotter noticed a field gun with its detachment retreating at the trot towards Beersheba. The unarmed stretcher-bearer galloped forward to stop the gun. He yelled for the Turks to surrender. They threw down their weapons. Cotter bent down to rein in the detachment's lead horse. One of the 'surrendered' men was now behind Cotter. He noticed the Australian had not produced a weapon. The Turk ripped out a hidden revolver, took a step forward and shot Cotter in the back of the head. He fell from his horse, dead.

Six troopers witnessed the sly killing. They galloped forward, revolvers drawn. They reined in the detachment horses, dragged the 10 Turks clear, and without singling out the 'culprit', gunned down all of them.

In another incident, Lieutenant Ben Meredith, accompanied by trooper Moon, dismounted and approached a redoubt, revolver aimed at the 20 men in it. They all held their hands high. Meredith turned away. He signalled for Moon to take charge of them. One Turk picked up a rifle. He aimed, fired and hit Meredith in the back. Moon ran at the Turk, who was turning to shoot again, and bayoneted him in the stomach.

'You bastard!' Moon screamed. He withdrew the blade, and thrust it into him another four times, each time yelling the same expletive.

Chauvel's force was fortunate. One German engineer had been assigned to destroy wells and vital installations with demolition charges laid ready at the wells and main buildings. The rest of the German officers had departed the town to the north or northwest along with the commander of the Turkish 3rd Corps, Ismet Bey. A desperate mass exodus left the one engineer to a certain fate. He was captured a fraction of a second before he could set off the bulk of the charges. All but two of 17 wells were saved.

And so, for the moment, was Allenby's campaign.

*

Soon all the surviving horsemen had broken through and overwhelmed the Turkish trenches, making it one of the most successful charges in history. In the end, the 400,000 litres were not enough for the soldiers, troopers and animals in the corps as its members swarmed into the conquered town.

The least in need among the men and animals would trek elsewhere for hydration. The rest took their fill. Troopers watered their horses at Turkish canvas troughs and fell on their knees to drink beside their thirsty mounts.

The decision to attack in a full-on cavalry-style action had been Chauvel's alone. It was a logical response to Allenby's order in the planning stage days earlier to take Beersheba before nightfall on the first day. The sheer recklessness of the two regiments' ride had forged the breakthrough that now made the toppling of Gaza a strong chance.

A message from Allenby (while at the imaginatively named El Buggar 20 kilometres east of Beersheba) received by Chauvel's staff at 6.05 p.m., 35 minutes after the main fighting was over, lay gathering dust on the Khashim Zanna mound. It was a response to a mistaken belief that Chauvel was thinking of pulling out of the battle to water his horses at Karm, 19 kilometres east. It read:

'The chief orders you to capture Beersheba today, in order to secure water and take prisoners.'

Chauvel never saw it. Had it been sent earlier and read at any time, it would have made no difference to his responses. One of his great strengths was patience. He claimed that he was less concerned with his decision-making than in any of the other tight situations on the campaign to that point. He was going to throw everything at the town with the intention of taking it one way or another. The risky charge was his last option.

After the charge and comprehensive victory, the 11th Light Horse Regiment historian noted that the troopers were 'swapping yarns around their campfires'. In the streets and roads of Beer-sheba, or 'lounging round the time-honoured wells of the town where Abraham, Isaac and Joseph, and the sons of Samuel watered their flocks'. Other troopers continued to mop up in the town, collecting hundreds of Turkish and German prisoners, and booty. The latter was quickly piled up. It included loaves of coarse Turkish bread, tins of poor-quality coffee, dried apricots, dates and figs. There was a hill of Turkish paper money. But it had no value for the troopers, although later in the conflict they would buy bread with it from an old woman despite its alleged zero commercial value. (After eating their purchase, the troopers swore that 'the old woman had robbed us, in any case'.)

Gold always did have value. One regiment was rumoured to have found a huge cache. If so, they kept it. No 'find' was reported.[4]

An 11th Regiment sergeant discovered a canvas bag filled with Turkish war medals, including many Gallipoli Stars, which were struck by the Turkish War Ministry to celebrate Gallipoli. The sergeant distributed the medals among his mates in a silent reminder, if any of them needed it, that every victory such as those in 1916 and now a big one at Beersheba was 'payback' for the failure on the Turkish peninsula and fallen comrades.

In the town's north-west, one group of troopers found a delight-ful hidden cellar of cognac, red and white wine. Before guards could be dispatched to mind it, the alcohol disappeared. Much of the cognac was consumed in celebration that night. One officer managed to retrieve a bottle for himself but had to buy it from a trooper who had beaten him to the cellar. It cost the officer 'five bob'. Just before midnight, a trooper from one squadron wan-dered into the lines of another, a bottle of cognac in each hand, singing a rollicking ditty. The front of his tunic was 'glittering with a score or more of Turkish war medals pinned closely together. In a loud, thick voice, punctuated with hiccups, he insisted that the sergeant major should come out of the tent and salute him.'[5]

The sergeant threw him in a guard tent to keep him out of further trouble. About midnight another trooper wandered into the lines making a great deal of noise celebrating his new-found wealth. He declared himself a 'Turkish millionaire' and emptied a feed-bag of Turkish bank notes near a campfire. He then crumpled on the bed of notes and fell asleep.

VC winner L. C. Maygar was found alive in the night by troops searching for the fallen and wounded after the battle. He had lost a lot of blood from several wounds. He was rushed to a field hospital, but too late. He died the following morning. His death was depressing news for the entire Light Horse. Maygar was a popular man apart from being a fearless leader who always wanted to take on the tough or perilous jobs from South Africa to Gallipoli and on the Eastern Front.

Harry Bell, the youngest trooper, was in a bad way also when he was found after being shot off his mount. He was taken to a field hospital and administered the soldier's 'friend', morphine. He had enough breath to ask a chaplain sitting with him how his regiment had fared. Harry was reassured that Beersheba had been taken. His mates and their horses were receiving a good drink. He wanted to know about his own horse before he fell unconscious again for the night.

The chaplain returned early the next morning. Harry was near death and in great pain. He managed to say that his real name was 'Bell', admitting he had taken on an alias so he would be recruited by the Light Horse.

'Make sure they get the headstone right!' were his last tortured words.

Harry was buried in a temporary cemetery on the outskirts of Beersheba. (His grave, along with those of Cotter, Maygar and the others that fell at Beersheba are in the British Commonwealth Cemetery there.)

In New South Wales, a Thomas Bell received an army telegram informing him of the death of his 'nephew' Harry. Bell wrote to army HQ informing them of their error. He did have a missing son of that name, he said, 'but he couldn't be in the army. He's only 16.'[6]

*

Bell was one of the 31 troopers killed. Another 32 were wounded and about 70 horses were killed, with another 10 having to be put down because of injuries. In military terms, Beersheba was a 'success'. More than 500 Turks were killed and 1,500 captured. Nine big guns were taken, along with a score of machine-guns and other material.

Allenby was elated. He bustled into Beersheba on the morning of 1 November to ring Chauvel's hand and congratulate him.

'Where's Grant?' he wanted to know. The lanky commander of 4th Regiment was summoned. Allenby decorated him by adding a bar to his DSO.

The relaxed atmosphere was disturbed by two German planes swooping low over the camps of 8th and 11th Regiments, bombing and machine-gunning. They scored a hit on the 11th's army medical tent, killing Sergeant Carney. The troopers scattered. Several propped and took aim with rifles, waiting for one of the planes to be almost overhead. Some of them hit the plane, but only one struck the pilot. And one bullet was enough. All the troopers watched as the plane wobbled and then plummeted into the hills to the west.

A terrific cheer went up.

In the troopers' collective mind, that 'kill' was for 'Elsie'.

At a camp inspection soon after the Beersheba 'win', Colonel Parsons commanding the 11th Regiment's C Squadron noticed that every man in a particular troop had placed a big round stone in the centre of his blanket.

'What is the purpose of the round stones?' Parsons asked a trooper.

'Those stones, sir,' the trooper relied poker-faced, 'represent the pebble you told us about at Khalasa. We now carry them in our kits to quench our thirsts.'

The rest of the troopers burst out laughing. Parsons again joined in.[7]

45

An Early Declaration

Colonel Newcombe's Arab detachment had moved at a leisurely pace from Asluj on a wide detour east to create a headquarters at Yutta on high ground 24 kilometres north-east of Beersheba. It overlooked the road to Hebron, which ran north-east out of the town. Newcombe surprised the Turks by cutting communications and setting up a road block.

Chauvel and Allenby did not expect much from this small camel force, which was meant to protect the right flank and to harass the Turks leaving Beersheba in a hurry. But Kress thought it was part of some wider conspiracy of action, especially when it made its appearance soon after the 2nd Light Horse Brigade had seized the Hebron road at Sakati. On 31 October, the German commander believed Allenby could be attempting to bypass the Gaza–Beersheba fortification and strike up the Hebron road for Jerusalem. Newcombe's force was thought to be an advance guard for the Desert Mounted Corps. Kress overreacted and swung three divisions from Gaza to the east approaching the road. This move made Gaza most vulnerable to a British attack.

Six battalions—6,000 Turkish infantry—were sent to tackle Newcombe's 70 camels as they reached the Hebron road. He had two British machine-guns and two Lewis guns, hardly enough to fend off 600, let alone 10 times that many. With just on three days' rations, he found himself embroiled in a David-and-Goliath battle he could not win, and perhaps cursing the wise or fortunate Lawrence who had opted out of the assignment.

On 1 November, Allenby, now a bull at a gate, ordered Bulfin with his corps sweating on Gaza, to attack. At 3 a.m. on 2 November his force hit the city, which had been weakened by the movement of troops away, and uncertainty by Kress, who was confused by the ruse, reality and phantoms. The smashing of Beersheba had defied all German/Turkish intelligence. He had misjudged the movement of Newcombe's camels, and now faced the attack at Gaza, which had been expected as Allenby's opening move. It was part of a one–two British combination of punches, which had the Turks reeling. After a brief fight at Gaza, it was abandoned by the Turks.

Before midday on 2 November it was under British control.

Not coincidentally on the same day, Arthur Balfour, the British foreign secretary, sent a letter to Lord Rothschild (Walter Rothschild, the 2nd Baron), a leader of the British Jewish community. He had been lobbying on behalf of the Zionist Federation, a private group, for a Jewish homeland in Palestine. Soon after his friend Allenby had been appointed to run the Palestine campaign, Rothschild had sent a letter to Balfour about the issue. Now, perhaps on the verge of Palestine being in British hands, Balfour had replied on 2 November:

Dear Lord Rothschild,
I have much pleasure in conveying to you, on behalf of His Majesty's Government, the following declaration of sympathy with Jewish Zionist aspirations which had to be submitted to, and approved by, the Cabinet [on 31 October 1917]:
'His Majesty's Government view with favour the establishment in Palestine of a national home for the Jewish people, and will use their best endeavours to facilitate the achievement of this object, it being clearly understood that nothing shall be done which may prejudice the civil and religious rights of existing non-Jewish communities in Palestine, or the rights or political status enjoyed by Jews in any other country.'
I should be grateful if you would bring this declaration to the knowledge of the Zionist Federation.
Yours Sincerely
Arthur James Balfour

This was a quaint piece of British Empire over-confidence or optimism, or more likely, shrewd political manoeuvring. The cabinet had agreed this on 31 October, before the battle of Beersheba was over. The letter was written on 2 November when the result of Bulfin's push to break through in Gaza was not even acknowledged by Allenby.

That aside, the letter, henceforth known as the 'Balfour Declaration', was expected to become an important document after the war. It was also a useful teaser for American Jews, who would help influence the US government to commit further to supporting the Allies on the Western Front.

The Jewish community would be watching the progress or otherwise of Allenby's force in the Middle East with more interest than any other group in the UK. If the British were to win, the Zionists would be pushing hard for the beginning of a Jewish community of some size in Palestine for the first time since the Romans' destruction of the Second Temple in AD 70.

Allenby wanted Chauvel and Chetwode to push on after the Turks on 3 and 4 November. But they refused, explaining that water and other supply shortages would not allow it. Allenby was annoyed, letting his long experience with cavalry be overridden by his impetuosity. But he could not force his key commanders to move. He had to advance again on 6 November.

Newcombe and his camels continued their battle against the odds and incurred heavy losses. They were surrounded. Their ammunition and fortitude held out until 4 November when their rations and water did not. Newcombe surrendered.

Allenby was undeterred by this minor loss, but niggled by the apparent intransigence of his main force. He had haunting memories of the fine start in the battle of Arras that later saw a reverse. He wanted to push to make sure there were no repeats. With that in mind, he urged Bulfin and his 21st Corps on beyond Gaza and up the coastal road into Palestine.

*

On 5 November, Kress was another enemy victim of the Beersheba charge. He was replaced as head of the Desert Force by former German chief of staff Erich Falkenhayn. Kress was given command of the 8th Army in defence of the northern coastal sector.

Lawrence embarked on behind-the-lines operations timed to coincide with Allenby's breaking through the Gaza–Beersheba line. The main event was to occur early in November when Lawrence was set to blow up the westernmost rail bridge in the Yarmuk valley, which was on the Jerusalem-to-Damascus line. The interlacing steel structure spanned a deep ravine. The bridge was patrolled by eight sentries. If it was properly destroyed, it would take at least two weeks to reconstruct. This would bottle up Turkish troops retreating from Allenby's forces pushing into Palestine on the main route to Damascus. He and Lawrence agreed that this would be an opportune moment for an uprising among the Syrian peasantry, who could be expected to harass their retreat, especially if supported by Feisal's force.

The squad of 50 reminded Lawrence of recent Aqaba days. But it had a different make-up at the top, and he was looked to by the Arabs and British recruits alike as the de facto leader, or at least organiser and planner. In the vanguard this time were Warwickshire Yeomanry Trooper Thorne and Lieutenant Wood of the Royal Engineers. Lawrence would do the laying of the charge on the bridge. But they agreed that if he were incapacitated Wood would do that vital job. Another on the assignment was George Lloyd, a British MP/former Welsh banker and a colleague from the Arab Bureau, who had his batman with him. The official commander was brave, handsome 'Young Ali'—Sharif Ali bin Hussein al-Haritha. For appearances sake, on missions this size the nominal leader would always be an Arab. The British, apart from Lawrence, kept a low profile.

Winter was close. The nights were long. Lawrence was on edge. He was under pressure to deliver for Allenby. His reputation now preceded him and he was expected to come up with answers for everyone, including the young commander. On top of that, this was his most dangerous mission so far. There may have been a price on his head. Lawrence feared spies within Feisal's camp had sent a description of him to their Turkish and German masters.

Lawrence and his party left the former Roman Azraq Castle on the shores of a lake near Wadi Sirhan early on the morning of 7 November 1917. After a break in the day two hours east from the railway, they crossed it after dark. They rested in a shallow depression and had to wait until dusk the following day to begin the operation. They had 13 hours to move in the dark, destroy the bridge and depart, a round trip of 130 kilometres. Lawrence judged that his Indian machine-gunners would not have the stamina to make the distance there and back. He had watched their early progress and selected six who might just be able to make it, taking one Vickers. He took a party of 20 only.

At sunset they mounted their patient camels and drifted towards their target. They could not force the pace. The undulating gravel tracks and myriad rabbit warrens forced the ever-chewing camels to tread carefully and voice their disapproval, which unnerved the party. The Turks were everywhere. Any noise could betray them; every encounter, which in the Hejaz or around Aqaba would not be of concern, was here worrying. A barking dog was bad enough. A startled peasant firing his rifle a dozen times in their direction was nerve-wracking.

Lawrence was enveloped by a sense of foreboding. He was worried by an encounter in the night with a merchant and his family moving by donkey in the other direction. He decided they should be stopped and put under guard until the mission was over. Better to be one short, Lawrence believed, than to have the Turks informed and coming at them in numbers.

It began to rain, making him more miserable and the camels' tread more slippery. Yet there was a job to do. They passed under a telegraph line, indicating the railway and the bridge were close. Lawrence ordered the party to dismount. The camels were gathered. Wood helped the Indians assemble their machine-gun.

Lawrence led the way, heart in mouth, as the explosive gelatine was carried down a muddy slope to the base on the bridge. It hung over the ravine ominously, silhouetted against the star-studded night sky.

A train could be heard grinding along the track. Lawrence gestured that the whole party should not run. Instead, he lay flat in the mud. The others followed. The train clamoured by. Soldiers could be seen, thick in the carriage corridors. The party remained flat and slithered its way down the steep slope. They stopped a few metres from a pylon close to the edge of the ravine. Fifty metres away on the other side of the bridge, a solitary sentry, his gun slung over his shoulder, warmed himself in front of a fire.

Lawrence motioned for the explosives carriers to come forward. Just as he did, one of the party stood and dropped his rifle. It cartwheeled down the steep slope, clunking onto rock near the foot of the pylon. The sentry turned his head. He challenged the darkness, then dropped to one knee to fire several shots. This alerted the other guards, who scurried out of a tent, loading their rifles. After points and shouts, they too fired off a fusillade. Lawrence felt the sting of a bullet grazing an arm. Those carrying the explosives feared that if a bullet struck, they might be blown up. One panicked and tossed the gelatine into the ravine. The others did the same. Wood tried to help the Indians assemble the Vickers. It jammed without firing. Everyone ran for the camels.

Nearby villages lit up. Locals climbed onto their roofs and began firing as the party hastened to mount the camels. They felt their way in the dark. Lawrence and Ali slipped to the rear, urging their men and animals on.

Lawrence wanted a consolation prize and was not going to let a bullet graze stop him. Wood took the Indians back, while Lawrence and the bigger party of around 40 Arabs headed for the main Hejaz railway, the line of his successful demolitions. On 11 November, they moved to Jemal and derailed a train moving from Deraa to Amman. On board was Syrian governor Djemal

Pasha, who commanded Turkey's 4th Army Corps. His staff of
20 was with him. The train's boiler exploded. Lawrence was
clipped by metal splinters from it. Jamal Pasha's guards fired at
them. Lawrence was lucky to receive just a couple more grazes.
He also broke a toe. But his mind was not on minor wounds.
The 'failure' to blow the Yarmuk bridge weighed on him as the
bomber party crawled back to Azraq Castle on 12 November.

En route, they heard the distant boom of big guns in Palestine. Lawrence was distressed. He had been confident in front of
Allenby that he would pull off the bridge assignment, which in
the context of his experience was manageable and in the scheme
of the campaign was a minor event. Not being successful would
play on his mind and, he thought, diminish the legend. He was
mindful that had the bridge been blown there was no way of getting over the ravine. The Turks with all their weaponry, horses
and camels would have been cornered. He imagined an uprising
that would have ignited the long-awaited revolt in Syria. He had
been working towards this for months in the desert after years
of scheming in Cairo.

Lawrence was concerned too about Allenby's reaction.

46

Of Biblical Proportions

Allenby had other things on his mind as his three outstanding commanders, Chauvel, Chetwode and Bulfin
drove the Turks from the Gaza–Beersheba line to Jerusalem and beyond. He did not feel his Eastern Expeditionary Force
(EEF) had capitalised quite as he hoped after the Australians'
smashing of Beersheba. But he had kept the pressure on, urging

his commanders to drive through the strong Turkish resistance here and there. Bulfin's corps was aggressive. Its 52nd Division, showing the benefits of training during the summer months, was not far behind Chauvel's troopers, which was appreciated by the horsemen. They had serious backup for their work for the first time in the nearly two years of the campaign.

Chauvel felt the strain of his 52 years as his force fought on relentlessly. After the stunning Beersheba effort, the shock-waves of which were having a lasting impact on the enemy, it was slow going over the next few weeks. This period was frustrating for Chauvel, trying his patience and his stamina. He had almost no sleep in one period of three days and nights.

His letters to his wife were sparse in this period:

'I have no time to write,' he said, 'as we have been moving so quickly and fighting all the time.'[1]

Yet there were compensations. His Desert Mounted Column was almost at Jaffa, the ancient seaport on the Mediterranean 28 kilometres from Gaza, in its drive to push back and contain the Turkish 8th Army. The plan was to create a new defensive line in the Plain of Philistra, north of Jaffa, which would be a buffer against the main British communications in the south. The target was a river, Nahr el Auja, six kilometres north-east of Jaffa, where the Turks had set up a defence line. Chauvel directed his Anzac Division to push hard against the enemy there and hold it up. This would allow Allenby's main force of infantry, backed by mounteds, to advance to the Judean Hills north of Jerusalem, situated 52 kilometres east of the coast, and about the same distance south-east of Jaffa. He planned to encircle the holy city and at all costs avoid fighting in it. Destruction of even a part of it would make the British look like barbarians at the gate. This was in the light of the Turks, oppressive as they were for 400 years, not damaging any of the three main religious centres in the city belonging to the Christians, Muslims and Jews.

Allenby wished to strangle supplies to Jerusalem. The Turkish garrison, it was hoped, would be forced to surrender or withdraw.

*

The terrain around Jaffa and north of it was the best Chauvel had seen for cavalry work. He was stunned by the richness of the agriculture with cash crops such as citrus and bananas prominent. He was most conscious of this advance into country vital to his quiet, yet strong religious beliefs. He loved the country's history. He was enchanted to be in the territory where Saladin fought the British King Richard the Lion Heart in the late 12th century during the Third Crusade, where the Christians battled the Muslims. He expressed his amazement to Sibyl about passing through Ascalon, and recalled the battle there in 1099, considered the last action of the First Crusade. Chauvel did not see himself as a latter-day crusader, but because of his Christianity he was touched more than most by these experiences. Symbolism abounded, especially when he gave his orders on one occasion from a crusader castle. He was also conscious of the imminent taking of Jerusalem, which had been under Ottoman Muslim control for four centuries, and the ramifications of it for Christians. He was further inspired by being 'chauffeured' in his Rolls-Royce in this more amenable country through places of note from his Old and New Testament studies. Ashdod was one of many places that caught his attention.

He made an understated passing reference to this town controlled by King David in the 10th century BC in letters to his relatives.

Chauvel made his Desert Mounted Corps HQ at Khurbet Deiran (now Rehovoth), a pleasant Jewish village seven kilometres inland and south-east of Jaffa. It had abundant olive and orange groves, and vineyards. There was also plenty of water in wells with the pumping apparatus still intact. The Turks had rushed off but were still lurking in orchards to the north where cactus afforded them good cover. They were acting as a shield or buffer for escaping enemy transport further north along the coast. Cox's battery shelled them, but they kept firing, some sniping the Australians as they watered their horses. The orchards extended west to the sea and north-west for 13 kilometres.

Whereas the liberated Arab villages had greeted the slouch-hatted conquerors with their easy smiles and manner on horseback, the Jewish settlements were more hearty in their appreciation. They had experienced extreme hardship during the war. They had settled mainly from southern Russia, with a minority from Romania, Spain, Britain, the US and even Australia. The Jewish population had built towards 10 per cent of the Palestinian population (which stood at around 700,000). There were about the same number of Christians, most of whom belonged to the Orthodox Church and spoke Arabic. About 80 per cent of the population was Muslim, of whom only a small percentage were Bedouin.

Almost all the Jews there had entered the country since 1880. The migration started with a trickle in 1850. From then to 1880 a few hundred arrived. Russian pogroms led to a greater influx. The migrants began agricultural colonies. They developed the production of citrus fruits, particularly oranges, around Jaffa. They cultivated the vine; they manufactured and exported wine. They drained swamps. Much to the Australians' delight, they planted eucalyptus trees. More than 60 agricultural settlements were built (by 1917). The contrast was stark between these villages with their attractive stretches of cultivation and the primitive conditions of life and work that surrounded them.

Numbers of Jewish immigrants came to Palestine under a generous scheme founded and supported by wealthy Jews from several countries. They included the Rothschilds, notably from the UK where Lord (Walter) Rothschild, the 2nd Baron, had been active in pushing for and receiving the Balfour Declaration. Now that the British force was sweeping north with the intention of occupation and continued liberation from the Turks, the beleaguered settlers had their first signs of hope. Early in their arrival they had been harassed and pillaged by the local Arabs, who were resentful of the intrusion into the disputed homeland. The Turks had let this happen. When the Jewish numbers built they were forced to fend for themselves. They ran into the mania of the 'Young Turks', who developed a policy of action (genocide in the case of the Armenians), against all non-Turks.

The Turks were more menacing to Jews during the war. They had their vehicles, horses and barbed wire confiscated. This encouraged the Arabs to harass them further. The earlier British failures at Gaza had dashed hopes that the settlers would be saved from their two oppressors. Then rumours filtered up the coast of the Australians' devastating victory at Beersheba. The Turks and Germans, who had been full of bluster about the hold they had over the British forces, remained mute. Soon they made themselves scarce in hasty departures in the first two weeks of November 1917.

A quick and natural bond developed between the troopers and villagers, despite the language barrier. The settlements provided what the Anzacs saw as an attitude of hard work and civilisation not too removed from their own at home.

'The sense of straight-planted streets, the little white houses with their red roofs and gay gardens,' Henry Gullett noted, 'and the wide, rolling orchards and vineyards along the sand-hills, were an unfeigned delight to those simple, veteran campaigners.'[2]

The troopers enjoyed the large supplies of fruits, wines and white bread, all at affordable prices. They did not have the feeling that they were being 'robbed' as they had in the Cairo bazaars. Instead, they revelled in this lush garden area after the depressing and testing experiences in the desert living on bully beef, rock-hard biscuits and the occasional meal of dates. Palestine's lush offerings were part of the inspiration needed to fight on for Jaffa and Jerusalem. The villagers in turn were touched by the openness and friendliness of the Anzacs who were such a contrast to what had gone before.

It was discovered that a few of Chauvel's troopers were Jewish with relatives in the area and arrangements were made for reunions. At Wadi Hanein, a nearby village, a woman asked a New Zealand staff officer about her son in the Auckland Regiment. A letter was waiting for her from him. He was reunited with his mother.[3]

Chauvel occupied the empty home of a Perth businessman who had returned to Australia for the duration of the war. As winter crept over the Middle East, he did not expect the Light

Horse to be advancing very far. He needed an HQ base for the coming bad weather.

Khurbet Deiran was as good as he could expect.

On 14 November, Allenby's force captured Junction Station 16 kilometres south-east of Jaffa. This broke the enemy's main communications links between its 7th and 8th armies, and they were split. Without the capacity to coordinate, the 8th retreated north up the coast and the 7th retired into the hills to the north-east of Jerusalem. With the winter about to set in, fighting would continue but not with the big confrontations such as at Gaza. There would instead be pursuits, confrontations, small battles, patrol clashes and shoot-outs. Allenby was not Murray. He would not sit back despite shorter days and coming bad weather. But there were limits to pursuit in the bleak, rocky, close hills with an enemy in vantage points sometimes difficult for soldiers to access and impossible for horsemen, especially if the winter proved to be as awful as predicted.

Allenby pushed Bulfin into the wilderness north of Jerusalem. Chauvel continued the pursuit north, hugging the coast, and away from that vital city. The locals warned him that there would be a sudden change in conditions around the end of the third week in November. It would come with some shock and vengeance. The advice was accepted but not really understood. November had remained hot with tiring gusty winds. Then on 19 November the rains came hard, the wind dropped out altogether and the temperature plummeted. The British forces were short of greatcoats, with most supplies being sent to the Western Front. The troopers did not have blankets. The Philistia plain to the north of Jaffa, in which they were expected to pursue the Turks, was a quagmire. Horses weren't even considered for some operations. Camels, a long way from their natural habitat, collapsed and died. Only the hardy mules and donkeys could be used to carry supplies for the men, sometimes shin deep in mud. The roads were awash and often impassable as they broke up under the icy deluge and sudden rivers. The troopers and their horses became ill, with the men suffering from colds that could develop into influenza.

Turkish prayers seemed to have been answered at a critical time. Had the weather held perhaps another two weeks, Allenby may well have had a major victory. But it was far from his thoughts as reports came back to him of the struggle Bulfin's soldiers were having trouble scaling the stone and rock in the hills north of Jerusalem. The Turks dug in, repelling their British attackers as they fought ridge by ridge to reach the main enemy force. The Ottomans liked this kind of battle. Their endurance under terrible conditions was renowned. They had the advantages in defence of high ground and low weather.

While the weather lasted, there was very little chance of dislodging them.

The Turks had pushed back the limited British infantry presence and the New Zealand Mounteds from the north bank of the Auja during the first three weeks in November. On the night of 20 November, the 52nd Division of British 'Lowlanders' struck across the river in pontoons and coracles (animal-skinned boats). The torrent upturned many of them, but the soldiers helped each other onto the muddy north bank, formed up and attacked the Turkish trenches with bayonets. The attack caught the enemy by surprise. It was pushed north. By dawn the Infantry secured a line three kilometres north of the river. This daring manoeuvre was consolidated by the 54th Infantry. It was followed up by a thrust up the coast, with the navy assisting with artillery bombardment, until the sea-cliffs at Arsuf, 16 kilometres north of Jaffa.

The Turks were hovering in a lesser, defensive position north of the Auja, and Jaffa was secure for landing supplies and weaponry.

Despite brilliant pushes such as this, Allenby remained restless. He was frustrated by this sudden weather-caused halt to his force's momentum. He had not given much thought to the failure of the Newcombe-led Arabs on his right flank on the road to Damascus. Nor was he concerned with Lawrence's inability to destroy the bridge in the Yarmuk valley. The Turks were not on the run to the extent expected now. But again, Allenby was not about to sit back and let matters drift.

He urged Chauvel, Chetwode and Bulfin to find ways to overcome the elements.

47

At Jerusalem's Gates

Chauvel began a demonstration along the coast on 23 November 1917. Allenby wanted to hem in the Turkish 8th Army more than ever now to prevent it from moving close to Jerusalem to assist the 7th. The 54th Division marched up the coast under Chauvel's control. The Camel Brigade was also pushed into the area to back up the strong line of entrenched mounted riflemen posts running 10 kilometres to the coast, five kilometres north of Jaffa.

This move worked and was both hindered and helped by the weather over the next week. The 8th Army held its own but the key was them being locked into fighting. They could not move across to help their brother army.

Early in December, Chauvel sent Lieutenant McKenzie and the No. 7 Light Car Patrol on a mission to detain a Syrian spy in Beit Jibrin, a town a few kilometres from the Turkish-held Muslim centre of Hebron. When he arrived with his seven-vehicle convoy at Beit Jibrin he was told that that the spy had gone to Hebron. McKenzie, always gung-ho with a sense of invulnerability in his armoured vehicles, was not going to turn back. There was a mission to complete. He had with him Captain W. A. Mulliner, the assistant provost marshal of the Australian Mounted Division, who had orders to arrest the Syrian in question.

McKenzie cut across country by the old Roman road. It was a rough track. They ran into Turkish outposts, but were able to fend them off with their machine-guns. They reached a low stone wall surrounding a small village. The Turks forced them to stop and spread out. McKenzie ordered concentrated fire over the wall, killing all the Turks.

They moved along mountain tracks and ran into more opposition. But the element of surprise and their weapons allowed them to squeeze down into Wadi es Sunt to Solomon's Pools on the Jerusalem–Hebron road, four kilometres south of Bethlehem.

They motored on south towards Hebron, stopping again to battle with a Turkish outpost. McKenzie ordered the cars to form a semicircle facing the enemy trench. The Vickers opened up again and killed all the opposition. The convoy then resumed its drive onto Hebron, dominated by its heavy stone buildings. The cars entered the city cautiously to find that it was, as they were told, empty of Turks, except for the ill and wounded in the military hospital.

The locals cheered them in. McKenzie, Mulliner and the rest of the party relaxed. They were put up in comfortable accommodation and given everything they wanted, especially food and water. Mulliner asked the mayor for help in tracking the Syrian agent, but received no joy after a search for him. McKenzie's only request was that the mayor send a working party to repair the road where it had been destroyed by the Turks.

The next morning, the convoy's cars' radiators and fuel tanks were filled before it moved on south.

At that moment, Allenby was advancing more or less as planned to take Jerusalem. A little over half a year after his apparent demotion in the appointment to the Middle East, he was nervously anticipating the acquisition of this special religious centre as requested by his prime minister. With the war still in stalemate on the Western Front and no let-up on the massive casualties there, Lloyd George was waiting for the 'good news' in the Middle East. It would be the propaganda he needed to take the British collective mind off the misery in Belgium and France. It would begin to justify his belief that defeating the Turks would be the break in the war that would lead to success against their partners the Germans. Allenby now appreciated that driving the Turks from Jerusalem would be a terrific boost for his image and restoration of his self-esteem.

He had ample fresh troops ready for his hoped-for final drive. The 10th Division had replaced the 52nd. The 60th and 74th Divisions were in excellent shape. General Mott was advancing up the Hebron road from Beersheba with a detachment, including the 53rd Division.

Mott was aware he had to tread warily near Hebron and beyond it at Bethlehem, the birth-place of Christ. He was under strict orders not to engage in any battles in the vicinity of these holy places. This caused Mott to wait until the Turks had pulled away from the area.

He was surprised to meet McKenzie and his convoy and be told that the road ahead was clear. Hebron had been evacuated. The Turks were pulling back.

Chauvel's sense of history and respect for the significance of the holy city of Jerusalem saw him send the 10th Light Horse with a small contingent of New Zealand Mounteds in the advance towards it. They would represent the Anzac forces, and be the first mounted riflemen there. Chauvel was mindful too of the 10th's performances and history, especially on Gallipoli at the Nek. He had witnessed the courage and obliteration of that regiment and that of the 8th under impossible conditions. This honour was a small compensation, and a reward for consistent, always courageous performances in battle and patrolling.

The 10th had been in the hills alongside the railway to Jerusalem toiling in extreme cold on road-making and reconnaissance.

They had frequent skirmishes with the enemy in their support role for infantry moving on their left. They patrolled over the rough hills and cleared the 75th then the 60th Division's right flank as it marched and fought on. The 10th Light Horse then moved between the 60th, coming from the north to Suffa, and Mott's now confident 53rd coming from the south, and linked these two British forces.

Allenby's final assault was timed for 8 December. On the night of the 7th, the Turks had been pushed back to a line of defence covering Bethlehem two kilometres south of Jerusalem, where Mott was engaged in hot fighting. The enemy line snaked north, then three kilometres north-west of Jerusalem to Suffa.

The Turks faced torrents of rain and British artillery in the freezing night. The combination broke their resistance after 12 hours in the sodden, flooded trenches. They left them before dawn and abandoned their strong line in the hills. Yet there were about 40 other important defensive positions in the Judean hill territory, the greatest of them near Jerusalem. The city was well-placed for resisting assaulting forces as its inhabitants had done for thousands of years. The outer rim of rocky hills formed a massive natural edifice. Then there were the deep gorges on three sides and the high thick walls of the old city.

Bad weather also stopped the British assault, which was suspended. The advance line was strengthened with a Worcester Yeomanry regiment joining the 10th Light Horse to bolster the gap between the 60th Division in the north and the 53rd in the south.

The Turks defended stoutly on 8 December, but this was only a delaying tactic. Refugees began pouring out of the holy city. At night some enemy troops became a rabble, choking the Jaffa road into Jerusalem. They preferred to pass through there than endure being run down by Chauvel's horsemen. Memories and stories of the Beersheba attack were fresh. The Turks knew that if the Light Horse could charge heavily defended trenches, they would have no fear at all in coming at them if they were isolated in redoubts, trenches and posts, or on the roads around Jerusalem. But while the Turkish infantry were in chaos, their batteries continued to pound the British forces, and to delay them while the last of their soldiers left the holy city by 7 a.m. on Saturday 9 December.

The Turkish governor Izzet Bey had a bizarre early morning. Just before dawn, he dictated a formal letter of surrender and handed it to the mayor (a Turk, whose family had traditionally supplied men to this post). Izzet was hell-bent on relieving his frustration, caused by him being the first Ottoman governor in four centuries to capitulate. What better way, he thought than to take a sledgehammer to the equipment in the telegraph office. After acting like a petulant teenager for 10 minutes, he fled the city via the Jericho road.

Dawn filtered over Jerusalem at about 7.30 a.m. on 9 December. The mayor, done up in his traditional fine robe, stiffened his back and marched out of the main gates. He was flanked by two Turkish police, who each carried a white flag. They were met by two moustachioed British sergeants from the Londoners, who saluted him. They then marched him to officers of the 302nd Royal Field Artillery Brigade, who in turn passed the governor's letter to General Shea, commanding 60th Division, while the mayor waited in open ground outside the holy city. Shea took a guard of honour to formally accept the surrender. Enjoying his moment in the drizzle, he drove into the new city, which lay on a rolling plateau just west of the walled old city. His car was surrounded. The crowd, made up of many nationalities, was wildly happy as he reached the Jaffa gate of the old city. The Muslim Arabs were less enthusiastic. They watched more curious than cheerful at this development, wondering what it would mean for them. The Turks had been harsh, but they were of the same faith. After 674 years (and the 'Sixth Crusade') the holy city passed again into the hands of a Christian power.

'The nightmare of anxiety in which the people had lived at Jerusalem and elsewhere was due not to the brutal behaviour of the Turks in their midst,' Henry Gullett noted, 'but to the fear that one day they might be treated as the Armenians had been treated [by the Turks] further north.'[1]

For the moment, that concern had drifted out along the Jericho road.

British troops followed Shea into the new city. Officers made their headquarters in imposing residences set in big gardens, a few still remarkably well manicured. Military police began to search for supplies, hidden weapon caches and saboteurs. Engineers began to repair the telegraph office. Outside Jerusalem the thoroughfares were clogged with every kind of motor and other transport forms except tanks. Trucks, armoured cars, wagons, pack-camels, mules and donkeys were moving close together. Even caterpillar tractors were in the throng.

The changeover of power did not stop the conflict as the 53rd Division continued to encircle the city. They battled the Turks off the Jericho road and took them on at the Mount of Olives to the north-east. The 74th Division moved around outside the city's west and took the Nablus road.

The 10th Light Horse Regiment in the morning heard the news of the Turkish capitulation. The weary Western Australian Horsemen broke away from their duties flanking the divisions. A and B Squadrons moved at the trot through the congested traffic to Jerusalem. Major C. G. Dunkley went to the head of the first two squadrons to lead them in. The horses were slowed to a walk as they entered the main gates.

First to acknowledge them inside was a nun repairing tiles on a roof. She smiled, waved and greeted them in French. The horsemen lifted their emu-plumed slouch hats to her. Soon they were surrounded by many of the inhabitants of the city. They had never seen horses like the big, long-tailed, fit-looking walers as they clip-clopped along the cobblestones.

'The [new] City presented a most gloomy appearance on our

entry,' Arthur Olden noted in the 10th Regiment's history. The inhabitants had greeted the British. But as the day wore on it was evident that 'they had not yet the full confidence in our arms to thoroughly believe that we were "there to stay". The reception for our troops was of a half-timid, half-wistful nature.'[2]

The British troops were struck by the stench in the city and the 'filth', mainly caused by the lack of drainage and overcrowding.

There were a few dim lights in the houses and shops. The city was just about out of oil or even tallow. But the adaptable merchants were back at the stalls pushing for more trade from the hopefully better-paid British troops and the Western Australian troopers. Greek priests, Syrians in Western dress (shirt and trousers), Arabs in raggy or spectacular robes, Jews in greatcoats, and peasants in sheepskins surrounded stalls. They watched every move of the Tommies—English soldiers—in their steel helmets and shorts, and the unshaven, mud-splattered Australians. The locals looked on in awe at the swift banter between them in variations on the English language that was beyond local comprehension. Yet they noticed the smiles from both these alien groups. They were tough-looking yet funny men, who bartered knowingly after their experiences elsewhere in the campaign. Some expressed their distaste of the shoddy souvenirs and religious relics on sale. But everything was done in good humour. The locals were encouraged to think that the new 'masters' of the holy city might be benign in their 'rule'.

A common early local phrase was that the 'good English' had arrived.

The next morning, 10 December, the Light Horse trotted out along the Nablus road for 13 kilometres and ran into heavy shell-fire. The Turks were aiming to contain the British push at Jerusalem. It also indicated that a counter-punch could be imminent.

The big moment in the Middle East pushed events going on in Belgium and France from centre stage. Lloyd George was thrilled, and felt somewhat vindicated. He would milk the propaganda even though the capture of Jerusalem in the grand scheme of the war was meaningless. Given a straight military campaign, taking the holy city was nowhere near the importance of the break-through at Beersheba and would not be as important as winning Damascus. Tiptoeing around the holy city was a digression in the drive to push back the 7th and 8th Turkish armies. Yet Lloyd George was a shrewd politician. There was the Christian vote. Headlines about Christianity's cradle being in the 'right' hands abounded in the Western press.

There was rejoicing in London. A solemn Te Deum was to be sung in St Paul's Cathedral, All Saints in Margaret Street and Westminster Cathedral.

'For the first time since the beginning of the war,' London's *Morning Post* reported, 'the big bell of the Cathedral was rung . . . at short notice a large congregation assembled.'

There was also the Jewish vote. Jews lobbying for access to the ancient homeland of 'Israel' were excited everywhere. London's chief Rabbi, Dr Hertz, told the *Post*:

'Jerusalem, which for ages has been the magnetic pole of the love and reverence of the world, is now in British hands; and this soul-thrilling news reaches us on the day that the Jews are celebrating the Maccabean festival.'

Much was made of the coincidence that Judah Maccabeus (the Jews' greatest warrior next to Joshua, Gideon and David) had his final victory on the same date 2070 years earlier in the revolt against the Seleucid Empire when he 'drove the heathen oppressor from the Holy City'.[3]

The dream for Jews everywhere of re-forming their own nation in Palestine seemed to have substance after a 1,900-year wait.

At Khurbet Deiran that evening, Chauvel was guest of honour at a local Maccabean festival. He took the moment to announce to the several hundred from the Jewish community the 'liber-ation' of Jerusalem. It brought an emotional response. Many cried, especially among the elderly. They told him they never thought they would live to see the day when the Turks were forced out. Chauvel received a spirited, spontaneous eulogy in Hebrew from a rabbi that when translated embarrassed the shy leader. He had been well liked by the local community, receiving every kind of invitation from planting commemorative trees to witnessing circumcisions. After the announcement, he was feted even more. He and his men were invited to drink wine and enjoy various citrus fruits, cakes, raisins and sweetmeats.

Up the road at Wadi Hanein, General Ryrie and his officers from 2nd Brigade were guests at a feast and dance celebrating the deliverance of Jerusalem. It was attended by 60 teenagers from the local school and about 100 others. The school's headmaster gave a long and demonstrative speech in Russian with references to Oliver Cromwell, Lord Byron and former British prime minister Gladstone. It drew few laughs but great applause. Ex-parliamentarian Ryrie responded. His words drew plenty of laughs from the Australians present and wild applause from the locals. Then the dance began with the younger Australian officers leading off dancing with the schoolgirls and other young women from the village.

The gaiety and celebration drove home to the troopers how important their war operations were to the Jewish population.

Lawrence took an X Flight to Allenby's headquarters and joined his entourage (including Meinertzhagen) for the ride and formal entry into the holy city at 2 p.m. on 11 December. He shed his Arabic robes for a cobbled-together uniform, but without decorations, which he disdained.

The motorcade made its way along the Jaffa road. Near the city, Allenby switched to the handsome, tall charger picked out for him by Banjo Paterson when he first arrived in the Middle East. He rode, flanked by cavalry guards, towards the new city and the wide representation of the British force, including the Light Horse under Lieutenant Hugo Throssell, the VC winner from Gallipoli; Mounted New Zealanders who had raced from Jaffa to be there; Gurkhas; Scots; Welsh, Indians and British from all the divisions. There were also diplomatic representatives based in Jerusalem from the US, the French infantry, who added colour with their pale-blue uniforms, and the Italian Bersaglieri (light infantry).

The locals were out in huge numbers for a glimpse of the new British 'conqueror'. They pushed against the soldiers and crowded every balcony, stair and roof vantage point. The populace added more colour against the new city's soiled white buildings and the dull stone grey of the old city.

Just as Allenby reached the beginning of the long guard of honour, he dismounted. He would have preferred a response more like that of a cricket crowd at Lord's, with polite clapping. Instead he received cheers from the throng as if he was the prize bull at a carnival. He could not plan against that, but he did have a clever strategy for this formal takeover. Allenby had done his homework. He was the 24th leader in history to take over the most famous spiritual centre on Earth, but he was mindful of not appearing the conqueror. In 1908, the German Emperor, Kaiser Wilhelm II, done up in all his pomp, entered the old city on horseback through the main gates with a band and much ceremony.

Allenby went the other way. He kept it simple. There was no band in sight. There wasn't even a Union Jack. Fanfare was replaced by quiet symbolism as he bypassed the huge gateway which had been made in the wall to accommodate the German emperor. Instead, the British commander-in-chief was greeted by the new military governor and escorted into the holy city on foot through a side entrance at the narrow old Jaffa gate.

Allenby was led to the terrace of the ancient citadel near the Tower of David. A proclamation placing the city under martial law was read in English, French, Italian, Arabic, Hebrew and Russian. It emphasised the protection of all sacred places and institutions. Lawful business could carry on.

The repetition in so many languages irked the general. He became agitated.

The Turks weren't far away and he had a war to prosecute.

*

The enemy had not given up on the holy city. The Light Horse fought as infantry from the stone sangars (reinforcements) of the Judean Hills and helped push back a major Turkish assault.

Christmas approached. The weather worsened and the supply problem increased. A few months earlier the Australians had been in desert heat that caused delirium. Now the nights were freezing. The rain made it more miserable, seeping through clothes and blankets and under groundsheets.

There was little relief from the Turks, who were making Jerusalem's defenders work hard under tough conditions. One night a small party of 20 from 4th Regiment could hear the Turks advancing on the hill to the right of a Light Horse position. They had to hold it. With the numbers coming at them there was a strong chance they would be wiped out.

About midnight, the party was startled then relieved to hear the sound of bagpipes. Scotsmen from the 52nd Infantry Division had arrived to relieve the Light Horse. They joined the Australians and counterattacked ending the Turkish encroachment and forcing them to retreat.

'I like the bagpipes,' trooper Red Hutchinson wrote, 'but they never sounded as they did in the hills that night. It was the most beautiful sound I'd ever heard. It was salvation.'[4]

PART FOUR

1918

48

Weather Wait, Surprise Win

Christmas Day 1917 was bleak for man and horse in Palestine. At Chauvel's Khurbet Deiran base there was sleet, freezing rain and winds that reached gale force. He was concerned about the morale of his men and decided to visit every camp to boost them on an occasion that was important to most of his troopers. He knew they would be homesick. Many of them would be spending their fourth successive Christmas abroad. They would be thinking of hot, sunnier climes in the bush and country towns around Australia. He gathered Brigadier General Trew, the English manager of his administrative staff and two orderlies. They could not use the Rolls, which Chauvel and his staff had become used to, until the shift in the weather from 19 November. No car, not even their dependable vehicle, could make it far over some of the terrain in the wet, flooded conditions, which had become so bad that all motor transport had been suspended. Without that option, Chauvel was happy to demonstrate that as commander he was prepared to share the hardships that his men had to endure every day.

He jumped on his waler.

They rode to the sandhills where the troopers' camps stood, with their lines of canvas bivouacs close to the railway to avoid transport problems. The little party then moved through the torrential rains, overflowing valleys onto the plains, now a slosh of deep mud, some of it moving glacially down slopes, which made further military operations impossible. The railway bridge over the Wadi Ghuzze was washed away and would be out of action for a week. The railhead at Esdud was more than a metre deep in water.

Mid-morning Chauvel spotted a horse on a rail bridge over a valley and a flooding river. It seemed in difficulty. As they reached a second bridge running parallel to the rail, they could see the horse was slipping, its legs jammed between the sleepers. Chauvel moved fast. With rain drenching them, he, Trew and a trooper left their mounts with one of the orderlies and climbed onto the rail bridge. Treading carefully, they made their way to the stricken animal. A front and back leg were trapped. Chauvel, lying flat on the sleepers, struggled to ease the horse's legs free. With the help of the trooper and Trew, he rolled the animal onto its back and then off the bridge into the torrent two metres below the bridge. The three men watched as the horse lifted its head and swam for the bank. They cheered as it scrambled up the bank and was away galloping along the valley.

Chauvel continued on his goodwill Christmas-cheer tour, his good deed done on the special day, and something those accompanying him would remember for many years to come. It was a bright moment in a bleak last week of 1917. Another was the thoughtfulness of the local villagers on Christmas night when they spruced up a local hall for communion for the troopers, and left gifts of food, wine and other hand-made items. These 'luxuries' augmented the other little presents, such as cigarettes, tobacco, sweets, shaving soap and toothpaste, which were raised for the troopers' Christmas funds.

Another uplifting moment for Chauvel came on New Year's Day 1918 when he learned that he had been awarded a KCB (Knight Commander of the Order of Bath). This came at Allenby's recommendation. His early attitude to Chauvel had changed, especially after Beersheba. That moment gave the Australian a certain kudos and power. Allenby had wanted to go harder after the Turkish 8th Army on the coast in the last weeks of 1917. But Chauvel would not be pushed against his will. The tough weather conditions from 19 November, including an unforeseen serious lack of water, at first led Chauvel to regroup and build up the Desert Mounted Corps, rather than attack the Turks in

circumstances that he felt would have been fruitless and weakened his corps further.

In effect, Chauvel was carrying out Allenby's directive to keep
his troopers fresh for later, bigger action. Yet it led the impatient,
contradictory Allenby to appear unhappy with a perceived tar-
diness in disposing of the enemy along the Mediterranean. But
Chauvel stood firm. He knew what was right for his corps and
how it was faring. When he was ready in December, his force
drove the Turks up the plain of Philstra and ended their chance
of attacking with any impact south of the river. Any counter-
moves were thwarted. This allowed Allenby to plan his pursuit
of the 7th Army without the fear of the 8th Army coming to its
aid.

Allenby's appreciation for Chauvel's way and style was seen
when Lieutenant Colonel Wavell, his liaison officer to the War
Cabinet and Robertson in London, wrote a draft report with
just a few sentences of criticism about the 'cavalry's' failure to
cut off the enemy north of the Nahr river in November. Allenby
blasted Wavell, who had touched on a sore point. Allenby himself had been responsible for Chauvel's approach that would
prepare his men for a later, more important thrust. It was superfluous to mention anything about it in the report. When Wavell
still wished to include the negative remarks, Allenby gave him
a fearful tongue lashing.[1] The criticism was edited from the
report.

The appreciation went both ways. Chauvel had not been
impressed with the generals at Gallipoli, except for Birdwood.
After the initial feeling out, when Allenby tried to impose himself with staff appointments, Chauvel began to appreciate the
commander-in-chief's good points. He wrote to Sibyl in praise
of him, especially when Jerusalem fell, noting that he was
ubiquitous.

'He is the most energetic commander I have yet come across,'
Chauvel wrote. 'I like him immensely and he appeals to my
Anzacs tremendously. He is just the kind of man we wanted
here . . . The great thing is he gets about among the troops, like
in at hospitals, etc., has a cheery word for the wounded, he does

not have a fit if he is not saluted. All those appeal to the Australians and I think the other troops also . . .'[2]

By the end of 1917 and early into the New Year, Allenby's force had pushed back a fierce, concentrated Turkish counterattack on Jerusalem. The British now held a line north of the holy city running further north to the coast beyond Jaffa. The last few months had been exhausting for both man and mount. Allenby ordered both infantry and mounteds to take five weeks off to recuperate during the worst of the winter after a huge job well done. It was after all, just two months since the smash-through at Beersheba.

Many of the Light Horse were ordered to take their break in a nicer clime on the coast south of Gaza at Belah. The walers enjoyed the break just as much, if not more than the troopers. The horses needed rest, nourishment and time to get over leg soreness. Picquets reported that on the first night in Belah the leaders of the pack began to relax and roll around after their evening feed. Soon every horse was doing it until every single mount was on its back rocking and rolling.

In this extended rest period, the charge at Beersheba was re-enacted, but the 'actors' refused to ride at full gallop, despite the exhortations of the official cinecamera photographer, Captain Frank Hurley.

The disappointed director had something to show for posterity concerning the most extraordinary and important action to that point in the Middle East War.

Most of Chauvel's winter was spent in restitution of his force and carrying out the wide duties that went with his position. Problems were never ending in everything from embezzlement by officers to medical issues, especially malaria. He had to educate new officers, make sure his artillery was sufficient, keep his remount numbers right and attend to the usual incidents that were bringing his force into disrepute. These ranged from the

trivial concerning the non-saluting of officers to the more contentious drunkenness. Chetwode and Allenby seemed to have
surmounted their fixation over the Australian troopers' careless
and apparently disrespectful attitude. It was insignificant beside
the outstanding performance of the horsemen throughout the
campaign, of which they had been a part for a lot longer than
the two officers concerned. The wild behaviour, however, continued to plague Chauvel as he looked to everyone from padres to
officers to resolve the niggling issue. One factor was the Anzac
pay-packet. It was bigger than that of the other forces, making
the troopers a target for every whore and wheeler-dealer in the
region. Once the Australians thought they had been cheated,
there would be reprisals, some of them violent. There had not
been another 'Battle of Wassa'. But it nagged Chauvel that something like it could boil over at any time, which nearly happened in
Bethlehem and Jerusalem when the troopers were on leave over
the New Year. Not all of them cared much for the history, and
even those that did search for a possible manger or climbed the
Mount of Olives, were soon bored.

The long spells in the desert or hills, fighting, patrolling and
waiting caused many of them to be keen for carousing with
prostitutes wherever possible.

Chauvel was so concerned that he addressed those about to visit
Jerusalem in mid-January. He did not hector or lecture them, but
at two months off 53, he was a father-figure to the troopers. Most
listened and absorbed his advice, but a minority was hell-bent on
trouble no matter what the highly respected commander said.

Not even an appeal to the honour of the Light Horse could
change their attitude or intent.

Small parties were granted leave to visit Port Said and Cairo.
Some troopers underwent training. The horses had been rested
when the troopers were dismounted in the hills, and they continued to enjoy continued good grazing. The Light Horse was
well-prepared for drilling, especially for recruits, who had to
undergo bayonet work while mounted.

It was not all training. A race day was enjoyed at Port Said. In the Gallipoli Handicap, there were entries such as 'Beachy Bill', 'Anzac', 'Whiz-bang', 'Abdul', and 'Shrapnel'.

Abdul, perhaps inappropriately, won.

Chauvel made his headquarters for several weeks at the desolate Talat ed Dumm in the Jordan Valley. Not a blade of grass or tree was visible for several kilometres.

'If rain had ever fallen there in the history of man,' the 11th Light Horse historian noted, 'there was no visible sign of it.'[3]

Troopers had to travel five kilometres into a precipitous gorge to the Wadi Farah to water the horses. By the time they were back at their lines, men and horses were exhausted. Talat ed Dumm was the place where a victim of thieves was befriended by the biblical 'Good Samaritan'. The troopers felt the bleak, forbidding setting was just the place for an ambush and mugging, as it had been nearly 2,000 years earlier.

49

Tactics Against the Odds

While Chauvel and his troopers marked time waiting for Allenby to direct a 1918 spring offensive, the taking of Jerusalem began to have an impact across the Middle East. It drew off Turkish reserves intended for other campaigns. The Turks were pulling troops from other theatres and this led to securing the British capture of Baghdad. It meant that the progress for the offensive across Mesopotamia (Iraq) would not be held back. Predicted strong oil reserves would be held.

The Light Horse advancing on Beersheba

After the battle...

The railway between Maan and Amman, with a block house today

Damaged Turkish trucks after an Australian attack on the railway line

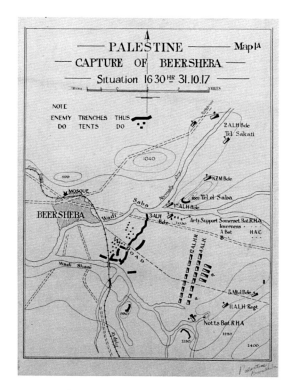

A contemporary map of the battle

The hill at Beersheba from which Chauvel launched his attack

A wrecked tank near Gaza

The 3rd Light Horse on the move near the Sea of Galilee, September 1918

The Light Horse in the Jordan Valley

A Light Horse camp at Ramleh, late 1917

The famous Daughters of Jacob bridge over the Jordan,
being repaired by Chauvel's engineers

The Light Horse on the move in Jerusalem

1st Light Horse in dune country, Belah, January 1918

Ryrie at the head of the 2nd Light Horse, Esdud, January 1918

Sir Harry Chauvel

The Turks were suffering heavy losses. Until early 1918, 11 of their divisions had been defeated. Their 28,443 casualties were nearly 10,000 more than the British forces. On top of that, 12,000 Turks had been taken prisoner and there was the usual high count of weaponry acquired by the British.

Jerusalem's acquisition was an inspiration for Lawrence's Arab Revolt on the far right of the British front. He was able to take back first hand to Feisal, Nasir, Auda and the other leaders the experience of Jerusalem and the Turkish retreat.

Lawrence believed that the big showdowns that would settle events would occur in 1918. He wished to play a leading part in them. To provide some insurance, he hand-picked a bodyguard of 30 Arab mercenaries, which included some brutal murderers and assassins, many of whom Auda vouched for. They were paid well and would allow him to sleep better at night. He had a price on his head. He would have been a useful kidnap target with which to harass Allenby. Lawrence had no compunction about surrounding himself with such a mob of cut-throats, and didn't think himself any worse than Feisal and Allenby with their protective entourages. In Lawrence's mind, such a guard on his person was not about lack of courage. It was about practicality. He believed the Arab Revolt would not be cohesive enough to achieve its aims without his unifying and motivational force behind and in front of it.

Among his British peers he was everything from a bombastic curio to an eccentric hero. But to the Arabs, from Auda to the lowliest old peasant, he was a legend. Hundreds of them had witnessed his fearlessness under all circumstances in battle, espionage work, guerilla activity, leadership and diplomacy. Many had experienced his endurance, compassion and justness. He symbolised their cause, which he articulated better than they did. In the first half year since he began on the long, circuitous trek in May 1917, Lawrence had pangs of guilt about the integrity of his work, given that he was aware of British aims. But as the revolt gathered force apace, he thought less and less about his deeper motives, or those of his masters in Whitehall and the EEF. He was fortified too in the knowledge that the Arabs now had no doubts about him after his eighth month of operations on their behalf.

He may have begun by aping them in dress, manner, speech, attitude and style like a super-chameleon. But he was now energised by the whole experience. He may also have been a writer by intent and a thespian by nature. But he had now taken method acting beyond any performance ever given. When he was in the desert with the Arabs he was one of them. So much so, that when he flew back to the British camp to consult with Allenby, he had trouble shaking off his Arabisms. It had been a struggle to get him into his officer's uniform. He eschewed all decorations for his acts of bravery that would have been proudly worn by any other soldier or trooper. His close friends such as Hogarth may have noticed the changes. But newer acquaintances like Meinertzhagen found him 'odd'. His moods were unpredictable, mainly because he would have had trouble 'morphing' back into Lawrence, the strange little Englishman, after being 'El Laurens' the Arab champion of the desert.

Lawrence knew he had to survive 1918 if his cause was to make it too. He would chance fate here and there. But the bodyguard meant he was unlikely to fall victim to an assassination plot. If he died in a spying operation or battle, that would be one thing. It would make a martyr of him. This would be the next best thing to him seeing his mission through to its completion one way or the other. Yet to have his throat cut by a paid assassin as he slept in the night would be a humiliation that the movement could do without.

Hence the fearsome, well-remunerated bodyguard.

On 16 January 1918, Auda and Nadir had an easy capture of the town of Tafilah, 150 kilometres north of Aqaba and 20 kilometres south of the Dead Sea. Its importance now was its position 90 kilometres south-south-east of Jerusalem. If Lawrence was to provide full support and strength on Allenby's right flank, Tafilah was useful. The Arabs could move their base there from Aqaba for the further push north to link up with Allenby in his next drive—to Jericho. They would connect up also with 3,000 northern Arabs gathered under Jafar Pasha.

The Turks were determined to take Tafilah back. They sent a cavalry advance party ahead of three infantry battalions mustered for the purpose. Lawrence, who had not been in a battle since before taking Aqaba, opted to take control of strategy to meet this threat.

His first move was to send out a small unit of 40 Arab horsemen and peasants, armed with two machine-guns, to fight off the advancing cavalry. They were successful. The horsemen pushed them off the plateau north of Tafilah and back into the camp of the main body of Turkish infantry. These troops then counterattacked with howitzers and machine-guns against the Arab horsemen, and pushed them back to the plateau. The Arabs retreated behind a ridge not much more than a metre high. They sent a message to Lawrence for help as the Turkish infantry advanced with artillery and 15 machine-guns, which pinned the Arabs down.

They returned fire but were no match for the welter of automatic weapons arrayed against them. Just when they were running out of ammunition, Lawrence arrived with another 25 Arabs after placing a further 20 riflemen on a ridge three kilometres back. He was barefoot. He had no visible weapon. A revolver was jammed into an ornate belt under his robes. Lawrence took a few seconds to size up the situation. Then he strode about 30 metres in front of the ridge. To the amazement of friend and foe he strutted along, almost as if he were daring the Turks to hit him. After the first few seconds of shock at his bravado, the Arabs intensified their fire. Noting this weird antic from an unidentified enemy (Lawrence), some of the Turks scrambled to adjust their machine-gun, artillery and rifle sights to pick him off. While they did this, shells still fell between him and the ridge. He strode to some unexploded bullet casings.

He bent down, almost theatrically, and picked one up and examined the artillery calibre the Turks were firing. He bowled it back in the direction of the Turks, turned and strutted behind the ridge.

Seconds later, shells fell in clumps where he had just been. Machine-gun fire kicked up the sand for 50 metres and bullets ricocheted into the ridge. But the flamboyant, foolhardy target was not in view any more. Perhaps he had taken a calculated risk to stir his defending force. They were outgunned and would be wiped out within an hour, or two at the most, if they remained where they were. Possibly Lawrence needed to test his courage yet again. Or maybe it was just another example of him seeking a thrill. This had marked his precarious existence since the revolt began.

The plateau 'dance' was a form of Russian roulette. But it appears that he was not on a death wish. Lawrence, spy, guerilla and writer, had turned intrepid battle commander. With these unpredictable desert men, it was not so much about giving orders as a mix of begging, cajoling, bribing and urging. He ended up imploring a few horsemen to hold the position for a quarter of an hour while the rest retreated, most on foot. After his mad histrionics parading in front of the small ridge, the half a dozen horsemen found it hard to deny him. They did their job while the rest hurried for the ridge where Lawrence had placed 20 riflemen and machine-gunners. Their numbers had been swollen by local village peasant supporters and more Arab horsemen.

Lawrence was the last one on foot to leave the plateau. He ran without panic, pacing himself for a three-kilometre distance. The last-stand horsemen held out and then galloped off, soon overtaking him with Turkish cavalry out-riders charging after them. The leader of the Arab horsemen stopped to pick him up and they scampered across the plateau for the protective ridge. His men had him and his retreating little force so well covered that the chasing Turks, led by cavalry, ran into a wall of fire from a vantage point that forced them to stop, fall back out of range and regroup.

Lawrence scrambled up the steep, chalky escarpment where his men were settled into pits with their gun emplacements near a set of ancient, decaying Byzantine masonry blocks. They looked down on a treeless undulating terrain featuring yellow goat-grass interspersed with clumps of black and grey rocks and boulders.

To the left (west) was a long ridge where the Turks were placing their machine-guns, with their range of about 2,600 metres. On the right was a flatter, scrubby hillside that ran to a sharply crested ridge. It was steep on each side and sloping gradually at each end where more Turks were forming up. Beyond it was an escarpment and out of sight behind it was the enemy base.

Lawrence considered tactics, using modest logic and daring, but calculated more on instinct than any grand design. His inclination against superior numbers (600 Turks as opposed to about 130 of his own men) was to take the initiative and counterattack. The most obvious move with that approach in mind was surprise. That could be achieved by sending half his tiny contingent around the rear of the west ridge so that it came up behind the machine-gunners. The task was given to a group of peasants who had joined them from a nearby village, which was just to the left of the west ridge. These locals were motivated to keep the Turks out of the area. They had been maltreated in Tafilah. Lawrence's determination, along with his spirited Arab contingent, boosted the locals' confidence to join in the battle. Usefully too, they knew every square metre of the territory. Lawrence sent them off at about 3.30 p.m. At the same time he discussed the more problematic approach to the right (east) with the Arab artillery officer, Rasim Sardast. They decided he should move off on a wide arc with about 80 horsemen, a mix of Arabs and peasants, to the right of the hill leading to a road that would take them to Tafilah. The idea was for Rasim to double back to the steep ridge on the right, but it would be his own judgement as to whether he should risk a raid. The two counter-punching forces were meant to make their surprise attacks at about 4 p.m. But it would all depend on their progress.

The peasants, carrying two machine-guns, gathered on a hill a kilometre from the west ridge. The machine-gunners, led by an Arab officer, decided to run across open ground to the base of the ridge. The peasants followed them. The gunners then scrambled up the ridge's west face.

*

As luck would have it, the Turkish officers had moved off down the slope to the east side to a meeting with their strong, experienced commanding officer, 60-year-old Hamid Fakhri, leaving no leaders on the ridge.

The Arab machine-gunners set up their Vickers and fired from just 30 metres at the unsuspecting Turks. More than a hundred were mown down in the first few minutes, giving the attackers a huge edge. The Turks scrambled to change their position. The peasants, thinking they were retreating, rushed them, yelling as they attacked. The stunned enemy abandoned their guns and ran. Leaderless Turkish contingents close by caught the panic and hastened off with them, the peasants in hot pursuit. Commander Fakhri screamed for his men to return to their lines and pick up their rifles. But it was too late.

'I never saw rebels fight like these!' he yelled, 'Enter the ranks!'[1]

Fakhri ran to his horse, mounted it, wheeled around and galloped straight to his soldiers, attempting to rally them. Just as he was ordering his men to stop and go back, he was hit by bullet through the chest. He rolled off his charger, badly wounded. Seeing this, his troops kept running.

Just at that moment, Rasim Sardast came over round the rear of the eastern 'hogback' ridge and cut off many of the retreating force. Lawrence, who had watched the outcome of his hurried and unscientific plan with nearly as much surprise as the Turks, led the rush down from his ridge with the remaining Arabs. They dashed across the plateau.

The result was a resounding victory for the Arabs. They killed 200 of the enemy, including commander Fakhri, who died of his wound. They rounded up 250 prisoners, leaving no more than 150 who retreated to the Turkish base. The Arab haul included two Skoda mountain howitzers, 27 machine-guns and 200 horses and mules.

Lawrence knew it should never have happened. A combination of surprise by the attackers, shock for the Turks, and the topography, which was so well understood by the motivated locals, created this fluke battle win. He was aware more than anyone that it was accompanied by an enormous amount of luck.

Lawrence was struck by the irony of such an unlikely outcome. He sat down in a euphoric mood to write a report. Cynically using the language of a seasoned battle commander (which he was not), he described the battle as if he had planned it with the skill of an experienced or even a great strategist. He had in mind his audience: his superiors at the bureau and Allenby's staff. They were trained in the methods of big-name military thinkers such as the French generalissimo Ferdinand Foch, and particularly Carl von Clausewitz, the Prussian soldier, who had captured many of the British High Command's minds with theories expounded in his treatise, *On War*.

Lawrence received enormous satisfaction from learning that his superiors fell for his ruse, at least in the writing. He commented, sardonically, there would be more glittering chests in the armed services if others were to compose their own battle reports.[2]

His adaptability with words, as much as his courage and questionable battle skills, earned him a DSO (Distinguished Service Order). But it would never glitter on Lawrence's chest.

He was not disposed to wear it, feeling it was unjustified.

50

Topping Up with Talent

Chauvel had no such disdain for decorations as he stepped forward onto the makeshift podium to be greeted by the smiling Duke of Connaught. The place was Jerusalem's Barrack Square under the shadow of the Tower of David. The time was early March 1918. It was a bitter, cold mid-morning. The duke pinned the gold and silver KCMG (Knight Commander of St Michael and St George) on Chauvel's left breast in front of an assembly of military personnel and local dignitaries. They shook hands. The duke then pinned the CB (the badge of a Companion of the Order of the Bath) on the right of his chest and shook hands again. Chauvel turned to go. But there was more. The duke found room on the general's 'bright breast' for a third decoration: the blue and yellow Order of the Nile, which had been instituted in 1915 by Sultan Husayn Kamil for 'service to the nation' of Egypt.

In contrast to Lawrence, Chauvel saw the merit in such awards. He was a career soldier at the top, and they meant something, especially among his peers. It was a competitive business and part of the 'game' of soldiering, particularly among officers and especially among the generals. If Monash on the Western Front or other Australians doing well in the main war venue received a new pretty badge or ribbon, then Chauvel would want one too. But there was more to it than simply being a battle for decorations. Dominion commanders such as them had to prove themselves much more than their counterparts among the British. The Australians had not been in the 'British Club'. But sheer performance was sorting all that out in the pressure cooker of war when abilities were found out one way or the other. Chauvel rightly felt that in 1916 he had been ignored for honours when he deserved them in front of everyone on the Eastern Front. Anything he had pinned on him now would help make up for that.

It was also recognition for his corps and the achievements of his mounted riflemen.

One of Chauvel's continuing responsibilities was the topping-up of his Light Horse with new recruits after the attrition caused by war and illness, particularly malaria.

The AIF depletion, especially on the Western Front, caused the Australian government to change its recruitment policy to attract more men. Volunteers from the ranks of Aborigines were allowed to join up, if they had 'European' blood. In mid-1917, Queensland's chief protector, J. W. Bleakley, announced that:

'Half-castes will now be accepted into the Australian Force provided they satisfied the medical authorities that one parent was of European origin.'

'Origin' did not mean the parent had to be completely European, which opened the door for recruits among Australia's Aboriginal and Chinese communities. They could not vote. They could not move interstate, even represent the state in sport, without the written permission of the protector. Yet now they could fight and die for Australia.

Preventing Aborigines volunteering was a loss for the Light Horse. Many an outback stockman could have added to the forces' performance in the Middle East, especially in the desert regions. They also had special tracking skills, which were used on occasions, but would have been employed more often had there been more Aboriginal servicemen. The insidious attitude of authority towards the original Australians robbed them of their right to represent the superimposed European (mainly British)-originated nation.

One of the scores of Aborigines to be allowed to volunteer for service in August 1917, and who joined the 11th Light Horse regiment in early April 1918, was Frank Fisher (the great grandfather of Olympic sprinter Catherine Freeman). He was from the Barambah Mission (now Cherbourg) in Central Queensland. Fisher (born on 27 August 1880) turned 37 soon after he joined up, which was 'mature' for a recruit. He was a labourer, and could not read or write. He made his mark with a cross and nominated himself as a Catholic having been 'cared for' by the church mission. The moustachioed, round-faced Frank was married with three children. He was above average height for the era at 173 centimetres (5 feet 8 inches) and was heavily built at 93 kilograms.

He was a crack shot and a good horseman, ideal for the Light Horse, which he joined with thousands of others heading for the Eastern and Western Fronts. They were needed to keep the momentum on the eastern flank push towards Amman, then the key destination of Damascus.

*

On Allenby's right flank, the Lawrence-led success at Tafilah was a boost for the Arab cause. It demonstrated that perhaps Feisal's force could do more than harass the Turks with hit-and-run guerilla tactics. However, the revolt was yet to have anything like the impact of Allenby's army, which in March 1918 was fighting crucial battles against strong enemy resistance. Chauvel did not take part, but provided his Anzac Mounted Division and Camel Brigade to Major General Shea of 60th Infantry Division (the Londoners) in an operation under Chetwode. The horsemen would support the foot soldiers in the move to capture Jericho, famous in a Biblical story for having been destroyed by Joshua, Moses' successor, allegedly in 1550 BC. In those ancient times, this town was penetrated by nomads and semi-nomads from the desert in the east travelling to the fertile lands closer to the coast. Jericho's position in the Jordan Valley at the foot of a passage through the Judean Hills made it of strategic importance in history, and now.

C. F. Cox's 1st Light Horse and the New Zealand Brigade began from Bethlehem and eased down towards the Dead Sea on goat tracks and other paths through the yellow-brown, vegetation-free eastern slopes of the Judean Hills. They could not always ride their horses on the narrow tracks. As they moved they could hear the battles being fought on the main hill road between the 60th Division and the Turks, backed by a German contingent. The infantry would take the brunt of the enemy force. The road to Jericho began to be studded with little crosses bearing the names of Londoners, poignant reminders of brutal clashes and quick burials.

Dismounted New Zealanders branched out on their own, attacking Turkish hill positions, while Cox's troopers edged down to the Dead Sea at the floor of the Jordan Valley, 400 metres below sea level. Unless there was a well-concealed enemy force hidden in caves or trenches, there seemed no opposition as the brigade approached Jericho. Cox sent out scouts, who reported that the town appeared deserted. He ordered a single troop of 32 horsemen to take it. They encountered about a dozen enemy soldiers, who were forced to surrender without much of a fight.

The troop was thrilled at the thought of acquiring such a

well-known town. But the men were let down. It was one of the most unattractive conquests of the long campaign. Squalid mud huts featured in a village dominated by a towering mosque and the unpopular Jordan Hotel, which endeared itself to no-one that stayed in it. Historian Henry Gullett, who had the displeasure of spending a couple of nights there, remarked that he would rather have camped out. A cloying whiff of sewage prevailed. The food was inedible; the water undrinkable. The rooms were rat-infested; the beds flea-infested.

The main bulk of the Turkish force had retreated across the stone Ghoraniye Bridge, which they blew up. The raging, 30-metre-wide Jordan could not be easily traversed. It gave the Turks temporary respite from the relentless pursuit by the trudging, fighting infantry and the sweeping, speedy Anzac horsemen, who were so ready to use their bayonets or rifles.

The Turks consolidated in the light-brown hills on the other side and the more jungle-like vegetation on the west bank, setting up their machine-guns to cut down any soldiers brave enough to swim the torrent.

51

Spring to Offensive

Allenby now decided to push hard 65 kilometres east of Jerusalem to Amman, which was on the Hejaz railway. Its hoped-for acquisition would shore up the British right flank and support the Lawrence-generated Arab Revolt, which was advancing north in parallel with the British. This in turn would cause the Turks in the south to be more isolated. The 7th and 8th enemy armies caught up in conflict in the Judean Hills and closer to the coast would be forced to assist with reinforcements on the eastern or right flank.

Allenby's main target was the 1,200-metre-high Moab Mountain, which was held by the Turks. The two following aims would be to destroy a rail tunnel and viaduct at Amman.

Before a force could come anywhere near those targets they had to cross the Jordan River 25 kilometres from the holy city. Chauvel trained an Anzac Light Horse engineering contingent in quick time for the challenging task of throwing a bridge across the river. They made an attempt at the site of the destroyed Ghoraniye Bridge, but the swiftly flowing water, along with machine-gun fire from the west bank, defeated their efforts. Heavy rains and turbulent waters delayed the mission three days until 22 March. The engineers trekked south to the bank claimed as the site where John the Baptist baptised Jesus. This was the point of least resistance by the torrent and the enemy machine-gunners. Australian and English engineers stripped down and hauled a raft-load of soldiers across. The soldiers fended off attacks while the engineers worked hard through the night to build four bridges. They were made up of 10 pontoons roped parallel to the banks with a wobbly wooden construction laid over it. Soldiers clamoured over them easily enough but they were not safe for riding across. At first light, New Zealand troopers dismounted and led their horses gingerly over the bridges. They then rode out past the infantry and attacked the Turks, who were forced back nine kilometres to the foot of Moab.

Allenby was relying on Lawrence and his Arabs arriving from the south to support the infantry and horsemen by cutting off any Turkish reinforcements from the south coming to help their comrades on Moab. It was to be the second test of the hoped-for combination with the Arabs, as the two forces headed towards Damascus. The 'experiment' with Newcombe and his contingent had met with mixed success five months earlier north-east of Beersheba. They had drawn off 6,000 Turks from Gaza, but had been heavily defeated.

The British force—the soldiers, horsemen and the cameleers—

began the march on the heavily defended Amman and further on north-west to Es Salt. The latter was taken by the 3rd Light Horse Regiment, and then held by British infantry, but nature intervened on the night trek further south on the approach to Amman. Torrential rain made the going tough in the slush on the undulating goat trails. All were forced to go single file. Vehicles and artillery were abandoned. The horses coped, but the camels found it near impossible. Some were led by the men, which slowed the camel contingent. The horsemen had to wait for them on a flooded tableland. After another freezing night in the wet, the whole attacking force linked up about 11 kilometres from Amman.

On the third night, the railway was destroyed. It was the signal for the thrust at the target, but it was protected by a half-circle of ridges harbouring 4,500 Turks and Germans, who were being reinforced by the hour via the railway from the south unhindered by Lawrence and his Arabs. The enemy used artillery and machine-gun fire to counter the attack by the courageous Londoners, who trudged through the mud. Rain-sodden, they still moved unhindered in pace, direction and determination. But the barrage began to take its toll. Soldiers were cut down. The ranks thinned.

Binoculars remained trained on the horizon to the east and south in hope of seeing the banners of the Arab force. But Lawrence and his army were nowhere to be seen. Instead, German engineers were viewed reconstructing the railway, which would bring Turkish reinforcements from the south. They began coming in mid-afternoon on the third day of action. After day six the British had made no headway as the defending ranks built up.

A telling moment occurred when 96 horsemen from the 6th Light Horse made a bayonet charge. But it was not to be even a mini-Beersheba. All but one was brought down by intense machine-gun fire. It was the worst moment since the Nek for the horsemen and it had a similar impact.

Still the enemy numbers increased. Now they began flowing in by train from the north. If ever the Arabs were needed to show their importance to Allenby, Chauvel, Chetwode, Chaytor and the other generals it was now. But apart from a token trickle who snaffled bully beef and bullets and then disappeared, never to be seen again, there was a 'no show' by Feisal's force. In those last three days, many men of the Egyptian Camel Corps froze to death. Chetwode called his venture off.

On 30 March, the British were ordered to withdraw. It took them two days to limp back with the wounded to the Jordan Valley. The British infantry had 447 fallen officers and men. But the Anzacs and Camel Brigade fared worse, losing 671. Troopers were disgruntled at the abortive nine-day operation overall, and the let-down by the Arabs. Once more they were downcast about leaving their fallen comrades on a battlefield with a mission unfulfilled. It reminded those who had been at Gallipoli of setbacks there.

Scapegoats were sought for the failed mission. Fingers were pointed at Lawrence. He admitted he had failed to deliver and apologised to Allenby, which was not much use to the force that had depended on his assistance. No substantial reason was given for the Arabs not turning up. They were known to not enjoy full-on battles, preferring guerilla tactics. Excuses of lack of water and food were proffered. None were acceptable. But when Lawrence begged for another chance, Allenby granted it.

This was the first success for the Turks since Second Gaza. Much credit had to go to the 63-year-old Field Marshal Liman von Sanders, one of the oldest commanders of the war. He had been a key figure behind Turkish strategy on Gallipoli in 1915, after creating the Turkish 5th Army for its defence. In 1916 and 1917, Liman von Sanders had been based in Istanbul. As the crisis in the Middle East escalated, he took command of the force in Palestine.

Liman von Sanders ordered General Falkenhayn to concentrate a new Turkish force at Qatrani, on the Hejaz railway between Maan and Amman, and just 40 kilometres from Tafilah. Much to Feisal's shock, this fresh enemy detachment took back the town and pushed the Arabs out, their first setback on the push north. Putting on a brave front over the loss, Lawrence now claimed that Tafilah was 'not worth losing a man over'. Showing a remarkable tactical flexibility, he said that if the Turks kept a sizeable force there, they would weaken either the Maan or Amman garrison, which would work in favour of the British and Arabs.

Feisal remained disconcerted. Lawrence lifted his spirits by telling him Allenby was rewarding them for their drive to the Dead Sea by placing £300,000 worth of gold 'to my independent credit'. The chief had thrown in a train of 700 pack-camels complete with personnel and equipment.

Gold, it seemed, not only talked in the desert war. It also strengthened resolve.

Turkish confidence was up and boosted even more by the massive breakthrough by the Germans on the Western Front, which began on 21 March 1918. Commander-in-chief Erich Ludendorff thrust forward 50 German divisions (more than a million men) on an 80-kilometre front. The Germans smashed through Gough's 5th Army and dislocated the British 3rd Army. It was the first major penetration since the Western Front had shaped up initially on a line running from northern Belgium to northern France. Ludendorff had been emboldened by the big increase in German troops coming from the Russian Front after the Bolshevik Revolution, which led to the Russians opting out of the 'Imperial War'.

The resultant German attack, which pushed nearly 70 kilometres through the Allied side, was only stopped by brilliant action by Australian divisions, the 3rd commanded by Lieutenant General Sir John Monash and the 4th run by Major General Ewen Sinclair-MacLagan.

The consequences for Allenby's campaign were dire. The British in Belgium and France needed reinforcements fast and he was asked to supply them. Like Murray, he responded by offering to send 60,000 troops over the next three months. Unlike Murray, he was not prepared to sit back and wait until something happened or until he could obtain more troops, which depended on events on the Western Front. He asked for and was promised the Indian cavalry in France. Allenby was also promised Indian infantry, but they had to be trained. That process would not be completed for half a year.

Before he could continue the way he had intended before the huge German assault from 21 March, he had a mighty reorganisation and training program to instigate.

Chauvel remained the most unscathed in terms of the force under him. He did lose the yeomanry, which were replaced by the Indians. Despite their experience in France, they still had to be trained in the different conditions, which would delay his corps being more or less at full strength until after April.

With the infantry in disarray until reconstructed, Chauvel would have to provide the main attack focus for the EEF campaign. Allenby boosted the mounted/cavalry force in a reorganisation that saw Chauvel's corps up to four divisions. It was to be bigger than any other mounted/cavalry force in history.

It would be four months before it was properly organised, providing there were no setbacks in the meantime.

52

Daunting Dawnay, Peeping Thomas

On 18 April Lawrence drove a Ford car to the Hejaz railway under orders from Allenby to join a force that would aim at destroying such a large part of the track that the Medina garrison would be cut off for the rest of 1918.

He met with Lieutenant Colonel Alan Dawnay, a military strategist who had an appreciation of guerilla tactics. He agreed with Lawrence that a recent Arab assault on a Turkish garrison at Maan had failed because of a conventional frontal attack. Lawrence had advised an encirclement, which would have gradually strangled the enemy stronghold.

Dawnay was overseeing a mixed force of British, Egyptian Camel Corps and Bedouin non-regular fighters preparing for an attack on the rail, a culvert, bridges and a station. Lawrence was acting as an interpreter. He was also observing the cohesive use of an array of weaponry and vehicles including nine armoured cars and Rolls-Royce tenders (wood-bodied, unarmoured), a battery of 10-pounder Talbot guns mounted on Ford cars, and a plane squadron.

Dawnay had planned every facet of the operation down to the second. At dawn on 19 April, he and Lawrence sat in one of the wooden 'Rollers' on a ridge to observe the exercise unfold. They could have been at an athletics meeting at Oxford. All they needed were chicken sandwiches and champagne to complete the picture. Lawrence had binoculars. Dawnay had a notepad. A map was spread on his knees. He clicked the button on a stopwatch as soon as the fleet of armoured cars appeared in a cloud of dust and chugged their way towards the Turks' trenches at Talish-Shalm station.

The enemy was caught by surprise. The shock caused soldiers in a group of trenches to give up without a fight. Dawnay clicked off his stop watch and made notes. He had predicted a small firefight. But the Turks' surrender caused him to raise his eyebrows and mark down the time, which was 10 minutes shorter than expected.

He turned his attention to two Rolls tenders that hurtled down to a culvert. A bomb was attached to it. The tenders moved away. The culvert was blown up with such force that the two observers felt the vibration from their distant vantage point. Dawnay made another note with a satisfied smile. This one was on time almost to the second.

Pandemonium broke out in the station's blockhouse. Turks manned four machine-guns behind a foot-thick stone sangar on a small ridge and began firing. They were answered by the turret-mounted Vickers on the armoured cars that featured half-inch-thick steel plating.

Dawnay looked at his watch and then clicked a second stopwatch as the Bedouins rushed from behind a knoll and fired at defending troops in the station.

With the Turks now preoccupied, Lawrence called for another Rolls and two protective vehicles. He set off down the track to attach guncotton charges on rails and bridges, firing them off one after another.

Dawnay continued to scribble notes. He pressed his timepieces and watched Bedouins and their camels attack the Turkish fort at the south end of the station. The animals were urged on in a cavalry-style charge up the gentle ridge and over the tight trench system, causing panic among the defenders. Then the Egyptian Camels attacked from the north from a longer approach of hills and ridges.

Dawnay glanced at his watch. The Talbot guns were a minute late when they opened up. The explosions were so loud that he was deafened for a few seconds after the opening salvo as the station blockhouse walls collapsed. Right on cue, two planes buzzed overhead and rolled bombs out onto the Turkish trenches not yet reached by his force. The combined explosions of the 10-pounders and bombs sent a wall of smoke and dust high, allowing the vehicle to move forward unhindered. They crunched over the flint surface with their Vickers rotating on the turrets and spitting bullets.

Lawrence was making his way back in his Rolls and was within striking distance of the station when he saw some white flags go up. The Turks had suffered enough from the clamour and concentrated, varied attack. Their surrender was the signal for looting. Lawrence, quickly on the scene, set the questionable lead and mayhem in the rush for souvenirs. He grabbed the brass bell used to announce meals and calls to arms. Dawnay, his timekeeping almost done, motored down as the Bedouins and Egyptians swarmed over the crumpled station and fought for anything that was not nailed or bolted down.

Dawnay made for the Turkish commander's office and laid his hands on a ticket-punch machine, which would sit in his home workshop. His driver, caught up in the rush, pocketed a rubber stamp in this most crude of desert sports, where looters bumped each other aside and fought over things both useless and practical. Dawnay, Lawrence and the British went for curios, things they could show other officers back at the club in Cairo and take back to England as reminders of their times in the Middle East war. Egyptians and Arabs went more for items they could sell, eat, wear, fight with or use in their modest abodes or in their desert wanderings. They did not care if they were on the living or the dead and they went nearly berserk in their fury to ransack the destroyed buildings. The frenzied rush saw many of them firing weapons in the air as they announced their acquisitions.

A fight broke out between Egyptians and Arabs over an ornate desk clock. Lawrence had to move swiftly to adjudicate before the conflict turned deadly. But not even he could stop a feud when stores of rifles and ammunitions were broken into. Disputants began shooting each other and did not stop even when a camel set off a trip mine and blew itself up. British officers rushed to separate the antagonists, and just succeeded without being targeted themselves. They directed that the Egyptian Camel Corps troopers could have first go at the scavenging. After 15 minutes, it was the Arabs' turn. The Bedouins scrambled for what was left 'like a solid mass of ejected inmates from Bedlam'.[1]

A surge of bodies hit the door of a locked storehouse, snapping it open. Most of them loaded up their camels with goods and took off into the desert shrieking with the joy.

Lawrence, an unabashed and well-rehearsed looter in the Bedouin tradition, would report back that the multi-pronged and 'international' raid had been in the 'deluxe' class. Given his style of humour, this could have been referring to the pillaging as much as the battle.

Dawnay with his time-and-work fetish, made light of the Turks for their 'ignorance and haste' in surrendering 10 minutes earlier than he had anticipated. Lawrence, matching the cynicism, noted that this was 'the only blot on a bloodless day'.[2]

The destruction of the station was only the beginning of this mission. It disabled the main Turkish defence, giving Lawrence limited time for the chance to demolish a large section of track. He sent an armoured vehicle south to the next station at Ramleh to distract the small fort of Turks there. He then motored in the same direction in the Rolls, enjoying the luxury and the thrill of the moment, accompanied by teams of dynamiters. Bridges, rail and culverts were the targets. After almost a year of experience, he moved fast and confidently, slapping charges on bridges, pushing them into culvert drainage holes and planting them under rails.

He gained pleasure from blowing them himself. He especially enjoyed the discordant, cacophonous opera of his destruction and the visual artistry of his explosions.

On the night of the 19th, he returned to the destroyed station, slept well and the next day prepared for an attack on Mudowwara, another station on the track. But he was less optimistic. The Arabs had disappeared. He was not confident about the Egyptian Camels' fighting capacity.

They left in armoured cars early in the morning with plenty of swift traction on the smooth plains of sand and flint. When they were within seven kilometres of the new target, they noticed that a train was there. Lawrence wondered whether it was evacuating Turkish troops or bringing in reinforcements.

He could not ponder for long. The Turks spotted them. Within minutes they were aiming four guns at the little attack party, two of them Austrian mountain howitzers. Even at that distance, they were accurate enough to force Lawrence and his party to rush for cover.

That caused him to lead his men on a wide detour to a place on the track where he had carried out his first-ever demolition raid 11 months earlier. This time he destroyed 450 metres of culvert.

His lust for twisted track was not sated. He hurried off to Ramleh to plant more of the 'tulips' (charges) under the line. Mid-afternoon he sent a force of Howeitat to buckle the rail north of their first night's handiwork.

By the night of 20 April 1918, the British and Arabs had put out of action 130 kilometres of the Hejaz railway. Seven stations were in their hands. Lawrence had now made impotent Fakhri Pasha's force in Medina, which had troubled the planning of Murray then Allenby and Feisal for so long.

Chicago reporter Lowell Thomas was being given a tour of Jerusalem by its British governor, Ronald Storrs, when he spotted a fair-skinned, blue-eyed man in an Arab prince's garb.

'Who's that?' Thomas wanted to know.

'That's the uncrowned king of Arabia,' Storrs replied with more admiration than cynicism.[3]

Thomas and his cameraman Harry Chase managed to join Lawrence for about a week in the desert to film him in action. Lawrence seemed to be a willing 'model', judging from the images that emerged from this sojourn.

The eccentric, alluring young Englishman was perfect for Thomas's aims. The Americans had entered the war a year earlier in the spring of 1917, but the move was not wholeheartedly supported by the American people. The US government, led by President Wilson, wanted more enthusiasm for the growing number of American soldiers entering Europe. Strong, emotive propaganda through the mesmerising new medium of film was needed. Thomas was commissioned to find the right footage to convey and make palatable the war effort. Thomas reckoned on a budget of US$75,000 (about US$1.4 million in 2009). His ambitious mission superseded the US government's means for such a project. Thomas secured the funds from 18 wealthy Chicago meat-packers who owed him a favour.

He toured the Western Front and found it unsuited to his

promotional needs. There was nothing 'sexy' about trench warfare. It was all about blood and death, factors that would turn
the American public off supporting the war. Thomas learned
about Allenby's fight to drive the Ottomans from the Holy
Land. He was told of vague stories about Arabs prepared to
revolt after centuries of Turkish oppression. This was far more
attractive. He could 'sell' this story much easier than trying to
make the Western Front attractive, especially after the German
offensive of 21 March 1918, which tipped the scale of the battle
in the enemy's favour.

This led the reporter to gain accreditation as a war correspondent attached to Allenby's army.

Thomas's week of documenting Lawrence's activities
convinced the American that he had 'gold', and not just for government propaganda purposes.

The Englishman could be exploited well beyond that original
aim.

53

Turks Hold Amman

The success on the railway encouraged Allenby, who was
under pressure to act fast or be forced to sit out the rest
of the 1918 spring and summer until the next opportunity
for a further big push to Amman, Deraa and Damascus as late as
the next autumn. He put a plan to Chauvel. It was in three stages.
First he had to capture two enemy strongholds at Es Salt, where
the Turkish 4th Army had its HQ with 1,000 men, and nearby
Shunet Nimrin where there was a garrison of 5,000. Second, once
his forces consolidated in the area he had to take Amman.

Third, he told Chauvel:

'As soon as your operations have gained the front Amman-Es Salt, you will at once prepare for operations northwards, with a view to advancing rapidly on Deraa.'

Deraa was a local capital 104 kilometres north-east of Jerusalem, which acted as the rail junction between Damascus and Amman. (Amman was connected to the Hejaz railway running south to Maan and on to Medina.) It was the point where the Hejaz railway threw out its western branch, crossing the Jordan River south of the Sea of Galilee.

Allenby knew Deraa would take a big operation to win. Yet once it was taken, Damascus would be the next important Syrian city to fall, and a less difficult proposition.

One risk among several came in Allenby's assertion that the Arabs in the area east of Jerusalem, the Beni Sakhr, would come to Chauvel's aid. 'The closest touch must be maintained with them,' Allenby directed. Perhaps he had been influenced by Lawrence's optimism concerning the Arabs, despite the letdown in late March in the assault on Amman. But it was not simple. The Arabs had to be wooed and won everywhere by every means possible. The British force in general still had a distrust of the Arabs, who to them seemed to drift with the wind. If it blew for the Turks, they would stay with them. If it blew for the British, they might go with them. But they distrusted all 'invaders'. Unless they were persuaded by Lawrence himself, they were most unlikely to do the bidding of the British, and he was not called on to help out. Nor was his liaison officer with this tribe, Hubert Young, an Arabist he first met at Carchemish before the war (and the man he had nominated as his replacement should be he 'incapacitated', which was a euphemism for killed). Allenby's HQ representatives had been heavy-handed in dealing with the tribe. They had not communicated their plans and what was expected of it. Young later reported the British envoys had 'perplexed and frightened' them.

The envoys wrote to Allenby that the Beni Sakhr would only

help out before early May while their sheep were still grazing in the area. After that, they would have to move on to other pastures. It sounded like a 'thin' restriction (and in reality an excuse for not helping out) that would never have been put to experienced Arabists Lawrence and Young. Nevertheless, Chauvel was informed that the Arabs would march on the village of Naur, 14 kilometres east of Shunet Nimrin, cut the Turkish communications and attack them as they withdrew.

Allenby also put a time constraint on Chauvel by saying that the spring wheat and barley harvest on the plains west of the Jordan would be important to the Turks.

For these reasons, Allenby claimed, it was imperative to strike before the beginning of May.

The commander-in-chief, then, was giving the impression of being dictated to by the agrarian gods and the eating habits of a flock of sheep. It was out of character. He could see his grand plan to take Damascus and defeat the Turks slipping away. There was not quite the whiff of panic in Allenby's directive. But at the least it was rushed and over-ambitious. There were more risks than most pragmatic generals would accept.

Chetwode was asked to 'demonstrate' against Shunet Nimrin to make the Turks think the British were going for Amman first. In private, he thought this a 'stupid' plan (and said so later). Why alert the Turks to something big with a feint that would have them prepared for a sizeable attack? This took away the element of surprise, especially for the mounteds, whose advantages over the infantry included speed of attack, and shock.

Chauvel did not like the idea of this feint. It worried him that the 5,000 well-entrenched, forewarned Turks were waiting for his force to attack. At a conference with Allenby on 24 April he asked for an infantry division to help out. He was granted the 60th Division, minus one brigade of three, which was to sit in reserve with Chetwode. But Chauvel felt he needed a full division. He became uneasy about the entire scheme. He was a diligent planner who left little to chance. There were too many 'what ifs' in this scheme. On top of that, intelligence reports informed him that German infantry would most likely be enlisted to come from Amman. The enemy would have a big supply of artillery and machine-guns.

He used the legitimate yet convenient excuse that his transport capacity would only stretch to Es Salt. He wrote to HQ and asked that plans two and three be 'postponed'. Allenby was perhaps aware that he had suffered from a rush of blood over the three-part plan, or maybe his staff gently persuaded him against it. Whatever the influence, he agreed to Chauvel's request.

This still did not make the first aim any easier, although it did relieve Chauvel of worrying about the improbable logistics beyond it.

He sent the two brigades of the 60th Division across the Jordan at 5 a.m. on 30 April and on another eight kilometres to tackle Shunet Nimrin. The Londoners fought with their usual tenacity, but they were up against a powerful force of fire from artillery, machine-guns and rifles. They needed that third brigade.

Despite repeated thrusts, they could not make a breakthrough.

At first light, Chauvel sent out one of his favourite attack commanders, Brigadier General Grant. He was to strike further north with his 4th Brigade up west (left) of the Jordan. If he made it across the plain of Mafid Jozele, he was to swing across the Jordan and aim for Es Salt, which was 16 kilometres north-east of Shunet Nimrin. The 4th would be followed by more Australian Mounteds.

The Light Horse swept 15 kilometres north and brushed aside Turkish posts en route to the plain, despite big guns firing on the stream of mounted riflemen. By 8 a.m. the 4th Brigade's 4th Regiment had reached a small tributary to the Jordan another 10 kilometres further north. A squadron of the 11th Regiment, including recruit Frank Fisher, was aiming to reach a crossing on the river at Damieh. But the Turks had a string of big gun emplacements and were making the passage difficult. They attempted to pulverise the oncoming horsemen, who were forced to disperse.

Grant brought up his own considerable artillery in the hope of clearing a way for his riders.

At 6.30 a.m. on 30 April 1918, Brigadier Lachlan Wilson, the quiet Queensland city lawyer, arrived with his 3rd Brigade on the Mafid Jozele Plain. He and Grant had a quick conference. Grant informed him that his men had cut the telegraph wires at Damieh, which meant that the Turks at Es Salt might not know of the impending assault from the north. Grant thought he could hold his ground and at the same time cover Wilson and his riders, who would make for the Damieh crossing.

Wilson made his move, leading the horsemen over the crossing and then onto a plain and a winding climb of 23 kilometres south-east towards Es Salt. The road became a narrow, dangerous track as it left the plain. It rose so sharply for two kilometres that the men dismounted and led their horses single file. No transport could make it, but a train of 360 camels, not used to acting like mountain goats, scrambled up. Twenty-nine camel cacolets for the wounded were included. Some carried the six guns of the Hong Kong and Singapore Mounted Battery and their ammunition. Each man carried 230 rounds of ammunition. For each Hotchkiss gun there were 3,100 rounds; for each machine-gun there were 5,000 rounds.

Wilson sent Scott out ahead with the 9th Regiment. They were surprised to see nothing of the enemy, especially as the track past the steep part was surrounded by hills where snipers and machine-gunners would have strong vantage points. Enemy scouts could have warned the Turkish 4th Army base at Es Salt.

So far there was no opposition.

Scouts for the 9th came across their first three Turks six kilometres from Es Salt. They crept up on them, shooting one and capturing the other two. Next encounter was with a Turkish cavalry troop of 32. The Australians rushed them. The enemy fled on horseback and foot across the rocky ground. Wilson's brigade had come 17 kilometres in a climb of 4,000 feet and were on a tableland.

The third confrontation came about 800 metres further on. The Turks had set up small fortifications on a high ridge running for a kilometre to the left of the track and on hills either side of it.

Wilson was determined to take Es Salt by nightfall after he received a radio message from Chauvel saying it had to be done. The slow camels were holding up Wilson's advance. With the afternoon wearing on, he did not hesitate to take on the Turks in the hills and on the ridge, sending his men on foot. The horsemen revelled in their mission. They were aided by broken ground, which allowed them to close in on the Turks, who would have been unnerved to see how the Australians did not hesitate to go into action. Wilson let loose three of the Hong Kong battery guns with 12 of the machine-guns, which softened up the enemy. The Light Horse turned infantry and attacked in three directions. The machine-gun fire and shells kept coming until the horsemen were almost at the Turkish fortified stone barricades. Many of the enemy soldiers were still crouching when the Australian attackers, armed with revolvers or bayonets, came over their fortification at them. German officers tried to make their Turkish charges stay and fight. But the stories of the Australians at Beersheba had filtered back to the entire army. This assault had something of the intensity of that historic charge, again brought on by the urgency of reaching their objective before nightfall.

Some of the Germans in the defence stood and fought but they were soon overwhelmed.

Wilson could see this first battle going his way. He ordered Major Shannon to prepare for a mounted dash of 3.5 kilometres to Es Salt itself. By the time the 8th's squadrons were ready, Wilson gave the signal for them to take the town. The 250 horsemen trotted off. They ignored fire from the hills and broke into a gallop but then met intense fire from sangars two kilometres further on. They were forced to stop and take on the 60 Turks by the road. Shannon ordered his troopers to flank and break the opposition, which was done in less than 20 minutes. The Light Horse regrouped and continued on the approach through several small valleys flanked by stony hills. They met occasional opposition, which necessitated troopers thrusting in bursts at the enemy, who were soon broken and running.

Shannon and his men were now galvanised to take the town at a rush. This was their moment. Every trooper lived for these isolated chances to be part of a hot-blooded charge, the shock of which was part of the impact on the enemy.

Lieutenant Charles Foulkes-Taylor, a 28-year-old London-born Western Australian, led the first troop into Es Salt. The town was at the head of a valley on a hill dominated by a medieval castle. Its basalt houses and buildings rose one above the other on the hill slopes. On its western and southern sides it was protected by a system of steep terraced hills.

Preferring the revolver to the bayonet, Taylor fired at some of the 300 Turks and Germans still left in the 4th Army HQ as he charged down the cobblestone lanes startling inhabitants and enemy alike. Most had evacuated in the last hour knowing that the Australians were coming. The remaining soldiers were under orders to fight.

Taylor saw a German officer in a courtyard trying to rally some Turks to make a stand. He spurred his horse at them, aiming his revolver at the German. Taylor pulled the trigger and found he was out of ammunition. He kept coming, still aiming his weapon and with bluff, forced his quarry to hand over his own revolver.

With the town under control, Taylor gathered eight troopers and tracked down transport leaving the town on the road to Amman. They overtook them on a narrow track beside a steep slope into a valley.

'The Light Horsemen forced teams and carts over the edge of the roadway,' Henry Gullett wrote in his official history, '. . . they tumbled into the deep-bed of the water-course.'[1]

Taylor had lost two men wounded and was down to six. He ploughed on only to be stopped by intense machine-gun fire four kilometres along the road. He was forced to stop and retreat. This small band with their reckless drive had captured 200 armed enemy troops, weaponry, food, water and other supplies.

Taylor was soon reinforced by other troopers from the secured town. They turned back to Es Salt, satisfied with their afternoon's 'work' and haul. (It would later earn this newly commissioned officer the Military Cross.)

German radio traffic was intercepted after the town was taken.

'Es Salt had been captured,' it said, 'by the reckless and dashing gallantry of the Australian Cavalry.'

A German officer noted that the 8th Regiment's rush on Es Salt featured troopers galloping their horses in places where 'no-one else would have ridden at all'.

Further documents captured later in Nazareth confirmed that the Es Salt action had caused more problems between the Germans and Turks running the war. The shock debacle at Beersheba had begun the rift. Es Salt had deepened it. Liman von Sanders was most unhappy about the way Djemal Pasha conducted the operations east of Jordan before Wilson's fierce attack from the river to Es Salt. The German commander condemned Djemal's 'failure' to guard against the ride up the Jordan Valley and the taking of Es Salt. Liman von Sanders said it should never have changed hands. The Turks, he claimed, should have held it at all costs.

The battle was far from over, but internal enemy friction was already exposed.

The town was soon covered by the regiments on the routes north and east. A spirited search for 'booty', always the consequence of a new town acquisition, was carried out. It didn't have the intensity or intent of the local Arabs' looting. But the Australians were buoyed by their finds, especially five lorries, six German cars and 28 new machine-guns yet to be unpacked. There was also a tonne of ammunition and small arms.

One captured German officer spoke a little English.

'Well,' he said in a guttural accent to a 10th Regiment officer, 'and how long are you going to make the war with us?'

'Until we lick you,' the Australian replied.

'Lick? Lick? What do mean lick?'

'Until we beat you.'

'Oh,' the German said, shrugging his shoulders, 'then it will be a very, very long war!'[2]

54

Arab Let-Down, Summer by the Jordan

The 10th Light Horse Regiment found the night sky over Es Salt strange. It began in pitch black at 6 p.m. except for the odd flickering of primitive oil lamps in some of the stone buildings. By 9 p.m. the moon forced its way through a dark bank of clouds and threw fitful light on the wet cobblestones. Here and there the ghostly shapes of naked, dead men in the streets were visible and then gone as the moon or the clouds moved on. They had been stripped in the Arab scavenging tradition that none of the Australians could come to terms with.

The silence was broken by the groans of the wounded and dying, somewhere in a lane or a back alley. The helpless sounds were overridden by the howls of stray dogs.

'Occasionally a rifle shot reverberating through the basalt piles,' the 10th Light Horse Regiment's Major Olden wrote, 'told of the native [Arab] making trial of his new-found toy—probably improving the happy circumstances of our presence in his domain by settling long standing grievances with his neighbour.'[1]

There was a disturbance in a courtyard in the town's centre where 800 Turks were guarded by the 8th Regiment. Prisoners were caught looking up to a building high on a hillside. Regular lamp-light flashes were seen at a window. The guards watched. The code being signalled was not an Allied one. The enemy had to be sending the signals. An Australian marksman fired at the window, shattering it. The lamp stopped flashing. But half an hour later signals began again from another window. The same sniper fired again. The light went out once more. This happened again several times, and the Australians were now alerted to this probable espionage activity. A volley of shots from several trooper snipers snuffed out the light for the night, and most likely the agent.

Wilson was satisfied with the day, but there was no call for celebration. The yeomanry and the 5th Mounted Brigade had not been as quick or successful and were not going to be at Es Salt until the next morning. At last he made direct radio contact with Chauvel. The revised plan was to pursue the enemy 11 kilometres along the Amman road to Hill 2900. Wilson complied with this but not with the force he would otherwise have done if the others had arrived overnight. He sent out 37-year-old dentist Olden with two squadrons and four machine-guns. He covered nine kilometres in the moonlight by midnight before encountering stiff opposition. Olden encamped and remained on watch. His orders were to meet up with the Beni Sakhr west of Hill 2900.

The idea was that they would combine to stop any counter-punch by the Turks from Amman towards Shunet Nimrin, where Shea's 60th Division and the Turks in the fort there had battled to a stalemate.

German dissatisfaction with events was premature. During the night the Turks threw a new bridge over the Jordan opposite the Mafid Jozele plain. The next morning Chauvel sent the Camel

Brigade to attack and destroy it, but it was too late. Liman von Sanders was annoyed about the loss of Es Salt, but realised that Shea's 60th Division had not been able to take Shunet Nimrin and was in trouble. The German sent more troops of the Turkish 8th Army to the town.

At the same time, the Beni Sakhr failed to show west of that town. Had they done so, the reinforcements of enemy troops and supplies from Amman would have been cut off, or at least held up, perhaps enough to have an impact further east at Shunet Nimrin. It was the second time in a month that the Arabs had failed in their support of the British. Lawrence was not to blame this time. But the pattern disturbed the British officers and rank and file. The distrust from earlier incidents, beginning with the massacre of the yeomanry in the Sinai in April 1916, was maintained. If the Arabs were to play a significant part in the capture of Damascus, as Lawrence hoped, more leadership and determination had to come from them. Questions were raised about their value, although they could not be left out of Allenby's overall plans. They were a political necessity, no matter how poorly they contributed in combined operations. Besides this, they were doing well coming up through Jordan.

Early on 1 May, Chauvel sent up air reconnaissance to find the Beni Sakhr, but they had dispersed. He ruled them out of his wider force and concentrated on options without them. Reinforced Turkish infantry and cavalry attacked, outnumbering Grant's 4th Light Horse forces by four to one.

A mound called Red Hill on the west Jordan bank was held by just one squadron of Grant's 4th Brigade. It was overwhelmed. The Turks were now either side of the Jordan and threatening to march south. Chauvel felt Grant's communications were now under threat. He ordered him to dispose his artillery so that if he were forced to withdraw he could take them with him. But events were happening too fast for such rational plans.

Grant, who had expressed his concerns on the previous

afternoon to Chauvel when he visited him at the front, decided on a hasty withdrawal. He did not think he had time to take his big artillery pieces with him. Nine of 12 were lost to the enemy, along with other weaponry and supplies.

There was a danger now that the Turks would overrun his retreating force. But the experienced troopers fell back with typical discipline over broken ground and steep slopes.

Chauvel sent Chaytor with a regiment of the reserve brigade and part of the New Zealand Brigade to protect Grant's retreating flank as the 4th Light Horse slipped back down the territory east of the Jordan. Chauvel ordered Shea to push harder against Shunet Nimrin, preventing pressure on the horsemen, who with Chaytor's reinforcements were soon repelling all Turkish attacks. Meanwhile Hodgson's Australian Mounted was pressing on with the plan to attack Shunet Nimrin from the rear. But there were concerns that with all tracks held by the Turks, except the one he had arrived on, he too might be cut off.

On 2 May, Chauvel directed more air reconnaissance. A huge number of enemy troops were photographed arriving at Amman. Already outnumbered by the Turkish forces in combat, and with ammunition, water, food and medical supplies a growing problem, he made contact with the Australian Mounted. It was under pressure from the north and east.

Chauvel decided on a general withdrawal. But he had to consult Allenby first. The chief visited Chauvel's battle HQ four kilometres south of the front on the Jordan at Ghoraniye. Allenby examined all the evidence. He concurred with Chauvel without showing emotion either way about the situation.

At 4 p.m. on 3 May, the order went out for the entire force to pull back.

Wilson and his 3rd Brigade had the longest trip from Es Salt but their passage along the tracks back to the Jordan was helped by the Australian Flying Corps' 3rd Squadron. It piled up its flying machines with bombs and dropped them on the Turks in the path of the horsemen and followed this up with machine-gun strafing.

By midnight on 4 May the last of the Light Horse brigades crossed to the Jordan's west bank.

The four-day enterprise, more than a raid and less than a success, was over.

Chauvel expressed his disappointment at the failure to Allenby.

'Failure be damned!' a surprisingly ebullient Allenby responded. 'It has been a great success.'[2]

Chauvel, the realist, was unsure about this response. The casualty figures were one way of giving the outcome of Es Salt a positive 'spin'. His force had 1,649—split two-thirds infantry, one-third Light Horse; the Turks had more than 2,000. Chauvel's force brought back nearly 1,000 prisoners, and normally in this type of more-than-a-raid mission that would constitute a near-win. Yet Chauvel factored in the loss of the big guns and the withdrawal. He would never claim it as a victory, even when Allenby later circulated a congratulatory message to all the troops which referred to the 'unity which led to success'.

In the compulsory post-mortem, the chief was mildly critical, the way he would be even in a clear-cut victory such as at the last Beersheba–Gaza battle. Chauvel was rapped on the knuckles for not strengthening Grant's Red Hill flank when he had called for reinforcements. He was further criticised for not directing Grant to tighten his defence. It was considered too dispersed. The report concluded that this led to the big guns being lost, which provoked some pertinent questions from Robertson in the War Office, London.

Allenby's overall rosy assessment would have been in part because he wished to bury his own blunders. His 'demonstration' on 18 April 1918 that alerted the Turks was a fundamental mistake. He erred over Beni Sakhr. If he had called for Lawrence to liaise with the Arabs, or if he had ignored them and waited two weeks for another British infantry division, the outcome may well have been different. Again, the Arabs' 'no show' at a pivotal point in a battle was critical. It led to Turkish reinforcements moving from Amman towards the Jordan without opposition just when Chauvel's combined infantry and trooper dispositions could have tipped the scales his way. This was especially so after Wilson's sensational taking of Es Salt by nightfall on the first day.

Another factor was the rushed planning by Allenby and his staff. He had been clutching for a big breakthrough before he would be forced to hold his positions and feed off his troops to the Western Front. Every part of the plan had to work for this to come off and it did not.

This left the EEF in limbo until events unfolded in Europe.

Allenby and his staff called this second attempt at victory over the Jordan a 'raid' to further diminish its significance.

Chauvel's Light Horse base and HQ after Es Salt was in and around Ghoraniye, just east of the Jordan and 10 kilometres east of Jericho. From early May it was a time of inertia and consolidation. The biggest decision for Chauvel was whether he should sit out the summer where he was on the banks of the lower reaches of the river valley or move into the hills. The locals had warned him that the area was nearly uninhabitable from late May to late September. Even the Arabs took to higher ground. The people of Jericho stayed in the town as long as they could to sell to the pilgrims and tourists. But come the last week of May, all but the most impoverished departed for the hills. Only beggars and homeless were left. Most would not make it through the summer.

If Chauvel shifted their base west, the Turks would move to the valley and occupy the river low land from the Dead Sea to about 25 kilometres north. The enemy would pour down the road from Amman and seize the river crossing at Ghoraniye. Once the area was under its control, it would have Chauvel and his force on the defensive and could attack in strength.

Allenby left the tough decision to Chauvel, having complete faith in his judgement. He was in command of the diverse corps with key commanders—three Englishmen (Hodgson, MacAndrew and Barrow) and one New Zealander (Chaytor). In turn, Chauvel gave these commanders considerable discretion once he gave out his orders and objectives.

The dilemma here was clear. Staying put would mean many deaths from disease, especially malaria. Heading for the less suffocating hills, where the mosquito infestation was not as strong, would mean losing more troopers trying to get back control of the area after the summer. He also wished to 'hoodwink' the Turks into believing he was preparing something big when Allenby was considering a push north-west towards the coast. Chauvel was influenced here by the interception of many Turkish messages. They stated in different ways that the Light Horse was feared. Wherever they were, the enemy believed, they were likely to strike at any moment. Chauvel also worried about the lack of water and space in the hills for the more than 30,000 troopers and 50,000 horses. After having a good look at the hill region, he also concluded the climate was only a fraction better anyway. With all these factors in mind, Chauvel weighed up these poor options and went for the lesser of two evils.

He decided to stay in the valley and face the worst dust they had experienced, the fierce heat, the flies and the inevitable spread of malaria.

To the Sword

The lull in fighting allowed time for the ceremonial and some medal-giving. Allenby decided to award decorations for the battles around the Jordan and chose a parade area near a road five kilometres north of Jericho. The Anzac Mounted Division lined up. Chauvel, Trew and Allenby were chauffeured to the division's HQ and switched to horses for the trot up the road to the parade. Allenby mounted, twisted around and belted the mare on the rump. The waler was not used to this.

'She put her head down and pig-rooted into the bush and dust,' a witness, Lieutenant Colonel Sir Michael Bruxner, said.

Chauvel took off after the chief, praying he would not fall off, reached him and reined in the indignant horse and startled Allenby. As they trotted back, Chauvel saw that Trew on the other side of the road was also in trouble with his waler, who had reacted after his sister horse had taken off. Chauvel galloped after Trew, settled his waler and drew him up with Allenby. The three riders proceeded to the parade area to receive the salute and carry on with the ceremony.

Not a word was said about the incident. But all who witnessed it knew who the gifted horseman was among them.[1]

Summer hit hard and early. By the end of the first week in May 1918, the heat was wicked and the flies vile. The temperature climbed a fraction each day until 40 degrees Centigrade was considered cool. The heavy traffic needed to service Chauvel's mighty corps of men and horses (the 2,000 camels had been 'retired' from this region) ground up the fine dirt, which became dust. Within weeks the whole area had been transformed into a light bed of powdered clay.

Lawrence applied to Allenby for the redundant camels.

'What do you want them for?' the chief asked.

'To put a thousand men into Deraa any day you please,' Lawrence replied. The town was becoming more important as the battle for the Middle East and the two forces, Allenby's and his, began their long convergence. Lawrence's plan was to create a contingent of Arab regulars on camels, and march them north 240 kilometres from Maan to Azraq. This town was just 120 kilometres from Amman, and about 135 kilometres from Deraa. The Arabs were closing slowly but surely on the Turks, and Deraa was uppermost in Lawrence's mind, and thanks to him, the chief's too. Lawrence was drawing up plans for an attack with the camels, artillery, machine-guns, armoured cars and planes.

It would take 14 days. Lawrence wanted to attack the railway with Rwalla irregulars in unison with Allenby making his autumn offensive, which was aimed at Damascus.

The chief did not automatically give his blessing to the camels going to Lawrence. The latter was throwing out ideas at this critical stage with the enthusiasm of a bright schoolboy. Many of them were not thought through in the military sense, especially in his lack of appreciation of fall-back positions and the consequences of failure. Yet Allenby appreciated him and encouraged his expression.

After considering the request, Allenby kept some camels for his quartermaster for the upcoming plans to take on the 8th, 7th and 4th armies, and gave the bulk of them to the fair-haired boy of his force. Lawrence, keeping up his youthful fervour, hurried to meet Feisal the next day to tell him he had been granted the means for final victory. Then he swapped the Egyptian Transport Corps camel men with Arab camel-drivers from Mecca, who Lawrence believed would be more reliable for the purposes he had in mind for them.

He gave the task of working out the logistics to Hubert Young, his 'understudy'. Lawrence had a high regard for his combined skills as a military man and Arabist, which, in theory, made him more useful than Lawrence himself in the desert campaign. His main flaw, which would keep him an understudy, was his temper.

Lawrence characterised him by telling of one incident when he went too far in verbally abusing some Arab officers. Lawrence soothed their injured egos by telling the Arabs that Young did not discriminate.

He shouted at the British just the same.

By mid-May, the temperature in the Jordan Valley was close to 45 degrees Centigrade and occasionally near to 50 degrees. This brought out scorpions in plague proportions, black spiders bigger than most of the Australians had ever seen at home, and snakes. A variety of insects joined the myriad flies, including the biting variety, and mosquitoes to disconcert the troopers. Many of them swore that taking on the Turks in rain and sleet would be far preferable to the conditions they now faced.

Soon the troopers were lining up at medical tents with painful scorpion bites. But not long after they infested all the camps, the troopers countered them with the only weapon possible: humour. The biggest of them would be put in a ring and forced to fight each other. Bets were laid on the outcome of their 'battles'. Then it was black spiders versus the scorpions. The troopers could not wipe them out, but they learnt to coexist with them.

The men were informed about the 'asp', a venomous snake that infested the wilderness. A scientific squad at military HQ in Jerusalem required specimens for research purposes. The troopers were offered rewards for bringing one in. When not in action or on patrol, the men tramped the nearby hills armed with forked sticks and went on searches.

'Literally no stone was left unturned in the treasure hunt for asps,' the 11th Light Horse historian said. 'Many other varieties of snakes and even lizards were brought in for classification.'

Soon a frantic note came down from the scientists cancelling the order for 'live snakes'.[2]

Through all this, they had to labour at building trenches and fortifications under the engineers' direction, and to clear the area of all standing water in an attempt to limit mosquito breeding. Many of the scrubby swamps could not be drained and the troopers camped away from them as much as possible. Even the watering of horses had to be restricted to the canvas troughs to which water was lifted by pumping. Otherwise puddles breeding mosquitoes could form in the holes made by hooves.

The methods worked at first. But malaria spread by late May and threatened Chauvel's entire force.

The only relief for man and horse was swimming in the streams and shallow fords. Fish were plentiful, but were so well-fed that rod and reel could not entice them. The Australians resorted to Mills bombs to blow them out of the water until this action was banned.

In early June, the men were lifted by the news that the 'angel' Rania MacPhillamy had opened a canteen in Jerusalem with Allenby's blessing and assistance.

The troopers worshipped her for bringing them a tiny slice of home with food and other items (magazines and papers included) that for the brief time they could be there on leave was a distraction from the hell of their camps in the Jordan Valley. Her devotion inspired Major J.J. Trickett, a sales manager from Melbourne, who started a mobile car canteen. This at first brought the wrath of the chiefs until its harmless benefits to the troops were endorsed by Chauvel and other commanders. Trickett soon had car canteens with every brigade. They came to the troopers in the camps and often followed them to the battlefields.

His greatest treat, however, went a step further. He opened an ice soda fountain in a store near Jericho.

'Let's go to Trickett's,' became a catchcry for the heat-depressed troopers during that oppressive northern summer of 1918. It created a welcome respite. There was further relief by rotating the units. Cox's brigade was moved into the hills in late June. In early July it had a wonderful break in the Jewish settlement at Wadi Hanein where the climate was hot but pleasant, and the fruit and wine appreciated. The New Zealanders and Ryrie's brigade were sent to a camp near Bethlehem, where Chaytor had his HQ in a Carmelite monastery.

Training in the use of the sword in the olive groves near the coast also lifted many of the troopers from their lethargy. By late July, the 3rd, 4th and 5th Light Horse Brigades had been trained and were waiting to use them. Grant was next to be trained with his 4th Brigade. He and Wilson had been keen to take up the tradition. Chaytor had not. He and his men preferred rifle and bayonet.

The Australians took to the new weapon with zeal. It brought a focus to their work as they waited for orders to move out on another mission.

Henry Gullett noted the joke that abounded in the villages near the sword-training camp:

'Not a wild dog has been left alive', in the region.[3]

This was repeated in the Jerusalem bazaars so that Turkish spies would pass back the chilling propaganda: 'The horsemen of Beersheba and Es Salt now have long swords.'

The men not on rotation for rest or sword-training faced the growing dust and grime of mid-summer in the valley of dreariness and debilitation. More and more men fell sick, mostly with malaria, recurrent fevers and stomach complaints. The corps was at its lowest point during the entire campaign so far. The troopers also had to contend with shell-fire and snipers. The losses may not have been heavy but they kept a steady pressure on Chauvel's force. Those who were wounded would end up back in the line after treatment when they otherwise may have been invalided out. There were no troopers to replace them.

In the tight manpower months of mid-1918, hospitals far away in Cairo and elsewhere were not options.

In mid-August, the mood of the EEF changed. News was coming through that the Allies had won a huge battle on the Western Front on 8 and 9 August at Amiens, 120 kilometres north of Paris. This 'Battle of Amiens' had been masterminded by Monash after his smaller success with tanks in the 'model'

Battle of Hamel five weeks earlier. The Australian general had shown what tanks could do if properly deployed with planes and infantry, when the British High Command had been loath to use them after failures earlier in the war. The result at Amiens was devastating for the Germans, who lost the equivalent of two armies inside 48 hours. They were ready for total capitulation and were surprised when the British did not force the issue as Monash had urged after 9 August. Nevertheless, the Germans for the first time acknowledged, according to their military dictator and commander-in-chief General Erich Ludendorff, that they could not now win the war, but only defend.

After Amiens, it was only a matter of time before the war was over. The state of affairs in the 'main game', which would go on thanks to the intransigence of the British High Command, had wide ramifications for the minor war in the Middle East. Allenby sniffed victory wafting from the Western Front.

It was time to drive home the sword, literally, on the Eastern Front.

56

Phantom Horsemen

There was commotion at Fast's Hotel in Jerusalem early on 4 September 1918. Officers, American journalists and an assortment of other patrons were informed that they had to vacate the building that morning. The word came from the manager, Monsieur Caesar, who had received official yet confidential instructions from a high place. Guests had to be cleared out. He was a legend after a long time as the head waiter at the Continental Hotel, Cairo. Those who objected were assisted in their packing of belongings and helped out into the street. Sentry-boxes were placed at the front door of this former German house. It had been taken over in December 1917 by the British Canteens Board and mainly used by officers over the past 10 months. All rooms were booked out. Notices headed 'GHQ' were pinned on every bedroom door.

Something big seemed to be happening. Stories spread that commander-in-chief Allenby and his vast staff would be based there soon. Rumours filtered into the bazaar that Fast's would be his advance headquarters for a mighty push east from the Jordan Valley. This was it. The holy city buzzed with the news. Before noon, the enemy heard the story and believed it. Just like the feint at Gaza when Beersheba was taken, Chauvel and Allenby were up to their tricks that may have had their roots in schoolboy pranks. They were creating a vast and elaborate illusion. Even Monash, the finest trickster on the Western Front in Europe, who had been a teenage illusionist with cards, could not have bettered this sophisticated war fraud. Allenby wished to give the impression that a big move east was on.

The detail of how Chauvel would wave his magic wand was left to him and his staff. It needed the coolest of characters, and the front of a world class poker player to pull off this giant 'con'. The Australian had always played his cards close. He was a quiet disciplinarian, who had the utmost respect of the officers under him. Here his underlying strength as a man and leader was to be tested in conditions only surpassed by the strictures of battle itself. The secrecy required on so many levels reflected the trust every officer and commander had in Chauvel. He was not a leader by bluster. But bluff was a strong suit, the conundrum being that bluff only worked because beneath it lay a mind and leader of substance. If he wished to fool the enemy with trickery, then every man so assigned responded. They knew that if Chauvel directed it, there had to be something special behind it. His every move since the dark days of mid-May 1915, when huddled 'cheek by jowl' with Monash in the valley of death at Gallipoli, had been in the interests of the men under him. From the humane, sane and logical decision to pull out of the futility of the advance from Courtney's Post on 7 August 1915 through the entire Middle East campaign, Chauvel had calibrated prudence, patience and an instinct for the kill in a formula only such a refined, clinical and confident mind could manage.

This grand charade was cover for a serious punch west, first with the 20th and 21st Infantry Corps. When a hole in the enemy defences on the Plain of Sharon near the coast was apparent, Chauvel and a large slice of his force would crash through it, ride hard in the direction north-east and tackle the enemy in their HQ and communications centres at Nazareth and El Afule.

It was bold, daring and plausible, but only if the enemy was taken by surprise. Chauvel and his commanders gave no written orders. The troopers were not allowed to sight-see, which left them with only a few options, such as playing cards. Some of them sneaked down to the coast for a swim at dawn. During the day they had to be out of sight or still. Horses were kept hobbled as they drank from irrigation channels. All cooking was by smoke-free cubes. Mules and camels, with their groans and rumbling, were kept well clear of the eight-kilometre strip from Jaffa to Ludd inland where the Light Horse hid. Jaffa, which they could see from their camps in the orange, lemon, almond and olive groves, was out-of-bounds. Waiting in the heat was boring, even if it were preferable to sitting around in the Jordan Valley.

Early on 17 September and two days before the attack, Allenby arrived at the mess tent of divisional HQ to meet Chauvel and his commanders and brigadiers for a pep talk.

'I came here, gentlemen,' he said, with his characteristic certitude, 'to wish you good luck, and to tell you that I consider you are on the eve of a great victory. Practically everything depends on the secrecy, rapidity and accuracy of the cavalry movement.'

*

That morning a devout Muslim Indian sergeant went AWOL from General Barrow's cavalry division and reached the Turkish stronghold at Nablus, 55 kilometres from Jaffa. He had been tormented by the thought of his brother Muslims being defeated on a massive scale and decided to defect and tell all. He was taken to a Turkish officer, saying he wished to defect and inform him of a massive plan of deception. His breathless divulgences brought a sceptical response at first from the experienced Turkish officer, who knew of the feint at Gaza and other British tricks. But when the Indian had laid out what he knew, the officer was convinced that the defector was telling the truth. The wily Mustafa Kemal, who had been appointed the head of the 7th Army by the sultan himself, was alerted.

He believed the story and sent a rushed message to Liman von Sanders 60 kilometres north of Nablus at his HQ in Nazareth.

The Indian sergeant's disappearance and assumed defection was reported to Barrow, who passed on the bad news to his commander, Chauvel. With Allenby's terse comment about the need for secrecy still ringing in his ears, the Australian considered the possible crisis but decided not to change anything in the schedule. Too many wheels of the attack were in motion.

He would have to pray that the defector would not be believed.

Liman von Sanders dismissed the defector's report out-of-hand. He did not have the benefit of the sincere Indian in front of him with all the detail in his head. On paper, the claims seemed fantastic and far too elaborate to be true. The scheme ran contrary to every military intelligence report the German commander had read in the past week.

'It is just another British ruse,' Liman von Sanders said.

Part of the grand Allenby plan was to take risks on the Jordan. Chaytor was to stay in the valley with his sick and jaded Anzac

Division (made up of three Australian brigades and one New Zealand brigade), which had been there the longest and had been most debilitated by malaria. Its numbers were swollen to keep up the impression that Allenby was putting everything into a bash east. Next to the Anzacs now camped two battalions of British West Indians, two Jewish battalions and the 20th Indian Infantry Brigade. To the enemy from a few kilometres away, and even spies close by, this was a build-up in keeping, at least in numbers, with the rumours. Much play was made of them arriving in daylight, with the amount of dust kicked up an indicator of thousands of soldiers being marched into the area. Dust clouds were generated by mules dragging wagons and tree branches. Anzac patrols, which were precursors to large-scale attacks, were stepped up, alerting the Turks to a projected move east. Makeshift pontoon bridges were strung across the Jordan. Had the Turks stepped on them they would have realised they could not have supported traffic. But they looked real from 50 metres. There was a flurry of horse-feed purchasing, giving the appearance to locals that a big movement of cavalry was coming. Some would pass such suspicions onto the Turks. False wireless messages, which had the whiff of Meinertzhagen's cynicism, were sent from the old Desert Mounted Corps HQ.

Fifteen thousand dummy horses made of canvas were eased into the valley and along the lines during the night. In the morning, they looked realistic from a distance. Any observer concentrating on these equine marvels for any length of time would have been impressed, then suspicious of how still they were. Chauvel also put it about that there would be a race meeting at a track in a small village near Jaffa on 19 September to mark the end of the long, hot summer and change of seasons. It was advertised as 'The Great Horse Show'. Hundreds of horses were said to be committed to the event of eight races. Programs were printed. The publicity in effect designated the Jaffa area as a 'play' or 'dead' sector. The movement of horses would be seen as connected to the event.

The local population was expected to turn out to see the parade before the races.

Back in the Jordan Valley, the West Indian and Jewish troops were marched around, again creating the sense of a considerable force kicking up further walls of dust.

Away to the east near the Hejaz, Lawrence was playing his part in the ruse concerning the decoy Light Horse invasion east. He gathered a mounted force of Arabs, supported by British armoured cars and a French mountain battery at Kasr el Asrak, 80 kilometres east of the big Turkish/German base at Amman. This contingent was set for raids on the railway north, east and west of Deraa, a vital rail junction. These raids were timed to distract the Turks and make them believe that the Arab attacks were part of the push east from the Jordan Valley. Lawrence even went to the trouble of using his agents to filter into the Arab farming area around Amman where they used gold to buy up the entire local barley crop as feed for horses.

Without spelling it out, the agents let slip that the feed would be needed for an imminent massive British cavalry push in their direction.

The air force helped. The six British squadrons of the Royal Air Force, and the No. 1 Squadron, Australian Flying Corps carried on their superiority in the skies that began to be apparent from early in the year. When the summer began there were more than 100 German planes in any week buzzing above. Some spied, others bombed and strafed. By the end of the summer they were down to under 20. The dominance of the Australian Flying Corps in this 1918 shift of power above the battlefields was acknowledged when Captain Ross Smith, the trooper turned pilot, was given the only big 'bomber', a Handley-Page, to be used on the Middle East front. This was in part due to his devastating performances in the air against the odds. A classic encounter in the hot summer came when he and another pilot flew into the midst of seven enemy planes and took them all on. They engaged in the most stunning dogfight of the Middle East war, shooting down four planes. The other three, seeing their companions spiral into the sand and hills, departed the scene.

In the eight weeks build to the mid-September secret mission, the Australian Flying Corps destroyed 15 enemy aircraft that entered war zone air-space. Another 27 were forced to ground. The German pilots and spotters in the plane were harassed off their job. There was no photograph reconnaissance that would have picked up the positional changes in a substantial part of the British force. With so many enemy planes being brought down or beaten off, the troops on the ground were also better protected than at any time in the desert war. This dominance allowed the Australian Flying Corps to carry out more reconnaissance and attacks with bomb and machine-gun on ground targets.

It all added to the cover for the big clandestine movement of men, animals and machines from one front to another.

Lawrence continued his part in the overall Allenby scheme, moving from pretence over horse-feed to his demolition specialty that would distract the Turks at Amman and Deraa. On 15 September he took off once more for the much-abused railway, this time at Mafraq with two Rolls-Royce tenders, two armoured cars and two officers (his commander Lieutenant Colonel Pierce Joyce, and Lord Winterton, who had a new job after the disbanding of the Imperial Camel Corps).

They trundled across the Hauran plain and in mid-afternoon reached their target, a four-arched bridge near a fort at Kilometre 149. The two-pronged attack was swift and merciless. Winterton headed for the fort and opened up at the surprised Turks, while Lawrence motored to the bridge. His gunner fired the on-board Vickers at the four guards, killing two. Lawrence took the rifles from the others and then set six charges in the bridges' spandrel drainage-holes. He fired them and ran for the cars.

Seconds later, the four arches shattered. Lawrence, Winterton and Joyce took off at speed. They had gone 300 metres when their Rolls stopped with a broken spring-bracket. They and the driver worked feverishly to fix it with the Turkish patrols not far behind them. Their nerves were sorely tested as bullets pinged close by. They gingerly tried the car's suspension. It worked.

They drove off again to their base, escaping the enemy pursuers.

Chauvel's mounted riflemen were eased silently and secretly west for Ludd and the orange groves around Jaffa where they would be hidden. Some, such as the 10th Light Horse Regiment, had the benefit of sight protection from a wall of high cactus, which had been such a problem when the British attacked Gaza. Chauvel was driven to his new HQ at the German village of Sarona, five kilometres north of Jaffa, while leaving his old camp 80 kilometres away as if it were still in use. Its worst feature—the dust—was now its best from his point of view. It created cover. Only someone 50 metres from the base would have realised that it was a ghost camp. None of the big tents in a few acres of high ground at Talat ed Dumm were pulled down. Sentries patrolled and cars moved around it as if it were still Chauvel's HQ. Five troopers were detailed to keep lights operating at night. Camp fires were built. From a distance it all seemed like business as usual in the valley.

This charade was continued close up too. Chauvel turned elf in manner in keeping with his physical appearance. He kept out of sight in the new HQ. His staff denied even to brigadiers and divisional commanders that he was there. Only a handful of staff men in his corps knew what sleight of hand was transpiring.

Captured enemy intelligence maps of 17 September showed the Australian Mounted Division was still believed to be in the valley next to the new arrivals from India and the world's Jewry. Barrow's 4th Cavalry Division had also tiptoed west. The Turks still believed the big base to be at Jericho. Shea's 60th Infantry Division was marked on the maps in the hills east of the Nablus roads, when it too had shifted like a phantom in the night.

Allenby had also boosted his artillery on his western front from 70 to 301 pieces.

Everything was in place for a shock assault on an unsuspecting enemy.

Demolition Derby

Here were the Arabs believing in me, Allenby and Clayton trusting me, my bodyguard dying for me: and I began to wonder if all established reputations were founded, like mine, on fraud.

T. E. Lawrence

Confident that the bridge-blowing had put the railway out of commission for a week, Lawrence, Winterton and Joyce early on 17 September motored after the main column of a thousand camels and caught them by 8 a.m. Lawrence was not about to miss the attack on Deraa, the major rail terminus south of Damascus, and its surrounds, beginning with an assault by regulars at a small fort eight kilometres north.[1] A Rwalla squadron rushed to the fort followed in a Ford tender by Young and Nuri Said, the former Arab Baghdadi staff officer in the Turkish army. Lawrence, always the conscientious espionage operative, had contacted him when he was ill in a Cairo hospital and had helped 'turn' him to Feisal's cause. His skills as a military man had seen him soon rise to second-in-command of the Arab regular army.

Everyone slowed down close to the fort, thinking it had been abandoned. Young was just pouring himself a whisky from a hip-flask when Turkish machine-gun fire caused him to spill more than a drop. The fort was not empty. The 20 inhabitants had just been having a lazy morning sleeping in. A Turkish officer, clearly upset at his reverie being so rudely interrupted, rushed out of the fort in his night-shirt waving a sabre. Young called for French artillery, which soon silenced the protests from the fort. Rwalla horsemen then continued their assault and captured it.

*

Lawrence was more interested in Deraa itself. He and Joyce climbed to a hill crest to view it and stations to the north and west. He decided to lay 600 charges with the aim of crippling 6.5 kilometres of track and disrupting traffic for at least a week. After breakfast, he directed Egyptian sappers and Algerian gunners to paste the tracks with tulip mines.

Lawrence went back to the hill crest to survey Deraa. His binoculars lingered on the aerodrome. He was disturbed to see nine German planes being pulled out of the hangars.

He had no air cover for the mission.

Lawrence swung his binoculars back to the track to see the demolition teams working. Could they do their job in time? He thought he had the answer seconds later when the first tulip went off and sent a black plume skywards. Seconds later, Lawrence was not so sure. He had to dive for cover as a Pfalz spotter-plane burst over his vantage point. It was soon followed by two lumbering Albatross bombers and four Haberstadt scouts humming from the Deraa drome. The planes attacked like a swarm of mutant killer bees, unleashing bombs, and spraying machine-gun fire.

They caused pandemonium among Lawrence's party. Everyone scattered. Machine-gunners and artillery-men scrambled to position themselves for a response, which soon forced the planes high. Then another uninvited plane—a British Bristol—wandered into view. The German aircraft turned their attention to it. The Egyptian sappers and the Arabs continued their charge-laying.

Ever the opportunist, Lawrence directed a detachment to ride out by camel along the Palestine branch of the line running west to Mezerib, where they were to blow it up as part of the isolation of Deraa. He and this squad were just about to mount up when the Bristol came whistling into view with the enemy planes doing their best to machine-gun it. The lone British fighter could be heard to falter. It seemed like a stricken bird. Either it was hit or its fuel was low. Lawrence and Young yelled for a landing strip to be cleared. Camels, cars and artillery were dragged clear. The Bristol pilot turned for a fitful run at the makeshift strip, then dropped altitude, seemed to correct and then hit the ground hard. It bounced once, twice, then crashed into a boulder, flipping over. The pilot jumped out of the dented cockpit, scrambled to hoist some of his weaponry clear and made a dash for a car coming to collect him. Seconds later the German Halberstadt swooped in low and slow enough to release a bomb right towards the upturned Bristol. It exploded and was soon a ball of fire.

Having viewed this episode with bated breath, Lawrence got astride his mount and trotted off towards Mezerib with Nuri Said and his men. He hoped the German planes would not notice. But frightened off by the machine-guns on the ground, they spotted Lawrence's squad and came after it, dropping three bombs on the camels, which were spread out. The force of a fourth bomb shook him, spun his mount and disabled two camels belonging to his bodyguard. The men were sent flying, but managed to stagger to others and were quickly hoisted up.

Lawrence felt a searing pain from the blast. His left arm went numb. He panicked, thinking it may have been shot off. Fumbling under his cloak he unpicked a thin shred of shrapnel. It left him with another mark on his battle-peppered body.

Nuri's machine-gunners and artillery men took about 25 minutes to finish minor Turkish resistance in the two small forts at the target railway station, Mezerib. Nuri and Lawrence snipped the telephone wires, and Lawrence took his time doing it, almost ceremoniously.

He was closer now to cutting Deraa off.

If all went close to plan on this day, the city would be segregated from the Turkish forces and useless as a supply or escape route. But there was still plenty of 'gardening', as Young called it, to do, planting the tulip bombs along the track to the east and the points at the station itself. Their work was interrupted by the sound, then the sight of a train rumbling along the track from Deraa. Young struggled to finish and rushed clear, only to see his fuse ignite the tulips prematurely. The puffs of smoke from them were noticed by the train driver. He stopped, and put the seven carriages into reverse back to Deraa.

Mezerib was at least temporarily in Arab hands with the consequent looting of the forts. They were sullen, spare homes of sorts for the 80 Turks who had lived their uncomfortably, separated from civilisation for the past three years. Anything bolted down was soon worked free by the Arabs, who disappeared at sunset with yet another haul.

This was their climax and reward after fighting. The thought of gaining booty often drove them on, and meant more to them than any hate for the enemy. If Lawrence couldn't buy them with gold, which was rare, they could be lured on by the prospect of Turkish souvenirs from swords to wristwatches, which could fetch a year's living expenses in the town bazaars.

Lawrence relaxed for two hours at night in Mezerib. Then he set out again for one more mission before retiring. This was to blow the bridge at Tel ash-Shehab, which he and Sharif Ali had not been able to destroy earlier in the year.

Lawrence, Young and a small squad crept to within 200 metres of the bridge. But once more it defeated him. Because of his earlier effort, there was now a strong artillery battery defending it. Lawrence, fatigued and grumpy, retreated with reluctance.

He returned to Mezerib. It had been a long day—perhaps the longest of his campaign—in the saddle, and in blowing bridges and rail. It was also the most important and satisfying 24 hours so far. He had been the key organiser in cutting off Deraa to the south, east and north. There was nowhere to go west but to a desert of oblivion. That vital city was now cut off from any main escape. The Turkish garrison was isolated, and in only a matter of time, finished.

He savoured the moment, but just for a few minutes, scribbling in his diary without reflection. He was so active that there was not much time for other than saying where he was. He was too exhausted to even put pen to paper for more than a line or two. Lawrence had begun his 'adventure' as the disembodied writer, taking copious notes on every event, every wadi and most characters. Blowing a bridge, even killing or seeing people killed had his creative juices running. Something shocking or spectacular was worth describing. Now none of these things were new. Killing, destroying and moving on for more were constant. He was not detached from any of it. He was a leader, if not the most crucial captain of the creaky, dysfunctional Arab army. He had become used to blood, death and demolition, things he would never believe in himself as an archaeological student when the main thrill in his life was finding another intriguing ancient castle.

Lawrence fell into a deep sleep, waking at dawn with the usual things preoccupying him. Were the enemy pressing? Which bridges were to go? Could he muster an Arab force, or had the looting caused them to disappear into the night? The regulars would be there. The non-regulars or 'blow-ins' would be as unreliable as ever, except that now there was a real sense that events were happening; the Turks were being overthrown, not so slowly now, but surely. It had taken several years for the local Arabs, who had an uneasy relationship with their Turkish masters for centuries, to comprehend that huge change could be afoot. The Ottomans had ruled by brutality and fear. They had played up the Muslim brotherhood when it suited, but they were, and always had been, the oppressors. To think they were going when 16 generations had experienced nothing else was not easy for the locals to digest, let alone appreciate. They disliked all foreigners, a natural response to thousands of years of abuse by those passing through, and others who wished to stay, subjugate and control them. Fear and loathing for non-Arabs was part of the Bedouin DNA. They remained sceptical about those replacing the Turks. Nevertheless evidence that the Arab Revolt had real voltage was seen in the number of local peasants that arrived at the camp that night.

Up to 5,000 men were in and around the area.

*

In essence, this mission to sever Deraa's main arteries was over. At breakfast on 18 September Lawrence had to set his mind more on leaving the area than worrying about any more demolition, before the Turks could pursue them in numbers or pinpoint them with their artillery and planes.

By 10 a.m. Lawrence had caught up with Nuri's party and was on his way to the base at Umm Tayeh to meet Joyce and the armoured cars. The Germans were following. There might also be a force in front of them. There was always the threat from the skies. The Germans had been defeated in the air in the west between Jerusalem and the coast. Their squadrons were now hovering east without much opposition for the moment, looking for easy prey. Along with this, peasants from a town en route, Ramtha, were hostile to Lawrence's force, due to a tribal feud and some loyalty to the Turks, who had sided with them in disputes.

Lawrence's retreating column of camels was therefore a target in three ways. This caused him to ride ahead of the column to mine the railway near Nasib, which could be used as a base for the enemy to attack his force. When night fell, Nuri Said ordered an artillery bombardment on the fort there. This distracted the Turks while the entire column crossed over the track.

'Long and lanky' Alec Kirkbride, a young officer in the Royal Engineers, caught up with Lawrence for this assignment. His job was to demolish a section of track while Lawrence destroyed a large bridge just north of the station fort. Kirkbride was well aware of his habit of using excessive amounts of explosives.

'Give me plenty of time to get away before you blow it,' Kirkbride called.

'Oh, alright, alright!' Lawrence replied tetchily. 'Don't fuss!'

He was feeling drained after the rush of the day before, which was not the mood to be in when laying charges. Lawrence fired them.[2]

'There was a deafening roar,' Young noted, 'and a blaze which lit up the country for miles. By its lights one saw the abutment arch of the bridge sheared clean off and the whole mass of masonry sliding down into the valley below.'[3]

Flying debris from the bridge fell all around Kirkbride and his men. They were fortunate not to be killed or injured. He approached Lawrence and abused him. Lawrence sat on a rock and roared laughing. He then invited the irate young officer to join him for coffee with his bodyguard, which placated him. Kirkbride knew this was an honour. Lawrence the legend was not in the habit of entertaining British officers. He restricted this kind of desert largesse to Arab leaders.

He tried to justify his careless work and his using so much explosive.

'It was strategically most critical since we were going to live opposite it at Umm Tayeh,' he said, '[and] I was determined to leave not a stone of it in place.'[4]

Kirkbride was mollified, especially as none of his men had been hurt. He was stressed enough himself and could only wonder at the pressures on Lawrence.

They were beginning to take a toll.

58

The Light Horse Breaks Out

As soon as night fell on 18 September, the lazy countryside east of Jaffa, bathed in late summer heat, became a seething mass of movement under moonlit skies. The artillery, cars, men, horses, camels and mules brought up to the front in the last few hours jammed every thoroughfare going north. Silence was imposed, although the groaning of wagons, purr of lorries, crunch of boots on metallic roads, the odd groan of the camels or whinny of the horses could not be avoided. Despite the Indian defector, it seemed the secrecy had worked in fooling Liman von Sanders and Kemal. The latter was the only Turkish commander who had not experienced defeat. He had an image of invincibility after his mighty leadership at Gallipoli. Kemal was no great strategist or tactician. He was more than that. He had inspired his troops to defend Turkey and they had succeeded. His late appointment (in March 1918) was welcomed by the Turkish troops.

Chauvel, who had learnt through intelligence that Kemal was commanding the 7th Army, was very keen to defeat him. Without making propaganda through the ranks, he quietly informed his senior officers of Kemal's appointment, just to add an alertness and dedication to winning. Chauvel was not aware of the friction between Kemal and Liman von Sanders. The German head of his country's military mission in Turkey for five years often overruled the Turks. He did not agree to Kemal's demands to amalgamate the three Turkish armies in Palestine and Syria. Kemal thought his disparate force was undernourished, listless and ripe for demoralising and defeat. By coordinating the three armies, he believed he could focus them on winning.

The fact that a Turk put up such a radical development meant it was going to be rejected.

The moonlight was helpful for the Flying Corps. Ross Smith went up in his Handley-Page 'bomber' with three lieutenants. At 1 a.m. on 19 September, the plane dropped bombs on the rail junction at El Afule, which was to be the target for Chauvel's Light Horse during the day. Now it was softened up and shaken. With moonlight still good, the ebullient Smith decided to fly back to base and reload. This time he dumped an ever bigger weight of bombs on the German aerodrome at Jenin. This would have the dual impact of grounding the enemy pilots and stopping their support for the enemy forces.

The moon set at 4 a.m. Chetwode's 20th Corps and Bulfin's 21st troops made their last-minute adjustments to weapons and gear. They were to attack on a 13-kilometre front between the railway and the coast to confront an enemy less than two kilometres away. A smash-through would open the gap for the cavalry.

By 4.30 a.m. the first fingers of dawn crept over the Judean Hills. The big gun symphony began with 300 artillery pieces blasting off in a 15-minute bombardment. The second-most important day (after Beersheba) in the battle for the Middle East was underway involving 540 guns, 12,000 horsemen with either sabres or bayonets, and 57,000 soldiers carrying rifles.

The infantry of the 20th and 21st Army Corps stomped off on time. The cavalry and light horse waited. They were travelling light. Most took rations for two days, which in itself was an indicator. This mission was more than a raid but expected to be less than a protracted battle, if the intelligence Allenby and Chauvel had received was accurate. Many horsemen discarded groundsheets and greatcoats, although some retained them knowing that it would be freezing in the heights at night. Most blankets, tents, horse rugs and any 'surplus' kit were left behind.

When the Turkish trenches were penetrated, the cavalry would pour through the breach first led by Barrow's 4th Division and MacAndrew's 5th Division consisting of yeomanry and Indian regiments armed with lances. The 4th would thrust north towards Liman von Sanders' HQ. The 5th would cut through a pass towards Samaria and then Nablus, 70 kilometres north of Jerusalem and 80 kilometres in from the coast.

They would be followed by Light Horse from the Australian Mounted Division, including a brigade of Australian and New Zealand companies, a remnant of the Imperial Camel Corps, and a Scottish Horse machine-gun squadron.

Chauvel had to wait for the result of the first few hours knowing that engagement would begin within the first hour. At 7.30 a.m.

he strolled from his tent at Sarona to a pool in a nearby valley and had a relaxing morning swim. He had prepared painstakingly and had left nothing to chance as far as was possible in a project full of imponderables. The mission—to have his force ride 80 kilometres in a day to a key Turkish communications centre and rail junction at El Afule—was simple enough on paper and allowed him flexibility.

Just after he arrived back at his tent, he learnt that the British infantry in four hours had broken through the Turkish 8th Army, leaving a massive breach in its trench defences on the Plain of Sharon. It was the chance for the contingent of cavalry then the Light Horse to ride through and swing north-east with Chauvel following in a 50-vehicle convoy. His corps was under instructions to avoid the fight on Sharon and to move at speed to make sure that the Turkish 7th Army at Nablus to the east was well south of them by the afternoon.

This was a moment the Light Horse revelled in. Their advantage of mobility was marked, and the sleeping enemy would be unaware for hours that a mighty cavalry force was striding north of them and heading for a vital centre.

The intelligence that Allenby relied on was accurate. Barrow and MacAndrew encountered no opposition through the narrow passes that led south of Afule. But Liman von Sanders' force had been alerted. At dusk, a captured Turkish officer informed Barrow that an infantry brigade heavily armed with machine-guns was marching 12 kilometres south from Afule to block them at the 23-kilometre, shallow, stony pass at Mus Mus.

It was now dark. Barrow and his Australian chief of staff Colonel W. J. Foster galloped ahead of their long column, moving two abreast, to urge the leading brigade to speed up its movement through the dangerous, tight pass. It moved up from an elevated ridge, which rose from 100 metres above sea level to 400 metres.

Troopers were forced sometimes to ride then walk single file. One slip would see a horse tumbling into an abyss. Here and there, the troopers took some of the load off their horses and carried it themselves to make sure the mount could be eased through.

The aim was to be well clear of Mus Mus before the enemy arrived. At dawn the entire 4th Division was almost through and moving onto the Esdraelon Plain at Megiddo, the Armageddon of ancient times. This was the site that St John predicted in the Book of Revelation would host the last great battle on earth. For the moment, the plain was a mundane Bedouin grazing area. From a century earlier, it had been a non-combative wheat growing district.

The 4th Division reaching it coincided with the 5th Division moving closer to the coast, hitting the plain of Abe Shushe (25 kilometres south of Haifa).

The vanguard of the 4th Cavalry was just onto the plain when it ran into the lead battalion of the Turkish force sent to intercept it. The enemy began deploying its column and machine-guns. The British leader of the Indian 2nd Lancers bringing up the rear (of the 4th) made a decision to charge. Before either side could think, the attack was on. The Indians, wielding their lances, crashed through the unsettled Turkish lines, wheeled around and attacked again, using their frightening weapons to devastating effect.

In a few minutes, they had killed 46 soldiers and taken 476 prisoners. The first engagement of the big attack had been a resounding victory.

During the battle, Liman von Sanders was still asleep at the predominantly Arab town of Nazareth 30 kilometres away to the north-east. He knew about the British army's smashing through of his 8th Army and its retreat. But he believed there was a buffer of his own infantry and cavalry that would block any significant further advance.

He half-expected possible setbacks, but not so fast.

Chauvel and his convoy reached Megiddo early on 20 September and made it his HQ. He used wireless communication and contact with the air force to keep in touch with the various Light Horse forces on the move. When the morning fog lifted, he could see Nazareth in the distance. Chauvel was quietly yet definitely religious, and the thought of capturing the town in which Jesus Christ spent most of his life excited him. So did the prospect of taking Liman von Sanders, the most senior German military figure in the Middle East.

But there were no gloating or even expectant remarks in his letters written at the time. His experiences touched his deep beliefs, although he kept his thoughts private. Chauvel did not see himself as a latter-day crusader. Yet he was very conscious of the importance of victory and what it would mean to his Light Horse, especially those who had been at Gallipoli and had experienced the dark days. Thoughts such as those, buried but not forgotten, spurred on every commander and trooper.

Nothing but a complete rout of the enemy would do.

The 13th Cavalry Brigade's Brigadier General P. J. V. Kelly led his men towards Nazareth, but took his time. He stopped at each village en route and scoured it for Turks, picking up the odd surprised soldier and adding him to a growing group of prisoners. At dawn on 20 September, he reached the outskirts of the city nestled in a hollow plateau between two 500-metre-high hills at the southern point of the Lebanon mountain range. His men and horses were exhausted after riding for 20 hours over 80 kilometres without rest from Arsuf on the coast north of Jaffa. His decision to divert to search in the small towns en route drained the energy of his force and affected his own decision-making as he entered the city.

Wearing pyjamas and armed with a torch, Liman von Sanders rushed from his headquarters when told by a breathless officer that 'the British cavalry' had entered the town. He yelled for his driver to bring his car. The chauffeur awoke to his commander's bellowing and obeyed. Then the German commander-in-chief scurried back to his rooms to dress and grab some vital papers, which he stuffed into a satchel. They drove off, the chauffeur being ordered to put his foot down. The exits seemed blocked except for the road north to Tiberias, on which they scurried away.

Kelly erred in not blocking off every road out of Nazareth. He built his prisoner numbers up to 1,200 and searched the buildings until they found Liman von Sanders' HQ. There the 13th Brigade collected important papers that the German commander had not had time to grab in his haste to depart. Plenty of booty in the form of cars—a fleet of Mercedes among them—and a big cache of arms, was gathered. Reluctant members of Liman von Sanders' staff led the captors to an abundant stock of champagne and sweet wine.

The 5th Cavalry Division's MacAndrew arrived a few hours later and was disappointed to hear that Liman von Sanders had managed to flee. Yet he accepted Kelly's argument that his squadrons were depleted and exhausted after the arduous day.

MacAndrew commandeered one of the fleet of Mercedes and was driven south to report to Chauvel.

Chauvel had Afule in his safekeeping. He was aware Nazareth had been taken. But he wished to know about Liman von Sanders. There had not been any word either way. Had he been taken? Perhaps he had been killed. Maybe he had escaped. Chauvel wanted this biggest of fish netted and was concerned that no news was bad news.

That aside, he was feeling confident. The two target towns had been taken with the lightest of losses. The infantry, still some distance away, was progressing without serious opposition. He could safely report back to Allenby that he had achieved his mission. It had taken 30 hours.

Without waiting for further directives, Chauvel ordered Barrow to move at once on Beiran, 24 kilometres east of Megiddo. With two of the enemy's three armies in disarray, Chauvel knew

without higher reference to strike on. He called a midday conference at Afule and arrived at 11 a.m. Impatient for news on
Liman von Sanders, he decided to drive on to Nazareth. Coming
his way was a large Mercedes. Chauvel was excited. Was someone bringing him the trophy of Liman von Sanders? Much to the
Australian's chagrin, only MacAndrew alighted from the vehicle.

Chauvel was furious to learn that Liman von Sanders had
escaped. The British commander gave his quick report. Chauvel
quizzed MacAndrew and established that Kelly had been tardy
in his approach to Nazareth. His biggest mistake was not to
have his squadrons surround the city.

Chauvel had been used to his Australian and New Zealander
commanders barging into places such as Beersheba and Es Salt,
sometimes too recklessly. They never would have dallied in villages wasting energy and time. Nor would any of them have
failed to surround a town and secure every exit. He didn't vent
his displeasure at MacAndrew, but he would report to Allenby
the detail of this 'failure'. He predicted the chief would be deeply
aggrieved. Capturing Liman von Sanders would have been the
individual prisoner coup of the Middle East war.

There was little doubt Kelly would lose his command.[1]

Missing the German commander had no impact on the progress
of the war. By the evening of 20 September the British infantry
divisions were marching relentlessly towards the retreating Turkish armies that were being pushed east. The Royal Flying Corps
and the Australian Flying Corps were bombing and strafing them,
making life uncomfortable even if there was no major conflict.
Chauvel's self-imposed directive now was to cut off the Turks
and round them up. He controlled the communications and his
squadrons were eager in pursuit. The Turks, without leadership,
fatigued and underfed, were providing little resistance.

Chauvel was more confident than ever before in the war. On
the evening of 20 September, he took time to correspond with
Sibyl.

'I have had a glorious time,' he said. 'We have done a regular

Jeb Stuart ride . . . I am writing from a hill close to Lejjun [Meg-
iddo] overlooking the plain of Armageddon [Esdraelon] which
is still strewn with Turkish dead "harpooned" by my Indian
Cavalry early this morning.'[2]

From his tent door he could see Nazareth, Mt Tabor, El
Afule, Zerim (Jezreel), Mt Gilboa and Jenin. He told his wife
of MacAndrew's success at Nazareth without mentioning the
escape of Liman von Sanders, which would have not passed the
censor.

'Barrow took Efule with nearly 1,500 prisoners having got
into them with the sword,' he added, 'for, tell it not . . . to Curly
Hutton [Chauvel's former army mentor], I have armed all H's
[Hodgson's] lot with that weapon at their own request! All this
miles behind the enemy's front line through which B. [Bulfin]
made a gap for us on the coast and which he and P.C. [Philip
Chetwode] are now attacking.'

Chauvel also reported that it was the first time in the war the
cavalry had managed to get through a gap in the enemy lines.

'I am feeling very pleased with myself,' he said. 'No time to
write more darling.'[3]

This was near-euphoria for him. For someone so circumspect,
this mood was a clear indication that the war had swung his way.

59

Enemy Collapse

Ross Smith, fighter/bomber pilot and reconnaissance
reporter, informed Chauvel that a 10,000-strong enemy
infantry force was marching towards the town of Jenin
15 kilometres south-west of Megiddo. The advance guard of

the Australian Mounted Division had just reached him after coming 90 kilometres in 22 hours, which meant no sleep for two days and nights. After watering, feeding and a brief rest, Chauvel ordered Wilson and his 3rd Light Horse Brigade to ride to Jenin to intercept the Turkish force. This brigade and the 4th were almost over-keen in their exuberance. They and the New Zealanders had taken the mounted lead in the Sinai and Palestine. They were not impressed with following either the Indian Lancers or the British cavalry on this, the most massive and definitive attack of the Middle East war. Chauvel had held them back, calculating that the toughest fights might occur in protracted battles after the first day. He had proved clever in holding strong, fresh reserves for the coup de grace, as seen at Beersheba and Romani. The same strategy on a far broader scale was in play in these 'Megiddo battles'.

An added factor was the desire of these brigades to use their swords for the first time. Wilson unleashed his 9th and 10th Regiments for the ride to Jenin. The Notts Battery clattered its way with them, while the 8th Regiment remained as a reserve and to protect Megiddo.

Arthur Olden, who had been active at Es Salt in the last important Light Horse mission of late April and early May, was temporarily in command of 10th Regiment. It had been given the honour of leading the advance at a steady 16 kilometres an hour, with the 9th Regiment bounding along as a flank-guard. After covering about five kilometres of fairly even, cultivated ground, with 'only crab holes and countless stinging hornets to mar its perfection as "real cavalry country",' it had to step up its pace to make Jenin by dusk.[1]

They encountered a small Turkish outpost half-way to Jenin at Tannuk. It was dealt with by the 9th, which caught up with the 10th as it reached Jenin just before sundown.

An enemy force of more than 1,000 soldiers was encamped in olive groves to Jenin's north-east. Lieutenant P. W. K. Doig with a troop on the right flank of the vanguard, was assigned to attack. Swords were drawn. Doig led the charge straight into the camp of Turks. After a few of the shocked enemy had been wounded, the rest surrendered. The footsore soldiers, looking gaunt and weak, were in no shape to fight, especially after realising they were being assaulted by Australian 'cavalry'. Doig organised the taking of the entire force, which included 300 Germans, and 400 horses and mules. The enemy prisoners were marched to the rear and handed over to a troop of the 9th Regiment. Doig then assisted the advance on Jenin by picketing the heights on the right flank.

Wilson did not stop for this swift action. He moved his main troop body forward, swept around Jenin and closed the roads leading out north and east. The 10th then moved into the town from the north as darkness settled. Seeing the columns galloping in, with the troopers' swords drawn, the Turks surrendered. But German snipers and machine-gunners in some of the houses made clear their intention to fight. The Australians moved fast and efficiently, pinpointing the places from where they were being attacked. They moved in their machine-gunners from Captain G.H. Bryant's squadron. A firefight ensued. The defending Germans decided to try to escape but were cornered by the machine-gunners and surrendered.

The Australians reflected that although they had rushed to reach Jenin before sunset, the fact that they had entered the town in semi-darkness, which soon faded to black, had worked in their favour. The enemy's impression was a large force, especially with the horses thundering in, the troopers wielding swords and the quick deployment of machine-gunners.

In reality, Wilson had just 280 troopers. They captured 3,000 Turks and Germans, 90 per cent of whom were armed. The attacking force moved so fast and brusquely in rounding up this big group of prisoners and herding them out together in the town that they had no time to assess the imbalance of the forces.

The collapse of Jenin's defenders was the signal for 'countless hordes' of Bedouins that appeared from everywhere to commence looting the stores of food, clothing and equipment. The narrows streets were soon blocked. All transport was brought to a standstill.

'Men, women and children,' Olden wrote, '. . . [were] all the time screaming "Arab! Arab!" as if that was the password with the "Inglese" to permit them to rob and pillage.'[2]

The Australian force did not have the numbers to stop the mayhem. Not even firing rifles and pistols over the heads of the rioting Bedouins could prevent the frenzy. They were hamstrung by the orders to keep the peace with the Arabs at all times. The regiments were not about to enforce anything. A guard was placed over a Turkish hospital in the main street, which was overflowing with sick and wounded enemy soldiers, along with two brave German nurses. Troopers tried to put out a fire of ammunition and bombs at the train station two kilometres south of the town. They gave up, allowing the bullets to fire off and light up the night sky.

Wilson was confident that the Turks were unlikely to make a stand. He placed the 10th Regiment on the Nablus road. R. R. W. Patterson, a 23-year-old Victorian grazier with the machine-gun squadron, was sent with two guns and 23 troopers to support it.

The moon had disappeared leaving the area in pitch black apart from the occasional ammunition dump fire. Patterson moved out on the road well ahead of the regiment. The small contingent of troopers had been on the road a few minutes when 21-year-old Western Australian contractor, T. B. George, dismounted and put his ear to the road. He signalled for his good mate Patterson to do the same. They could hear the muted tread of feet coming their way. Within two minutes, the crunch of the marchers was audible on a road that narrowed between hills.

Patterson was in two minds. The oncoming force sounded considerable, perhaps a few thousand enemy soldiers. He could turn and go back to the 10th and alert them. Or he could stop and fight.

'Let's try to bluff 'em,' George whispered, 'get 'em to surrender.'

Patterson thought it might be too late to retreat anyway. He spread his men on both sides of the road in elevated positions seconds before the 3,000-strong force of Turks and Germans came close.

Patterson called for his gunners to fire over the heads of the enemy. The head of the column halted in fear and confusion. They could not scramble easily up the hills. They could fall back or charge forward. Patterson yelled for a ceasefire.

'You are outnumbered!' he blustered, 'I call upon you to surrender!'

There was a silence among the enemy commanders, then an urgent conversation. A woman called out in English. She suggested they meet on the road. Patterson wished to know who she was. The woman replied she was a German nurse travelling at the front of the column with the commanding officers. She said that she spoke for them.[3]

Patterson summoned his considerable courage and walked onto the road, meeting her half-way between the forces.

Keeping a stern manner, he informed her of his 'superior' force. He demanded that her side should give up and avoid a massacre, knowing that it would be his tiny contingent, outnumbered 100 to 1, which would be slaughtered if a firefight ensued. The nurse dutifully passed on his conditions to the enemy commanders. They conferred and decided to surrender. Patterson ordered them to lay down their arms and to march on to Jenin.

This was the most audacious bluff of the Middle East war. It indicated that the enemy was so demoralised and hungry that they had little interest now in making a stand.

None of the 60 Australian light horsemen left in Jenin that night had any sleep. They spent a nerve-wracking time minding close to 6,000 enemy troops, including many high-ranking Turkish officers and 300 Germans. All through this ordeal, the ammunition and bombs at the train station fire continued to explode. It intermittently lit up the black, moonless sky and made the Australians' hazardous guard activity a fraction easier. Yet the sporadic illumination worked against them too. The Turks could see the small number of Australians on duty. They realised they had been duped. Disgust turned to anger as they were rounded up in the town's only sizeable square. Four machine-guns were trained on them. On three occasions, groups thought they might try to escape. Each time the troopers mounted and waded among them, swords at the ready. This managed to quell any serious mass attempt to break out.

The weary guards were pleased to see the dawn. Wilson did a count of his prisoners and the booty, including five artillery guns, 12 machine-guns, two planes, and a wagon loaded with £250,000 worth of gold and silver coins.

First light also attracted the local Arabs. They swarmed in along all tracks to Jenin with their women, donkeys, mules and carts, loaded them up and departed. The Australians were unhappy about the Arab men letting their women bear the burden of every kind of weighty 'trophy' while they drove the animals off into the morning heat. But the troopers had long ago stopped forcing the men to carry things. They had to accept this custom so alien to their own culture, where the men did the heavy lifting.

An hour after dawn on 21 September, the 8th Light Horse took the massive haul of prisoners to an ancient prison at Megiddo. Dysentery had taken its toll in recent weeks. Malnutrition and dehydration were further weakening enemy soldiers. They begged for water, which the troopers could not spare. Soon their ranks were swollen by other prisoners taken by George Onslow's 5th Brigade on the west side of the Samaria ranges.

Only half of the Turkish 7th and 8th armies were left. They struggled on a north-east track across mountains to Besain, which lay 25 kilometres from Jenin and just eight kilometres from the Jordan. Their fate as a force to be reckoned with was sealed by the relentless air force. The No. 1 Australian Squadron did the reconnaissance and spotted the long column of enemy transport and soldiers following the tracks along the valleys. They used wireless radio to let the various British aerodromes know of the targets. Within minutes British pilots were aloft carrying full loads of bombs destined for the retreating enemy lines.

Inside an hour, they located the main Turkish force plodding along. It had just entered a gorge when six British and Australian bombers climbed down low towards them. They dropped their loads and strafed the cars, lorries, horse-transports and troops as they swooped. There was an immediate traffic jam as the planes turned and made their runs over the hapless troops, who could not surrender even if they wished to. The air force was relentless and pitiless. As soon as they ran out of bombs and ammunition they hurried back to their bases to refuel and reload. With hardly a few minutes break, a new wave of planes dived at the enemy convoy. There was nowhere to hide or take cover, except under the transport, which was targeted and destroyed.

Many of the pilots, showing a lust for killing and a desire to finish the opposition once and for all, made up to four separate attacks during the morning massacre. Even those enemy infantrymen who made dashes through side tracks and gorges were hunted by the 'sky demons'. Some Turkish soldiers were still unfamiliar with planes and believed they were sent by Allah as retribution for past transgressions. Many of those who did escape the air attacks and scrambled their way towards Besain were confronted by Barrow's yeomanry and Indian lancers, whose weaponry was the dread of all those who faced it.

Among those on the run from the Australians was 7th Army leader Mustafa Kemal. The wheel of fortune had come a full turn, as it was apt to do in war. The Australian mounted rifle-men had been under siege at Gallipoli from Kemal and his Turks, and had been lucky to escape. Chauvel and thousands of troopers had been among them. They had been humiliated. Losing was not part of the Anzac psyche. But the no-win finish on the peninsula had forced acceptance of failure. Now, close to the Jordan, Kemal and his Turks were feeling the pressure of defeat, hounded on the ground by the Light Horse. They were being harassed from the air by pilots such as Ross Smith, P. J. McGinness, and Wilmore Hudson Fysh, all Gallipoli veterans who had swapped horses for Bristols.

Kemal had been one of the first away from Jenin when he knew the Light Horse was bearing down on the 7th Army base. He was better off alive and leading than dead or captured. Kemal was aware that complete defeat was imminent but while there was not wholesale surrender, it was his duty to do what he did best: command.

At the Jordan, he steadied the rump of his rattled army. The British cavalry and Light Horse were closing. The Turkish and German soldiers wanted to cross the river and keep running. Kemal waited until most of them were over it, especially at the 14th century Bridge of Jacob's Daughters. While other commanders urged him to make the dash over the muddy waters, Kemal, cool as ever, realised that if that three-arched, grey bridge was blown, it would slow their pursuers enough to enable them to make Damascus. If the bridge was left open, there would be a danger that the remainder of his army would be caught and cornered on the stony path to the Syrian capital.

Kemal could see the British 11th Cavalry Brigade in the distance coming at the double from one direction, and closer still the 10th Light Horse from another. The commander began running, calling for his German demolition crews to set the charges, and for the machine-gunners and Turkish soldiers left stranded to halt the Light Horse. He was barely over to the east bank when the first arch collapsed. He was up the slope when the second went and out of sight when the 500-year-old monument collapsed.

After a bloody fight, involving also French colonial Spahis, who had arrived in support of the Light Horse and British, the Australians sent out two flanking squadrons to look for a place shallow enough to cross the river. It was evening. Darkness was coming fast.

It took an hour before a local directed them to a shallow enough spot. The Light Horse began the tricky manoeuvre. The water was freezing and the current was strong. The leading horses and men were half-way across when German machine-gunners opened up. A few were hit; four men were swept away. But it was not the Nek. They kept coming. The gunners saw they could not stop them and ran.

It was dark when the Australians reassembled on the east bank. They had to dry themselves and their mounts and settle them down. Many of the horses were unhinged by the crossing. They would not drink or feed. There could be no mounted attack on the rearguard of Germans and Turks on the east bank the next morning.

The 10th Light Horse would have to wait.

Chauvel and his corps still had work to do west and east of his base at Megiddo. He sent a small force to take the port of Haifa, which the air force had led him to believe had been evacuated by the enemy. But the force was met by a strong artillery and machine-gun defence. MacAndrew was then sent to clean up. He too met stiff resistance. He ordered the Indian Lancers and the cavalry to charge and they broke through. Haifa and nearby Acre were secured.

Chauvel turned his attention east again to the battles on the Jordan. In the early morning of 22 September, Chaytor's New Zealanders took Jisr ed Damiye from the Turkish 4th Army. A Jewish Battalion cleared the west bank. Most of the enemy 4th had crept away in the night east of the river aware that the British force was squeezing them from the north coming down from Besain, and from the south (Chaytor's international force—Australians, New Zealanders, Jews and West Indians) coming up from Jericho. The north-south pressure was on a front of 25 kilometres and closing. The only enemy option was to pull back east to Amman.

The Turkish 4th Army headed towards Amman and the Hejaz railway even though it was aware that Lawrence and the Arabs had cut them off from the main junction at Deraa. The Turkish commanders now had to hope the railway could be rebuilt and their force could join up with the 4,000 soldiers in the town and 6,000 more at Maan. This was the vague option or plan, now wishful and turning wistful. Enemy communications had broken down everywhere.

The chance for consolidation and any form of solid defence was slipping away.

60

Beyond Armageddon

Major Lawrence goes out with a few of his dusky cut-throats and a few camels loaded with guncotton and blows up trains and the line to Mecca. The Arabs stop him in the street to kiss his robes.

Australian Flying Corps pilot Lieutenant Stanislaus Nunan, 1918

Chauvel held the plain from Haifa on the Mediterranean coast to Besain a few kilometres from the Jordan. The 7th and 8th Turkish armies had been broken and there was little impediment to an advance to Damascus. Yet there would still be resistance elsewhere. The rumps of the 7th and 8th and the retreating 4th Army, which was on the run, would provide it, especially if they were able to link up. Chauvel's 20,000 horses employed on the mission had enjoyed some rest and plenty of water in the past day or two and the local Arab threshing-floors supplemented the horse-feed. There were no major problems with transport. Most of the men were still fit and well. The air force ruled the skies. Casualty figures were not complete, but Chauvel was relieved to learn he had lost no more than 60 troopers in the past 72 hours of hectic engagements on a wide front and over a large territory. This was a remarkably low figure for such a wide-sweeping action by several prongs of the light horse and cavalry, which had already resulted in the dislocation of two enemy armies. A combination of a brilliant strategy and tactics, and the weakened condition of the impoverished enemy were responsible for the result.

Chauvel was in high spirits when Allenby arrived at Megiddo on the morning of 22 September.

'How many prisoners have you taken?' was one of the chief's first questions.

'15,000,' Chauvel replied.

'No bloody good to me!' Allenby replied with a laugh. 'I want 30,000 from you before you're done!'

At that moment, the chief was well-pleased with the outcome of these battles.

His next question was: 'What about Damascus?'

Chauvel was all in favour of taking it and confident it could be done. But Allenby gave no orders concerning the main prize. A move on that city would depend on developments in the next few days.[1]

That final coup was very much up to Chauvel's judgement, and the chief's order when it was imminent. The first steps were to direct Hodgson to seize Semakh and Tiberias on the Sea of Galilee and then take the important nearby bridges of the Yarmuk River.

Lawrence, who had conferred with Allenby just before Chauvel, flew back to his base south of Umm Tayeh on the morning of 22 September in the observer's seat of an Australian Flying Corps Bristol. It was accompanied by two other planes, one flown by Ross Smith. The airmen, fresh from their 'kills' in the gorges approaching Besain, were eager to engage German planes in the Deraa area, which was now the last frontier of the Middle East war. The three planes and Lawrence were greeted by thousands of Arabs who cheered and waved weapons near the makeshift landing strip.

It was 10 a.m. and the airmen were just in time to join Young and Kirkbride for breakfast of porridge and fried sausages. The discussion over the meal was all about the success of the cavalry and infantry in the western plains and hills; how the Jordan was almost secure in British hands; and how the Turks were descending on Amman and pushing out from there.

All these men were excited. The enemy was in chaos and on the run. The war was reaching a climax. They were interrupted by a report that German aircraft were in the area.

Ross Smith and another Australian pilot, Lieutenant E. S. Headlam, put down their food and stood up.

'Our Australians,' Lawrence wrote in *Revolt in the Desert*, 'scrambled wildly to the yet-hot machines and started them in a moment. Ross Smith with his observer [Lieutenant E. A. Mustard] leapt into one and climbed like a cat up the sky.'

The enemy craft were two Pfalz scouts and one DFW two-seater. The enemy turned for home as soon as they spotted the two Bristols.

'Ross Smith fastened on the big one and after five minutes of sharp machine-gun rattles, the German dived towards the railway line. As it flashed behind the low ridge, there broke out a pennon of smoke and from its falling place a soft dark cloud. An "Ah" came from the Arabs about us.'

The plane crashed at Mafraq, killing one German on board. The Australians then set it alight, making sure it would not enter the fray again. Five minutes later, Smith and Headlam landed their planes.

'Ross Smith . . . jumped gaily out of his machine swearing that the Arab Front was the place [now that the German Air Force was defeated near the coast]. Our sausages were still hot; we ate them and drank tea.'

Smith told Lawrence he wished he could stay in the area with an enemy plane every half hour but after breakfast he had to go back to the west to pick up his big Handley-Page bomber. He would then bring back a load of petrol, food and spares for the Arab front, which was where the action would be from now on.[2]

Just as he finished eating at 10.30 a.m., his remark about German planes coming every half hour proved prescient. Three more Pfalz scouts were reported in sight. Ross Smith and Mustard once more dashed for their plane. Retrieving the Handley-Page would have to wait. They soared aloft again and pursued the German machines, which were forced to ground. Two landed near the railway and ran along the ground to Turkish forts, which they hoped would provide some protection. The Australians chased the third to the well-defended Deraa. Smith and Mustard turned around and went looking for the two Pfalz scout planes. The Australians strafed them from close range, pumping 50 rounds into each.

Smith and Mustard flew back to their base on the coast. Observing their departure, the Germans attempted some retribution for the morning's attacks. In the afternoon another DFW (biplane) two-seater flew low and bombed Lawrence's camp. Lieutenants Peters and J.H. Traill took off to engage it. They flew close. Traill pumped his Lewis gun at the lumbering enemy machine. It faltered and began to smoke. The Germans made an emergency landing near the aerodrome. Fulfilling air combat etiquette, which was uncompromising, Peters dipped low and made a run over the stricken plane seconds after it came to a halt. The German pilot and observer were attempting to escape the plane before its fire spread. Traill let go gunfire, killing the two enemy airmen.

Smith returned later in the day with the Handley-Page. The Arabs lining the airstrip welcomed it in with even more enthusiasm than the Bristols, cheering and firing their weapons. Much to Lawrence's joy, the next morning another AFC Bristol dropped 16 bombs on the Deraa aerodrome. This attack set a hangar on fire, obliterated two DFWs, and disabled two others. After this softening up, Smith was airborne in the Handley-Page, heading for Deraa. He throttled back as much as he dared, dipped to 1,000 feet and swung in low over the aerodrome and the station, depositing nearly a tonne of bombs with great accuracy and to devastating effect.

Every enemy plane and all the stores at Deraa were destroyed.

This attack decommissioned Deraa as a junction of importance for the rest of the war and ended the activities of the German air force based there.

Commander Grant of 4th Brigade was sent to Semakh, a small village of mud huts 1.5 kilometres from where the Jordan entered the Sea of Galilee (Lake Tiberias), to take on a German/Turkish defence there. Planes had seen troops evacuating by motor launch on the lake. Grant took his machine-guns, and part of the 12th Regiment and the 11th. The latter had been on reserve at Beersheba and had to observe its brother regiments gain legendary status for the most daring charge of the war. The 11th's troopers were highly motivated to make their own reputation as they trotted along by moonlight in the early hours of 25 September.

They arrived just before dawn and were met by heavy machine-gun and rifle fire from the enemy force. No-one knew its strength or the nature of the terrain they would have to cross in the dark. Grant had two choices. He could wait until he had more support, which would mean he had to take the town in daylight. This would mean high casualties. The alternative was to charge immediately, in the Beersheba manner. Grant had no time to weigh his options.

He decided to act.

This move would be regarded as either brave or foolhardy after the event. He lined up the machine-guns on the left and sent forward an order to Colonel Parsons, who bellowed:

'Form a line and charge the guns!'

The 11th Regiment troopers drew their swords for the first time in conflict. The Aborigine Frank Fisher was one of the forward scouts. Parsons was leading the main body of troopers. A squadron commander, Major Costello, was close behind. His squadron would be first out, followed by a second led by 55-year-old Major J. Loynes, a fearsome Boer War veteran. A minute after the order, they galloped straight towards the flashes from the guns. At first, this attack seemed easier than Beersheba as they overran machine-gun nests. Fire from the railway station and other stone buildings 1.5 kilometres away quickly disabused the attackers of any thoughts of a walkover.

As the chargers drew closer, several horses went down in the rough terrain's potholes. Others were hit by the fire that intensified as the defenders—Germans and Turks—realised the force of the charge. The wall of bullets caused the troopers to split. Loynes swung to the left at the village. Costello moved right of the troublesome station, from which the gun flashes were coming. Most defenders were in the buildings, but some were concealed in rail trucks and carriages.

This was the most dangerous time for the troopers; their vulnerable moment. They could be picked off by snipers and machine-gunners shooting from windows down into the streets. Several troopers and their mounts were felled. Loynes swept around and ordered his squadron to dismount and head for the station. He picked out a drain and a stone fence running along it and ordered his squadron to dash for the position, just 20 metres from the station.

A firefight went on for an hour. No-one could gain the advantage until Grant's machine-gunners moved in close and focused on the windows being used for enemy fire. They soon hit their targets. The flashes from the buildings diminished. The German members of the defence in all positions could see they were losing the fight, despite outnumbering their opponents two to one. They began passing round liberal amounts of rum. This fortified their spirits. They began to throw hand grenades, not with great accuracy, but still enough to cause the troopers trouble.

It took the mature, headstrong Loynes to lead a charge at the main station to break the impasse. His men battered down the door. They filed in wielding bayonets and swords and pursued the enemy in the darkness into every room. The Germans scrambled up the stairs. They were stalked 'from floor to floor and room to room' until everyone was killed or captured.

Outside, the surviving enemy soldiers made a run for the railway line east. The chasing troopers brought them down with Hotchkiss fire. About 30 Germans rushed for the lake. They scrambled onto a motor launch pursued by the gunners. The launch took off, but not before the gunners by the lake let loose, hitting the boat. It caught fire. Only one enemy soldier survived. He could be seen swimming for the shore and dashing off.[3]

This fight was one of the bloodiest since Chauvel's cavalry took off six days earlier. Fourteen Australians were killed. So were 61 horses with another 27 wounded. The enemy had 98 killed. Another 365 prisoners were taken, 150 of them German.

The increased number of Germans at Semakh indicated a forward defence for Liman von Sanders, who had been at Tiberias, another 7.5 kilometres north and on the east of the Lake.

But after his embarrassing experience at Nazareth, the enemy commander-in-chief had long since fled the area.

By the same day, 25 September, Chaytor's Anzacs had shoved the 4th Army east beyond Amman, captured the city and snared the enemy force's rearguard, taking 2,500 Turkish, German and Austrian prisoners. Chauvel directed them to hold their gains, then to attack the Turkish force of an estimated 6,000 soldiers coming up the Hejaz railway from the garrison at Maan, 190 kilometres south. The enemy had fought off the Arabs from there for months. Now cut off from supplies, they were compelled to come north in the hope of joining other Turks from the 4th Army.

It was a forlorn hope. The weakened force was in no shape for a prolonged battle. Their main concern was the marauding Arabs, who they knew would massacre them if they could without regard for the conventions.

Young visited Lawrence's tent in a camp at Nuwayma at midnight on 25 September and suggested that the Arabs should be taken out of the war and retired to the Druse Mountains. They had done their bit, he said. They could wait until the British took Damascus.

Lawrence would have none of it. He wanted the Arabs to be seen to take Damascus. It was what he had entered the fray

for in the first place. A lot was at stake now, not the least factor being Lawrence's own integrity. He had promised the Arabs
Damascus. He wanted to deliver it, no matter how cosmetic the
act.

Young had played along with Lawrence's whims and aims,
knowing of his strong relationship with Allenby. In the military
adviser's mind, the main objective was for the British to take
Damascus. Yet he understood Lawrence's sensitivities and position. He did not press the issue. The Arabs would move on at
the same time as Chauvel's front-line cavalry/light horse force
to Damascus, where all the issues about control and ownership
would culminate.

The next day, Young and Lawrence, with four Arab tribes,
including Auda and the Howeitat, blew up bridges and took
forts, prisoners and weaponry, including big guns, as Turkish
resistance disintegrated in every direction.

Just as the Arab regulars and non-regulars swarmed north on
26th September, Chauvel motored to Jenin for a conference
with Allenby. The chief asked about the Desert Mounted Corps'
state-of-play. Chauvel told him that two of his divisions were
hovering at Nazareth and Tiberias. The third, led by Barrow,
was crossing the Jordan as he spoke. Chauvel had given him
orders to take Deraa and link up with the Feisal's Arabs, who
would come under his control with the final step in mind: a
drive up the stony, old pilgrims' road to Damascus. This was
the longer route into the prized city. The aim was for Chauvel,
coming by a shorter route north, to be there with the rest of his
corps at the same time as Barrow.

Chauvel intended his corps to travel 'light'. The transport,
including lorries, would be left behind to speed movement.
When rations and forage ran out, the troopers would live off
the land.

His only reservation was how the Arabs would cooperate.
He had been let down by the Beni Sahkr in the second attempt
to take Amman. With this in mind he had given Barrow specific

orders that he and his 4th Cavalry Division would take charge of them.

Allenby approved the plan.

Chauvel wished to be clear on how he was to handle the 300,000 population of Damascus. Allenby had not informed his Mounted Corps leader, the most important field commander in the war, about the secret Sykes–Picot agreement. Chauvel had heard vague rumours about it. They had not concerned him until now he was about to take the capital. It was not his role as a soldier to immerse himself in the politics.

'What should I do about the administration of the city?' he asked.

'You know what we did in Jerusalem,' Allenby replied, 'Do exactly the same. Send for the Turkish vali [civil governor] and tell him to carry on, giving him what extra police he requires.'

Chauvel was aware of this. He had taken plenty of villages in the last two years. But he knew there was more at stake. He probed further.

'What about these Arabs? There is a rumour that they are to have the administration of Syria.'

'Yes, I believe so,' Allenby said, evasively, 'but that must wait until I come.' There was a pause and the chief added:

'If Feisal gives you any trouble, you are to deal with him through Lawrence, who will be your liaison officer [with the Arabs].'[4]

Chauvel thought these orders were 'sketchy' and very un-Allenby-like. He was to go off with the vague hope of meeting up with Lawrence before entering Damascus. If he did not, Chauvel would have no guidance on how to deal with the Arabs in what he was certain would be a shambolic, even chaotic situation, which offended his ordered military sensibilities.

On 27 September the squeeze on the enemy was apparent. Ross Smith dropped Lawrence a note telling him that Chauvel's advance cavalry led by Barrow was just 25 kilometres away at Ramtha. An estimated 8,000 Turks in two parties were now converging between the British and the Arabs around Deraa. These were mainly enemy troops from the defeated 7th and 8th armies, which had been pushed east from Besain to Lake Tiberias.

Despite being fatigued and on edge, Lawrence savoured the moment. It was what he had longed for.

Lawrence, Nasir and Nuri decided to direct their regular Arab contingent to tackle the smaller Turkish force of around 2,000, which was close to Mezerib, and the fort Lawrence had already dealt with. The bigger enemy force would be harassed by the horsemen of the Rwalla and Huaran tribes, who would track, flank and surround them like a huge pack of hyenas.

Lawrence's aim was to defeat this smaller force. There was talk of 'taking no prisoners', which would always be the Arab way given the history with the oppressors and the desert culture of the tribes, who had no use for prisons or prisoners. Lawrence tacitly approved of this approach. He did not favour a massacre, nor would the other British military advisers, especially as enemy prisoners could be passed to the British army. But he turned a blind eye to the increasing brutality. In the climactic days of the Middle East conflict, there were no guarantees that the Arabs, massing more every day in their thousands, could be stopped from doing what they wished.

Lawrence for one, would not try.

Retribution

Lawrence, Auda, Nasir and Nuri and their Arab regulars reached the outskirts of the village of Tafas north of Mezerib on the afternoon of 27 September. Blue smoke swirled from houses. Shots and bursts of fire punctuated the otherwise still and hot atmosphere. The Turks began to file out in an orderly manner; guards of lancers at the front and rear. The force was flanked by machine-gunners. The transport was in the centre of the column with the most protected vehicle being that of Djemal Pasha, Syria's military governor.

The Arab artillery boomed out, catching the Turks' rearguard force by surprise. Its commander panicked and ordered the massacre of the villagers, including 40 women and 20 small children.

With the enemy distracted, Lawrence and a troop of Bedouins on horseback moved down a track to the village. They were met by a little girl of about four running away. One of his bodyguards, who happened to be from Tafas, dismounted and reached out as she fell into his arms. Her dress was bloodstained from a lance wound in the neck. The child tried to wriggle away, screaming, 'Don't hit me Baba!' before she collapsed and died.

Lawrence and the troop rode on in stunned silence until they reached a point just outside the village where the massacre had taken place. The bodies of the women and children lay where they had been lanced, stabbed and shot.

A few wounded Turks wandered into their path. They were shot at point blank range. The troop galloped on. They were in sight of the departing Turkish column under fire from the Arab artillery. It was too much for Talal, a sheikh of the village travelling with the troop. He cried out, spurred his mount and charged straight for the retiring Turkish column. Lawrence went to follow, but Auda restrained him. They watched on helplessly as Talal, screaming his own name, was mowed down by enemy machine-gunners.

A few moments after this suicide act, Auda said with force:

'We will take his price!'

The Arabs attacked the rearguard force, which had been scattered by the artillery fire, while Jamal Pasha in the main body slipped away on the horizon. One section of the rearguard defended by Germans and Austrians could not be broken. The Arabs turned their attention to two other sections and broke through.

'In a madness born of the horrors of Tafas,' Lawrence wrote, 'we killed and killed, even blowing in the heads of the fallen and the animals; as if their death and running blood could slake our agony.'[1]

The massacre seemed out of hand when 250 Turkish, German and Austrian soldiers surrendered, only to be machine-gunned to death. Lawrence and an Arab officer tried to stop the slaughter, but could not.

Fred Peake and his camel detachment arrived on the horrific scene a short time later. Lawrence, appearing disturbed by the bloodthirsty hysteria, asked him to restrain the Arab killing and to protect the other enemy prisoners. Peake ordered 100 troopers to dismount. They were marched into Tafas with fixed bayonets. This sobered the Arabs, but they still had a lust to kill. Many of them rode after the main retreating column only to find that its soldiers were prepared to fight. The Arabs fell back. Many of them felt justified in their frenzied slaughter after the Turkish killing in the village. British officers were now concerned for enemy prisoners as they increased in number as the conflict drew to a close.

Could the vengeful Arab tide be held back? Lawrence did not seem to think so. Despite the debacle at Tafas, he appeared to let events take their course without interference.

It was a major problem too in the south near Maan. The Turkish force of 6,000 had left the garrison. They had run out of supplies, food and water and were forced to make an attempt to join up with their other armies floundering in the north.

Early on 28 September, this rogue force was reported by a British Bristol pilot to have reached Ziza, a few kilometres south of Amman. He flew low to observe the Turks hurrying to dig trenches. They were being hounded by a swarm of an estimated 10,000 Arabs on horseback and on foot. They prowled wide of the Turks, not prepared to take on the rifles and machine-guns, but content for the moment to encircle and harass with yelling and firing their rifles into the air.

The pilot dropped a note into the camp for the Turkish commander warning him that Chaytor's Anzac force controlled the region and all its water and food. There was no point in putting up a fight. Their plight was useless. If he did not surrender, the pilot concluded, the camp would be bombed in the night. The message here was clear. After such destruction, chaos would rule. Then the Arabs would move in.

There was no response from the Turks. The pilot informed Brigadier Colonel Donald Cameron of Anzac's 5th Regiment and prepared to join a bomber force to attack the Turks in their camp that evening.

Cameron had further intelligence that the Turks were so weak they could not fight. He sent two squadrons of Queenslanders to explore the enemy situation and to see if there was any chance to negotiate a surrender. The easy approach by the troopers gave clues. There were many enemy soldier stragglers in the region. They had broken from the ranks in a desperate search for food and water. The troopers gave a couple of stragglers sustenance in exchange for finding them the enemy commander, Ali Bey Wahaby. A meeting was arranged with Cameron.

At the rendezvous, the Turkish commander said he was prepared to surrender. But on looking around at the few hundred Australian troopers on horseback he was not ready to capitulate and give up arms to such a small force. He feared that once he did, the Arabs would then massacre his men. He would only give in to a British contingent big enough to defend his unarmed men against the Arabs.

Cameron assured Wahaby that this would be arranged. In the meantime, his two squadrons would stay with the Turks. Wahaby still would not lay down arms. Cameron was forced to agree that they could keep them while they were technically under Anzac control.

He was anxious now to prevent the air raid.

Cameron sent a telegraph message to Chaytor asking for urgent reinforcements and to make sure the aerial bombing was not carried out. The air force could not be reached. Cameron improvised by sending a dozen of his troopers into the camp to lay out ground signals for the air force to make sure no bombs were dropped. But there was no guarantee that the signals would be understood or even picked up. The prevention of the raid was no certainty, Wahaby was informed. He just shrugged. Reflecting the general attitude of many of the Muslims regarding the likely outcome of the war, he said:

'It is the will of God.'[2]

The Australians, less convinced of divine intervention, did all they could to prevent an attack from the skies. Chaytor was kept fully informed. He realised the gravity of the situation, especially with such a massive haul of prisoners, whose lives were now in his hands. He ordered Ryrie to round up as many of his troopers as possible, then motored to meet Wahaby himself before they arrived. The enemy commander tried to convince Chaytor to stay away while the Turks fought the Arabs. The Anzac leader would not have been tempted by this option, no matter what his sentiments, but he did understand the Turks' predicament.

Chaytor had a division to run. He left the area, telling Cameron to pass on his order to Ryrie to sort out the problem.

Ryrie was informed his mission was urgent. He left the pack-horses behind and led his support squad at the double, arriving just before dark. He found the Turks in the trenches fending off the Arabs, with the Australian troopers grouped to one side awaiting orders.

To the relief of all, Cameron had received a message that the air force had called off the bombing raid. That left Ryrie with some difficult negotiations with the Arabs and Turks. He first met two Arab sheikhs. They urged him to wipe out the Turks, saying they would fight with the Australians. Ryrie was wary. His experience over three years in the desert campaign was that the Arabs were more inclined to loot than fight.

He then consulted Wahaby and his Turkish commanders. They again tried to convince him to let them destroy the Arab force. But like Chaytor, he would not countenance such a solution. The Turks pointed out that the darkness would cause the Arabs to close in. Would he stand by and let the Turkish force be attacked, possibly wiped out?

Ryrie believed the Turks were his prisoners, and therefore his responsibility. He would not like a repeat of Lawrence's experience in the north where Turks were massacred. The Australian weighed his options and decided that the Turks could keep their arms. His troopers would join the Turks in their camp and stand by in support if needed.

Ryrie, accompanied by six armed troopers, had a second meeting with the two sheikhs. The articulate, no-nonsense brigade commander remained on his horse, saying he wished to be brief and was too busy to dismount.

Ryrie eyeballed the sheikhs. He said he wished to make it very clear that the Turks were his prisoners. He was obligated to protect them. His men would be in the camp with them. If the Arabs invaded during the night, Ryrie said he would hold the sheikhs responsible.

The sheikhs asked indignantly what would happen if the Turks attacked *their* men. Ryrie said he was in charge and that would not happen. He paused and reiterated that if the Arabs invaded, their leaders (the sheikhs) would be held responsible. They would be arrested and executed.

With that chilling remark hanging in the air, he bid them good evening and galloped off.

Pushing Barrow

Lawrence arrived in a hurry at Deraa in withering heat. First, he wished to be ahead of the British force all the way to Damascus and he needed to learn Chauvel's plans. Second, Barrow and his cavalry were closing in on the town, under orders from Chauvel to take it, not realising the Arabs had already done the job. Lawrence feared there could be disaster. He knew Barrow and his mounted swordsmen would not be able to distinguish between Arabs in the pay of the British and tenuously on their side, and those controlled by the Turks. Under the circumstances, Barrow could be expected to attack and ask questions later.

Lawrence and an Arab regular took a huge risk in riding out on camels to meet the general, galloping through the cavalry lines. The British were expecting to fight. They were prepared for it. An Indian machine-gun post challenged him and took him 'prisoner'. Lawrence was flustered. He tried to convince them he was a British lieutenant colonel with an urgent need to see Barrow. As they spoke a squadron of Bristols swooped low over the road to Deraa and bombed a contingent of Arabs led by Nuri Said. Lawrence was furious. He ignored the Indian gunners and rode on through the lines. He was next confronted by a troop of yeomanry, who were ready to kill.

'I'm Lawrence,' he said, his manner impatient. 'Where's Barrow?'[1]

He was shown to a British officer who directed him to the British general. Barrow listened to Lawrence's emphatic pleas. Barrow had his orders from Chauvel, which had been endorsed by Allenby, regardless of Lawrence's claims. Barrow was taking Deraa, no matter who was in there.

'. . . my head was working at full speed,' Lawrence said, 'to prevent the fatal first steps [of a British attack] by which the unimaginative British' made an error that could undo all Lawrence's work over the past two years.

Lawrence, ever the intelligence analyst, had 'studied Barrow and was ready for him'.

A few years earlier the general had published an article in which he elevated 'fear' as the key motive for 'common people' in war and peace. This set Lawrence's mind against the general, who was short with him.

'I find fear a mean, over-rated motive,' Lawrence wrote, 'no deterrent, and though a stimulant, a poisonous stimulant, whose every injection served to consume more of the system to which it was applied.'

For his part, Barrow was hostile to the Arab need to massacre their opponents. He had been educated (as Chauvel had) to offer surrender where possible, and if accepted, take prisoners and treat them fairly. This was the British and Australian way. Barrow and Chauvel were horrified at the Arabs' desire to kill to the last man, no matter if they had surrendered or not.

Lawrence's close association with the Arabs was regarded with suspicion by the generals in the field such as Barrow and Chauvel (not to mention some, but not all the rank and file). It made them wary of him, especially as he seemed to approve of the Bedouins' propensity to slaughter. They did not appreciate Lawrence's acceptance of a culture whose members fought outside the conventional, and who had felt oppressed and used by the Turks for hundreds of years. It was payback time as if the current Turkish masters were responsible for every atrocity visited upon them over the centuries.

An edgy discussion with Barrow followed in which Lawrence, tetchy and fatigued, attempted to explain the situation. The general was not happy with reports and evidence of Turks being massacred in Deraa. He censured Lawrence for allowing it. Lawrence pointed out that the Arab irregulars were not part of the British army. They were not under his direct control, but that of Nuri Said. What he did not tell Barrow was that he was the overall motivator, organiser and key strategist for the revolt. Yet when it came to the point of these heavy engagements with the enemy, he did not have control in the field. He still defended the Arabs' actions, citing the Turkish massacre of Arab villages, about which Barrow knew nothing.

Any other officer challenging a general like this would be in trouble. But Lawrence's reputation had long preceded him. In effect, he had the same power as the general, albeit unofficial, because of his record, his influence with the Arabs and his personal connection to Allenby.

Barrow intended to surround the town and take charge of it. Lawrence said his Arabs, who were on the British side, were already running it. Barrow talked about inspecting the wells and getting them functional. Lawrence explained that his men had already done that. The general turned his thoughts to the railway, on which he had specific orders from Chauvel. Speaking as if he were a commander-in-chief, Lawrence claimed his Arab engineers already had this up and running.

As irritated as he was, Lawrence kept his manner civil. He was telling Barrow that he was superfluous at Deraa, which, if taken the wrong way would have offended the general. Instead, as the tense conversation progressed, Barrow realised the Arabs were in charge. Lawrence had the muscle, and therefore, in the general's eyes, the mortgage on any local 'fear' if he wished to exercise it. Once Barrow weighed the situation he realised he would not have to expend men and resources in fighting the Turks.

Lawrence felt he had 'won' a mental battle, one of his motives being to make sure the Arabs, not the British, took all the credit for acquiring Deraa. Newspaper reports to the world would reflect this. They would help create the impression, which Lawrence desperately wanted, that the Arabs were winning the war against the Turks. The British forces were just there to help out. In fact, the War Cabinet supported this. It made sure the censor stopped any other perspective or report being published.

The general, Lawrence noted, 'surrendered himself by

asking me to find forage and foodstuffs'. The tension between them eased. Lawrence turned on the charm, as only he could do when he wished, with flattery and encouragement. Barrow responded. He was a good soldier, with the attitude of a subtle bully, although he would never countenance the butchery that had occurred in and around Deraa, no matter what the revenge or 'fear' motive. Instead of blustering his way into the town, he moved with his entourage at a walk and stopped in the town's main square in front of the burnt serial (town hall). Lawrence pointed out Nasir's silk flag hanging from the balcony. Barrow threw his shoulders back and saluted it, much to the pleasure of Lawrence, and the Arab officers and men.

A relieved Lawrence had also overcome a problem that could have ended his dreams and plans right there in a nightmare fight between the trigger-happy British force and a combustible Arab army. He had been the most prominent and passionate 'educator' of his army leaders in the way they should treat the Arabs to get and keep them on their side for the push to Damascus. They had almost done their job in the east of the Middle East battle zone, holding up, harassing and now defeating their former Turkish masters. Much of this was due to Lawrence's juggling act. He had managed to keep all his options open, turning this near-catastrophe into a minor diplomatic triumph.

As night fell on 28 September, the Australian troopers south of Amman filed into the Turkish camp in one of the most extraordinary moments of the war. They were outnumbered about 10 to one and felt vulnerable. But the Turks, grateful that the Australians were not leaving them to the Arabs at night, welcomed them. These two fierce foes, who had fought each other for three and a half years since Anzac Day 1915, sat down together at camp fires. They exchanged food. The Australians handed out cigarettes. After a short time, there was laughter and attempts to communicate. The Turks managed to express their admiration for their long-time enemy, and the Australians reciprocated.

Those Turks in the trenches exchanged machine-gun fire with

the Arabs during the night, but there was no attempt by them to close in. Ryrie's blunt warning had been heeded.

Dawn broke. Tensions eased. The Australians stayed in the camp and had breakfast with the Turks. Then the New Zealand Brigade arrived at 8 a.m., swelling the number of Anzacs to the point where Wahaby felt comfortable about giving up all his weaponry.

The Arabs stayed clear as the 6,000 surrendered Turks were marched out of the camp and on to Amman.

The 29th was exhilarating for Lawrence. He had surmounted the problem at Deraa. He was ready for the ride to Damascus, his two forces, British and Arabs, in harness and harmony on a grand scale for the first time. Barrow's cavalry had marched out early with the Arabs under Nasir on their right flank. Lawrence had waited patiently at Deraa for Feisal, coming from Azraq in his Vauxhall car. After a brief meeting, Lawrence drove off with Stirling in their Rolls-Royce Blue Mist driving along the tracks of the disused French railway.

They caught up to the cavalry. Lawrence, always ready to make others believe he was a very speedy camel jockey, borrowed an animal and rode up to Barrow, who was with some of his men watering their horses at a stream.

At Deraa, Barrow, like most horsemen, had shown contempt for the camel. He did not expect Lawrence to keep up with him.

The general was amazed that he appeared to have ridden so far so fast.

He asked Lawrence where he intended to spend the night.

'In Damascus!' Lawrence said. Before Barrow could say he should see Chauvel about that, Lawrence was riding away chuckling to himself after fooling the general.

Lawrence and Stirling caught up with Nasir's Bedouin cavalry and Nuri's Rwalla. They had never stopped pressuring the larger Turkish column that had done its worst at Tafas and had been too big and fit there to tackle, despite the destruction of part of its rearguard. But that was two days ago. The Turkish troops had not had any major food replenishment and their physical condition was deteriorating. The Arabs stalking and hounding them had reduced their numbers. Auda, the most ruthless jackal of all, was ahead of the column gathering Bedouins for an ambush.

Lawrence, now the guerilla general with his tactical brain working overtime, instructed Auda, Nasir and Nuri to slow down the plodding Turkish column. He then raced back to the yeomanry and its horse artillery and convinced them to hurry up to the Turkish rear and attack it. Hammered now from behind, the enemy force began to fall apart. Hundreds fled their transport and guns and headed for the hills in the east.

Auda was there waiting to deal with them as they reached their hoped-for refuge at night.

'The old man [Auda] killed and killed, plundered and captured until dawn [on the 30th] showed them the end,' Lawrence wrote.

Barrow's force was still fighting the bulk of the depleted 4th Army, having agreed with Arab commanders to move up the west of the Hejaz railway while they moved east. He was in no hurry especially as his cavalry had to pick their way north looking but not finding the path taken by pilgrims to and from Mecca. They passed abandoned Turkish equipment surrounded by hundreds of bodies, the carnage from the Arab attacks on the vanguard of the 4th Army.

It was only a matter of days before this nemesis of the Arabs over two years would not exist.

A City in Turmoil

D amascus was in chaos. The Arabs, who had been waiting for this moment, stopped their subservience towards the Turks and were hostile to their 'rulers'. There was even rebellion in the ranks, with Turks and Germans attacking each other over the desperate need to acquire transport out. Gunfights began over the governor's fleet of Mercedes cars. Liman von Sanders had fled days earlier on the way, 320 kilometres to Aleppo in Syria's north.

His last notes on the town mentioned how the Arabs had become threatening; the city unruly:

'Armed bands of Arabs arrived there daily, which though they did nothing but arrange fantasies and fire into the air, formed an ominous element in the city . . . [It] was full of Sharif Feisal's agents who incited the population. The four-coloured flag of the sharif was displayed from many houses. Baggage trains were tangled in the streets. More and more Turkish soldiers left their ranks and scattered through the city . . . there were fires at the station at Kadem, terminus of the Hejaz railroad, and the German depots there.'[1]

Liman von Sanders was trying to organise the dwindling remnants of the 7th and 8th armies outside Damascus. Mustafa Kemal had straggled with the survivors of his 7th Army into the city, but was on his way out again. First he had planned to head west to Beirut, but learned Chauvel was moving to block the road. Now he was left only with a push north. He had decided to give up Syria and form a line of defence in front of the Turkish border, with Aleppo the last major town in the north to be defended.

On 30 September, Feisal's flags increased in number, poking from many buildings. Messages about Arab rule and freedom were hung from many balconies, which in the past would have received swift punishment. Now the Arabs were openly defiant. No-one was pretending any more about how they felt about the Ottomans. The worst aspect of this was the abandoned hospitals. Thousands of wounded and sick Turks were left without medical or any other kind of help. With no sanitation and clouds of flies, many were dying in the wards and corridors.

Djemal Pasha, well protected by a strong armoured force, had managed to make it back to Damascus. The Turkish military governor let the city's leading citizens know he was departing this time for good. In an orderly act, he passed his temporary control to Emir Said al-Jezairi, grandson of the Sultan of Algiers. He was pro-Turk. His record in standing up to imperial European powers was well established. In the late 19th century, he had created the nationalist movement in his country, which had been annexed by the French. He had defied them for 15 years before being captured and sent into exile in Damascus. These credentials were the reason Djemal Pasha favoured him. The Turk would rather leave a Muslim in charge, someone who opposed the British and French, the two powers with covetous eyes on Syria. Emir Said would not be looking for a short tenure. He was ambitious as was his brother Abdul Qadir, who Lawrence always suspected was a spy, especially after he dropped out of the assault on the Yarmuk River bridge in November 1917.

Chauvel disagreed with Lawrence. He did not think Qadir was a spy and regarded him as 'definitely anti-Turk'. But he had no use for the Hejaz Arabs either. Chauvel thought him a closet French supporter, despite his claims that he was 'anxious to see the British in control of Syria'.

Chauvel believed that he and his brother were still drawing 'the huge subsidy granted by Louis Napoleon in 1852 to their grandfather', when he agreed to live in Turkey and stop disturbing the peace in French North Africa.

Given Lawrence's hatred of the French, this would explain his questioning of the brothers' bona fides. In reality, he may well have seen them as French rather than Turkish spies. In either case, viewed from Lawrence's prism, they were active against

British interests. Chauvel, who had nothing against the French, was more sympathetic to the brothers.[2]

The connections of Lawrence and key Arabs such as Feisal, Nasir and Auda had been slipping into Damascus and were plotting to take control when the chance arose. But with the turmoil, all these key figures would need to be there to sort out the conflicting interests.

After this handover of power, Djemal Pasha made his hurried departure from Damascus just as the big guns of Chauvel's approaching Australian Mounted Division became audible.

At 8.50 p.m. on 30 September, a Turkish troop train left Damascus, with soldiers and other passengers forming a desperate throng on the roof and hanging from the sides of carriages.

It was the last one for the night.

At the same time, the Australian Mounted Division was on the city's outskirts. In what had become a conventional move, Chauvel had ordered his troopers to begin to block every road out. Hodgson's brigades were sent to bar the way north to Homs, Hama and Aleppo. MacAndrew and his 5th Cavalry Division had been instructed to leave operations against the crushed 4th Army to Barrow and to move up in support towards Damascus. Chauvel, marching north from Kiswe towards Damascus, directed MacAndrew to detach a brigade to cut off a rogue Turkish force, which had been spotted by an Australian pilot. The 14th Brigade of Indians and yeomanry were selected. It galloped into the Turks with lance and sword, destroying the main part of the force. The commander and staff of the Turkish 3rd Cavalry Division was among the big haul of prisoners. It was a fitting end. This outfit had not once in the entire campaign taken on Chauvel's Light Horse. Before Beersheba, they stayed clear of them.

After Beersheba, the Turkish cavalry was never seen until this humiliating capture.

Chauvel asked Hodgson to cut the road west to Beirut, which ran through the tight, vulnerable track of the formidable Barada Gorge with its massive overhanging rocks and steep cliffs, green, yellow and brown by day, black and forbidding at night. Any force attempting to escape, no matter how well equipped, would be no match for the Light Horse, who would make clear their capacities as riflemen. They would dominate an unfair fight. Wilson's 3rd and Macarthur-Onslow's 5th Light Horse Brigades positioned themselves in vantage points on the cliff-tops overlooking the V-shaped, 100-metre-wide gorge. It wound between near vertical mountains of the Anti-Lebanon range's eastern buttress. The waters flowing from the mountains, which were snow-capped until June, formed the Barada River, which crisscrossed the narrow path. The road and rail route to Beirut via the Lebanons was carved along its banks.

The brigades were engaged from mid-afternoon with a column of about 4,000 enemy soldiers, including hard-fighting German machine-gunners, who were attempting to escape Damascus by heading west. The Germans operated from the top of trucks and trains. They were defiant but no match along the gorge for the Australians, who held the heights. The Light Horse machine-gunners raked the pass, causing mayhem and confusion. The trapped Turkish/German force could not move forward. Their vehicles could not turn back, especially with the line of trucks, vehicles and horses behind them in the slim pass. They could not take refuge either side of the road. There was no way of challenging the Australian snipers and machine-gunners by clambering up the cliffs. They would be even easier targets if they attempted to claw somewhere near the heights.

The enemy was forced to turn back to Damascus, but was caught in the passage of death. There was nowhere to hide from the incessant rain of bullets from above. The ease of the slaughter took many minds back to 19 May 1915, when

10,000 Turks attacked Monash Valley on Gallipoli without artillery support and were picked off as if, one digger put it, at a 'wallaby hunt'.

The light horsemen fired until their weaponry was too hot to handle. By nightfall the column in the gorge was still.

'All night long continuous fire was maintained,' Olden of the 10th Light Horse wrote of an unnecessary precaution, 'sweeping the head of the Gorge . . . making it practically impossible for any living thing to escape.'

No enemy troops entered the gorge in the night. About 700 of those trapped became casualties, he recorded. There were also the hundreds of animals killed, including camels, horses, mules, donkeys, sheep and dogs.

'Truly,' Olden concluded, 'the net was fast closing on the doomed city!'[3]

64

With Swords Drawn

Chauvel gave orders to Hodgson to begin the city's encirclement at first light on the morning of 1 October. Hodgson chose Wilson's 3rd Brigade for this mission.

Allenby, playing along with Lawrence's scheme, which suited both for reasons common to them and otherwise, sent crisp orders to Chauvel, who passed them on to all his commanders:

'No troops are to enter Damascus unless absolutely forced to do so.'

Brigadiers were directed to arrange posts on all the roads to make sure this was adhered to.

This would ensure that the Arabs, led by Feisal, would be seen to be first into the city. Allenby and Lawrence hoped it would be a case of first in, best dressed, but not quite in the black and white way some Arabs did. It was widely thought among leading Syrians that whoever entered Damascus first would have the best chance of ruling Syria. This belief had spread when, in June, Mark Sykes released a document, virtually a clarification of the Sykes–Picot agreement, to seven leading Syrian exiles in Cairo, who were making claims in anticipation of taking over once the Turks were forced out. In short, this group felt they would be entitled to any territory they 'conquered' from Turkey in the war. This so-called 'Declaration of Seven' had no binding clauses in law, but in the build-up to the Turks' defeat and banishment from Syria, its effect was electric. The thought reached fever pitch in the minds of acquisitive Syrians, who saw all sorts of riches, wealth and power emanating out of them being in Damascus and making claims at the right moment.

Allenby had not been consulted on the extra Sykes declaration and viewed it as unauthorised. None of the key leaders of the revolt had been party to it.

Allenby's aims on behalf of his government were more limiting for the Arabs and subtle. He wanted to make it seem as if the Arabs had taken Damascus. This would lessen French rights to the country, which was his government's wish. It would also increase Britain's chance of major influence.

Lawrence's thoughts were in accord with Allenby's over the French. But he fervently hoped that the Arabs being first in would lead to their control of Syria as a 'Brown Dominion' as he called it. In other words, Syria would be like a Canada or Australia in terms of British influence. They were both former colonies. Lawrence's creation would bypass the colonial era in this country and move straight to stage two as a dominion. He hoped the strong link forged by him with the Arabs would mean also that the French would not get a look in, in spite of the Sykes–Picot agreement, which had handed them Syria.

*

The 3rd and 5th Brigades spent the freezing night of the 30th in the hills above the Barada Gorge. Those not engaged in super-fluous firing on the beleaguered and silenced enemy force were kept awake by the one-sided battle and fireworks of exploding ammunition dumps, which the enemy had set to destroy as they departed.

Wilson noted the instruction to keep out of the city. He sent out scouts to reconnoitre all exits and a way across to the north. They rode out from the conquered Barada Gorge and found the track crossing south-west to the ancient caravan route to the Jordan, Judea and Egypt. They also discovered the path south: the old pilgrims' road to Mecca via Deraa. But they could not find a track around the city to the north.

Wilson had no option but to go through Damascus itself.

There was a considerable enemy garrison in the town, and intelligence reports spoke of the Arabs' 'excitement', which could mean anything in terms of responses to foreign troops. No-one knew how the Arabs would react. Were they still under Turkish/German control? Would they be forced to defend the city against invading horsemen? This job required the best of the best.

Wilson in turn decided that the hardened, brilliant 10th Light Horse Regiment, which had experienced so much against the Turks all the way from the Nek, would be the brigade's advance guard.

Just before 5 a.m., Arthur Olden, second-in-command of the 10th Regiment, ordered the A, B and C squadrons—400 horse-men (half the size of the force that took Beersheba)—to saddle up. It was still dark. Most of them had not slept much with the noise coming from every direction around their bivouac near the gorge. Yet still these troopers were ready. Olden sensed that this could be *the* moment of his career, if not his life. The Ballarat-born son of a Swedish mining agent had given up his dental practice to join the Western Australian Mounted Infantry in January 1913. He had enlisted in the AIF in October 1914 and embarked for Egypt in February 1915 as lieutenant with

C Squadron, 10th Light Horse Regiment. He landed at Gallipoli on 20 May and was wounded twice in May and July. Olden had 'survivor's guilt' for being spared because he missed the carnage at the Nek when his fellow troopers were butchered. This fact above all others drove him on in the Middle East conflict. An element of revenge propelled him. But more than this, he remembered the hundreds left where they fell in that suicidal attack. He should have died on that totally exposed, tiny killing-ground. It nagged deep in his subconscious, and would forever, he thought, even if he survived the war.

Olden, promoted to captain then major early in 1916, was detached to other units for most of the Sinai campaign, but his mind was never far from the 10th. His record and the respect he had throughout the Light Horse allowed him to be placed back with the Western Australian Regiment for the attack on Beersheba on 31 October 1917. Olden assumed temporary command when the regiment's two senior officers were wounded in the failed incursion across the Jordan from 30 April to 4 May 1918. Fate seemed to be pushing him to greater challenges and dangers. But he felt less a sense of self-preservation than most. He believed he should have been left with his mates at the Nek. Every battle was a bonus. An instance was his direction—as second-in-command—of a dismounted bayonet-charge by the 8th Light Horse against a sizeable Turkish stronghold guarding Es Salt. He was never in two minds about what should be done. This decisiveness reached his men. There was nothing reckless about Olden's tactics and style. He planned well and measured caution against daring. Consequently, his troopers attacked with the confidence and certainty of invincibles.

Eight days earlier on 22 September, the 10th, with temporary Lieutenant Colonel Olden up front and commanding, led the Australian Mounted Division in the encirclement of the Turkish armies in Sharon and Samaria. He captured Jenin with a brilliant charge by just one squadron. In a 48-hour operation, he took 8,107 prisoners and five field guns. This earned him the DSO.

It was no surprise that Wilson went to him for the lunge at Damascus, even though he knew Olden and his men would be fatigued after the all-night massacre of the Turks. They would ride on adrenaline. None wanted to miss the moment. They saw their assignment as a great honour. It could be the culmination of the regiment's much longer journey that began in Cairo early in 1915, and was sidetracked to the hell of Gallipoli before it returned to Egypt, refreshed and reconstituted by early 1916. From there, the regiment had ridden through the Sinai, then Palestine and now Syria. The troopers had experienced many hardships, which were compensated by regular 'wins' along the way until this final, major 'event'.

Olden and his troopers did think in terms of war as a sport, although not quite the 'point-to-point' that Lawrence accused them of sarcastically after the war (in a different context). Their contests were less like steeplechasing and more like football grand finals, or even boxing contests. The only difference was that in their 'matches' not just injuries were expected. Death was part of the competition.

This regiment, and all those that had been at Gallipoli, had a terrible start. Only a complete victory, where the enemy had been obliterated, would salve some of the pain suffered and memories of mates killed. Winning, to the Anzacs, had been part of their character and make-up when they joined as callow youths. Now after three and a half years for the longest serving of them, it was nearly everything. They had put up with privations that would have surprised even the hardiest before they began the journey. The act of seeing the fight right through to the last round was their motivation to carry on.

This regiment of 400 men and 400 horses was perhaps the prime example of an assassination squad. They believed they had no peer in this war or any other. The troopers behaved and performed as if it was beyond debate, yet rarely with boast or bluster. Instead there was a clinical, laconic professionalism about their work when they went on patrol or an assignment.

Lawrence, always the analyst, observed them from the air, on horses and on the ground, in action and at play over two years. He noted: 'These Australians, shouldering me in unceremonious horseplay,' he wrote, 'had put off half civilisation with their civil clothes [presumably he would have appreciated them more in Arab garb]. They were dominant to-night, too sure of themselves to be careful: and yet:—as they lazily swaggered those quick bodies, all curves with never a straight line, but with old and disillusioned eyes: and yet:—I felt them thin-tempered, hollow, instinctive; always going to do great things; with the disquieting suppleness of blades half-drawn from the scabbard. Disquieting: not dreadful.'[1]

Even these hardened troopers were excited at the prospect of the next day, 1 October.

The oasis between the mountains and the desert, set in bleak surrounds on two rivers, was now the key city in the Middle East war.

Olden and his 400 were on the ride of their lives. They intended to conquer Damascus.

65

The 10th 'Conquers' Damascus

The 10th Regiment's three squadrons began their advance by descending from the steep hills to the Barada River where they watered their horses. They then crossed the river and headed for the Dumar station where a train had drawn up. The horsemen of the lead squadron drew their swords and charged round a bend in the road. About 800 Turks were crowded close, hoping to board the train. They were called on to surrender, which they, and all on board, did. The Australians looted the train, finding four chests of gold and silver coins, which were commandeered. There were also boxes of cigars. They were not Cuban but German and of a good enough quality to entice many of the troopers to light up. They rode off puffing and pleased with the fruits of the diversion early in the mission.

A troop was left to guard the prisoners and the advance continued.

The troopers, en route to Damascus, were blocked on the road at the head of the gorge by the carnage created in the night by the two Australian brigades. Human and animal bodies and broken transport littered the way and the regiment had to clear a path. The troopers cursed, chomped on their cigars, dismounted and began the unappealing task under occasional fire from hidden snipers in the gorge. They carried wounded enemy soldiers to the river bank where they would be picked up by ambulances. The dead were put on one side of the road. They made an eerie sight as the first hint of dawn slid over the gorge. Wounded animals were shot and dragged clear, leaving enough space for the column to move on.

At the next turn, the troopers could see the tips of Damascus's minarets, sparkling in the day's first light. They began the direct ride to the city and its spread of green gardens, made even more colourful by flowering fruit trees. The cool orchards included jasmine, whose aroma along with the whiff of the citrus flowers was sharp and pleasant in the crisp autumn air along the 30-kilometre, half-hour ride to the city.

On the left was the gorge. On the right was the river and the railway separated from the road by a high stone wall. On the right after 500 metres were military barracks on the other side of the river. The horsemen could see a big body of troops, estimated at 12,000, in the parade ground. Some gathered with rifles by the wall. Others disappeared into the building. These were Mustafa Kemal's troops. They looked bedraggled and disorganised. But even in their sorry state, had he been there they may have rallied to take on this modest invading force. Yet this was not Gallipoli. The commander had slipped away on the road to

Homs, just avoiding the road blocks set up by the Australians.

The troopers drew swords at the sight of lifted Turkish rifles. But they were not fired on. Olden ordered them to keep their column formation. Riding at the front, he lifted their rating to a gallop, which brought up a shroud of dust, and created a rumble like rolling thunder that was heard in the city. It drew crowds into the streets that had been alive during the night. The Light Horse eased back a fraction. There was no target, no opposition. But the momentum of the initial move kept them thrusting forward, almost as if they were inviting an enemy to emerge. None did. Damascus was in turmoil, not from military confrontation, but because of expectation mingled with fear.

The troopers reined in their mounts and placed swords back in scabbards as they neared the city centre. Hundreds of Arabs in different types of garb approached. They were not hostile but exuberant. The Australians were seen as the long-expected and awaited 'British' troops, who were liberating them, and who would make sure, they hoped, that the Turks would never come back. Some in the crowd revealed the identity of their allegiances. There were the rugged Druse from the Hauran mountains; uniformed gendarmerie; European-suited Syrians (including some of the 60,000 Christians living in the city of 300,000); Jews, Greeks, Armenians and even some Turkish civilians. They were excited. Rifles were fired into the air. The Australians, unaware at first that this was not hostile fire, reached for their revolvers.

The column followed the road onto a bridge that crossed the Barada River near the Victoria Hotel. They had to force a passage through the throng as it surged close. The Australians were in no mood to acknowledge men and women trying to touch them and their horses. They were alert and grim. They had not expected a festival. Nor had they expected the enemy to have fled or be impotent.

They made a path through the crowded streets to the serial. The steps were busy with officials and well-dressed locals. It was not yet 6.30 a.m. but there was more activity than any midmorning. Olden halted his column. An interpreter was called for. An official stepped forward.

'Where is the Governor?' Olden asked.

'He waits for you in the hall,' the official replied.

Olden and three lieutenants dismounted and drew revolvers.

They were led up a marble staircase to the governor's salubrious antechamber. The little party walked in and holstered their revolvers as they were in the presence of various officials and important locals in their robes. They stood as Olden and Co. burst in. It appeared to be a solemn, important moment. Emir Said, loving the pomp, was sitting on a high-backed gold inlaid chair in front of a conference table. He was wearing a suit and tarboosh. He looked dignified and quite pleased with himself in his rule of Syria and its capital, which had been his for less than a day.

Officials approached Olden. They stood in the centre of the room. They asked Emir Said to come forward. The Australians realised they were in the middle of something rehearsed and ceremonial. In the mind of Emir Said and his brother Abdul Qadir, this official handover would legitimise their power in the city and the 'nation', no matter how it was to be constituted post-war. If the 'British' accepted Emir Said's position, and then protected it, he would truly be in charge.

Emir Said reached to shake hands with Olden. Speaking in Arabic, which was translated, he said:

'In the name of the City of Damascus, I welcome the first of the British army.'

The Australian was handed a document which began:

'You are the first British Officer to enter Damascus, in the bravest manner known of the Saxon race . . .'

He would have preferred the paper to have said 'Australian' rather than 'British' officer. He was bemused by the reference to 'Saxon race' which to him was uncomfortably close to a description of at least part of the enemy. But he was in no mood for editing such niceties. Nor did he have the time.

Olden informed Emir Said that the city was surrounded by Chauvel's troopers, which was no bluff. Resistance, the Australian said, was futile.

'Does the city surrender?' Olden asked.

'Yes. There will be no further opposition in the city.'

'What then, is all the firing in the streets?'

'It is the civil population welcoming you.'

'Who are all the uniformed men in arms?'

'They are gendarmerie. What are they to do?'

'They may retain their arms for the present, prevent looting by the Arabs, and otherwise maintain order.'

Olden paused as Emir Said digested the information and nodded. Then Olden added:

'As for the shooting in the streets, issue orders that it must cease immediately, as it may be misunderstood. You will be held responsible for this.'

'You need not fear,' Emir Said replied, 'I will answer for it— that the city will be quiet. We have expected the English here and have prepared for them.'[1]

Olden demanded that he write out his surrender. The governor was being most agreeable, deferring to the new military ruler. By doing so he thought he was keeping his job. He then began a speech in Arabic. The other Arabs present applauded often. Olden put his hands up and asked him to save it for the more appropriate commander-in-chief, Allenby, who was expected later. This surprised the assemblage. Emir Said pointed to a table of food and drink. Olden declined the offer. He had to hurry on to the Aleppo Road north in pursuit of the enemy, a thought which would have galled the new governor much more than the rejection of refreshment, given that the Turks had commissioned him.

Olden asked for a guide. Emir Said turned to Zeki Bey, an Armenian, who obliged this request. The Australians bid their farewells. They were not quite certain of their status as conquerors of Damascus and Syria. But at that moment, technically at least, A. C. N. Olden was the next in line after some great names in history including Egypt's Rameses II, Greece's Alexander and France's Napoleon.

Undaunted by such exalted historic company, Olden and his men hurried down the steps to their waiting column of troopers, who had not dismounted. A huge crowd now squeezed around the town hall to witness the event and get close to the new rulers. A huge cheer went up when Olden and Co. emerged.

'The march now assumed the aspect of a triumphal procession,' Olden noted, 'the dense masses of people rapidly becoming hysterical in the manifestations of joy.'[2]

As dawn began to settle on Damascus at 6.45 a.m. on 1 October, the populace viewed the horsemen as their saviours and emancipators. 'They clung to the horses' necks, they kissed our men's stirrups; they showered confetti and rose water over them; they shouted, laughed, cried, sang and clapped hands.'

Rugs, silks, flowers, perfumes, fruit and other 'delicacies' were thrown from windows to the troopers. Arab women high in building windows lifted their dark veils and shouted:

'Meit allo wesahla!' (a hundred welcomes). The call was taken up like a Mexican wave and carried along the column in one continuous chant. Olden and his men were mystified as to why they had been greeted with such fervour. They were unaware of the build-up and preparation for the moment when 'liberators' and 'conquerors' (the 'English') would arrive. The Australians' grand flourish of a galloping entrance, swords drawn or pistols in hand, had confirmed their status. There had been rumours that the Germans were planning to burn the city on departure. The explosion of ammunition dumps at the station seemed to support this fear. But the arrival of the horsemen had alleviated any possibility of such an act. Hence the Arabs' greeting, which had a sense of relief as much as joy.

The Armenian guide was either revelling in the crowd adulation at the head of the 'parade' or he was following Emir Said's instructions to delay the Australians. Whatever the motive, he led the troopers on a merry dance around the city, and every way except the route they wished to go. Olden became irritated. He asked if anyone in the crowd could show them the shortest route to the north-east road out of the city. A Greek stepped forward and helped. The man mounted a horse and joined the head of the column.

Seconds later a British pilot who had been released from prison rushed up and joined the ride on a pony he had 'borrowed' from an onlooker. (He would later fight with the troopers.)

The new Greek guide directed them, single file, through the

narrow, winding streets of the bazaars, where there was a second wave of welcome and appreciation. Storekeepers pushed close, offering fruit, sweets, cigars and cigarettes.

'They neither asked—nor would they accept—any payment,' Olden wrote, adding dryly that this was something 'miraculous in the east'.

By a little after 7 a.m. the amused and bemused 'conquerors' of Damascus trotted out along the road north to Homs and Aleppo. They were glad to have left the city, which they found suffocating and squalid, with a stench that they had breathed in elsewhere in cities such as Jerusalem. It suited the troopers to ride freely along poplar-lined avenues with sweeter smelling orchards either side.

Having accepted the city's surrender, they were part of the sizeable Light Horse and cavalry force that would now lock it down and pursue the enemy north.

66

Town Hall Troubles

Lawrence could not sleep on the night of 30 September. Damascus was the climax of two years of hard work, exhilaration, agony, hope and false promise. At last he had a chance to deliver the Arabs what they wanted and he had promised. Allenby was a long way behind the front and would not be on the scene for three or four days. This, Lawrence thought, gave him his chance to deliver and present the chief with a fait accompli. The Sykes–Picot Agreement was after all, only a paper document drawn up two and a half years earlier. Events since then had been fluid and momentous. In the minds of Lawrence and Feisal, the carve-up was not even a rough blue-print or worth the paper it was printed on.

Sykes–Picot was not in his thoughts as he tossed and turned to the sounds from the ammunition dumps. If they had been blasts at set intervals, he may have slept. But his tumbling brain was being pierced by the noise of bombs and bullets exploding. They painted the sky white and yellow in uncertain splashes and shook the earth where Lawrence camped 15 kilometres south of Damascus.

In the middle of the night, when blackness, sound and fear distort the mind, Lawrence was convinced the city was burning, not knowing that the dump was at a station well outside it. This depressed him. For its incineration would mean his dreams would go up in smoke too.

At dawn, he drove to a ridge overlooking Damascus to the north. To his delight, instead of a collapsed and smouldering heap of buildings, the city was still there, a 'pearly' in the shimmering mist.[1]

Damascus was his oyster again.

He and Stirling in the Rolls-Royce Blue Mist let Nasir and Nuri gallop in ahead. It was their moment. Lawrence may have been the architect of the revolt's success, but it was for the Arabs, not him. The two Englishmen stopped to clean up for the event with a wash and shave in a little tributary to the potent Barada, which was giving hints of the torrent it would be in less than two months.

Their brief interlude was rudely curtailed by some Indian troopers, who arrested them. Lawrence may have been a god to the Arabs, but Indians had little care for a strange little pasty-skinned Englishman in Arab robes. It took time to talk their way out of incarceration. Lawrence became nervous that he was too far behind Nasir.

They drove on into the city on the heels of the advance guard of the 5th Cavalry Division. It was 8.30 a.m. The streets were still crowded but not as they were when the Australians rode in and out. A photograph of Stirling driving and Lawrence in the front seat next to him shows people looking on but without enthusiasm. The car and its occupants seemed nothing more than curios. Excitement in the streets was high yet not quite as it had been earlier. (It would reach the heights again later in the morning when Lawrence, Nasir, Nuri, Auda and other Arab leaders toured the city by car.) The main event in the mass's collective thoughts had occurred at 6.30 a.m. when the first of the 'British'—Olden and his 10th Light Horse—had taken the surrender and sanctioned Emir Said.

Lawrence arrived at the city administration and hurried up the crowded steps to the antechamber, where he found Nasir and Nuri in confrontation with Emir Said and his brother Abdul Qadir ('my old enemy', Lawrence wrote).

The brothers were claiming they had formed the government, along with 'Shakri el Ayubi, of Saladin's house'.

Lawrence was stunned. This was not even half the way he intended it to happen. In June 1917, he had anointed Ali Riza al Rikabi as the governor-to-be. This had been confirmed and understood in the 15 months since. Shakri was supposed to be his deputy. But where was Rikabi? No-one could find him. Lawrence quizzed Shakri about the usurping of power by the Algerian brothers Said and Qadir.

Lawrence claimed that Shakri told him that the Algerians had stood by the Turks until they ran from the city. Then they stormed the committee set up in Feisal's name and took over. They, not the absent Rikabi, had greeted the all-conquering Olden and his troopers.

Lawrence was furious and 'dumb with amazement'.

At that moment, he may have felt it was better if the place had gone up in smoke after all.

In despair he and the others kept asking, 'Where is Rikabi?'

Rikabi had left Damascus in search of Chauvel. He wished to submit his services to the real power, which he knew lay with the British. He found Barrow and passed on all his ideas for the planned transfer of governorship from the Turks to him. He proved a disappointment to Lawrence and of little consequence to Chauvel. The plans were next to useless. Events had moved too fast. They had already bypassed yesterday's schemes.

Lawrence was distracted by a fracas in the middle of the ante-chamber. Auda had accused Sultan el Atrash, chief of the Druses, of siding with the Algerians, and by implication, the Turks. Atrash had the temerity, or foolishness, to strike Auda across the face with a stick. They tore into each other. Lawrence and an Arab pulled them apart. Atrash was hustled into another room. Lawrence and several others had to restrain Auda, the 'old man', as he was known. He was in a fury. He had murdered those 75 men on battlefields and in other forums *before* the Arab Revolt. He may have doubled that number in his butchery of the Turks in recent weeks. Atrash would have been just another notch on his dagger.

Lawrence and the others manoeuvred Auda into the quiet great state hall and held him down in a chair while he fumed and ranted. It was half an hour before he calmed down and listened to anyone. Lawrence asked for three days to handle things. Auda promised to wait before he did 'something', which was a euphemism for murder.

In the meantime, Lawrence had Atrash removed from Damascus for his own good.

Chauvel, his chief of staff Godwin and an aide-de-camp went on horseback from Kaukab in the morning to see Barrow, whose division was in reserve. He also wished to see Lawrence, who should have been with Barrow.

'I met Barrow at 7.30 a.m. a few miles south of the city,' Chauvel wrote. 'He told me that Lawrence, who had been his guest for the last three days, had slipped off early that morning without saying anything to him . . . I was anxious to get the civil administration of Damascus arranged for without delay. Here was my only political adviser gone off without any instructions and without, so far as I know, knowing what those instructions would be.'

He told Barrow to bivouac outside Damascus and directed

his aide-de-camp to select a spot for his own camp in the same area. He then borrowed a staff car and drove with Godwin to the city, arriving at about 9.30 a.m.

'I found Lawrence in his white and gold Arab costume on the town hall steps,' Chauvel recalled, 'surrounded by a large crowd. With him was another magnificent person whom he introduced as Shukri Pasha.'

The general wished to know why Lawrence had left Barrow without seeing him or leaving instructions. Lawrence's 'excuse' was that he *thought* Chauvel would like him to come in (to Damascus) at once, assess the situation and then make a report to him. Lawrence informed the general that Shukri was the new governor.

'Shukri was quite obviously an Arab,' Chauvel observed. He asked to see the Turkish Vali at once, as instructed by Allenby.

'The Vali fled the city yesterday with Djemal Pasha,' Lawrence claimed. 'Shukri has been elected Military Governor by a majority of the citizens.'

This was not true. Emir Said was officially the governor. There had been no election. Lawrence himself had 'appointed' Shukri as the stand-in since Rikabi had disappeared. But Chauvel had no way of knowing of the double deception.

Lawrence also told Chauvel that Shukri was 'a lineal descendant of Saladin' as an additional reason for accepting him as Governor. (Shukri 'indignantly denied' this at a lunch he gave Chauvel soon afterwards. 'He said "Salla Haddin" was a Kurd and a man of no family. He added, "I am descended from the Prophet".')

'I took Lawrence's word for it [Shukri's election],' Chauvel said, 'and agreed to Shukri's appointment, arranging for Lawrence to be liaison between us and telling him to let me know as soon as possible what police would be required.'[2]

Lawrence did not think any aid would be needed. It would be better, he added, to keep troops out of the city.

Chauvel then departed.

*

A sleepless Lawrence was becoming irritable. He called for a meeting with Emir Said and Abdul Qadir. They had been sleeping after the long night in preparation for meeting Chauvel's troopers and formally taking power. They arrived with bodyguards but, according to Lawrence, were intimidated by his overwhelming support, mainly from the Rwalla in the square outside the hall. His own bodyguard was lounging in the antechamber when the Algerian brothers walked in.

Lawrence's deception of Chauvel meant he had the ultimate backing for Shukri of the Desert Mounted Corps' big force of troopers installed around the city and settling into camps. He announced the sacking of Emir Said and his replacement by Shukri.

Emir Said reacted angrily. Lawrence ignored his passionate outburst. Emir Said drew his dagger. Auda leapt forward to protect Lawrence. The Algerian realised he was outnumbered. Nuri Said reminded the brothers that the Australian Light Horse and Rwalla were behind Lawrence. Emir Said and Abdul Qadir left the antechamber in bad temper.

Someone suggested that they be executed. Lawrence was against it, for the moment. He claimed he did not fear them. Nor did he wish to set an example of institutionalised murder as a way to get things done in the politics of the new government.

67

Capital Clashes

Chauvel drove off from Damascus, after his tense meeting with Lawrence, in search of Hodgson, to learn the situation with the Australian Mounted Division. He came across the war historian Henry Gullett, who filled him in on that force's status. Chauvel then went to his own HQ and sent a message by plane to Allenby informing him of his approval of Shukri's appointment. Next, he became immersed in the usual problems for a corps commander 'of supply, collection of prisoners, orders for the morrow, etc'.

In the middle of this, the 'bronzed and bearded' Captain Young, wearing Arab head dress and a British uniform, arrived from Damascus. Chauvel had sent for him. Young was senior supply officer with the Hejaz forces. Before they got down to business, he asked him for an update on Damascus.

Young informed him that Shukri had not been elected by a majority of citizens, but 'only by a comparatively small faction, i.e. the Hejaz supporters'.

Chauvel realised he had erred in appointing him governor. It meant that 'by installing him, I had virtually admitted the rule of King Hussein over Syria'. This was not going to thrill the large minority of Christians. Nor did it excite the city-living Syrians, who had little time and some contempt for their desert-dwelling cousins, who had followed Lawrence, Nuri Said, Nasir and Auda into the city. They were mounted and armed with rifles, swords, daggers and revolvers. Their horses were weighed down with ammunition. There were also Joyce's 300 mounted khaki-clad regulars of the Hejaz Camel Corps, the only troops who had accompanied Feisal, who was yet to make an appearance, all the way from southern Arabia. The rest were from the country north of Deraa. In the northern advance, tribe after tribe had been enticed into 'service' by gold and the prospect of looting.

'The better class of inhabitants,' Chauvel noted, 'was appalled at the idea [of King Hussein ruling the city].'

The consequences seemed to be already being played out in the streets.

'There is chaos in the city,' Young informed him. 'The bazaars are closed. Looting is going on.'

The Hejaz supporters were trying to downplay the British role in driving out the Turks. They were telling the populace the Arabs had done it.

'That was quite evidently why I had been asked [by Lawrence] to keep my men out of the city,' Chauvel realised, 'and why I had not been asked for any police.' This was even though Lawrence and Shukri knew that 'I had a whole regiment of Australians standing by for the purpose [of policing] in the grounds of the Turkish barracks. The Hejaz people were trying to cope with the situation with their newly formed gendarmerie.'

Young advised 'a show of British force as soon as possible'. He also suggested Chauvel should not take over the British Consulate, which was being prepared for him.

'By doing so,' Chauvel noted, 'I would define the British as well-meaning allies—not the conquerors of Damascus.'

Young thought it would be better if he took possession of 'Djemal Pasha's house, which was the best one in the place'. Lawrence was reserving it for Feisal.[1]

This heralded a big power play. Chauvel would display a representation of the force that had swept the Turks up from the Sinai, Palestine and Syria in the last two years. This would be a cold reminder to any rebels, rioters, potential coup leaders and assorted thugs that there was military muscle ready to act against them. Furthermore, he was not about to let a 'nuisance' (as Chauvel viewed him at that moment) of a subordinate officer deceive him, or usurp his role, whatever his purpose.

Chauvel felt he could not undo the Shukri appointment because he had already told Allenby of it.

'But I could put up a show of British force and take possession of Djemal's house,' he said. 'I could also police the place if necessary.'[2]

Lawrence busied himself in the evening of that first very long day with the administration of the city. He heard reports of disturbances that had closed the bazaars but did not think they were a major problem. Early on 2 October he woke to the news that Abdul Qadir was rebelling with support from the Druses, who were looting shops owned by Christians. The rioting of the previous evening that Young had reported had been stepped up. The problem had been compounded in the night by desert Bedouins swarming in, lured by the vision of a good loot in Damascus. Many had already made off at dawn with their women, camels and asses laden with army stores and merchandise.

Lawrence contacted Chauvel and called for help. The general sent a second Light Horse regiment to the barracks in the town as a precaution. Its troopers intended to take on a policing role. The gendarmerie had proved inadequate.

Then Lawrence enlisted Nuri and Auda to push the 'rioters' towards the river districts in the middle of Damascus. There, he noted the streets crossed bridges, which could be controlled. He and Kirkbride toured the streets.

'When we found anyone butchering Turks,' Kirkbride said, 'we went up and asked them in a gentle voice to stop, while I stood by brandishing my firearm [a large service revolver]. Occasionally someone turned nasty and I shot them at once before the trouble could spread.'[3]

There were three such 'occasions'. Nuri's machine-gunners cornered other Druse troublemakers. Lawrence, wishing to counter the sensational headlines and claims in the press, said that only five were killed and 10 wounded in the attempted 'uprising'.

Emir Said was arrested and jailed in the town hall. Lawrence wanted to execute him. But when Qadir was discovered to have fled the city for the country, and with Chauvel's intimidating column lining up for all to see outside the city, the main crisis was past.

Emir Said was spared.

In a moment of elation, Lawrence strode alone to the heart of the old city, and approached the Umayyad Mosque, the oldest place of worship in the Muslim world. It was the most important religious structure in Syria, which ranked architecturally and in its decorative splendour with Jerusalem's Dome of the Rock. Lawrence removed his footwear in deference to the sanctity of the building, which in that respect was second only to the holy mosques of Mecca and Medina. He paused in front of its elaborate façade, before making his way behind the building to the small archaeological garden that lay along the north wall. He darted past a few columns dating back to the original Roman Temple of Jupiter and entered the Mausoleum of Saladin, a small white building topped by a rust-red dome. The famed adversary of the Western crusaders died in Damascus in 1193 and the original tomb was erected on the site in that year. It was restored by funds supplied by Germany's Kaiser Wilhelm II when he visited Damascus in 1898.

Lawrence related to Saladin's well-documented personal austerity, which the visitor felt was reflected in the mausoleum. He found inside it two cenotaphs. On the right and holding Saladin's body was a walnut tomb, decorated with motifs typical of the 12th century. On the left was a more expensive modern marble tomb donated by the Kaiser.

This was his third visit to this part of ancient Damascus to pay homage to Saladin. In 1908, aged 18, he had been on a strenuous walk studying crusader castles for a thesis at Oxford. In 1912, he returned as a graduate while working as an archaeologist studying the Hittites.

This time he felt connected to the fabled figure. He prised away from the walnut tomb the gilt wreath presented to the Sultan of Turkey by the Kaiser on that 1898 visit.

It was a symbolic act of both defiance and victory.

Chauvel called for Lawrence to meet him at his camp outside the city and told him of his plan to parade his force. Lawrence protested against this, telling him it was unnecessary. The general was adamant. Lawrence had bluffed Barrow at Deraa. He had to try Chauvel. Lawrence asked him if he would salute the black, white and green Hejaz flag hanging from the town hall balcony as he rode past.

'I declined,' Chauvel noted. 'I was by no means sure that it had any right to be there.'

This was the moment of frustration where the Australians

irritated Lawrence the most and precipitated his 'after the fact' uncomplimentary remarks in *Seven Pillars of Wisdom*:

'The sporting Australians saw the campaign as a point-to-point [a steeplechase], with Damascus as the post; [where the best horse would pass first]. We [Lawrence and the Arabs] saw it as a serious military operation, in which any unordered priority [of how Damascus was entered, for instance] would be a meaningless or discreditable distinction. We were all under Allenby and Damascus was the fruit of his genius.'[4]

This was a thoughtless slight. Lawrence confused the approach of the front-line troopers with the mentality of the commanders. Chauvel and his key generals of course saw it as a 'serious military operation'.

The clash between Allenby's two key 'players' was also the result of him not letting his left hand know what his right was doing. His vague directive to Chauvel about taking Damascus and Lawrence's role left the general in the dark, which was part of his game. Lawrence had no real idea of Chauvel's command or his role as the most senior battle commander in the field. He did not seem to understand or care that the final push into Damascus was Chauvel's plan, which Allenby had approved. Lawrence believed, or tried to make out, the plan was Allenby's when it was not.

Lawrence did not seem to comprehend (or again did not care) that Allenby had instructed Chauvel to set up the administration in Damascus similar to that in Jerusalem. It had to have a civil governor and Chauvel was obligated to provide whatever extra police the governor required.

Lawrence tried in his writing to present Chauvel as a lightweight overly concerned with protocol and ceremony. This was an attempt to strengthen his case for claiming that the Arabs took Damascus first. Chauvel became his bete noire, and he had to colour him in this way.

Chauvel did not know the detail of Sykes–Picot, although, as he expressed to Allenby he had heard rumours about some agreement for Arab takeover of Syria. Lawrence now knew it in detail.

These two very different characters had contempt for each

other. Chauvel was old enough to be Lawrence's father. He studied history but was a typical general, whose life had been in the military. Chauvel's experience on Gallipoli and in three years of battles meant he had few peers as a successful senior commander in World War I. Lawrence was distant in rank and had one experience of running a small battle. Chauvel understood better than most the impact of guerilla and terror tactics. He had seen them close up in the Boer War. But he much preferred the challenge of a set-piece battle. Almost all Lawrence's experience was of guerilla warfare. Each saw taking Damascus as the culmination of years of work: the main goal in the Middle East war. They were both fighting for British victory from different perspectives. Allenby's distance from the front caused both men to fill the vacuum of leadership in Damascus. They both saw the other man as threatening what each believed was the best conclusion to the campaign, as instructed by Allenby.

The British War Cabinet, pulling Allenby's strings, did wish to make it appear as if the Arabs had won Damascus from the Turks. It would be useful in their power play and rivalry with the French. The propaganda element here behind the scenes was clear. Henry Gullett experienced it. He wrote to Chauvel soon after he had taken Damascus.

'On the question of the Arabs v Australians and the entry to Damascus,' he said, 'we are, I fear, butting against policy laid down from London. Apparently the Arabs were to have entered first but did not fancy the job until the Light-Horse made the way safe for them. Like the other correspondents I was advised of the policy and asked by GHQ to say anything I could in favour of the Arabs. I disregarded the request and made repeated efforts to disclose that the Australians were first into the town. But the Censor each time took steps to prevent it.

'The same policy was adopted in regard to British and Indian troops at Deraa. The Arab was glorified all the way by GHQ. A passing reference I made to the fine work done by the little band of British officers, who directed the Arab operations, was cut out.

'I enclose an article I wrote . . . giving in some detail the story of the 3rd Brigade's entry. I headed it "First Into Damascus." The Censor altered this to "Entry into Damascus." And in the text where I wrote "the first troops into the city were the Light Horsemen from Western Australia"—the Censor altered the sentence to read "first British troops." '[5]

Chauvel, if not given a political directive, would act according to military priorities for the aims of defeating the Turks, and protecting the Syrians in the city and his own men.

This put him at odds with the secretive Lawrence, who seemed to Chauvel to be running interference with his war operations.

Lawrence, bearing in mind his desperate efforts to make it appear that the Arabs were in charge, made a last demand of Chauvel: he wanted to know if he objected to a small detachment of the sharif's gendarmerie riding in front of the column to 'clear the way'. This was part Lawrentian petulance, part cheek and part attempted one-upmanship. Chauvel reacted generously.

'This seemed a quite reasonable request,' he felt, 'as police in any large city would do the same thing.'

He agreed.

'When these people arrived at the rendezvous,' he recalled, 'about every second man was carrying a huge Hejaz flag, which he was waving about in a most unmilitary manner. Some of my staff wanted me to despoil them of these but I decided to let it alone. It could not detract from the object I had in view.'

Chauvel thought 'it showed a sense of humour on the part of Lawrence, which was worthy of recognition!'

Chauvel led the 'show of strength' on horseback at noon with a squadron of the 2nd Light Horse Regiment acting as bodyguard.

'It [the military column] was representative of every unit in the Corps,' Chauvel said, 'including artillery and armoured cars, with the three divisional commanders and their staffs riding' also in the show.[6]

The parade featured British Yeomen and gunners, New

Zealand Light Horse, Indian lancers and a detachment of French cavalry (which would have infuriated Lawrence) from Onslow's brigade.

The effect was 'electric'. The bazaars were opened. The city went about its normal business. The impact was what Chauvel wanted. He laughed good-naturedly at Lawrence's attempt to upstage him, believing that the Arabs and their flags made his (Chauvel's) point stronger. The long, sombre and fearsome column of artillery wagons, machine-guns, armoured vehicles and tough, slouch-hatted troopers on their walers spoke for itself. This line-up of grey hardware contrasted with the bright, 'carnival' impression of the Arabs at the front.

Everyone in Damascus was now fully aware of where the real power lay. To drive home the point symbolically at least, Chauvel took over Djemal's house as Young had advised and allotted the British consulate to one of his divisional commanders.

This upset Lawrence even more. The clash between the most outstanding battle commander of the Middle East war doing his job, and the brilliant 'guerilla' leader/adviser of the Arabs and British had peaked.

Chauvel was alerted to the terrible state of the big Turkish military hospital by Lieutenant Colonel Bourchier of the 4th Light Horse. It had been neglected since before the Turkish leaders made their escape from Damascus. The Arabs were certainly not going to do the wounded and sick former occupiers any favours.

'It was cleaned up,' Chauvel said, 'the dead were buried by the fatigue parties of Turkish prisoners.'

They were supervised by his corps' medical staff. Australian doctors directed Turkish medicos and orderlies before the hospital was handed over to the Arab administration. Lawrence wished all hospitals turned over to the new regime. Chauvel refused. He kept the European ones, knowing he would need them for his corps. (The new rulers failed to reach any suitable standard with the Turkish hospital. Chauvel took it over a second time after just four days.)[7]

By the night of the 2nd, electric light had been restored. The city was calmer.

68

The Chief's Resolution

Chauvel received a message from Allenby late afternoon on 2 October. The chief was making a quick visit to Damascus the next day and would arrive at 1 p.m. Early on the 3rd, Lawrence let him know that Feisal would arrive in the afternoon by special train from Deraa.

'He [Feisal] wished to have a triumphal entry,' Chauvel noted, 'galloping in like an Arab Conqueror of old at the head of about 300 horsemen.'

The idea did not appeal to him, given, Chauvel mused, that Feisal had 'very little to do with' taking the city. But he didn't think it would do any harm.

Mid-morning, Chauvel too took a few minutes to visit the tomb of his hero, Saladin. He paid his respects to someone who had captured his imagination long ago, and would take time to reflect on the amazing link he now had with a legend from history. Perhaps if the gift from the Kaiser had been there, he may have removed it as Lawrence did. To both of them, this would not have been an act of desecration. They believed that the placement of the gilt wreath in the first place had been sacrilege.

Chauvel and Godwin then drove to Kaukab to greet Allenby. Chauvel wanted to know if the chief thought he had done the right thing in appointing Shukri.

'Yes, Harry, you did,' Allenby replied, 'under the circumstances

as they were. But there are complications with the French. I want
to see Feisal at once.'

'He won't be in [Damascus] until 3 p.m.,' Chauvel said. 'He
wants to make a "triumphant" entry.'

"I can't wait until 3 p.m., Harry. I must get back as far as
Tiberias tonight. You must send a car for him and request him
to come in and see me at once. He can go out again for his triumphal entry.'

Chauvel dispatched his aide-de-camp and an officer of the
Hejaz mission (Young) 'in my best Rolls-Royce' to get Feisal and
then lunched with Allenby at the Hotel Victoria.

'He [Feisal] managed to dodge my emissaries somehow,'
Chauvel said. In fact, he refused the ride in, 'and arrived at the
Hotel Victoria on horseback at a handy gallop followed by forty
to fifty Bedouin horsemen. As a triumphal entry, it fell a little
flat. It was an hour before the populace expected him.'

A conference was held. Present were most of the main players
in the entire Middle East conflict for the Allied side. At the table
were Allenby, Chauvel, Godwin, Feisal, Nuri Said, Nasir, Joyce,
Lawrence, Stirling, Young and Lieutenant Colonel K. Cornwallis, of Cairo's Arab Bureau. Perhaps only two people, Auda and
Bertie Clayton, were missing from the diverse and unlikely team
that changed history in the region.

Lawrence acted as interpreter. Allenby in his usual crisp style
cut to the main points, directing his comments to Feisal. Chauvel took his own notes, as he always did at such meetings.

'France is to be the protecting power over Syria,' Allenby said.
Before Feisal could react through Lawrence, Allenby went on:

'You, as your father's representative are to have administration over Syria—less Palestine and the Lebanon—under French
guidance and financial backing.'

Feisal did not like what he was hearing. Allenby ploughed
on:

'The Arab sphere [of influence] would include the hinterland
of Syria only. You will have nothing to do with the Lebanon,
which stretches from the northern boundary of Palestine [about
Tyre] to the head of the Gulf of Alexandretta.'

Feisal began talking in Arabic to Lawrence as Allenby concluded: 'You are to have a French liaison officer at once, who will work, for now, with Major Lawrence, who will give you every assistance.'

Feisal could now get a word in. He objected.

'I know nothing of France in this matter,' he claimed, which was a touch disingenuous. Lawrence had sugar-coated his articulation of how events would unfold politically once Damascus was taken. He had made obstacles to Feisal's rule appear surmountable. Nevertheless, the hard facts were a shock to Feisal. He would not have expected the underlying 'truths' of Sykes–Picot, namely French imperial control, and no Lebanon, to be thrust at him without equivocation.

'I am prepared to have British assistance,' the stunned 'Prince of the Hejaz' said. 'I understood from the Adviser [Lawrence and/or Young] whom you sent me that we were to have the whole of Syria including the Lebanon but excluding Palestine.'

Allenby listened as Lawrence translated.

'A country without a port is no good to me!' Feisal added, 'I reject any French Liaison Officer and will not recognise French guidance in any way.'

Allenby turned to Lawrence and asked:

'But did you not tell him that the French were to have the protectorate over Syria?'

'No, sir,' Lawrence said, also disingenuously, 'I know nothing about it.'

'But you knew definitely that he, Feisal, was to have nothing to do with the Lebanon?'

'No sir, I did not.'

There was further discussion around the points made, some of it heated. Then Allenby addressed Feisal again:

'I am commander-in-chief, and you, for the moment are a lieutenant general under my command. You will have to obey orders. You must accept the situation until the whole matter is settled at the conclusion of the war.'

Feisal digested the blunt words in the translation. He was unsettled.

'Do you accept this [decision]?' Allenby asked.

Feisal indicated that he did. He got up, shook hands with Allenby perfunctorily and left with his entourage.

Lawrence remained.

'I will not work with a French Liaison Officer,' he said. Before the chief could comment he added, 'I am due for leave. I'd better take it now and go back to England.'

Allenby did not like being defied over his instruction to work with the French.

'Yes!' he said. 'I think you had!'

Lawrence was stunned and humiliated. All the subterfuge, plans, schemes, deceptions, hopes and dreams seemed in one blinding moment to have been destroyed. The game, after all, was to install the French as controller of Syria. It was the moment Lawrence dreaded. The duping of his beloved Bedouins was a reality and exposed.

Lawrence left the room without shaking hands or acknowledging anyone else.

There was a nervous silence in the room. Chauvel, not given to filling such vacuums, said to Allenby:

'I think you were a little hard on him [Lawrence].'

Chauvel did not record in his notes if he gave reasons for defending Lawrence, whom he did not care for then (or later). But he recognised his hard work on behalf of the Arabs, and the British cause, as Allenby did.

The chief responded:

'Very well, send him down to my headquarters and tell him I will write to Clive Wigram [King George V's equerry and right-hand man] asking him to arrange an audience with the King. I will also give him a letter to the Foreign Office so he can explain the Arab point of view.'[1]

With that, Allenby left by car for Tiberias.

Chauvel and Godwin visited Lawrence in his hotel room and 'thanked me outright', Lawrence said, 'for my help in his difficulties'. This generosity made him feel 'mean'.

'I have come to feel that the trouble between us,' he added, 'was a delusion of the ragged nerves which were gangling me to distraction these days. Certainly Chauvel won the last round.'[2]

As a last gesture of goodwill, Chauvel gave Lawrence one of his cars for the long drive back to GHQ Cairo.

On 4 October, Lawrence of Arabia was on his way, never to return to Syria.

69

The Long Mop-Up

Damascus did not mark the climax of the war in the Middle East. It would not be over while Mustafa Kemal still had the will to fight. He retreated to a top suite at the grand Baron's Hotel in Aleppo 350 kilometres north of Damascus, and managed to cobble together a force of two divisions from the remnants of the 4th and 7th armies.

The Ottomans, who had built Aleppo as a trading city, had always felt more comfortable in this north Syrian town, which was connected more to Turkey to the north and Iraq to the east. Aleppo was set on a large, featureless plain where the valley of the Qweiq River entered it. Kemal believed he could defend better in this ancient (8,000-year-old) place than in Damascus. If he could not, he was closer to home if he was forced to run or retreat further.

Allenby kept the pressure on in pursuit, urging Chauvel to mop up the remains of the Turkish resistance. His corps was depleted by illness, mainly malaria picked up in and around Damascus. But he sent MacAndrew and his 5th Cavalry Division to Aleppo. They were supported by an Arab force and with Barrow and the 4th Cavalry as backup at Homs.

MacAndrew's advance cavalry arrived five kilometres south of Aleppo on 23 October. He was encouraged by the sight of traders and locals coming in and out of the city unhindered. It did not appear like a town under siege. He sent a demand for surrender into the Turkish fort. It was passed to Kemal. His response was:

'The Commander of the Turkish Garrison does not find it necessary to reply to your note.'

MacAndrew directed in his weakened (by illness) 15th Cavalry Brigade and his squadron of armoured cars. They were beaten back. The Arabs under Nuri then attacked the defensive Turkish trenches south of the city on 25 October. The enemy held their entrenched positions once more. But that night, 1,500 Bedouins went around them to the east and broke into Aleppo. Kemal for the third time left a city in haste, taking his garrison and two divisions with him north.

The next day, MacAndrew rode into Aleppo to a positive reception (after having an earlier one on the way at Homs, where 70,000 citizens greeted him and his conquering cavalry warmly).

A hot fight ensued in the north. Kemal, just as he did at Gallipoli, oversaw his soldiers' defence, ordering them to stand and fight. Only at night did he withdraw. MacAndrew held Aleppo and was content with that for the moment. Chauvel arrived in the city and ordered Hodgson to come there with his Anzac Mounted Division to aid the 5th Cavalry.

The Anzacs were on their way on 27 October for one last swipe at Kemal and his Turks. But they had not even reached Homs when they heard an armistice had been concluded with the Turks at Mudros on 31 October.

The war in Syria was over. (But not quite elsewhere. Britain captured Mosul, Iraq's northernmost province, 15 days *after* Britain and Turkey signed the Mudros armistice ending hostilities. This bold act secured the oil territory the British wanted so much and drew protests from the Turks that grew louder at the Lausanne Peace Conference four years later.)

*

The last push from north of the orange groves at Haifa from 19 September to 31 October 1918—a space of 42 days—had been an overwhelming success for Chauvel and his Desert Mounted Corps. They had taken about 80,000 prisoners while covering up to 800 kilometres. In so doing, they had suffered only 649 casualties (compared with 5,666 over all by the EEF). He would sleep well. No commander of such a big force of men and horses could expect or dream of better. If wars had to be fought, the performance of his multi-pronged, speedy and highly flexible corps in conjunction with a strong infantry and backed up by a spirited air force, was what any general would regard as perfection.

Chauvel could not bask even modestly in his glory just yet. He had many chores to cover, with the main one being repatriation. There was a shipping log-jam around the world as capitulation by Germany on 11 November led to a huge problem in returning soldiers to their various homelands across all oceans. That was the biggest headache administration-wise.

A second worry was occupation. No 'peace treaty' ever left an occupied nation happy. There was always disgruntlement and issues for the occupier. A large force had to sit on the Rhine to make sure Germany honoured the armistice. There was continuing trouble on the Afghanistan border with north-west India. Civil war in Russia would see Anzacs volunteer to fight with the White Russians against Lenin's Bolsheviks.

Supervising troops were needed in several spots in the Middle East. The British Mandate and interests in Palestine, Iraq and Egypt had to be adhered to and policed. The worst trouble-spot in the region appeared to be in northern Syria on the border with Turkey.

Allenby needed Chauvel's cool management. He kept him based in northern Syria to handle it. The Turks were still sabre-rattling north of Aleppo. They were feigning little knowledge of the armistice's detail. Mustafa Kemal had somehow mustered about 6,000 soldiers, who would be loyal to him. They were fatigued and bruised but still under arms. There was also the withdrawing 6th Army, which had been fighting the British in Mesopotamia (Iraq). It had another 10,000 armed men. A further 16,000 fighters in the 2nd Army, who had not divested themselves of weaponry, hovered in the north-west at Cilicia. About 32,000 hostile enemy soldiers therefore were defending Turkish borders as opposed to just 2,500 of Chauvel's horsemen at Aleppo. The Turks were supposed to be the other side of the border but they were still all in Syria. If Kemal and the other generals decided to confuse 'peace' with taking back a 'piece' of northern Syria, especially as the Ottoman Empire had lost so much, so suddenly, Chauvel would have real trouble.

The Turks were playing dangerous games. They spoke of their armies as 'gendarmerie', who they wished to leave in Syria. Kemal was less subtle. He told one of Chauvel's aides-de-camp that he had no intention of following the directives set out in the armistice.

Chauvel suggested two choices to Allenby in handling this. His first was military. He would need infantry support for his cavalry/Light Horse to move against Kemal. This was a tricky option, making Chauvel the aggressor when a ceasefire had been agreed to by both sides. But there were ways and means. He could move on the Turks and say they had threatened his men and had not complied with the armistice.

The other choice was diplomatic/political. Allenby should have Kemal removed and replaced with someone more ame-nable to the agreement. The chief moved fast. He sent a cable to the British representative in Constantinople (Istanbul). Soon afterwards, Kemal was 'out'.

Then trouble began in the towns to Aleppo's north. The Turks were whipping up anti-British sentiment making life tough for the patrolling troopers. The situation was serious. Chauvel responded by moving his HQ to Aleppo and calling up Barrow and his 4th Cavalry Division to the city. A British infantry divi-sion was also pushed north but the bad weather had destroyed roads and bridges, delaying their arrival.

The disturbances increased in the towns between the Turkish border and Aleppo. Chauvel moved to occupy them, learning that the main culprit was the 6th Army under the troublesome

General Ali Ihsan. He was breaking every clause in the armistice declarations.

Allenby was fed up. He organised meetings in the Turkish capital and took a French battleship there, accompanied by Wavell. The 'Bull' was in good form. He told the Foreign Minister and key figures in the Turkish military administration that they were flouting the armistice agreements outrageously. They were to dump Ali Ihsan forthwith as commander of the 2nd Army or he would make other moves to ensure it was done. Allenby did not specify what they would be, but his red face, words, decisive manner and size had an impact.

'I met the Minister of Foreign Affairs and the Minister for War,' Allenby wrote. 'I gravely told them why I had come, and refusing to hear any arguments, I left them with the text of my demands in English and Turkish. They were taken quite aback; and I do not think they will forget it while they live.'

The 2nd Army general was recalled before Allenby had even returned to his battleship.[1]

70

Full-Circle: Return to Gallipoli

The Light Horse experience came full circle early in December 1918 when a group of Anzacs were sent attached to the 28th British Division to Constantinople and Gallipoli. The men from the 7th Light Horse Regiment and the New Zealand Canterbury Mounted Rifles had almost all served on Gallipoli. Despite their weariness, all Anzac units had fought for this honour.

The Anzac contingent embarked from Kantara on 27

November and arrived at Chanak on 5 December. The Mediterranean crossing was rough. Many of the fatigued and physically vulnerable men contacted influenza. They were billeted in a rat-infested hospital between Maidros and Kilid Bahr. The weather remained bad during their six-week stay. Some Anzacs died. Their fate, it seemed, was always to end their days on Gallipoli.

A few of the more fortunate troopers visited Constantinople and found it crammed with refugees and soldiers from the defeated armies. They came from Russians fleeing the civil war, Armenians searching for safety and Turks on the run from armies in the Middle East and Europe. Tens of thousands were sleeping on the streets. There were as ever locals—Turks—who prospered. They were the criminals who dominated the black market and the prostitution trade, which was rampant. The Greeks, eager as ever to trample on their ancient enemy, were prominent. Their blue and white flag was hanging from doorways and balconies. They harassed Turks into removing their fezzes.

Constantinople, with its churches, mosques, frescoes, mosaics, palaces, covered markets and nearby fishing villages, was going through a period of decadence and mild hysteria with the change going on in the months after the armistice. The cafes were alive with dancing, boozing and drugs. The nightclubs had similar attractions, along with White Russians and others singing melancholy songs. Young female refugees offered their bodies for the price of a meal. In the rarified atmosphere, they rarely went hungry.

The troopers' main mission was to find graves of fellow Anzacs along the Gallipoli Peninsula, and to bury the remains of diggers. They were also engaged in collecting artefacts, 'trophies' and memorabilia for the Australian National Memorial Collection (later the Australian War Memorial).

It was an emotional moment for these men who had served on this barren finger of land before. The memory would stay with them forever. They wandered down to the already legendary Anzac Cove, then up into the hills, jagged ridges and ravines, searching for the remains of diggers, who lay where they had been felled on the Nek, Dead Man's Ridge and all the other chillingly but aptly named trenches in or closer to the Turks' former strongholds. Often they would find the bodies of comrades who had been the bravest and, briefly, the 'luckiest'; those who had managed to invade the Turkish positions before being cut down.

The returning troopers were not forensic scientists. Putting dog-tags, bones and the shredded remains of fatigues in bags was not pleasurable. But it was a duty that no-one would shirk. On the contrary, they did it willingly, caringly, knowing that, in the spirit of the Anzacs, it would be done for them if they were dead and the dead were them. This was part of the glue between comrades living or departed that was already an Anzac tradition. No matter how long their fallen mates had been left to the winds, rain, snow, heat, flies and maggots, the kinship was the same. For some, who had crept away in late 1915, leaving the fallen where they could not reach them, or in the makeshift graves at Anzac Cove, this return to the scene of battle was important therapy. The latter-day diagnosis of 'survivors' guilt'—the terrible black dog of depression that stayed with troopers who lived when their mates did not—was partly salved for some by this burial and retrieval operation. Some stopped and wept at the gravesides of their cobbers and friends. They spoke to the wooden crosses, swearing they would come back. They were angry that they had to leave. They sailed away with sad feelings that they were leaving their fellow diggers on foreign soil under the control of the 'enemy'. This would make many tough men break down, years, decades, even a lifetime later. The words 'they shall not grow old . . . we will remember them,' were never more poignant for those who survived Gallipoli. Others, not able to slay the black dog, would return to Australia and become drunks and social misfits.

The peninsula was now undefended. The Turkish army was almost all demobilised in the area. The locals were friendlier than the distracted soldiers in Constantinople (Istanbul), which was remarkable given the invasion of 1915. Some of the unemployed, ill-fed former Turkish soldiers who wandered the villages were enlisted to help the Anzacs in their sad, grim yet important work.

The stay was a deeply touching and intriguing interlude for the horsemen.

Everyone regarded the visit as a pilgrimage to a sacred place.

They re-joined the Anzac Mounted Division camps at Tripoli—a strategic spot on Lebanon's coast a short journey inland from Homs, which was half-way between Damascus and Aleppo. Many troopers were disappointed at the prospect of another freezing Christmas away from home. Without action, which had garnered wills and focused minds, frustration built. These soldiers were volunteers not regular army or garrison troops. They did not see why they could not be shipped back to Australia and New Zealand.

Their feelings were fuelled by their camps being in regions where Arabs harassed them with impunity. British policy did not allow the Anzacs to retaliate to the constant thieving and even the occasional murder. There were never prosecutions.

It had been going on for three years. Now that the Anzacs were idle and keen to go home, the situation had reached breaking point.

One night in mid-December, a New Zealand sergeant of the machine-gun squadron was asleep in his tent at the camp at Sarafend, in the sands near Tripoli. He awoke to a bag he was using as a pillow being pulled. The sergeant jumped to his feet and chased an Arab through the camp and into the sand-hills, shouting to horse-line pickets to help. The sergeant gained on the Arab. He stopped, turned and fired a revolver. The sergeant was hit in the chest and fell. The Arab escaped.

The New Zealander died as the pickets reached him.[1]

The entire camp was alerted. Three hundred Mounted Rifles tracked the Arab's footsteps through the sand back to his little village of Sarafend. The New Zealanders surrounded the place and waited until dawn. Then the village leader was approached. He was told that the murderer had to be given up. The leader conferred with Sarafend's sheikhs. They denied anyone from their village was involved. They were either ignorant of the killer's identity or they were covering up.

The hostile New Zealanders kept a strong, armed cordon around the village all day. Some Arabs tried to leave. They were forced back. A delegation of the troopers took up the issue with divisional staff and demanded justice.

Chaytor was informed. He dispatched his adjutant to nearby GHQ at Bir Salem but there was only a lukewarm response to the men's demands. No-one, from Allenby down, wished to antagonise the Arabs, especially not prior to the planned conferences that would attempt to sort out the post-war political structure in the region. Chaytor also sent a senior officer to take charge of the men surrounding the village. They were ordered to disband, but they refused.

Allenby either misjudged the feeling of the soldiers or did not wish to understand their grievance. Chaytor was forced to go to GHQ himself to make sure Allenby's staff comprehended that every effort had to be made to apprehend the murderer. Again there was no action taken. No-one from GHQ ventured near the village. No effort was made to even appear as if an investigation would take place.

Instead, the New Zealanders were ordered again to disperse and return to their lines. In the late afternoon, they reluctantly obeyed. When they later saw Arabs leaving Sarafend, they were incensed. The New Zealanders wanted retribution and to take the law into their own hands. They approached Australians in a nearby camp, who agreed to back their action, whatever they decided.

Early that night New Zealanders surrounded the village again. With a group of Australians standing guard outside the village in case Arabs arrived from other areas, about 60 New

Zealanders marched in armed mainly with sticks and chains. They gathered the women and children and pushed them out. Then they set upon the men.

'Many Arabs were killed,' Gullett recorded in the official history, 'few escaped without injury.'[2]

More than 30 men were murdered or wounded. Some of the victims were thrown into a well. A circular millstone was placed over it. All the houses were set alight.

Not content with this heavy act of reprisal, the New Zealanders, again supported by Australians, marched on to a nearby Arab camp, and burnt that too.

Satisfied that they had exacted revenge, the Anzacs returned to their lines.

Allenby wanted those responsible—the killers and the ringleaders—to be brought to account quickly. But the Anzacs remained mute. A subsequent inquiry, which they would have welcomed for their fallen comrade in the first place, failed to find any incriminating evidence. All those called before it claimed that they had seen or heard nothing. It was a case of one in all in, as it was in war. Allenby would have to charge the lot of them or none.

He put the Mounted Division on parade. He then marched in and addressed them. Allenby, his face on fire, vented his full fury at the men, whom he had grown to respect, until now.

'You are murderers and cowards!' he bellowed. 'By murdering the Bedouins you have taken away the good name Anzac!'

He paused, rode on between the lines, and continued his tirade:

'You have committed a worse atrocity than anything the Turks ever did!'

Allenby continued his abuse and remarked:

'I am no longer proud to be your commander-in-chief!'[3]

This brought a derisive laugh from the assembled troopers.

'As if rehearsed,' A. F. Nayton, military governor of Beersheba, said, 'the troops counted in unison, slowly from one to ten and ended with a roar of OUT. General Allenby's anger can be imagined. Undoubtedly an uncomfortable moment in an illustrious career.'[4]

Allenby rode away before the count was finished, according to other witnesses. He was well aware that if he and his staff had acted with alacrity he would have avoided the problem blowing up into a massacre. The New Zealanders' ultimate action was unconscionable, but they had not acted out of thoughtless reflex. They had waited impatiently all day. Then, when Allenby failed to even make a token response, they took matters into their own hands.

'Without making excuses for the Anzacs,' Gullett wrote, 'it may be said that the affair rose out of the simple fact that British regular officers entrusted with Australian commands in Egypt and Palestine, with a few notable exceptions, too often failed to grasp' the difference between handling men from the British Isles and those from the dominions.[5]

British regulars were too used to giving orders without listening to the genuine grievances of subordinates. In this case, the complaint was not petty. An Anzac had been murdered; authorities in the past and now had done nothing about bringing culprits to justice. Logic dictated that without deterrent the thieving and murdering would go on.

The result was vigilante justice.

The entire division was shifted down the coast to Rafa, with orders that all its members be confined to camp until repatriated. Allenby's further 'punishment' centred on withdrawing all recommendations for decorations. He would never praise the Anzacs again publicly. This was a petty response given his own mismanagement of the issue, and the fact that the actions of a minority would now end recognition for bravery in battle for representatives of the entire division.

Chauvel later visited the New Zealand Brigade involved. He made his own enquiries and ended in admonishing its members. The event would have offended his sensibilities, not the least being his sense of discipline. But his deeper attitude surfaced when he made every effort to have Allenby's ruling on decorations reversed. It was important to Chauvel to see that those who had distinguished themselves in the war were acknowledged.

It would become a cause for which he would keep agitating.

Later, historian Henry Gullett interviewed Allenby and told him about the bitterness towards him after his vitriolic speech to the Anzac Division at Sarafend following the village killings.

Allenby was surprised. He was the type that vented his feelings, walked away and held no grudges. Once he had said his piece in his overheated manner, he forgot about the situation that had provoked his outburst. That was his way. It had told against him more than once in his rise up the military ladder. The feelings from the Anzacs was not so much tied to his decision to hold back citations, but more to the apparent breaking of the bond between the commander and his force.

Allenby's remarks to the Anzacs had insulted thousands of men, when the incident applied to a small number. They had been his wide-sweeping strike force that had chased, charged, cornered, captured and defeated the Turks and the Germans. Without the commitment and skill of such a force, Allenby's reputation would not have been made. He would have been just another also-ran general who did not succeed on the Western Front, and was pushed away to an operation away from the main theatre. It happened enough in the military.

Gullett explained the sensitivity from the force that admired him.

'It (the incident) deserved all I had said at the time,' Allenby retorted defensively.

But he added that Sarafend could not shake the deep admiration he felt for the Anzacs. Without prompting from Gullett, who only expected to record a reaction useful in his future role in writing the official history of the campaign in Sinai, Palestine and Syria, Allenby volunteered to write a letter that expressed his admiration for the Light Horse.

The Short Goodbye

Late in 1918, many of the light horsemen faced the most painful act in their lives: shooting their horses. The order that led to this sad slaughter was as unexpected as it was shocking. It came from the Horse Demobilisation Committee at London's War Office. The cold, mindless directive from grey bureaucrats was not for the troopers to get rid of the mounts, but to hand them in. They would not be taken back to Australia or New Zealand, but sold to the British or Indian army. The horses were also to be sold to the local markets, or slaughtered. The committee would have had no clue about the relationship between man and his equine mount in the desert, and what they had been through together. Many of the troopers would rather put the animals down themselves than let someone else take them.

The reasons given for the handing them in were mundane and meaningless to the troopers. There weren't enough ships; it would cost too much; the Australian quarantine regulations were too strict; the mares could not breed in case they had disease.

Lieutenant Colonel J.D. Richardson wrote in the history of the 7th Light Horse Regiment:

'Horses were handed into the Remount Depot, these being led away by men of the 6th Regiment and machine-gun squadron. These fine old comrades had carried us faithfully under all sorts of hardships; through long marches in the deep Sinai sand; through the steep and rocky Judean Hills. And then perhaps the hardest of all, in those long, exhausting treks across the Jordan and up the goat tracks of the Mountains of Moab, often going without water for nearly two days at a time, and sometimes much longer . . . These faithful companions, with a few exceptions, were to see no further service. After being kept in the remount depot for a few days, the greater number were to be taken out and shot.'

Banjo Paterson, who had spent two years nurturing, breeding, preparing, training and breaking in the mounts, was disgusted and upset by the directive. He was out of a job and took a boat back to Sydney. He would write about his experiences at the remount depots in Egypt and Palestine, but was less inspired to break into verse over what had happened to his beloved walers.

But some did put their thoughts to sentimental doggerel. The most memorable was written by Oliver Hogue, using the pseudonym 'Trooper Bluegum'.

The third and fourth verses of his 'The Horses Stayed Behind' touched the nerve with a very Australian mix of black humour and feeling:

I don't think I could stand the thought of my old fancy hack,
Just crawling round old Cairo with a Gypo on his back,
Perhaps some English tourist out in Palestine may find,
My broken-hearted Waler with a wooden plough behind.

No, I think I'd better shoot him and tell a little lie,
"He floundered in a wombat hole and then lay down to die,"
Maybe I'll get court-martialled, but I'm damned if I'm inclined
To go back to Australia and leave my horse behind.

Hogue never made it back to Australia himself. Shortly after penning these lines he was dead, one of the millions killed by influenza in 1919.

More than 20,000 horses were to be sold to the Egyptians. Others would be luckier. They would go to the British and Indian armies.

Disposing of them on a trooper's own volition as depicted by Hogue was illegal. They were worth something to the army alive or dead. If they were more than 12 years old, they were to be put down officially. Their parts—hides, manes, tails and horse-shoes—were to be sold off.

Right down the Mediterranean coast from Tripoli to Rafa the

orders went out that they be taken into the almond, orange and lemon groves, and tethered in picket lines with their feed bags on. Selected marksmen, who were not connected to them, were detailed to put them down.

But this was not good enough for many brave troopers. They felt they had no choice but to take the law into their own hands. They did not like the idea of some faceless marksman, or someone who had no affinity to these 'best friends', slaughtering them in this manner. Nor did the troopers like the idea of their mounts being sold into Middle East markets. They had witnessed the way the locals in Egypt, Palestine and Syria treated their animals, and how emaciated and flogged their horses were. Be damned if they would leave them to a life like that. It would be better on all counts to put them down themselves.

Most of the horsemen had done this sort of thing often enough in the bush. But they had never been as close to their animals. On many occasions these trusty mounts had saved the lives of the troopers by stopping short of a deep crevasse, or by riding an exhausted or wounded man to safety or base camp. The horses had also brought them glory in many rides to the battle zones from the deserts of the Sinai and the plains of Palestine to the mountains of Lebanon and Syria.

The humane way to carry out this agonising task was quickly after a good feed and a last ride. But it was that last ride that unhinged many of the toughest survivors of four years of battle. They galloped out into the desert, covered the animals' eyes and shot them in the forehead. The troopers were all such crack shots that the horses would not need a second bullet.

How many of those men would wake in the night in the near or distant future to the occasional nightmare experiencing the feel, smell and look of their horses, and then the sound of the shot, the sight of buckle at the knees and the dull thud on the sand?

The dreams of being in a parade in the main streets of their towns being cheered by a grateful public were shattered with that familiar rifle crack that they had heard a million times before, but never with such poignancy and finality.

72

Light Horse Legacy

General Sir Harry Chauvel and his 34,000 horsemen
wielding bayonet or sword, or with rifle, had the biggest impact on the defeat of the Ottoman Empire in the
Middle East War 1914–18. Their global legacy is even greater
than that of their digger brothers in General Sir John Monash's
army in Europe after they defeated two German armies in the
battle of Amiens that led to the end of the war.

The third battle of Gaza, when the 4th Light Horse Brigade
had its amazing breakthrough at Beersheba on 31 October
1917, was a key factor in the Middle East victory. But every one
of the 25 other major battles cumulatively pulverised (in combination with the indefatigable British infantry and supported by
Lawrence and the Arabs) the enemy over 30 months and ended
Turkish hegemony in the Middle East.

By doing most at the critical moments to defeat the Turks,
who had ruled the Middle East for 400 years, Chauvel's horsemen opened the region to the West (and vice versa), which then
extracted its lifeblood for the next century, oil. The troopers
would not have been conscious of their impact beyond the battlefield. But over the decades, those that followed developments
in the region they had once conquered would become aware of
the consequences of their success. In the years and decades after
World War I, oil was discovered in many places in the Middle
East, including the Arabian Peninsula, the Caspian Sea, Iraq,
Kuwait and the United Arab Emirates. The precious fuel was
the object of desire again in World War II. When the Nazis took

France and created the Vichy puppet regime, the Australian government, early in 1941, urged British Prime Minister Churchill to seize Syria—French forces were about to give their new German masters access to the country. The operation to take on the Vichy French was viewed as a gamble. After a short period Australia's (2nd AIF) 1st Corps took command of the operation, led by Major General Lavarack and his 7th Division. Many sons of Anzacs and light horsemen were among this force, which executed a successful campaign.

Also in World War II, the Australian 6th and 9th Divisions, again including many sons of Anzacs, fought in the North Africa campaigns of 1941 and 1942 against General Erwin Rommel's elite 'Afrika Korps'. At stake were the Middle East oilfields, Egypt, the Suez Canal and Britain's lifeline to India and Australia.

In January 1941, Australia's 6th Division took Bardia in Libya from the Italians, then advanced west to Tobruk. Hitler sent Rommel to Africa to prop up Mussolini's crumbling armies. By April 1941, Rommel, with his well-trained German troops, advanced tanks and artillery weaponry, had forced the Allies back. This led to the 'Siege of Tobruk' where Australia's Lieutenant General Leslie Morshead and his 9th Division, along with British and Indian forces, held off Rommel for eight months, saved Egypt and kept the Nazis from access to the oil wells of the Middle East.

This was followed in 1942 by two desperate battles: in July the first battle of El Alamein, and in October the second battle. The latter was a massive encounter, involving on the British side under Field Marshal Bernard Montgomery, 220,000 men, 1,100 tanks and 900 guns versus the Axis side of 180,000 men, 600 tanks and 500 guns. The 9th played a pivotal and disproportionate role (as part of the British 8th Army) in stopping the Afrika Korps, then throwing it back. The Australians made up just 10 per cent of the force, but took the brunt of Rommel's armoured attack and suffered 22 per cent of the casualties—1,200 killed and another 4,800 wounded.

This fearsome contest destroyed the myth of invincibility concerning Rommel and his troops, and decided the fate of North

Africa and the Middle East's oilfields. The oil became vital in the defeat of the Nazis in the second half of World War II.

As Western industry grew exponentially, especially in the second half of the 20th century, more and more oil was needed to fuel developments. In 1944, a prominent petroleum geologist, Everette DeGolyer, reported to the US government that he was certain the Middle East nations were sitting atop at least 25 billion barrels of oil—a third of which he reckoned was under Saudi Arabia. His report to the State Department commented:

'The oil in this region is the greatest single prize in all history.'

His estimate proved to be conservative. Chauvel or any former World War I trooper learning this would have reflected that a quarter of a century earlier they were responsible for the eventual exploitation by the West of this black gold.

The second legacy of Chauvel and his horsemen was the migration of Jews into Palestine. The troopers would have been aware of their impact at the time, but no one could have predicted the creation of the state of Israel 30 years later and the consequent developments and chaos in the Middle East that followed in the next six decades. A third legacy was the fulfilment of Arab nationalism in Syria, Iraq, Saudi Arabia and other states that could not have emerged however chaotically and at times, brutally, without the roll-back of the Ottomans.

Despite General Murray's remote-control command from early 1916 to mid-1917, Chauvel and his light horsemen took the initiative against the Turks in the Sinai. They were highly motivated. Those on Gallipoli had vivid memories of defeat, stalemate and withdrawal. Nothing much needed to be said to them about fighting against the Turks again on different terrain and a more even playing field. They had their main weapon of mobility, the horse. The walers were denigrated at first by Allenby, who preferred thoroughbreds. But he had long forsaken the horse for his Rolls-Royce. He thought differently when he saw the results of the horsemen on missions, charges and patrols in 1917 and 1918. The walers gave the Light Horse a terrific advantage with their staying power. Their loyalty to their riders too, if developed over time, was a further asset. Every trooper who stayed on one horse for any length of time had stories to tell about how he had been greatly helped, even saved, by his mount. They cited cases of the horses stopping at the edges of deep ravines, unseen by the men in the fog and mist; of how the horse had taken a wounded or fatigued trooper to a home base without any direction given. The desert and plains gave them the space to exhibit their special, unexpected qualities. Their riders could cover long distances at a pace that allowed the Anzacs to adapt to the conditions and make the elements theirs.

Those who had joined the force after Gallipoli were soon apprised of the attitudes and determination of the veterans from the conflict on the Turkish peninsula, and what it meant. The sense of a need to 'square the ledger' for mates killed and battles lost, along with the frustrations that manifested in 1915 in the infantry war for which none of the horsemen had been trained, was absorbed by the new misnamed 'recruits' post-Gallipoli. They, like the 'originals' from Gallipoli, were volunteers. Those who joined up to fight after Gallipoli were dubbed the 'dinkums' (from the slang 'fair dinkum'). They knew more or less what they were in for, even if the horrors of war were yet to be experienced. They realised early that 'winning' in battles was the prime function. No one wanted any more Gallipolis.

The terrain of the Sinai was not to anyone's liking, but the horsemen adapted faster and better than their adversaries. Those who had been in tight trench battles on Gallipoli were relieved, even with the prospect of the blistering heat and perpetual problems over water.

While Murray directed operations from faraway Cairo and squabbled with his number two, General Sir H. A. Lawrence, who was also too far from the action, Chauvel commanded his Anzac Mounteds into the isolated Sinai. His division was settling into desert patrol operations when the Turks raided British outposts covering the northern approach to the Suez Canal. The resultant butchery of the yeomanry after the battle by local Arabs in support of the Turks was a seminal moment. Those in the Anzac Division not initiated in the ways of war were galvanised for anything after seeing the way their British brothers-in-arms were treated.

Chauvel's horsemen formed the only desert-worthy force in Sinai. They stopped the second Turkish advance at Romani on 4–5 August 1916. Chauvel had only two of his four brigades under command, but with clever, decisive leadership and daring tactics, he out-thought the opposition in the oppressive conditions. His sense of timing was paramount. The Turks ran out of water and wilted. Chauvel pursued them but his force was too light to rout the enemy. This was due to the incompetence of the distant High Command.

Under British General Chetwode, Chauvel destroyed the Turkish garrisons at Rafa (December 1916) and Magdhaba (January 1917). This cleared the way for an assault on the main Turkish positions on the Gaza to Beersheba line. Even from a distance, Murray began to realise that Chauvel was his key and most effective commander. Without conviction, Murray ordered the first attack on Gaza on 26–27 March 1917. In the biggest blunder of the Middle East War his nervous commanders snatched defeat from the jaws of victory. Chauvel had forced his way into Gaza when he and the victorious British infantry were ordered to withdraw. Command believed, again from a distance that made it more guesswork than fact, that fresh Turkish troops were marching on Gaza. They weren't. Then in another major error, Chauvel's force was marginalised for the second Gaza attack on 17–19 April, against an enemy that had re-enforced. The British force was defeated again. The Turks were boosted. Murray had to go, but not before he realised his blunders.

His parting comment that 'these Anzac troops are the keystone to the defence of Egypt', was a realisation too late. But it was not lost on his successor, the more proactive General Allenby, who recognised the value of the horsemen and their outstanding leader. Chauvel succeeded to the command of the

Desert Column, making him the first Australian to lead a corps. Allenby calculated that the main defence force in the Egypt– Palestine war was also his best bet to go on the offensive, defeat the Turks and clear them from the Middle East. He reorganised the army into three corps, giving Chauvel the Desert Mounted Corps of three divisions and promoting him to lieutenant general. The Australian had leapfrogged over several British generals to take the top field command job in the Middle East War.

Backed, and indeed pushed, by British Prime Minister Lloyd George, Allenby used General Chetwode's plan to have a third try at taking Gaza. Yet he waited more than half a year to organise the attack. If they did not break through this time, it could have been a year before there would be another opportunity, which would be too late. The Turks would have defended the 70-kilometre line from Gaza to Beersheba by again building up a Western Front-style trench and fortification system to make it impossible for the British to win with the resources available. The delay would have taken the war to the time of the armistice.

If the British force had been held at Gaza–Beersheba, the Arab Revolt, guided by Lawrence, would have stopped and gone into reverse. Lawrence had to keep the tribes inspired with promises and handouts of gold and arms. It was a fluid, tenuous situation. Auda had his cohorts change sides temporarily for the gold, until Lawrence, using all his courage and diplomatic skills, lured them back to the British team. Had the British been stopped in Palestine, they would not have supported the Arabs in the Hejaz after they took Aqaba. There was no way that the British or the French would have let the Arabs attempt to take Damascus without controls from either power. Even if the Arabs had taken it upon themselves to move north towards Damascus, they showed no desire for conventional battles. They would have been easy pickings for the Turks, especially if they were not diverting large troop numbers to Gaza. (Even battered, footsore and hungry, the Turks fancied themselves against the Arabs, who late in the war surrounded them like jackals waiting for the Australians to disarm them. In one instance the Turkish commander pleaded with his Light Horse captors to let them attack the Arabs, which of course was not allowed given that the Arabs were on the British side officially. Though Light Horse sympathies in this case lay with the Turks.)

Effectively then, without the smashing of the Turks at Beersheba, at the time of armistice in October 1918, the Turks would still have controlled Syria, Palestine and the Hejaz, with Mustafa Kemal likely to be in charge of a combined operation of the three Turkish armies—the 7th, 8th and 4th.

The map of the Middle East at the end of the war without the defeat of the Turks would have looked much the same as it did at the start. The differences would have been in the Sinai and part of Iraq, where the British were to take control after setbacks and struggle. Yet the rest of the Middle East would have been still under the Ottoman yoke.

Victory against the odds at Beersheba was the turning point of the entire Middle East War, and a pivotal moment in 20th century history. Chauvel's brilliance as a tactician was to wait until the last possible moment to send his fresh troops into battle, as he did at Romani. His 4th Brigade light horsemen did the rest in an amazing show of daring and courage. But it was not just the unexpected victory that led to the collapse of the Turks at Beersheba then Gaza. There was also the psychological damage done to the Turks and Germans after the conflict; the impact of the charge was felt in all ranks of the enemy there and elsewhere. The Australians were thought to be truly crazy. As one German dispatch noted after a later charge: 'They are madmen, who take their horses where no horses should go.'

Beersheba was the catalyst for the British. But Chauvel was in no position immediately to finish the Turks. Four of his nine brigades had been detached. The remainder was nearly spent. Yet still, the Desert Mounted Corps, supported by the 60th Division, drove the Turks up the Plain of Philistia beyond Jaffa and the River Auja (now in the heart of Tel Aviv). With the 8th Army retreating north and away from Jerusalem, the British infantry entered the holy city early in December 1917.

After refreshment and reorganisation in the spring of 1918, a fourth division was added to Chauvel's corps. Allenby wanted quick results. But his directive to Chauvel to cross the Jordan east was too hasty. His force was under-strength for such a push at the main power base of the enemy. By early May 1918, the chance to take Amman and Deraa before the heat of summer took hold was lost. The next strategy, approved by Allenby and devised and implemented by Chauvel, was the big offensive up the Mediterranean flank. The attack began on 19 September 1918, four and a half months after the failure to thrust east over the Jordan.

The infantry sliced a gap in the Turkish defences just north of the orange groves at Jaffa, where the horses had been hidden. Then three divisions of cavalry barged through. After a day's hard riding, the corps was 80 kilometres beyond the disorganised Turkish armies. It took or destroyed communications between the 7th and 8th. Chauvel was soon directing the crossing of the Jordan.

At this moment, the psychology of the Beersheba win became apparent. So sudden and complete was the sweep across the Megiddo plain that any attack against sometimes vastly superior numbers was successful. Within days, an ever-weakening Turkish/German force was demoralised. The enemy desire for the fight was ever-dwindling.

Chauvel gave the Turks no time or chance to recover, destroying their forces around Haifa and Lake Tiberias (Sea of Galilee). Next stop was Damascus. Chauvel submitted his plan; Allenby, who was driving 100 kilometres behind Chauvel and the action, approved it after just one brief meeting in which the chief was fuzzy in his directives for the first and only time in the Australian's experience. The lack of clarity was over what was expected when Damascus was taken.

Chauvel drove the enemy across the Golan Heights and rode for Damascus with two divisions. A third, with Arab/Lawrence assistance, entered Deraa and pushed the Turks north.

After crushing the retreating Turkish and German forces in the Barada Gorge, 30 kilometres west of Damascus on the escape route to Beirut, 400 troopers of the 10th Light Horse rode to the city early in the morning of 1 October 1918. A garrison of 12,000 Turks, weakened and abandoned by Mustafa Kemal, took one look at the galloping Australian regiment and decided that they were in no state to act against them. The 10th rode on into the city and effected a surrender, which had not quite been in Allenby's plan, and definitely was not in Lawrence's. The Arabs had their chance to force the capitulation in the Syrian capital. But in the entire conflict to that point they had been reluctant to take the Turks head-on. Not being fully aware of the enemy strength, they decided that discretion was the better part of valour. It was wiser to let the Light Horse take the brunt of any action than to lose lives themselves. The Arab Revolt had been based on guerilla tactics and hit-and-run methods. Changing them now would not be productive.

Perhaps fittingly, 400 horsemen of the Western Australian 10th Light Horse Regiment, which had come a long way from the horrors of the Nek on Gallipoli, took Damascus from the Turkish governor. Then Chauvel sorted out the city, despite Lawrence running interference in his fever to instigate Arab 'control' of it, through *his* appointed governor, rather than that of the retreating Turks or the occupying British. His efforts were to no avail. Allenby arrived for one of his tight, to-the-point meetings. He made it clear to Prince Feisal and Lawrence that the French would be in control of Damascus and Syria. The Arabs had been duped by the British, something which Lawrence knew would happen despite his wishful thinking and deception of the tribal leaders. Lawrence was forced, or forced himself, to 'go on leave', leaving Chauvel's cavalry and Light Horse, accompanied by the Arabs, to chase the Turks north to Aleppo, which fell to them on 25 October.

Six days later the Middle East War was over.

In the five weeks since the opening of the offensive on 19 September, the divisions of the Desert Mounted Corps had advanced up to 800 kilometres, taken nearly 80,000 prisoners and acquired a huge amount of booty. Their battle casualties were a remarkably low 650.

The main reason for this overwhelming success lay in Chauvel's command. He planned his successive thrusts with care, sweetly coordinated his spread forces, and concerned himself with the logistical basis of all operations. With the infantry in support, he was the commander mainly responsible for the defeat of the Turkish 7th and 8th armies, and in the end the strangling of the 4th Army in the east after its continuing harassment by Lawrence and the Arabs.

The magnificent charge of the 800 horsemen at Beersheba began it all and should have been appreciated by both Jews and Arabs in the Middle East. The shock of it reverberated until the war was over and marked the beginning of the end of the Ottomans in the region. The Arabs, however, never appreciated the Light Horse or cavalry efforts in the striving for Arab nationalism. The military were under British control and therefore it was viewed by the Arabs as an invading force, similar to many others which crisscrossed the Middle East over many centuries. (The decades have not always improved the two-way attitude or relationship. At the time of writing, Australia did not have an embassy in Syria.)

It was different for the Jews. The smashing of the Turks cleared the area of the occupiers of Palestine right at the moment of the Balfour declaration. This precipitated increased Jewish migration to the area, knowing that at least in the short term, they would be afforded protection by the Light Horse. Without the stunning victory at Beersheba, the declaration would have been merely a paper tiger. There would have been no increased Jewish migration.

A bond developed between Chauvel and his troopers and the Jews. Their neat villages and farms around Jaffa reminded the Anzacs of their own country or outback towns and villages. For a time, the Arabs did not dare harass the settlers, knowing that there would be reprisals from the Australians, who held a thinly veiled contempt for the Arabs ever since the yeomanry massacre of 23 April 1916, and other incidents of theft and murder in the Anzac camps.

Where the British created the political conditions on paper for a build-up of the Jewish population in Palestine, it was the Light Horse in those heady days of late 1917 that provided the physical force that allowed it. The Turks were on the retreat for the first time in 400 years. This encouraged Jews to 'return' to the claimed 'homeland' of 2,000 years earlier, which was the Light Horse's second main legacy.

A special relationship between Australia and the burgeoning Jewish state began. Despite a small Jewish population (around 50,000) itself even after World War II, Australian diplomats were not insignificant players in the politics that led to the creation of Israel, which seemed a necessity after Hitler's attempt to liquidate the world's Jews, indeed anyone with even part-Jewish bloodlines. The late 1930s and World War II saw six million murdered because of this chilling, inhumane directive. Apart from the horrific loss of life, it caused a mass of refugees in Europe after World War II ended in 1945. The practical need and desire for a Jewish homeland drove the historical imperative, which had been yearned for over the centuries since the dispersal of Jews from the Middle East all those years earlier.

A United Nations Special Committee on Palestine (UNSCOP), chaired by Australia's Foreign Minister, Dr H. V. Evatt, drafted the proposal for the creation of the separate states of Israel and Palestine. This was put to the vote on 29 November 1947. To attain statehood, the Jewish people needed a two-thirds majority. The first country up for a decision was the Islamic Afghanistan. It voted No. Then Argentina abstained. Third up was Australia. It was the first country to vote Yes. So did Canada, France, the Netherlands, New Zealand, South Africa, the Soviet Union and the United States, along with 25 other countries. The Australian decision was a break from the 'mother country' and a sign of independence for the loyal 'dominion', as Britain abstained, one reason being the influence of its Foreign Office. It included some of Lawrence's old comrades, who did not wish to upset the Arab nations and their relationships with them. India, with its Muslim minority, also voted No. But it didn't matter. Israel had its two-thirds majority. It brought hostility from the Arab world, and the Jews had to fight hard to form the state in 1948.

Since then, Australia has been one of Israel's most consistent and strongest supporters, while attempting to maintain relations with most Arab states. Being such a strong ally of Israel has impeded some relationships. When the US and its allies attacked Iraq in 2003, Australian Special Air Services (SAS) went into action on the outskirts of Baghdad knocking out missile launchers aimed at Israel, the day before 200,000 American soldiers and their tanks arrived. The following day, there was joy, excitement and relief at the news in Tel Aviv, but media stories were suddenly censored. SAS operations were 'secret'. It was likely that the force involved would see more action in Iraq, then Afghanistan (which proved to be the case).

For Australians, even though the Light Horse efforts were never on home soil, there was historical significance of another kind. The war experience, beginning with the horrors and mainly failure of eight months on Gallipoli, followed by three years of battle success in the Middle East and on the Western Front, developed the spirit of a nation. Before those dark, frenetic years 1914–18, Australia—founded in 1901—was a nation in name only. In 1914, the country was still a collection of rival states with no real sense of cohesion outside the federal government, then based in Melbourne. The values of mateship, selflessness, courage, sacrifice and ingenuity were forged and squeezed out of those packed years of conflict on the Eastern and Western Fronts; values which form the backbone and overriding ideal of the nation.

That crowded, magnificent hour at Beersheba on 31 October 1917 was both an example and a symbol of what a young nation could achieve with determined, intelligent leadership, and courage and daring, against huge odds in war or any other major challenge in peacetime.

The light horsemen and their leader have largely faded from the national consciousness through time, and with the emphasis on the romance of *Lawrence of Arabia*. They should be remembered and revered for their enormous impact and their other controversial, lasting legacies. These include the defeat of the Ottomans in the Middle East; the chance to access vast oil reserves to fuel the West's rapacious appetite and industrial development for a century; the first steps in 1917 that eventually led to the creation of Israel; and the opportunity for the development of independent Arab states.

Notes

Chapter 1: Charge at Beersheba

1 Gullett, Henry S., *The Australian Imperial Force in Sinai and Palestine*, Volume VII, University of Queensland Press in association with the Australian War Memorial, 1984, p. 393.
2 *Spur*, April 1999, p. 25; 4th Regiment History, Australian War Memorial.
3 Chauvel to Gullett, Gullett, *op. cit.*, Notes on Ch. XXIII, p. 381.
4 Gullett, *op. cit.*, p. 397.
5 *ibid.*, p. 398.
6 Cox, John, *The Miraculous 'Lives' of a Man Called Jack*, Lime Leaf Publications, Melbourne, 2002, p. 129; Gullett, *op. cit.*, p. 400.

Chapter 2: Chauvel of Tabulam

1 Mitchell, Elyne, *Chauvel Country: The Story of a Great Australian Pioneering Family*, Macmillan, South Melbourne, 1983, p. 26.

Chapter 3: Change of Pace

1 Hamilton Papers (Lectures 1906, 1908).

Chapter 4: Fortune's Turning

1 Hamilton Papers, Ellison's letter, 9 March 1914, 14/1/5, CMA.
2 Hamilton Papers, 14/1/5, CMA.

Chapter 6: The Call, for All

1 HC letter to Fanny Chauvel, 7 August 1914, Chauvel Papers, Australian War Memorial.
2 *ibid.*
3 Ellwood, Robert, Interview, EJANZH, Australian Science and Technology Heritage Centre <http://www.jcu.edu.au/aff/history/net_resources/ellwood/016.html>.
4 Olden, A. C. N., *Westralian Cavalry in the War: 10th Light Horse AIF*, Alexander McCubbin, Melbourne, 1921, p. 16.
5 Cox, John, *The Miraculous Lives of a Man Called Jack*, pp. 53–4, Lime Leaf Publications.
6 Interview David Crawford, grandson of David Alexander Crawford, Service Record File, May 2007, National Archives of Australia.
7 Interview Major Warren Perry, October 2002.

Chapter 7: Parting and Much Sorrow

1 *Sydney Morning Herald*, 10 November 1914.
2 *Sydney Morning Herald*, 1 January 1915.

3   Ellwood, Robert, Interview, EJANZH, Australian Science and Technology Heritage Centre <http://www.jcu.edu.au/aff/history/net_resources/ellwood/016.html>.
4   *Sydney Morning Herald*, 10 November 1914.
5   Ellwood, Robert, Interview, *op. cit.*

Chapter 8: Culture Clash
1   HC to Sibyl Chauvel, 14 December 1914.
2   'Letters from a Pilgrimage', *Canberra Times*, 22 April 1965.
3   *Star*, London, 6 April 1915.
4   Jones, Ian, *The Australian Light Horse*, Time-Life Books Australia, Sydney, 1987, p.25.
5   Brugger, Suzanne, *Australians and Egypt 1914–1919*, Melbourne University Press, 1980, pp.34–5.

Chapter 9: Lawrence Shows His Hand
1   Knightley, Phillip and Simpson, Colin, *The Secret Lives of Lawrence of Arabia*, Nelson, London, 1969, p.38; TEL letters No. 81, 82; 18, 22 March 1915, Manuscript Section (MSS), British Library.
2   Knightley, Phillip and Simpson, Colin, *op cit.*, p.38.

Chapter 10: Invasion Preparation
1   Canning Diary, *Spur*, October 1999, pp.33, 37.
2   Birdwood to Munro Ferguson (Viscount Novar), Australia's governor-general, 25 February 1915.
3   24 March 1915, 16 September 1915, Novar Papers, National Library of Australia; Hamilton to Munro-Ferguson, 6 October 1915.
4   Birdwood to Munro Ferguson, 25 February 1915.
5   Hamilton, Gallipoli Diaries, Vol. 1, p.2.
6   Birdwood to Munro Ferguson, 25 February 1915.

Chapter 11: Wassa: a Very Different Battle
1   Canning Diary, *Spur*, October 1999, p.37.
2   Ellwood, Robert, Interview, EJANZH, Australian Science and Technology Heritage Centre <http://www.jcu.edu.au/aff/history/net_resources/ellwood/016.html>.
3   *Spur*, October 2003, p.12.
4   Ellwood, Robert interview, *op.cit.*
5   HC to Sibyl Chauvel, 29 April 1915.
6   HC to Sibyl Chauvel, 8 May 1915.

Chapter 12: Baptism of Fire
1   HC letter to Sibyl Chauvel, 29 May 1915, Chauvel Papers, Australian War Memorial.
2   Monash Diary, 13, 17 May 1915, Monash Papers, National Library of

Australia.

3   Pedersen, P.A. *Monash as Military Commander*, Melbourne University
    Press, Melbourne, 1992, p. 87.
4   *Spur*, October 2003, pp. 12–13.
5   Ellwood, Robert, Interview, EJANZH, Australian Science and Technol-
    ogy Heritage Centre <http://www.jcu.edu.au/aff/history/net_resources/
    ellwood/016.html>.

Chapter 13: Assaults in the Valley

1   *Spur*, October 2003, pp. 12–13.
2   Monash Diary, 19 May 1915, Monash Papers, National Library of
    Australia.
3   Hall, *Chauvel of the Light Horse*, pp. 54–5.
4   HC to Sibyl Chauvel, 23, 24 May 1915, Chauvel Papers, Australian War
    Memorial; Idriess, Ion L., *The Desert Column*, Angus & Robertson, Lon-
    don, 1982, p. 21.

Chapter 14: No Triumph

1   Idriess, Ion L., *The Desert Column*, Angus & Robertson, London, 1982,
    p. 21.
2   *ibid.*
3   Pedersen, P.A. *Monash as Military Commander*, Melbourne University
    Press, Melbourne, 1992, p. 87.

Chapter 15: Counterattack

1   HC to Sibyl Chauvel, 29 May 1915.
2   Hamilton to Birdwood, 28 June 1915, Hamilton Papers, Liddell Hart
    Centre, King's College, University of London.
3   HC to Sibyl Chauvel, 29 May 1915.
4   HC to Sibyl Chauvel, 13 June 1915.
5   Olden, A.C.N., *Westralian Cavalry in the War: 10th Light Horse AIF*,
    Alexander McCubbin, Melbourne, 1921, p. 47.
6   *ibid.*, p. 48.

Chapter 16: Insanity at the Nek

1   Captain Hore, letter to his mother, 9 August 1915, printed in *Argus*, Mel-
    bourne, 25 September 1915.
2   *ibid.*
3   Burness, Peter, *The Nek*, Kangaroo Press, Sydney, 1996, p. 108; Bean,
    C.E.W., *The Story of ANZAC: The Official History of Australia in the
    War of 1914–1918*, Angus & Robertson, Melbourne, 1940, pp. 606, 615.
4   Bean, *ibid.*
5   Bean, *ibid.*
6   Olden, A.C.N., *Westralian Cavalry in the War: 10th Light Horse AIF*,

Alexander McCubbin, Melbourne, 1921, p. 57.

Chapter 17: More Slaughter at Hill 60

1 HC to Sibyl Chauvel, 9 August 1915.
2 Olden, A. C. N., *Westralian Cavalry in the War: 10th Light Horse AIF*, Alexander McCubbin, Melbourne, 1921, p. 57.
3 *ibid.*

Chapter 18: Gallipoli End-Games

1 HC to Sibyl Chauvel, 20 September 1915.
2 *ibid.*
3 HC in an interview, *Australasian,* 30 April 1932.
4 HC to Sibyl Chauvel, 9 October 1915.
5 HC to Sibyl Chauvel, 16 and 25 October, 11 November 1915.
6 Birdwood to Pearce 8 November 1915, letter, Birdwood Papers, National Library of Australia.
7 HC to Sibyl Chauvel, 28 November, 14 December 1915.
8 Simpson, Cameron, *Maygar's Boys: A Biographical History of the 8th Light Horse Regiment AIF 1914–19*, Just Soldiers, Military Research & Publications, Moorooduc, Victoria, 1998, p. 282.
9 David Alexander Crawford died at Lone Pine 23 June 1915. He was in B Squadron, 8th Light Horse. His grave is at Ari Burnu, 1 kilometre north on Anzac Cove. See also National Archive service records, Boer War and World War I.
10 HC to Sibyl Chauvel, 20 December 1915.

Chapter 19: Lawrence's Ambitious Blueprint

1 Knightley, Phillip and Simpson, Colin, *The Secret Lives of Lawrence of Arabia*, Nelson, London, 1969, p. 58.
2 *ibid.*

Chapter 20: Birdwood's Push

1 Horsfield, Jennifer, *Rainbow: The Story of Rania MacPhillamy*, Ginninderra Press, Canberra, 2007, p. 67.

Chapter 21: Challenges to the Ottoman Empire

1 PRO, Foreign Office 882/15, 26 March 1916; Knightley, Phillip and Simpson, Colin, *The Secret Lives of Lawrence of Arabia*, Nelson, London, 1969, p. 49.
2 Paterson, A. B.(Banjo), *Happy Dispatches: Journalistic Pieces from Banjo Paterson's Days as a War Correspondent*, Lansdowne Press, Sydney, 1980, p. 83.
3 *ibid.*
4 *ibid.*
5 Idriess, Ion L., *The Desert Column*, Angus & Robertson, London, 1982,

p. 67.

6   *ibid.*

7   Horsfield, Jennifer, *Rainbow: The Story of Rania MacPhillamy*, Gin-
    ninderra Press, Canberra, 2007, p. 68.

8   PRO, Foreign Office, 882/7; Knightley, Phillip and Simpson, Colin, *The
    Secret Lives of Lawrence of Arabia*, Nelson, London, 1969, p. 63.

Chapter 22: Carve Up, Build Up

1   Levin, Leon, interview, 10 December 2007.

2   Horsfield, Jennifer, *Rainbow: The Story of Rania MacPhillamy*, Gin-
    ninderra Press, Canberra, 2007, p. 69.

3   HC to Sibyl Chauvel, 12 July 1916.

4   Idriess, Ion L., *The Desert Column*, Angus & Robertson, London, 1982,
    p. 95.

5   HC to Sibyl Chauvel, 25 July 1916.

6   Royston, Australian Dictionary of Biography <www.adb.online.anu.edu.
    au/biogs>; Gullett, Henry S., *The Australian Imperial Force in Sinai and
    Palestine*, Volume VII, University of Queensland Press in association with
    the Australian War Memorial, 1984, pp. 148, 157, 380.

Chapter 24: Chauvel from the Front

1   Gullett, Henry S., *The Australian Imperial Force in Sinai and Palestine*,
    Volume VII, University of Queensland Press in association with the Aus-
    tralian War Memorial, 1984, p. 151.

2   *ibid.*, pp. 151, 157; Jones, Ian, *The Australian Light Horse*, Time-Life
    Books Australia, Sydney, p. 52.

3   HC letter to Sibyl Chauvel, 8 August 1916.

Chapter 25: Push West to Katia

1   Idriess, Ion L., *The Desert Column*, Angus & Robertson, London, 1982,
    p. 71.

2   Gullett, Henry S., *The Australian Imperial Force in Sinai and Palestine*,
    Volume VII, University of Queensland Press in association with the Aus-
    tralian War Memorial, 1984, p. 175.

Chapter 26: A Tragedy Inscribed in Sand

1   HC to Sibyl Chauvel, 8 August 1915.

2   In 1919, Ronnie MacDonald's body (and the remains of many troopers
    scattered over the Sinai) was recovered and placed by the Commonwealth
    War Graves Commission in the Kantara War Cemetery.

3   Gullett, Henry S., *The Australian Imperial Force in Sinai and Palestine*,
    Volume VII, University of Queensland Press in association with the Aus-
    tralian War Memorial, 1984, p. 192.

4   *Sunday Observer*, 8 August 1916.

Chapter 27: The Anglo-Arabian

1 Nutting, Anthony, *Lawrence of Arabia*, New American Library, US, 1962, p. 79.
2 *ibid.*, p. 98.
3 *The Secret Lives of Lawrence of Arabia*, Phillip Knightley and Colin Simpson, Nelson, London, p. 64. (Italics are the author's.)

Chapter 28: Time Out

1 Wilson, Jeremy, *Lawrence of Arabia*, Athenaeum, New York, 1990, pp. 325–6.
2 HC to Sibyl Chauvel, 3 December 1916.

Chapter 29: On Firmer Ground

1 Interview with Trooper Ellworth.
2 Gullett, Henry S., *The Australian Imperial Force in Sinai and Palestine*, Volume VII, University of Queensland Press in association with the Australian War Memorial, 1984, p. 207.
3 Sibyl Chauvel's diary of letters and events 16 April 1917, Chauvel Papers Australian War Memorial.
4 Gullett, Henry S., *op. cit.*, p. 221.

Chapter 30: Feisal on the Move

1 Lawrence, Thomas E., *Seven Pillars of Wisdom*, Jonathan Cape, London, 1935, p. 143.
2 *ibid.*, p. 147.
3 Gullett, Henry S., *The Australian Imperial Force in Sinai and Palestine*, Volume VII, University of Queensland Press in association with the Australian War Memorial, 1984, p. 243.
4 Lawrence, Thomas E., *op. cit.*, p. 157.
5 *ibid.*, p. 166.

Chapter 31: The Turning

1 Idriess, Ion L., *The Desert Column*, Angus & Robertson, London, 1982, p. 176.

Chapter 32: The Executioner's Malady

1 TEL Papers, British Library, Additional Manuscripts Collection 45915.

Chapter 33: Blunder at Gaza

1 Idriess, Ion L., *The Desert Column*, Angus & Robertson, London, 1982, p. 177.
2 Richardson, J. D,. *7th Light Horse Regiment, 1914–1919*, pp. 29–34, 143.
3 HC to Sibyl Chauvel, 2 April 1916.
4 Gullett, Henry S., *The Australian Imperial Force in Sinai and Palestine*,

Volume VII, University of Queensland Press in association with the Australian War Memorial, 1984, p. 278.

5 *ibid.*

6 *ibid.*, p. 280; Hill, A. J., *Chauvel of the Light Horse*, Melbourne University Press, 1978, p. 104; HC to brother, 3 April 1916.

7 Gullett, Henry S., *op. cit.*, p. 282.

8 *ibid.*, p. 289.

Chapter 34: Demolition Man

1 Diary of Lieutenant Mackenzie, Australian War Memorial, cited in Gullett, Henry S., *The Australian Imperial Force in Sinai and Palestine*, Volume VII, University of Queensland Press in association with the Australian War Memorial, 1984, p. 288.

2 *ibid.*, pp. 286–9.

3 PRO, Foreign Office, 686/6, 24 April 1917.

Chapter 35: Gaza: Take Two

1 Gullett, Henry S., *The Australian Imperial Force in Sinai and Palestine*, Volume VII, University of Queensland Press in association with the Australian War Memorial, 1984, p. 314; 12th Light Horse Regiment, Official History, Australian War Memorial.

2 *ibid.*

3 *ibid.*

Chapter 37: Feints in the Desert

1 Massey, W. T. in *The Times*, London, 1 June 1917.

Chapter 38: Meeting the Terror

1 Lawrence, Thomas E., *Seven Pillars of Wisdom*, Jonathan Cape, London, 1935, Chapter 44, p. 256.

2 TEL War Diary, British Library, Additional Manuscripts, 45915.

Chapter 39: Corruption and Salvation

1 Paterson, A. B.(Banjo), *Happy Dispatches: Journalistic Pieces from Banjo Paterson's Days as a War Correspondent*, Lansdowne Press, Sydney, 1980, p. 79.

2 Sibyl Chauvel to HC, 13 June 1917.

3 Wilson, Jeremy, 'Sense and nonsense in the biography of T. E. Lawrence', (prologue to the authorised biography) <http://telawrencestudies.org/telawrencestudies/general_biography/sense_and _nonsense, p. 410>.

4 TEL War Diary, British Library, Additional Manuscripts, 45915.

Chapter 40: Bull Loose, Aqaba Taken

1 War Memoirs, George, (London, 1938) Vol. I, pp. 1089–90.

2 *Daily Telegraph*, 17 June 1917; Garner, Brian, *Allenby of Arabia*,

Lawrence's General, Coward-McCann, New York, 1966, p.115.
3 Paterson, A.B.(Banjo), *Happy Dispatches: Journalistic Pieces from Banjo Paterson's Days as a War Correspondent,* Lansdowne Press, Sydney, 1980, pp.81–2.

Chapter 41: Measuring Up

1 Lawrence, Thomas E., *Seven Pillars of Wisdom,* Jonathan Cape, London, 1935, p.320.
2 *ibid.,* p.330.
3 *ibid.,* p.324.

Chapter 42: Aid to the Arabs: Lewis and Stokes

1 James, Lawrence, *The Golden Warrior: The Life and Legend of Lawrence of Arabia,* Abacus, UK, 2000, p.225.
2 Chetwode to HC, 12 August 1917, Chauvel Papers, Australian War Memorial.
3 Lawrence, Thomas E., *Seven Pillars of Wisdom,* Jonathan Cape, London, 1935, p.370.

Chapter 43: The Prankster's Ruse

1 Garner, Brian, *Allenby of Arabia, Lawrence's General,* Coward-McCann, New York, 1966, p.129.
2 Hammond, Ernest W., *History of the 11th Light Horse Regiment, Fourth Light Horse Brigade, Australian Imperial Forces, War 1914–1919,* Published by the regiment, Brisbane, 1942, p.79.
3 *ibid.,* p.80.

Chapter 44: Charge of the 4th Light Brigade

1 Hammond, Ernest W., *History of the 11th Light Horse Regiment, Fourth Light Horse Brigade, Australian Imperial Forces, War 1914–1919,* Published by the regiment, Brisbane, 1942, p.82.
2 Jones, Ian, *The Australian Light Horse,* Time-Life Books Australia, Sydney, p.102.
3 *ibid.*
4 Hammond, Ernest W., *op. cit.,* pp.82–3, 95.
5 *ibid.,* p.83.
6 *Spur,* October 2002, p.24.
7 Hammond, Ernest W., *op. cit.,* p.84.

Chapter 46: Of Biblical Proportions

1 HC to Sibyl Chauvel, 10 November 1917.
2 Gullett, Henry S., *The AIF in Sinai and Palestine: The Official History of Australia in the War of 1914–1918,* Volume VII, University of Queensland Press, 1984, p.479.
3 *ibid.*

Chapter 47: At Jerusalem's Gates

1 Gullett, Henry S., *The Australian Imperial Force in Sinai and Palestine*, Volume VII, University of Queensland Press in association with the Australian War Memorial, 1984, p. 521.
2 Olden, A. C. N., *Westralian Cavalry in the War: 10th Light Horse AIF*, Alexander McCubbin, Melbourne, 1921, p. 201.
3 *Morning Post*, 11 December 1917.
4 4th Light Horse Official History, Australian War Memorial.

Chapter 48: Weather Wait, Surprise Win

1 Connell, John, *Wavell: Scholar and Soldier*, Collins, London, 1964, p. 133.
2 HC to Sibyl Chauvel, 8 December 1917.
3 Hammond, Ernest W., *History of the 11th Light Horse Regiment, Fourth Light Horse Brigade, Australian Imperial Forces, War 1914–1919*, Published by the regiment, Brisbane, 1942, p. 107.

Chapter 49: Tactics Against the Odds

1 Lawrence, Thomas E., *Seven Pillars of Wisdom*, Jonathan Cape, London, 1935, p. 479.
2 *ibid*, p. 492.

Chapter 52: Daunting Dawnay, Peeping Thomas

1 Rolls, S. C., *Steel Chariots in the Desert*, Cape, London, 1937, p. 230.
2 Lawrence, Thomas E., *Seven Pillars of Wisdom*, Jonathan Cape, London, 1935, p. 499.
3 Knightley, Phillip, 'The Making of a Legend', *Weekend Australian Magazine*, 19–20 November 2005.

Chapter 53: Turks Hold Amman

1 Gullett, Henry S., *The Australian Imperial Force in Sinai and Palestine*, Volume VII, University of Queensland Press in association with the Australian War Memorial, 1984, p. 613.
2 Olden, A. C. N., *Westralian Cavalry in the War: 10th Light Horse AIF*, Alexander McCubbin, Melbourne, 1921, p. 229.

Chapter 54: Arab Let-Down, Summer by the Jordan

1 Olden, A. C. N., *Westralian Cavalry in the War: 10th Light Horse AIF*, Alexander McCubbin, Melbourne, 1921, p. 263.
2 Hill, A. J., *Chauvel of the Light Horse*, Melbourne University Press, 1978, p. 151.

Chapter 55: To the Sword

1 Hill, A. J., *Chauvel of the Light Horse*, Melbourne University Press, 1978, p. 160.
2 History of the LHR, p. 121.

3   Gullett, Henry S., *The Australian Imperial Force in Sinai and Palestine*, Volume VII, University of Queensland Press in association with the Australian War Memorial, 1984, p. 676.

Chapter 57: Demolition Derby

1   Deraa was a contentious location in *Seven Pillars of Wisdom*. Lawrence claimed to have been raped there by the bey (governor), or a bey. The author's research, including examination of Lawrence's diaries at the time of an alleged incident in November 1917, concludes that this was one of the admitted fictions in his book. He had in fact removed certain relevant diary pages and then renumbered those concerned. James Barr in his *Setting the Desert on Fire* and Michael Asher in *Lawrence, the Uncrowned King of Arabia* both came to the same conclusion.

   Barr went as far as to have Lawrence's diary tested using static electricity and carbon powder to 'reveal' indentations made through an absent (read 'removed') page onto a sheet of paper below. The tests, according to Barr, revealed the imprint of a capitalised 'A' on 18 November 1917— almost certainly the A of Azraq, a derelict castle in an oasis 100 kilometres south-east of Deraa, where Lawrence had spent several days. Barr suggest that Lawrence stayed put rather than going to Deraa—a contention supported by a letter Lawrence wrote to his mother on 14 November 1917. In it he said he was staying 'here [at Azraq] for a few days'.

   It is possible that Lawrence fictionalised the rape scene to satisfy in fiction his sadomasochistic tendencies, which were exacerbated by his mental state during and after writing *Seven Pillars of Wisdom*. This book, including the rape scene, was written in the early 1920s when he was mentally unstable.

   When asked by the author (RP) in December 2007 about the issue, Jeremy Wilson, Lawrence's authorised biographer, said: 'Something happened at Deraa.' But he could not say what. In light of the new evidence, this seemed to be a shift in position from his previous acceptance of Lawrence's rape at Deraa. In reality, no-one today could really know if it occurred. Hence the decision to leave out this dubious aside and distraction from Lawrence's overall positive impact in the war against the Ottoman Empire.

2   Yardley, Michael, *Backing into the Limelight: A Biography of T. E. Lawrence*, Harrap, London, 1985, p. 123.

3   Barr, James, *Setting the Desert on Fire: T. E. Lawrence and Britain's Secret War in Arabia, 1916–1918*, Bloomsbury, London, 2006, p. 278.

4   *ibid.*

Chapter 58: The Light Horse Breaks Out

1   Allenby was even more displeased, at least outwardly, than Chauvel about Liman von Sanders' escape. Kelly was removed from his command.

2 James Ewell Brown Stuart, a cavalry commander for the Confederates in the American Civil War, led a 1,200-man force around the opposition Union Army in three days in 1862. He was doing reconnaissance work for General Robert E. Lee.

3 HC to Sibyl Chauvel, 20 September 1918.

Chapter 59: Enemy Collapse

1 Olden, A.C.N., *Westralian Cavalry in the War: 10th Light Horse AIF*, Alexander McCubbin, Melbourne, 1921, p. 263.

2 *ibid.*

3 Gullett, Henry S., *The Australian Imperial Force in Sinai and Palestine*, Volume VII, University of Queensland Press in association with the Australian War Memorial, 1984, p. 708.

Chapter 60: Beyond Armageddon

1 Gullett, Henry S., *The Australian Imperial Force in Sinai and Palestine*, Volume VII, University of Queensland Press in association with the Australian War Memorial, 1984, p. 728.

2 Hamilton, Jill, *First to Damascus: The Great Ride and Lawrence of Arabia*, Kangaroo Press, Sydney, 2002, p. 161.

3 Gullett, *op. cit.*, p. 733; 11th Regiment history; 12th Regiment history, Australian War Memorial; see also History of 4th Light Horse Brigade, including 11th, 12th, 13th Regiments by Lieutenant G. W. Nutting, R 940.41294n987h.

4 Chauvel, Letter to Australian War Memorial, 1 January 1936, p. 5.

Chapter 61: Retribution

1 Lawrence, Thomas E., *Seven Pillars of Wisdom*, Jonathan Cape, London, 1935, p. 654; Asher, p. 335.

2 Gullett, Henry S., *The Australian Imperial Force in Sinai and Palestine*, Volume VII, University of Queensland Press in association with the Australian War Memorial, 1984, p. 725.

Chapter 62: Pushing Barrow

1 Interview, *Toronto Telegraph*, 31 January 1963 with former Middlesex member of yeomanry, George Staples. He claimed Lawrence had about 10 bodyguards with him. Lawrence said he had one Arab Lieutenant, Ahmad az-Za'aqi.

Chapter 63: A City in Turmoil

1 Liman von Sanders, Otto, *Five Years in Turkey*, The Navy & Military Press, London, 1927, p. 296.

2 Report on *Seven Pillars of Wisdom*, Chauvel Papers, Australian War Memorial, p. 4.

3 Olden, A.C.N., *Westralian Cavalry in the War: 10th Light Horse AIF*, Alexander McCubbin, Melbourne, 1921, p. 279.

Chapter 64: With Swords Drawn

1 Lawrence, Thomas E., *Seven Pillars of Wisdom*, Jonathan Cape, London, 1935, p. 639. Lawrence implied he was watching them in an upbeat mood (on 30 September) before their mission to be first into Damascus early the next morning. But they were not at Keswe, where he said they were, but at least 10 kilometres away. His 'always going to do great things' remark may have been gratuitous given their record. His comments were in *Seven Pillars of Wisdom* and put together, not from raw notes before the events of Damascus, but after. The Australians upset and angered him and his plans. He had no idea on 30 September that they were going into the city before him and the Bedouins. Nor did Olden and his men.

By his own admission, Lawrence was unreliable in his writings about Damascus. 'I was on thin ice when I wrote the Damascus chapter,' he wrote to an early biographer and friend, Robert Graves. 'SP [*Seven Pillars of Wisdom*] is full of half-truths there. (See page 211, TEL letter to Graves, 3 August 1927, quoted in *T E Lawrence to his Biographers, Robert Graves and Liddell Hart*, Doubleday & Co., New York, 1963.

Chapter 65: The 10th 'Conquers' Damascus

1 Olden, A. C. N., *Westralian Cavalry in the War: 10th Light Horse AIF*, Alexander McCubbin, Melbourne, 1921, p. 283.
2 *ibid.*, p. 284.

Chapter 66: Town Hall Troubles

1 Lawrence, Thomas E., *Seven Pillars of Wisdom*, Jonathan Cape, London, 1935, p. 642.
2 Chauvel letter to Australian War Memorial, 1 January 1936, Chauvel Papers, Australian War Memorial.

Chapter 67: Capital Clashes

1 HC letter to Australian War Memorial, 1 January 1936, Chauvel Papers, pp. 7–8.
2 Richard Chauvel, Harry's grandson said his grandfather's light-hearted view of Lawrence was that he was rarely there when he was wanted and a nuisance when he was.
3 Barr, James, *Setting the Desert on Fire: T. E. Lawrence and Britain's Secret War in Arabia, 1916–1918*, Bloomsbury, London, 2006, p. 295.
4 Lawrence, Thomas E., *Seven Pillars of Wisdom*, Jonathan Cape, London, 1935, p. 643.
5 HC letter to Australian War Memorial, *op. cit.*, pp. 7–8.
6 *ibid.*
7 *ibid.*, p. 8.

Chapter 68: The Chief's Resolution

1 Chauvel's notes, pp. 9–11, Chauvel Papers, Australian War Memorial.
2 Lawrence, Thomas E., *Seven Pillars of Wisdom*, Jonathan Cape, London, 1935, p. 653.

Chapter 69: The Long Mop-Up

1 *London Gazette*, 8 August 1919; Allenby Papers, British Museum letter, 5 February 1919.

Chapter 70: Full-Circle: Return to Gallipoli

1 Gullett, Henry S., *The Australian Imperial Force in Sinai and Palestine*, Volume VII, University of Queensland Press in association with the Australian War Memorial, 1984, p. 195; Hill, A. J., *Chauvel of the Light Horse*, Melbourne University Press, 1978, p. 192.
2 Gullett, Henry S., *op. cit.*, p. 195.
3 *ibid.*
4 Letter to *The Times*, London, 24 November 1964 by A. F. Nayton, military governor in Beersheba, 1918.
5 Gullett, Henry S., *op. cit.*, p. 793.

Select Bibliography

National Archives of Australia
Bringing Them Home Project: Participation, Aborigine, Australian. June 2004.
—World War I and Boer War Biographical files.

Australian War Memorial, Canberra
Chauvel Papers:
Papers relating to Palestine campaign, 2DRL/0793
Annotated typescript autobiography of HC's military career, MSS1406
Collection of papers relating to HC—diaries, letters, photographs, reports and album. PR00535

Sir Henry George Chauvel Albums:
Album—Egypt, Gallipoli, Sinai, 1914–1917 PR00535003
Albums—Palestine, Syria, England, 1917–1919 PR00535004

The Australian Light Horse Association:
R 357.10994H17a

Brigades:
3rd: History, Wilson, 940.41294W749n; Narrative of operations 27 October 1917 to 4 March 1919, 224 MSS27
4th: Nutting G. W., R940.412994N987h
5th: Wynn, N. I., *Behind the Lines*, R940.400994W988

Regiments:
1st: *The Boys in Green*, R 357.10994B789
2nd: Bourne G. H., R940.41294B775h
3rd: Smith, Neil C., R940.41294S655t
4th: Smith, Neil C., *Men of Beersheba*, 940.41294 5655m
5th: Wilson L. C. H., R940.41294W749h
6th: Berrie, George, *Under Furred Hat*, R 94041294B533u
7th: Richardson, R940.41294R516s
8th: Simpson, Cameron, *Maygar's Boys* (see Select Bibliography)
9th: Darling T. H., *With the Light Horse in the Great War*, R 940.41294D221
11th: Hammond, Ernst, *History of the 11th Light Horse Regiment*, R 94041294H225h

Spur, October 1999:
Boer War, first casualty of Australians, p. 6
500,000 horses lost in SA, p. 11
Kitchener, p. 13
Chauvel at Coronation, p. 14
Chauvel and Boer War statue unveiled, p. 17
Breaker Morant, p. 20
Idriess on Suez . . . Battle of Romani, p. 22
Chaytor, p. 25
Bert Canning's brief diaries, p. 33

An Interim Report on the Civil Administration of Palestine during the period
    1 July 1920 and 30 June 1921, <http://un.org/unispal.nsf>

United Kingdom
Bodleian Library, Oxford Reserve Manuscript Collection
Public Record Office Kew: Foreign and War Office files; Arab Bureau Files;
    Intelligence files
British Library Additional Manuscripts Collection: various T. E. Lawrence
    correspondence, war diaries and pocket diaries
King's College, University of London, Basil Liddell Hart Centre for Military
    Archives
Imperial War Museum London: Knightley and Simpson Papers

Books
Asher, Michael, *Lawrence: The Uncrowned King of Arabia*, Penguin, Lon-
    don, 1999.
Barr, James, *Setting the Desert on Fire: T. E. Lawrence and Britain's Secret
    War in Arabia, 1916–1918*, Bloomsbury, London, 2006.
Bean, C. E. W, *Anzac to Amiens*, Penguin, Melbourne, 1993.
Brown, Malcolm, *T. E. Lawrence*, New York University Press, 2003.
Bruce, Anthony, *The Last Crusade: The Palestine Campaign in the First
    World War*, John Murray, London, 2002.
Brugger, Suzanne, *Australians and Egypt 1914–1919*, Melbourne University
    Press, 1980.
Carlyon, Les, *Gallipoli*, Pan Macmillan, Sydney, 2001.
— *The Great War*, Pan Macmillan, Sydney, 2006.
Churchill, Winston, *Great Contemporaries*, Mandarin, London, 1990.
Connell, John, *Wavell: Scholar and Soldier*, Collins, London, 1964.
Coulthard-Clark, Chris (ed.), *The Diggers: Makers of the Australian Military
    Tradition*, Melbourne University Press, Melbourne, 1993.
Cox, John, *The Miraculous 'Lives' of a Man Called Jack*, Lime Leaf Publica-
    tions, Melbourne, 2002.

Crombie, Kelvin, *Anzacs, Empires and Israel's Restoration, 1798–1948*, Vocational Education & Training Publications, Osborne Park, WA, 1998.

Cutlack, F. M. *The Australian Flying Corps in the Western and Eastern Theatres of War*, University of Queensland Press, St Lucia, Queensland, 1984.

Fisk, Robert, *The Great War for Civilization: The Conquest of the Middle East*, Harper Perennial, London, 2006.

Frindall, Bill (ed.), *The Wisden Book of Test Cricket, 1877–1984*, Guild Publishing, London, 1985.

Garner, Brian, *Allenby of Arabia, Lawrence's General*, Coward-McCann, New York, 1966.

Graves, Robert, *Lawrence and the Arabs*, Jonathan Cape, London, 1927.

Gullett, Henry S., and Barrett, Chas (eds.), *Australia in Palestine*, Angus & Robertson, Sydney, 1919.

Gullett, Henry S., *The AIF in Sinai and Palestine: The Official History of Australia in the War of 1914–1918*, Volume VII, University of Queensland Press, 1984.

Hamilton, Jill, *From Gallipoli to Gaza: The Desert Poets of World War One*, Simon & Schuster Australia, Sydney, 2003.

— *First to Damascus: The Great Ride and Lawrence of Arabia*, Kangaroo Press, Sydney, 2002.

— *Gods, Guns and Israel: Britain, the First World War and the Jews in the Holy City*, Sutton Publishing, UK, 2004.

Hammond, Ernest W., *History of the 11th Light Horse Regiment, Fourth Light Horse Brigade, Australian Imperial Forces, War 1914–1919*, Published by the regiment, Brisbane, 1942.

Hill, A. J., *Chauvel of the Light Horse*, Melbourne University Press, 1978.

Horsfield, Jennifer, *Rainbow: The Story of Rania MacPhillamy*, Ginninderra Press, Canberra, 2007.

Idriess, Ion L., *The Desert Column*, Angus & Robertson, London, 1982.

James, Lawrence, *The Golden Warrior: The Life and Legend of Lawrence of Arabia*, Abacus, London, 2000.

Jones, Ian, *The Australian Light Horse*, Time-Life Books Australia, Sydney, 1987.

Kartinyeri, Doreen, *Ngarrindjeri Anzacs*, South Australian Museum, 1996.

Knightley, Phillip and Simpson, Colin, *The Secret Lives of Lawrence of Arabia*, Nelson, London, 1969.

Lawrence, Thomas E., *Seven Pillars of Wisdom*, Jonathan Cape, London, 1935.

— *Seven Pillars of Wisdom*, Dell, USA, 1962.

— *Revolt in the Desert*, Jonathan Cape, London, 1937.

— *The Mint*, Jonathan Cape, London, 1955.

Liman von Sanders, Otto, *Five Years in Turkey*, The Navy & Military Press, UK 1927.

Macmillan, Margaret, *Paris 1900: Six Months that Changed the World*, Random House, London, 2002.

Mitchell, Elyne, *Chauvel Country: The Story of a Great Australian Pioneering Family*, Macmillan, South Melbourne, 1983.

Nutting, Anthony, *Lawrence of Arabia*, New American Library, New York, 1962.

Olden, A. C. N., *Westralian Cavalry in the War: 10th Light Horse AIF*, Alexander McCubbin, Melbourne, 1921.

Overy, Richard, *Collins Atlas of 20th Century History*, Collins, New York, 2006.

Parsonson, Ian M. *Vets at War: A History of the Australian Veterinary Corps 1909–1946*, Australian Military History Publications, Loftus, Sydney, 2005.

Paterson, A. B. (Banjo), *Happy Dispatches: Journalistic Pieces from Banjo Paterson's Days as a War Correspondent*, Lansdowne Press, Sydney, 1980.

— *Selected Verse of A. B. Paterson*, Angus & Robertson, Sydney, 1921.

Pedersen, P. A. *Monash as Military Commander*, Melbourne University Press, Melbourne, 1992.

Perham, Frank, *The Kimberley Flying Column: Boer War Reminiscences*, Timara, New Zealand, 1958.

Perry, Roland, *Monash: The Outsider Who Won a War*, Random House, Sydney, 2004.

Roberts, Paul, *The End of Oil*, Bloomsbury, London, 2004.

Roderick, Colin, *Banjo Paterson: Poet by Accident*, Allen & Unwin, Sydney, 1993.

Sheffield, Gary and Bourne, John (eds), *Douglas Haig: War Diaries and Letters, 1914–1918*, Weidenfeld & Nicolson, London, 2005.

Simpson, Cameron, *Maygar's Boys: A Biographical History of the 8th Light Horse Regiment AIF 1914–19*, Just Soldiers, Military Research & Publications, Moorooduc, Victoria, 1998.

Sluglett, Peter, *The Primacy of Oil in Britain's Iraq Policy*, Ithaca Press, London, 1976.

Starr, Joan, *From the Saddlebags of War*, Australian Light Horse Association, Beenleigh, Queensland, 2000.

Thomas, Lowell, *With Lawrence in Arabia*, Popular Library, New York, 1961.

Tuchman, Barbara W., *The Proud Tower: A Portrait of the World Before the War, 1890–1914*, Bantam Books, New York, 1967.

Wallach, Janet, *Desert Queen*, Weidenfeld & Nicolson, London, 1996.

Wavell, Archibald P., *Allenby: Soldier and Statesman*, Harrap, London, 1946.

Wilson, Jeremy, *Lawrence of Arabia: The Authorized Biography of T.E. Lawrence*, William Heinemann, London, 1989.

Yardley, Michael, *Backing into the Limelight: A Biography of T.E. Lawrence*, Harrap, London, 1985.

Articles

Adelson, Roger, Review of Wilson's official biography of Lawrence of Arabia, *Journal of Military History*, US, 1991.

Anderson, Perry, 'Kemalism', *London Review of Books*, 11 November 2008.

Australian War Memorial, *George Lambert: Gallipoli & Palestine Landscapes*.

— *Guide to the Papers of General Sir Henry George Chauvel*, Collection number: PR00535.

Bader, Rudolph, 'Lawrence of Arabia and H.H. Richardson', *Australian Literary Studies*, Vol. 11, May 1983.

Barrett, Roby, 'Intervention in Iraq, 1958–59', The Middle East Institute, Policy Brief, No. 11, 1 April 2008.

Binyon, Michael, 'Wise words survived desert but not change of trains', *The Times*, London, 1 March 2004.

— 'Lawrence: the man and the mirage', *The Times*, London, 8 October 2005.

Bou, Jean, 'The Palestine campaign 1916–18: causes and consequences of a continuing historical neglect', *Journal of the Australian War Memorial*, No. 40, <www.gov.au/journal/j40/bou.htm>.

— 'Cavalry, firepower, and swords: the Australian Light Horse and the tactical lessons of cavalry operations in Palestine, 1916–1918', *Journal of Military History*, 71, Australia, January 2007.

Sir Henry George Chauvel Albums (Private newspaper files); AWM PR00535003 Album—Egypt, Gallipoli, Sinai; 1914–1917; AWM PR00535004 Album—Palestine, Syria, England, 1917–1919.

— Letter to the Director, Australian War Memorial, Canberra, 1 January 1936, concerning T.E. Lawrence's book, *Seven Pillars of Wisdom*, Australian War Memorial PR00535003.

Coulthard-Clark, Chris, 'Aborigine medal winners', *Sabretache*, Vol. XVIII, No. 1, January 1977.

Daley, Paul, 'Straddling the divide', *Sunday Times*, 3 August 2008.

Day, Elizabeth, 'Legendary Lawrence of Arabia made up "rape"', *Daily Telegraph*, London, 20 May 2006.

Demirmen, Ferruh, 'Oil in Iraq: the Byzantine beginnings', *Global Policy Forum*, 25 April 2003.

Duffy, Denis, 'Lawrence of Arabia', *National Post*, US, 7 January 2002.

Ersavci, Murat, 'The Gallipoli legacy: a firm and abiding friendship', *Canberra Times*, 23 April 2007.

— 'Never Again', *Sunday Herald Sun*, 23 April 2006.

Faulkner, Neil & Saunders, Nick, 'Archaeology, Lawrence and guerilla warfare', *History Today*, UK, August 2007.

— 'Logical idea that could have prevented strife', *The Times*, London, 12 October 2005.

Fromkin, David, 'The Importance of T. E. Lawrence', The New Criterion online, 10 September 1991.

Furst, Barbara, 'Gertrude Bell and Iraq: déjà vu all over again', <American-Diplomacy.org>.

Fyfe, Hamilton, 'General Sir Edmund Allenby', *War Illustrated*, 12 October 1918.

Goldberg, Jeffrey, 'After Iraq', The Atlantic Online, January/February 2008.

Hill, A. J. *Official Histories—First World War: Volume VII—The Australian Imperial Force in Sinai and Palestine, 1914–1918. An Introduction.*

Hitchens, Christopher, 'The woman who made Iraq', *Atlantic Monthly*, 29 May 2007.

Hughes, Matthew, 'Review of M. Brown's T. E. Lawrence', *Journal of Military History*, Brunel University, UK, No. 1232.

Ireland, Phillip W., Reviews of *Lawrence of Arabia: The Man and the Motive* (Anthony Nutting); *Lawrence of Arabia: A Triumph* (Robert Payne), *Middle East Journal*, Vol. 18, No. 1, 1964.

Irwin, Robert: 'Ecstasy in the desert' (review, complete 1922 'Oxford' text of *Seven Pillars of Wisdom*), *Times Literary Supplement*, 2 April 2004.

Jerusalem Post, 'Saying it with flowers', 30 April 2008.

Kedourie, Elie, 'Colonel Lawrence', *Cambridge Journal*, Vol. 7, 1954.

Knightley, Phillip, 'Lawrence', *Sunday Times Magazine*, 2 October 2005, London.

Kroupnik, Vladimir, 'Emden and Sydney', <www.argo.net.au/andre/emden-forwebENFIN.thm>.

Tuchman, Barbara, 'History by the Ounce', *Harper's Magazine*, July 1965.

Leach, Hugh, 'Lawrence in Arabia', *History Today*, October 2005.

Mack, John E., Review of the Secret Lives of Lawrence of Arabia (Knightley), *Middle East Journal*, Vol. 24, No. 4, 1970.

Malvern, Jack, 'Lawrence of Arabia's Lessons on Fighting Iraqi Rebels', *The Times*, London, 13 April 2004.

— 'Lawrence's vision of Arabia and beyond', *The Times*, London, 12 October 2005.

Paul, James A.; 'Great power conflict over Iraq oil: the World War I era', *Global Policy Forum*, October 2002.

Ryan, Peter, 'Lawrence biography worth having', *Age*, Melbourne (undated); Review of *The Golden Warrior* by Lawrence James.

Sacks, David, 'Private Shaw', *New York Review of Books*, 16 April 2000.

Singh, K. Gajendra, 'Iraq's history already written', *Asia Times*, 15 July 2003.

Stewart, Rory, The Queen of the Quagmire, *New York Review of Books*, Vol. 54, No. 16, 25 October 2007.

Syal, Rajeev, 'Letters rekindle Lawrence suicide speculation', *Australian*, 2 September 1996.

Veitch, Alan, 'Queen of the desert', (Gertrude Bell), *Age*, Melbourne, 9 October 2002.

Wilson, Jeremy, 'Sense and nonsense in the biography of T.E. Lawrence', (prologue to the authorised biography) <http://telawrencestudies.org/telawrencestudies/general_biography/sense_and _nonsense>.

— Review comments on *Lawrence: the Uncrowned King of Arabia*, <http://www.telawrence.info>.

Other source material

The Battle for Zion (film), Daystar International.

GLOSSARY

Bey: Turkish governor
Redoubt: battlefield fortification
Tommy: English soldier
Wadi: valley

Light Horse

Section = four men
Eight sections = full troop = 32 men
Four troops = squadron = 128 men
Three squadrons = regiment = 384 men

Army officer rank

Second lieutenant
Lieutenant
Captain
Major
Lieutenant colonel
Colonel
Brigadier (in World War I, brigadier general, one star)
Major general (two star)
Lieutenant general (three star)
General (four star)
Field marshal (five star)

Acknowledgements

I would like to thank Tel Aviv-based Mike Guy, a former Israeli paratrooper, for his expert guidance through his country. He took us first to Beersheba and the ceremony to mark the unveiling of a Light Horse statue by Peter Corlett, and a children's park (concepts of Sam Lipski and funded by the Pratt Foundation) on 28 April, 2008.

Barrister/photographer Thos Hodgson, who accompanied me on research through Egypt, Israel and Jordan, taking many fine shots, eased into the mood in a desolate part of Jordan by changing into Lawrence of Arabia robes and dancing, *El Lawrens*-style, on a Hejaz railway bridge. Our Bedouin guide (in his four-wheel drive) was at first stunned, but then seemed pleased. He took us to a nearby village to acquire appropriate head-gear. We drove 150 kilometres that day in May 2008 for lunch in a café for tourists and local Arabs. Thos remained in his flowing white attire with gold embroidery, causing heads to turn. For a moment, Thos was the Lawrence curio incarnate.

Later, our guide was not so enamoured when I asked to see the home of Auda Abu Tayi at the village of Jefer near Mann. He drove the vehicle with some trepidation into the streets, reminding us more than once that no 'tourists' (he meant 'foreigners') ever visited the area inhabited by Auda's scores of relatives. His forehead glistened with sweat. I knew he was serious. He refused to let us take photographs or leave the vehicle. When the locals swarmed around us more curiously than menacingly, I understood his concern. Yet we did drive close to Auda's home—a white

THE AUSTRALIAN LIGHT HORSE

compound, which had been built by Turkish labour. Photographs were taken from within the vehicle, despite our guide's protests.

Advice from Susan Scollay on Syria and Lebanon was valuable for my research there. I am grateful to Aladin Rahemtula, who sits with me on the Advisory Council to the National Archive of Australia, for his searches on obscure material related to T. E. Lawrence. Research often involves endless reading of bland sources, but much of the appraisal of Lawrence seems to have lifted the articulation and readability of the authors. This enigmatic character attracted some of the best analytical writing of the 20th century from Winston Churchill and Basil Liddell Hart to George Bernard Shaw and Robert Graves.

I appreciate too, the assistance given by the Director General of the National Archive of Australia, Ross Gibbs. As a precaution in case I encountered roadblocks, I asked him for several letters of introduction to British institutions. When one obdurate soul in the British Library wished to stop me seeing Lawrence's diaries and notes, I produced the relevant letter, which overcame the problem.

My thanks also to Lawrence's official biographer, Jeremy Wilson. He was reluctant to engage me when he came to Australia late in 2007 for the excellent Australian War Memorial exhibition on Lawrence and the Light Horse. But as I encountered Wilson on several occasions and was able to question him at his lectures, I attained more than useful replies. They were broad questions, but his responses were invaluable whether clear or otherwise. The biographer, of course, could not know the deeper answers to all Lawrence's secrets. But his comments gave me a sense of what he and the Lawrence family knew or believed (they commissioned Wilson's biography), what they wanted the public and media to know, and also what they did not know.

My appreciation also to publisher Matthew Kelly at Hachette Australia for his support and encouragement on this project. His comprehension of the subject, and some of the issues being wrestled with, allowed him to provide wise counsel.

I would like extend further thanks to Bev Friend the following for interviews and/or information:

Major-General James Barry; James Barr; Mal Booth; John Burridge; Les Carlyon; Dr Richard Chauvel; Tom Dawson; Bernie Dingle; Ambassador of Turkey, N Murat Ersavci; ; David Evans; Milton Holmes; Major General 'Digger' James; Jack Grossman; Brad Manera; Sam Lipski; Billy McAuley; Lieutenant Colonel Malcolm McGregor; Leon Levin; Narelle Levin; the late Richard Pratt; Jeanne Pratt; Tony Millman; Richard Peterson; Angela Rodd; Warrant Officer Don Spinks; Ian Smith; Greg Thomas; Judy Thomas; Lyn Thomas; Jenny Horsfield; Robyn Van-Dyk: Adrian Jones; Gill Bozer; and the Ambassador of Syria, Tammam Sulaiman.

Photo credits

The photographs on the front cover (*top:* AWM H026770, *lower:* AWM A02684); and the portrait of Harry Chauvel (AWM ART1352) and photograph of T.E Lawrence (AWM B02170) on the back cover are courtesy Australian War Memorial.

In the second photo section, the images on p 1 (*top:* AWM J05674, *lower:* AWM P02400.026), p 2 (*lower:* AWM P0241.007), p 6 (*lower:* AWM B01619 by Frank Hurley), and p 8 (AWM ART13521) are also courtesy of the Australian War Memorial.

Other photos on the back cover and in both the first and second photo sections are from the author's collection, and courtesy of Carl Johnson, Judy Thomas and Thos Hodgson.

Index